# Making music with digital audio

## Direct to disk recording on the PC

### Ian Waugh

PC Publishing

PC Publishing
Export House
130 Vale Road
Kent TN9 1SP
UK

Tel 01732 770893
Fax 01732 770268
email pcp@cix.compulink.co.uk
web site http://www.pc-pubs.demon.co.uk

First published 1997

© PC Publishing

ISBN 1 870775 51 1

All rights reserved. No part of this publication may be reproduced or transmitted in any form, including photocopying and recording, without the written permission of the copyright holder, application for which should be addressed to the Publishers. Such written permission must also be obtained before any part of this publication is stored in an information retrieval system of any nature.

**British Library Cataloguing in Publication Data**
A catalogue record for this book is available from the British Library

Printed in Great Britain by Bell and Bain, Glasgow

# Introduction

Welcome to the cutting edge of music technology - digital audio. Major studios and recording artists have been using it for years but developments in this area have been so rapid that the cost of the technology has dropped to almost pocket-money prices.

In the 70s and 80s you had to budget for an analogue reel-to-reel multi-track recorder or cassette portastudio, a mixer, an effects unit, maybe a sampler, a sound module and lots of cables to plug them together. Now, you can get all these facilities in one box - the PC - and a good PC-based digital audio system costs much less in real terms than the analogue gear of yesteryear. And it can do a heckuva lot more.

We can't dismiss analogue recording completely - not yet, at least - and we look at the pros and cons of both systems later in the book. However, there's little doubt that it won't be long before the vast majority of music is recorded digitally.

Okay, you're convinced. You want to be at the leading edge of music recording. Or perhaps you're using analogue equipment and you're very happy with it, too, thank you very much, but you'd like to know more about digital recording - and there's nothing to stop you using both technologies. Or perhaps you're interested in making music but aren't sure what equipment you need and what's the best way to start. Or perhaps you have a PC with a sound card and want to do more with it than making it play random sounds every time it starts up.

If you fit one of those descriptions then this book is for you. It has been written for the thousands of musicians with home and semi-pro studios - or perhaps who have no studio yet at all - who want to get professional results for the minimum cost. But even though it concentrates on "affordable" equipment and software, you'll find that many of the items mentioned in this book are used in both home and professional studios. The difference between pro and semi-pro equipment narrows every day.

Inevitably, as with any new technology, there are a few new ideas to wrap your head around. These are explained as simply as possible and with the minimum of jargon - honest! A complete description of the technicalities of digital audio would take another book so I make no apologies for simplifying some of the concepts and glossing over others.

Another problem in deciding on the contents was what to put in and what to leave out, and how much detail to go into. Every chapter could easily be expanded into a book - or several books. The subject is vast. The criteria I used was to include the information you need to know to get the job done. This is a practical book which you can use to take you from the first stages of selecting a suitable system and software through to mastering your own album.

But as you delve into this exciting digital world, don't forget that your ultimate aim is to produce great music. Although the technology enables you to do many things which would otherwise be impossible, don't confuse technology with creativity. Master the technology, control it, bend it to your will, make it do what you want to do - don't let it determine or shape your ideas.

Welcome to the future of music making....

# Dedication

To Julia, my wife

...whose patience and support are greatly valued, appreciated and treasured and whose generous spirit is a constant source of delight and inspiration.

With much love

## Contents

**1 What is d-t-d recording? 2**
A short history of multi-track recording. Basic digital recording. Digital vs analogue recording. Digital processing. The digital myth. In praise of tape recorders. Digital audio is ... The full d-t-d potential

**2 What is sound? 9**
Sound is ... Measuring amplitude. The darned decibel. How loud is loud? Dynamic range. Signal-to-noise ratio. Measuring frequency. Frequency ranges. Flat frequency response. Of tones and timbres. The total sound

**3 Digital audio basics 21**
Sample rate. Hooray for Harry Nyquist. Oversampling. Bits and bytes. Vive la resolution. Resolution and dynamic range. Low flying noise. Will the real sample resolution please stand up? DACs and ADCs. Waveform formats. Summing up

**4 The PC system 32**
Buying a PC. Using high street stores. The Net Works PC. The processor. Clock speeds. The motherboard and chipset. RAM. The hard disk. Graphics card. CD ROM drive. Keyboard, mouse and case. Windows 95. The warranty. Add-ons. All together now

**5 The hard disk 44**
Hard disk basics. The essential specs. PIO. DMA. IDE, EIDE and ATA. SCSI. The SCSI evolution. SSA. It's a RAID. FireWire and associates. AV drives. Size counts. What's a megabyte? Using two or more drives. Partitioning. Summing up

**6 Storage and backup media 64**
Tape streamer. MO – Magneto Optical drives. Removable disks. CD-R. Backing up audio files to DAT. Good housekeeping. Hard disk maintenance. Summing up

**7 The soundcard 68**
Cutting through the tech spec jungle. Where the noise comes from. Beware the 'CD quality' promise. Sounds on board. Digital Ins and Outs. Soundcard city. External d-t-d systems. Summing up

**8 The software 80**
How digital recording software works. Non-destructive editing. Audio file storage. Flying edits. Of tracks and channels. Audio channel assignment by part. Audio channel assignment by track – method 1, method 2. Multi-track recording software. Stereo recording and editing software. Combined digital audio and MIDI sequencing software. Plug ins. Utility software. Summing up

**9 Recording and playback 109**
Basic recording techniques. Mic and Line level. Balancing tricks. Impedence. Noise - know your enemy. Clipping. Setting the recording level. Recording through a digital input. Selecting a sample rate and resolution. 44.1kHz or 48kHz? Playback. Playing back through a digital output. Hi fi in the studio

### 10 Editing  118
Non-destructive editing. Regions and Pools. Real-time control changes. Markers and Handles. Anchors and Q Points. Mixing it. Zero crossing points. Going loopy. Fades. Crossfades. The sound of silence

### 11 Processing and FX  131
EQ. Terms of EQ. Dynamics. De-esser. Change Gain. Normalise. Loudness maximisation. Enhancers. DC Offset. Invert Phase/Flip. Reverse. Pitch shifting and time stretching. Harmoniser. Reverb. Room simulators. Delay and echo. Chorus. Flanging, phasing and wah. Vibrato. Tremolo. Distortion. Noise reduction and other correctional facilities. Stereo expansion. Spectrum analysis and FFT. Sample conversion. Samplers and foreign file formats. Audio and MIDI cross-fertilisation. Summing up.

### 12 CD ROMs  180
Anatomy of a CD drive. CD ROM drive speeds. CLV and CAV. CD-R. CD formats. Multisession. ISO 9660. CD audio-to-disk transfer. Getting rid of the jitters. Digital audio transfer software. Wave file CDs. Recordable CDs. Preparing your system. Track-at-Once, Disc-at-Once. Gaps. Creating a CD ROM. Writing an audio CD with WaveLab. ISRC and UPC codes. Locks and emphasis. Ps & Qs and sub-codes. Buffer underruns. Going for the burn. CD-RW. DVD – the future of CD?

### 13 Digital audio for multimedia  200
What is multimedia?. Multimedia audio. Getting the right balance. Space savers. Stereo vs. mono. Sample rate and resolution conversion. Audio compression. WinZip. Codecs. Using codecs. Audio files for the Internet. Summing up

### 14 Audio and MIDI  211
Integrated audio and MIDI software. Synchronising to an external device. SMPTE and MTC. MIDI Machine Control. Converting tape tracks to digital tracks. Internal synchronisation. Master and slave. MIDI drivers. The missing link. Mixing MIDI and digital audio. Using sample loops

### 15 Mixdown and mastering  222
In praise of mastering houses. Creating your own master. Mixing a combined MIDI and digital audio recording. What speakers? Last orders. The final master. DAT. CD-R. DCC and MiniDisc. MiniDisc 2. Cassette. Packaging, artwork and promotion

### 16 Troubleshooting  229
System problems. Synchronisation problems. Audio problems. Calling for help.

### 17 Glossary  236

### Appendix 1  241
Copyrights and wrongs

### Appendix 2  243
Using the Internet. Useful contacts

### Index  247

# 1

## What is direct-to-disk recording?

Direct-to-disk recording is the process of recording sound and saving it to a hard disk. You could have guessed as much, couldn't you? D-t-d systems are the computer equivalent of the multi-track tape recorder but instead of recording to tape, sound is converted into a digital format and stored on a computer's hard disk.

Why would you want to do this? What are the advantages over using a multi-track tape-based system? For that matter, what is a multi-track recording system?

### A short history of multi-track recording

Strange though it may seem, in the very, very early days of recording – vinyl records, 78s and the like – performances were recorded and 'cut' live. If someone made a mistake it was either left in or the whole thing had to be recorded again. Imagine the pressure on the performers to get it right first time.

If we skip ahead a few decades we reach the era of the tape recorder which enabled a certain amount of editing to be done by physically cutting the tape. Then came the multi-track tape recorder which could record several different music lines – or tracks – in parallel onto a reel of tape. This allowed you to record alternative 'takes' or performances and keep the best one or even switch between them.

It also allowed different instruments to be recorded on their own track. If the singer didn't get it right first time, they could do another take on their own without the whole band having to play again. If the guitarist wasn't happy with his solo, he could record it again on another track and the best one could be used on the final version.

Multi-tracking also allowed one person to create an entire piece of music by themselves. In the early days you had to be a multi-instrumentalist to do this but with the development of the synthesiser – and later, MIDI – one person could create an entire rock band, ensemble or orchestra on their own by recording or 'laying down' one part at a time. One of the earliest examples of a 'one man band' album was Mike Oldfield's ground-breaking Tubular Bells which made him a fortune and put Richard Branson on the road to fame and fortune.

From four-track beginnings, multi-track recorders got larger until 8,

16 and 24-track machines were the norm. The Beatles' Sgt. Pepper album was reportedly recorded on a four-track although they actually used more than one machine synced together. Still, it was a magnificent accomplishment for its day. Now, however, anyone with a d-t-d system can produce recordings of higher quality at a fraction of the price. Whether the music will be as good is another matter...

During the early days of the multi-tracker, only studios or the rich could afford them but in the 70s, 4-track, 8-track and then 16-track recorders became affordable to the semi-professional and the enthusiast. A few years later companies developed four-track recorders which used cassette tape and these were cheap enough for the mass market. However, they were not without their drawbacks as we shall see.

But this was power indeed. Musicians with ideas but no money (the two seem inexorably linked) to hire a studio or other performers could create a complete song on their own using a multi-track tape recorder. The late 80s and early 90s was a boom time for DIY multi-track musicians. Now, as we head towards the next century, it's time to go digital.

## Basic digital recording

In order to highlight the benefits of digital audio and to illustrate its superiority over analogue multi-trackers, we'll run through a few digital recording basics. More comprehensive coverage follows in the next couple of chapters.

The principle of d-t-d recording is basically quite simple. Sound is recorded by a microphone and routed into an analogue-to-digital converter. This converts it into digital data, essentially a series of numbers so the computer can understand it, and then it's stored on the computer's hard disk.

One of the important differences between analogue data and digital data is that digital data consists of a series of discrete numbers. At any point in the recording, the data has a specific numeric value which you can home in on and edit. Analogue data on the other hand consists of continuously varying values so it's much more difficult to home in on a specific part of a recording and almost impossible to edit it in isolation without affecting the parts of the recording either side.

This is explained in more detail in the Chapter 3 so don't worry if it seems a bit woolly at the moment. However, even if you're not yet fully conversant with the theory, we can show how the two formats differ by comparing digital and analogue recording systems.

## Digital vs analogue recording

### Tape

With a multi-track tape recorder you are limited to the number of tracks the recorder physically has. On a cassette-based multi-tracker this may be four or possibly six tracks. On a reel-to-reel system it may be 8, 16 or 24.

You can bounce tracks together in order to free-up tracks for additional recording. This is a mixing process whereby you playback the tracks you want to mix and record them onto a new track. However, the mixing process adds noise to the sound (it's part and parcel of using tape) and when you record on the freed-up tracks you irrevocably overwrite what was on them losing that part of the recording forever.

### Digital
The number of tracks available on a d-t-d system is limited only by the storage capacity of the hard disk. Most d-t-d systems use virtual tracks which means you can record, store and arrange perhaps up to 256 tracks although using current (affordable) technology, you won't be able to play this many at once! However, it does mean you can record dozens of takes before deciding which one you want to use and the unused ones are never lost until you decide to delete them.

The number of tracks you can playback at once is limited by the system hardware. We'll look at this in detail later but it includes the digital audio card, the speed of the hard disk, the processing power of the PC and so on. With a high-end card and a fast PC you may achieve up to 20 mono or 16 stereo tracks. With a slower PC and a standard sound card you may have a capacity of four to eight tracks.

### Tape
With a tape recorder you have to record in a linear fashion – that is, from the beginning of the piece to the end. If you make a mistake you must re-record a section or, if you have nimble fingers, you can 'punch in and out' of a section to record over it. This involves hitting the record button just before you want to start recording and hitting stop as soon as you've finished so you don't record over existing material.

### Digital
D-t-d recording uses a pattern-based system very similar to that used by most MIDI sequencers. When you record a take, it's not stored irrevocably on tape at a specific point in the recording. It's stored on the hard disk and you can place its 'pattern' on any track and at any time position at all. The pattern simply 'references' the data on disk and you can, in fact, place the same recording on several tracks and at several different times within the same recording. This is an incredibly powerful and flexible method of arranging which is physically impossible to do with a tape-based system. Imagine, if a vocalist records the perfect chorus, you can use the same recording wherever the chorus occurs.

## Digital processing
You can do many things with a digital recording which can't be done with a tape recording. As the sound is stored as digital data, effectively a list of numbers, you can process it in a vast number of ways.

First of all, it's easy to copy so you can keep back up copies of all your recordings. Providing you have enough hard disk space or use a back up system, you never have to delete or overwrite a take. What's more, each copy is identical to the original so you don't lose any quality during the copying process. Tape has an inherent layer of noise which is magnified each time a tape recording is copied. No such problem with digital audio.

Using a growing range of processing software you can change the pitch of a recording, play it backwards (without reversing the tape in the machine) add reverb, echo, equalisation, apply compression and so on, all from within the PC. Some systems even apply the processing in real-time.

You can also select the smallest section of a recording for processing, safe in the knowledge that the data either side will not be processed. Use this to add reverb to a snare drum hit, for example. Impossible to do with tape.

If the potential of all this is starting to excite you – great! If you're still wondering what it's all about – keep reading. Everything is explained one step at a time in the following chapters.

The main point to bear in mind is that digital recording gives you more power, more quality, more flexibility and more versatility than tape recording...

## The digital myth

Well, almost. In the interests of accuracy – and honesty – we really ought to explore a few caveats and say a few words on behalf of those people who still use – and enjoy using and get good results from – tape systems.

It would be wrong to promote the impression that you can bung any old sound card into a 486 and produce a studio-quality recording. D-t-d technology and techniques are available to everyone but, as with most things, if you want top quality you have to pay for it. But that doesn't mean you have to spend a fortune. As with most aspects of the PC, if you pay a little more you get a little more performance, power or quality so you can tailor your system to suit your budget and the results you want to achieve.

As you read the following chapters, particularly Chapter 4, you'll understand the importance the various parts of a PC play in the digital audio process. We'll explore some of the limitations of budget systems and look at features that professional systems incorporate to achieve the highest quality possible.

But even with modest equipment you can achieve better quality sound than a cassette multi-tracker, for example, and, indeed, a typical four-track or eight-track reel-to-reel machine you may have used just a few years ago.

## In praise of tape recorders

So let's say a few words in praise of tape recorders.

For many musicians a tape machine was their introduction to multi-track recording and opened up a new world of musical possibilities. They realised, for example, that they could create an entire piece of music on their own.

And there are musicians and engineers who still prefer analogue tape. If you dismiss those who simply distrust or dislike computers (and there are several), the reasons for their preference are generally to do with the sound. They may say tape gives a more 'open' sound, that it's 'warmer'. Some also say that digital recording can't capture all the nuances or the full dynamic range of tape. Let's look at this a bit closer.

The warmth of most tape recordings can be attributed to 'over driving' the recording level. That is, recording a signal onto tape when it's clipping the recording meter. Tape is quite forgiving in this way and compresses the sound making it seem louder and warmer. If you overdrive a digital input it simply distorts. However, you can compress a digital recording afterwards using processing software. There's more about this later in the book.

As for the claim that digital recording can't capture the full dynamic range of tape, that's partly true. It depends on the recording resolution. At the moment the standard resolution is 16 bits although many pro audio systems use 20 and 24 bits and some are moving towards even higher resolutions. If you can hear the difference between 16-bit and 24-bit resolution and your equipment is hi fi enough to play it – you've got jolly good ears! There's more about this in Chapter 3 when we look at digital audio basics.

Other benefits include portability. A standard two-track 1/4 inch stereo master tape can be read by virtually every studio in the world. However, the use of DAT (Digital Audio Tape) is now so popular that it can be read by virtually every studio, too, and it's cheap enough for home users to use for mastering. With the growing popularity and ever-decreasing prices of recordable CDs, this is yet another alternative and CDs can be read by everyone with a CD player. So perhaps tape is losing its edge there.

## Digital audio is...

In order to put digital audio into perspective, especially for readers who may be new to recording, let's take a look at some other music making systems to compare and contrast.

### D-t-d vs samplers

The nearest relative to d-t-d is probably the sampler. In fact, you could say sampling is its mother. Both systems convert sound into digital data, allow you to edit it and then replay it. The two main differences are that samplers store their data in RAM and are designed to play it back at different pitches. This enables you to record a single note, for example, and by transposing it, pretend it's a complete instrument. You can't take the note very far away from its original pitch, however, before it starts to lose its character – there's more about this in Chapter 11.

It's obviously a lot faster to play something from RAM than it is to play it directly from a hard disk. Computers can shuffle data around in RAM almost instantaneously while it takes several milliseconds to read data from a disk – the difference is noticeable in music. Samplers work in real-time, transposing samples on the fly. D-t-d systems aren't designed for use in this way and while you can transpose d-t-d data easily enough, you can't really use a d-t-d system as a sampler. Not and remain sane.

Samplers are big on loops. If you repeat a middle section of a sample you can extend the sound indefinitely. You can do this with d-t-d recording, too, although as it's reading the data continuously from disk, if the loop is very short you may hear a glitch. Samples don't usually have this problem.

Most modern samplers are at least 16-note polyphonic. You can play 16 tracks at once on a d-t-d system but, as we mentioned earlier, the playback capability is directly related to the power of the hardware.

The storage capacity of samplers is limited by the amount of RAM they have. Stereo digital audio data of CD quality requires approximately 10Mb of storage space per minute. Many samplers can now be fitted with 32Mb, 64Mb or more RAM so they could possibly hold one track for a song but it's not terribly practical, and you certainly couldn't record a multi-track piece of music with ease. It's not what samplers were designed for – although having said that, several samplers now offer a direct-to-disk recording facility.

The storage capacity of a direct-to-disk recording system on the other hand, is only limited by the amount of disk space you have. A 1Gb hard disk – which is on the small side of standard in most PC systems now – could store over one-and-a-half hours of CD quality stereo music.

## D-t-d vs MIDI

When music met digital data, MIDI was the first widespread use of the technology. It differs significantly from digital audio data in one important respect – while digital audio data is the music information itself, MIDI data carries music instructions which have to interpreted or performed by a MIDI instrument.

Every music action such as pressing a key, twiddling the pitch bend wheel or pressing a button to select a different sound generates a corresponding MIDI event. When this is received by a MIDI instrument it responds by playing the note, activating pitch bend or selecting a different sound.

The important thing to note is that MIDI data contains no sound information as such, only performance information. An instruction to select a new sound is the equivalent of physically pressing a different preset button on the instrument's front panel. Now, if the recording instrument has a piano in its preset number 1 slot, for example, and the receiving instrument a harp, the music will play on a harp, not a piano.

This means that in order for a MIDI file to sound exactly the way it was intended, it must be played on the instrument which was used during the recording. Digital audio, on the other hand, is the entire music performance and can be played on any digital audio system. The quality may vary according to the hardware being used but the music content would be the same.

### ✤ RAM ✤

The world's entire supply of RAM is produced by a handful of companies which essentially 'fix' the price of RAM by controlling the supply as this, in turn, affects demand. In 1995 and 1996 when Windows 95 was launched, it was thought that users would upgrade their RAM because Windows 95 likes rather more of the stuff than Windows 3.1. However, the anticipated take-up did not occur, there were more RAM chips on the market than the producers expected and the prices fell accordingly. Nice.

But, unlike the price of hard disks which is technology and consumer lead, the price of RAM is still linked to production. During 1996 the RAM factories reduced their production and the price of RAM rose again in 1997...

The problem encountered when playing a MIDI file on an instrument different to the one it was recorded on has been partly addressed by the General MIDI (GM) spec, which basically states that every GM-compatible instrument shall have the same sounds in the same preset number slots. The result is a standard which does, indeed, enable a single MIDI file to be played on many different instruments but at the expense of individuality. Manufacturers can't do much with a GM sound set or it won't sound like the others!

Also, there are now two additional GM 'standards' which only serve to confuse the issue more. In order to make sure a MIDI file sounds, more or less, as intended, you have to cater for the lowest common set up which is plain old GM so in such cases the advantages of the extended GM specifications are lost.

But that's of little concern to us making music with digital audio. You can combine digital audio and MIDI in one piece and, in fact, many musicians work this way (there's more about this in Chapter 14) but unless your music is designed for mass distribution rather than recording or performance, there's no reason to restrict yourself to GM.

The problem with distributing digital audio is the size of the data although if the samples are small you may be able to squeeze a song onto a couple of floppy disks. If you are writing to CD (more about this in Chapter 12) then it's not so much of a problem.

MIDI data is very compact – a performance lasting several hours could be stored in a file a few hundred kilobytes in size – so it's an ideal way of distributing music on floppy disk and over the Internet.

### Digital audio editing vs sequencing

The final area in our compare and contrast section is editing. You can probably guess what the major differences are from what has been said but here's a quick summary.

As the data used by MIDI sequencing consists of individual items of performance data – essentially nothing more than a string of numbers – it is extremely easy to edit and process. By changing a few numbers you can change individual notes, their volume, pitch, duration, their position in the piece and so on.

Although digital audio data effectively turns sound into a string of numbers, the data contains within it all the elements of the sound. You may be able to isolate a note in a digital audio recording but you can't juggle numbers to change its tone or timbre, and although you could move its position in time, it would most likely overlap other sounds and the result is unlikely to be as clean as a similar MIDI edit.

However, digital audio can be processed and edited in many ways and you may be surprised by just how flexible digital editing can be – infinitely more flexible than working with tape. We get specific in Chapters 8 to 11.

> **INFO**
>
> Around the same time that GM was developed, Roland released a GS spec which allowed for more sounds known as variation tones and which included reverb and chorus effects which, oddly enough, were not included in the original GM spec. A few years ago Yamaha announced the XG standard which also allows additional sounds and offers greater control over the sound parameters.

## The full d-t-d potential

What can you expect to achieve with your d-t-d system? Well, with even basic hardware and software you can turn your PC into a multi-track recorder. The more powerful the hardware, the more tracks you'll be able to achieve. Processing software will enable you to add effects to your recordings.

You can mix digital audio with arrangements produced by MIDI equipment to combine the two into one production. Add a DAT machine or a recordable CD and you can create your own masters.

In other words, with digital recording you can house a complete recording studio inside a PC.

# 2

## What is sound?

Welcome to the techy chapter. Okay – semi-technical. In order to get the most from a digital audio system you need to know a few basics about sound – how it's produced, and how it's converted into a digital format and back to sound again. This inevitably involves a bit of science and a few sums but we aren't going to get bogged down in technicalities. Consequently, this is not an exhaustive explanation of the principles involved – there are plenty of text books containing all that stuff. We'll content ourselves with a light skirmish around the edges of the fray.

### Sound is ...

As the object of our attention in direct-to-disk recording is sound, it's a good idea to know what we're dealing with.

Quite simply, sound is a series of vibrations. These are produced when an object is, in technical terms, 'excited'. In practical terms an object – or musical instrument – is excited when it is rubbed, struck or blown into. You can see these vibrations when you pluck a guitar string, for example. The vibrations travel thorough the air and when they reach our ears, our eardrums send messages to the brain which are interpreted as sound.

Sound waves have three main characteristics – amplitude, frequency and tone or timbre. Amplitude determines the volume of a sound and frequency determines the pitch.

Figure 2.1 shows a sine wave with a frequency equivalent to Middle C on the piano (technically it's 261.63Hz). Figure 2.2 shows the same waveform after its volume has been increased; you can see that the height of the waves is larger. In Figure 2.3, the original waveform has been transposed up an octave and it has twice as many cycles in the same time period.

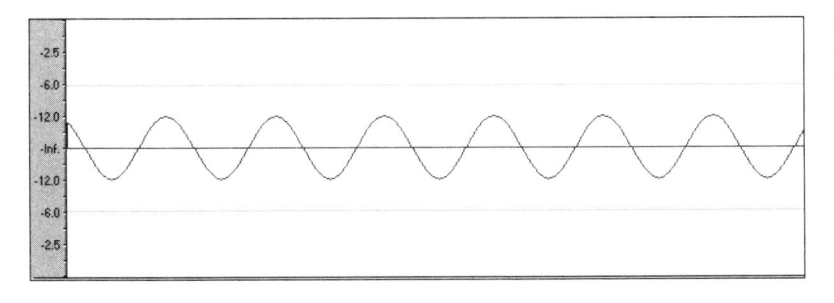

> **INFO**
>
> Skip this chapter if you know what it's all about, skim through it if you feel comfortable with the principles and delve into the text if you want a more detailed explanation. But read it if you're new to digital audio.

Figure 2.1 A 261.63 Hz sine wave, produces a pitch equivalent to middle C

Figure 2.2 The same waveform after its volume has been increased

Figure 2.3 The original waveform transposed up an octave has twice as many cycles

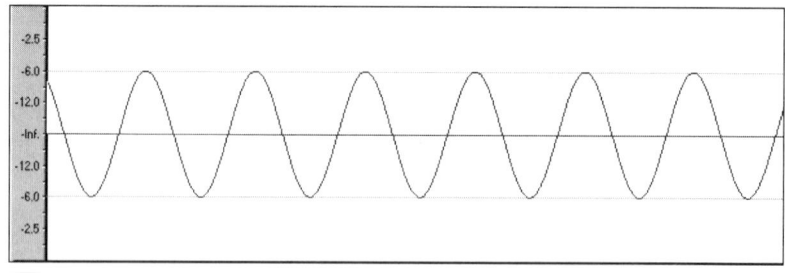

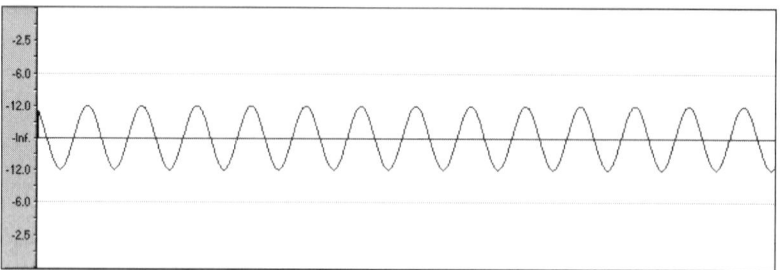

So, the greater the amplitude, the larger the waves. In other words, the vibration is stronger, it moves a greater volume of air (technically referred to as the air pressure) and we perceive this as an increase in volume.

Frequency is measured over time. The higher the frequency, the more vibrations (technically waveform cycles) there are in a given time period and we perceive this as a higher pitch.

The shape of the waveform determines its tone. The sine waves used in these examples produce a very pure tone with no harmonics or tonal content. Sine waves are used as reference tones in recording studios and sound a little flute-like.

A sine wave consists of a tones at one pitch only. If you add additional pitches the wave changes in shape and in sound. The square wave in Figure 2.4, for example, contains several harmonics and has a hollow sound, a little like a clarinet. A sawtooth wave, Figure 2.5, contains a different combination of tones and sounds rather buzzy.

Figure 2.4 Square wave contains several harmonics

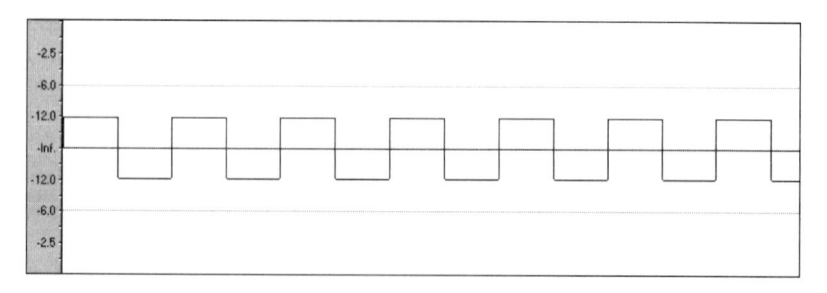

An important point to note is that sound vibrations travel through the air using a knock-on effect. A sound wave nudges (or shoves if it's a loud wave!) the molecules in the air around the object producing the sound. These nudge the molecules next to them and so on. Sound vibrations do

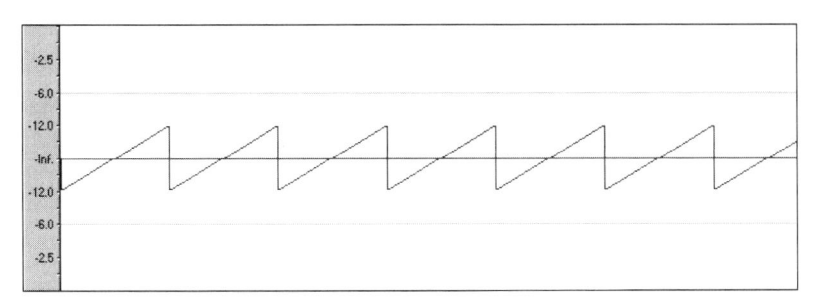

Figure 2.5 Sawtooth waves have a buzzy sound

not push the air forward or make it move from one side of a room to the other. If they did, every sound would produce a wind and if loud music didn't knock your socks off it would, at least, blow the papers off your desk and possibly rearrange the furniture!

## Measuring amplitude

Amplitude is not the most difficult aspect of sound to understand but it can seem that way when you try to measure it. We'll look at it first and after that it's downhill all the way.

Our perception of loudness is directly related to the amplitude of a sound wave. Technically this is referred to as intensity or sound pressure rather than loudness because – and here's a techy bit – our ears do not respond to changes in intensity in a linear way but in a logarithmic way. Figure 2.6 shows a logarithmic curve and you can see by how much the air pressure must increase in order to increase the perceived volume.

The difference in sound pressure level (SPL) from the softest sound we can hear to a sound loud enough to cause pain is enormous. Using SPL as a measurement would involve figures with lots of noughts on the end. Not only would they be cumbersome to work with, more importantly, they wouldn't accurately reflect our perception of how loud a sound was. So, a more suitable measuring scale was developed – the decibel, usually abbreviated to dB.

**INFO**

Sound waves travel through air much like waves move on the sea. If you watch an object floating in the sea and a boat passes by, the waves caused by the boat simply make the object bob up and down. They don't carry the object along with them. The water around the object stays pretty much where it is; the waves and ripples are caused by the knock-on effect. Sound vibrations in air work like that, too.

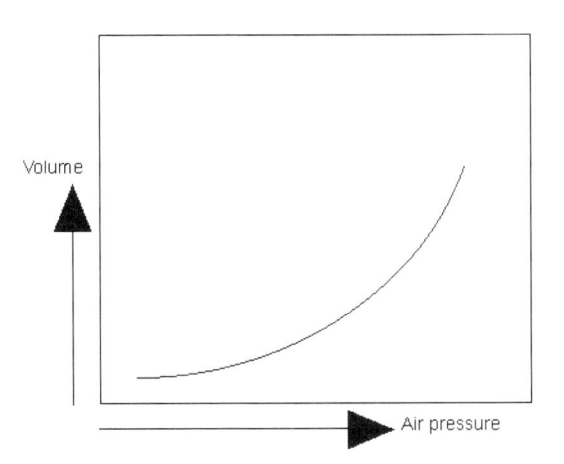

Figure 2.6 A logarithmic curve shows how air pressure must increase enormously for us to perceive a relatively small increase in volume

## The darned decibel

The use of the decibel measuring system is often a source of confusion for a several reasons. Firstly, it is used to measure different although related properties and secondly, it's not an absolute measuring system but a relative one. However, you'll find it referred to in many audio processes so you need to have a rough understanding of what it represents.

Don't worry, there'll be no attempt a technical explanation — it isn't essential for d-t-d recording at this level. If you are part of a large studio with professional audio equipment you may well need a more technical understanding of the system. However, for the most part, you can simply monitor recording levels on meters measured in dB and know that the higher the level is on the meters, the louder the sound. dB is also used in processing software which we look at in Chapter 11.

The main thing to understand is that a decibel is a ratio, not an absolute value. For example, if someone says that one sound is 6dB louder than another, we know how much louder it is although the figure does not tell us how loud either of the sounds are. They could be very quiet or extremely loud. All we know is the comparative difference in volume between them.

What good is this? Well, in the studio, setting volume levels is all about balance — making sure signals and volumes match each other. During balancing, the actual volume is often of secondary importance to the mix between the signals. Meters in hardware mixing desks and recording software which are used to indicate volume levels are usually calibrated in dB. You'll find the decibel useful in other areas of audio, too, such as filtering and for checking the audio quality of equipment.

So what's a 6dB difference in volume? Well, without going into the technicalities, in audio work an increase of 6dB is usually taken to be a doubling of the volume. To double the volume again, we add another 6dB and so on. 12dB, therefore, is four times the original volume and 18dB is eight times greater.

Having gone through that rather laborious — yet still simplified — explanation, you'll be pleased to know that many people working with audio don't know what a decibel is or exactly how the dB measuring scale works. But it's easy enough to set comparative levels for two or more signals simply by looking at the meters even if you don't know what the calibrations mean.

Here are a few bottom line statements to remember:

* A decibel is not an absolute value but a ratio used to compare the relative level of signals.
* If one sound is 6dB greater than another, it is twice the volume.
* To double the volume of a sound, however loud it may be, requires an increase of 6dB.
* The smallest change in volume most of us can detect is 3dB although some people may be able to detect changes of 1dB.

> **INFO**
>
> The decibel is one-tenth of a bel, a unit named after Alexander Graham Bell (1847-1922), a scientist best known for inventing the telephone.

> **INFO**
>
> If it's any consolation, I asked a few recording engineers if they could explain what a decibel was and although they all knew instinctively the part it played in the sound process, not one of them could lucidly explain exactly what it represents. Spooky, eh?

## How loud is loud?

If the decibel is only used to measure the relative difference between sounds, what do we use to measure absolute loudness? Is there a measure for loudness in the same way that there's a measure for distance and weight?

Scientists love to measure and quantify things so of course there is. However, there's more than one measuring system in use – you knew there'd be a catch, didn't you? – but none are particularly useful for audio recording. So we go back to our old friend the decibel.

Although the decibel alone can't tell us how loud a sound is, if we use a reference level, a volume we can compare the decibel difference of another sound against, then we will know how loud the other sound is. We can do this using the dB SPL (Sound Pressure Level) scale which takes as its reference point the threshold of hearing which is 0dB. This is so quiet that it's doubtful whether anyone in the Western world has even been in a 0dB environment!

At the top end of the scale when we reach 130dB or 140dB we are at the pain threshold where a sound is so loud it actually hurts. Prolonged expose to this level of sound can damage the ear. Jet engines and loud rock music appear at this point on the scale. The table shows some sounds and their typical dB SPL values across the range of human hearing.

*Sounds and their typical dB SPL values across the range of human hearing*

| dB (SPL) | Sound | dB (SPL) | Sound |
|---|---|---|---|
| 0 | Threshold of hearing | 70 | Loud conversation |
| 5 |  | 75 | Traffic |
| 10 | Dropping a pin | 80 | Loud music |
| 15 | Top of a mountain | 85 |  |
| 20 | Quiet recording studio | 90 | Motor bike |
| 25 | 'Empty' concert hall | 95 |  |
| 30 |  | 100 |  |
| 35 | Quiet conversation | 105 | Storm (thunder) |
| 40 | Very soft music | 110 |  |
| 45 | House environment without TV | 115 | Very loud music |
| 50 |  | 120 |  |
| 55 |  | 125 | Heavy metal |
| 60 | Clerical office | 130 | Threshold of pain |
| 65 |  | 135 | Loud siren |

## Dynamic range

The decibel is also used as a measuring stick to specify the dynamic range of a system. Dynamic range is the difference between the loudest and quietest parts of a performance or recording. In dB terms, it's the difference between the quietest signal and the loudest signal that the system is capable of producing.

A piece of orchestral music can have a dynamic range in excess of 100dB which almost spans the range of human hearing. If you want to capture all dynamic nuances in such a piece music, you'd need a recording system with at least a 100dB dynamic range. As we'll see later in the book, this is not yet possible with current affordable systems although we can get pretty close to it.

Tape systems typically have a dynamic range of 50 – 60dB which may at first seem limiting compared to the real world but it's actually not too bad. If we assume that the listening environment – let's say the front room in a semi – has a background noise level of around 40dB SPL, then the music must be greater than this in order to be heard. If we take this as our reference level and add 100dB to it in order to encompass the full dynamic range of an orchestra we get a top level of 140dB SPL which is actually far too loud. If this didn't cause ear damage it would certainly cause damage of another sort – probably inflicted by the neighbours!

Taking a modest dynamic range of 50dB for a tape recording and adding it to our 40dB reference level we get a top level of 90dB SPL. This is still loud enough to annoy the neighbours and quite loud enough to reproduce a wide dynamic range of sound.

A good digital audio system will have a dynamic range of 90dB or more. This doesn't give you a license to blast your neighbours out of their armchairs but it does mean you can have a greater range between the quietest and loudest passages in your music. There's more about this is the next chapter.

> **INFO**
>
> Recording engineers and audiophiles argue about the dynamic range required in order to accurately capture 'natural' sound. Theoretically it ought to be 130 – 140dB but such an extreme range is not essential for most recordings.

## Signal-to-noise ratio

You'll find signal-to-noise ratios are used a lot with audio equipment and often quoted in specs. As its name suggests, it's a measurement of the ratio between the music or sound you are recording and the background noise. In a tape system, for example, there is always background noise present – it's part and parcel of the medium. Again, it's measured using our old friend the decibel. It's often abbreviated to SNR or S/N.

The signal-to-noise ratio is closely tied in with dynamic range because the greater the ratio, the wider the difference there can be between the loudest and quietest passages without background noise interfering. To put this into perspective and to give you a few practical examples to hang the theory on, here's a few typical SNR figures:

- A Revox reel-to-reel tape machine: 60dB.
- A multi-track reel-to-reel recorder with noise reduction: 90dB.
- A high quality audio CD player: 93dB.
- FM radio: 50dB.
- Cassette player: 40dB.
- A cassette player with noise reduction: 50dB.

One of the benefits of digital recording is that it does not have the background noise inherent in tape systems so it's possible to achieve very high quality results with modest equipment. However, the most crucial part of the system is likely to be the digital audio card so if you want high quality results, check the specs carefully. There's more about this in the Chapter 7.

## Measuring frequency

If you've got your head around decibels, the rest's a piece of cake. An understanding of frequency and pitch is particularly important when applying filters or EQ to a recording. It also helps when constructing a piece of music as a well-rounded piece will contain sounds throughout the whole frequency spectrum.

Frequency is the scientific term for pitch. It's a measurement of how often or how quickly a sound wave vibrates. The faster it vibrates, the higher the frequency and the higher the pitch. The earlier examples in Figure 2.1 and Figure 2.3 show how it works.

Frequency is measured in Hertz, usually abbreviated to Hz, which is the number of times an event occurs in one second. Sometimes the term CPS (cycles per second) is used.

Although the relationship between pitch and frequency doesn't involve logarithmic curves and relative measurements, their relationship is not an even 1:1 ratio. If we increase the pitch by an octave, the actual frequency of the note doubles. Technically, it's known as an exponential progression. Don't worry – it's a lot easier to understand than decibels.

Let's take as an example a pitch and frequency which many people may already know – the A above Middle C which has a frequency of 440Hz. The A above that has a frequency of 880Hz and the A below it has a frequency of 220Hz. Figure 2.7 shows the relationship between frequency and the notes of the Western scale. This may look like a load of technotosh but it'll be useful when you start EQing as most EQ systems are calibrated in Hz and kHz so it's useful to know exactly where the frequencies lie in relation to the musical content of the material. You may want to refer to this while reading the EQ section.

### INFO

*The Hertz was named after Henrich Rudolph Hertz (1857-1894), a German physicist and the first person to produce electromagnetic waves artificially. But for the convention of naming discoveries after the scientist's surname, it could have been called the Rudolph!*

Figure 2.7 The relationship between frequency and the notes of the Western scale

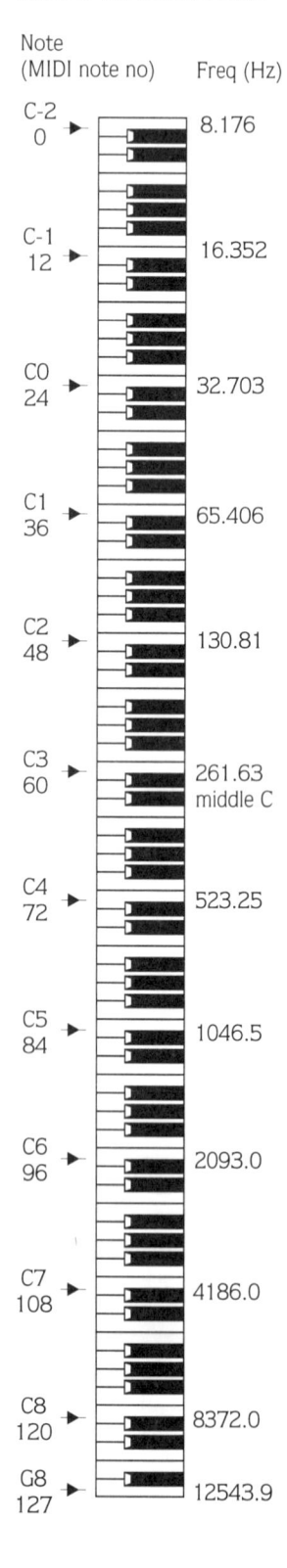

| Note (MIDI note no) | Freq (Hz) |
|---|---|
| C-2  0 | 8.176 |
| C-1  12 | 16.352 |
| C0  24 | 32.703 |
| C1  36 | 65.406 |
| C2  48 | 130.81 |
| C3  60 | 261.63 middle C |
| C4  72 | 523.25 |
| C5  84 | 1046.5 |
| C6  96 | 2093.0 |
| C7  108 | 4186.0 |
| C8  120 | 8372.0 |
| G8  127 | 12543.9 |

Our ears can detect frequencies from around 15Hz up to 20kHz. although some people may be able to hear sounds as low as 10Hz and as high as 25kHz. As we get older the range decreases, particularly in the higher frequencies, and this may fall to 15kHz or even 10kHz as we approach three score years and ten.

If you're looking at Figure 2.7 and wondering if we really can't hear the lower octave in the span of notes used by MIDI... Well, generally not. This refers to absolute frequencies which most people won't be able to hear. However, the sound produced by most instruments includes harmonics or overtones which are frequencies higher than the fundamental tones so we may be able to hear something from such sounds. The exception are instruments such as the flute whose tone contains few overtones and which can't play this low anyway.

## Frequency ranges

The representation of individual pitches as frequencies is not as useful in audio recording as the general pitch range which sections of the music fall into. As mentioned, however, it is helpful to know which frequencies occupy which pitch bands when you're twiddling with the EQ. Musicians work with pitches and notes as second nature but EQ uses Hertz. Obviously designed by an engineer, not a musician.

The human frequency range is commonly divided into three bands – bass, mid-range and treble. This is simply a grouping of convenience – there is no cast iron definition of where one stops and another starts. However, the following is a useful guideline which few would dispute:

- Low frequencies: between 20Hz and 200Hz
- Mid frequencies: between 200Hz and 5kHz
- High frequencies: between 5kHz and 20kHz

These categories can be further subdivided into more specific areas. Again, these aren't set in stone but they indicate how important the various frequency ranges are in a piece of music.

*10Hz to 80Hz*

The low end of the bass register. The very lowest frequencies in this range are felt rather than heard and the whole range provides the foundation and power on which the music rests. These frequencies can also provide a sense of depth. In this range you'll also find unwanted sounds such as background noise. This is the domain of low-pitched instruments such as the bass guitar, cello, bass tuba and bass sax. Many instruments can also dip into this range including the piano, harp, accordion, and bassoon.

*80Hz to 200Hz*

The upper end of the bass register. This, too, contributes to the power and drive of a piece of music. Rhythm licks usually inhabit this area. Most of the instruments mentioned in the previous frequency band can stretch up into this one and here we also find the bass voice, the trombone, baritone and tenor saxes, alto and bass clarinets, timpani and guitar.

*200Hz to 500Hz*
This spans the notes, roughly, from G below Middle C to the B above Middle C. With the exception of a few very low and very high pitched instruments, most instruments can play notes in this area. Almost anything can happen here – high bass notes, rhythm section, melody.

*500Hz to 2kHz*
This is the middle of the middle frequency band and it's where some vocals hang out along with the violin, flute, soprano clarinet, piccolo, chimes, marimba and xylophone.

*2kHz to 5kHz*
Now we're starting to move outside the range of most instruments. The piccolo, harp, xylophone and the upper notes of the piano are up here but these aren't found in every piece of music. However, it does contain harmonics and overtones, courtesy of the lower notes in the music, and these play a very important part in brightening the sound. You can increase the presence of a piece of music by boosting these frequencies although continued exposure to such boosted frequencies can grate upon the ear and lead to fatigue.

*5kHz to 10kHz*
This is beyond the range of virtually all instruments; the realm of overtones, high harmonics and tape hiss although as we're not using tape that shouldn't bother us – just be aware of the potential problems if you transfer a recording from tape to your digital audio system.

*10kHz to 20kHz*
We're right out of the normal music spectrum now at the very top of our hearing range. There may well be rare, fragile frequencies inhabiting this area although you'll need a good hi fi system – and good ears – to hear them. Sounds at the higher end of this range will probably be wasted on most systems – and most ears – although if you find yourself with a 24-bit digital audio system and the means to hear its full dynamic range you may be surprised at the added sparkle frequencies in this range can add to the music. Almost subliminal.

## Flat frequency response

It's worth saying a few words at this point about frequency response although there's more about it in Chapter 7 and in the section on EQ in Chapter 11. In an ideal world, recording and playback equipment would capture and play sounds exactly as we hear them. However, as you're probably aware, different hi fi systems, loudspeakers, CD players and the like, all sound a little different. In other words, they colour the sound.

**TECHY BIT**

kHz is short for kilohertz or 1000Hz which is one thousand cycles per second.

**INFO**

The frequency of 440Hz for A was fixed by international agreement in 1939. In the 19th century, A had been as low as 435Hz and prior to that it varied depending on whether one was playing chamber music, playing an organ and singing or in a town band.

> ### ✤ INFO ✤
>
> Many hi fi systems have a Loudness or Bass Boost button which boosts the bass frequencies so at low volumes you can listen to the music and still hear the bass notes without disturbing the neighbours.

In fact, virtually every recording and playback system colours the sound to some degree. If you've heard an audio CD being played through tiny PC Multimedia speakers you'll know how thin it sounds. Put the same CD on a hi fi system and it sounds totally different. This is because the systems cut or boost certain frequencies in the music. Small speakers, for example, tend to lose a lot of the bass frequencies. A good hi fi system retains all the high and low frequencies giving a much fuller sound.

The ideal recording or playback system has a flat frequency response. In other words, none of the frequencies in the signal will be cut or boost by the system. A frequency goes in at one level and it comes out at exactly the same level. This is obviously not the case in the above examples where the small speakers cut the bass frequencies.

In a system with a flat frequency response, if you plot the input level against the output level of all the frequencies you'd get a straight line – hence the term. However, such perfection is rare and a deviation of around 2dB or 3dB is usually accepted in analogue equipment and you may expect a deviation of 0.5-1dB in a good digital system.

The frequency response is worth bearing in mind as our aim in digital recording – as in any recording process – is to capture a sound exactly as it is. You can, of course, process it and EQ it just as you can in analogue recording but it's best if the recording is as close to the original sound as possible. It's also worth noting that our ears do not have a flat frequency response. For example, low frequencies have to have a far greater intensity – dB (SPL) – than higher ones in order for us to perceive them at the same loudness level. This is easily demonstrated by playing music containing low frequencies and seeing how low you can turn down the volume before it becomes inaudible. Now play some music containing mid and high frequencies and do the same. You'll still be able to hear the higher stuff at very low volumes.

## Of tones and timbres

> ### ✤ TECHY BIT ✤
>
> Strictly speaking, harmonics have a simple mathematical relationship to the fundamental such as 2x, 3x, 4x and so on. Partials with a more mathematically complex relationship to the fundamental are called enharmonics (also called inharmonics by some sources).

The final sound quality we're going to look at is timbre or tone colour. This is what gives a sound its distinctive character, what enables us to distinguish between different types of instruments playing the same note. Our perception of timbre is very much affected by pitch and loudness so all three sound parameters are closely tied together.

Timbre is determined by the harmonic content of a sound. Most sounds are made up of many frequencies at different volume levels. The basic pitch of a sound is determined by its fundamental which is the lowest frequency it contains. (This is usually the case but it is possible for a sound to contain frequencies lower than the pitch it is perceived to be.)

These additional frequencies are called partials or harmonics. The most pure sound is a sine wave which contains no harmonics at all. If you add two sine waves of different pitches or frequencies together the sound will take on an added 'characteristic'. In other words its timbre will change. If you add lots of sine waves at lots of different pitches, the sound's tonal character will change considerably.

You may have heard of additive synthesis. This is the process of creating sounds by adding waveforms together. A square waveform, for example, which has a hollow sound can be created by adding together odd harmonics. Conversely, all sounds can be broken down into their harmonic components. The process is a little more tricky but many pieces of modern software can perform a frequency analysis, sometimes known as a FFT or Fast Fourier Transform, which results in an impressive 'mountain' display. It shows the amplitude or loudness of the frequencies that the waveform under analysis contains.

Figure 2.8 shows a FFT display of a sine wave. It only contains one harmonic at 440Hz (the A above Middle C) and the graph only has one peak. Figure 2.9 shows a 440Hz square wave and you can see the individual sine wave frequencies from which it is constructed.

Figure 2.8 (below) FFT display of a 440 Hz sine wave

Figure 2.9 (bottom of page) 440Hz square wave

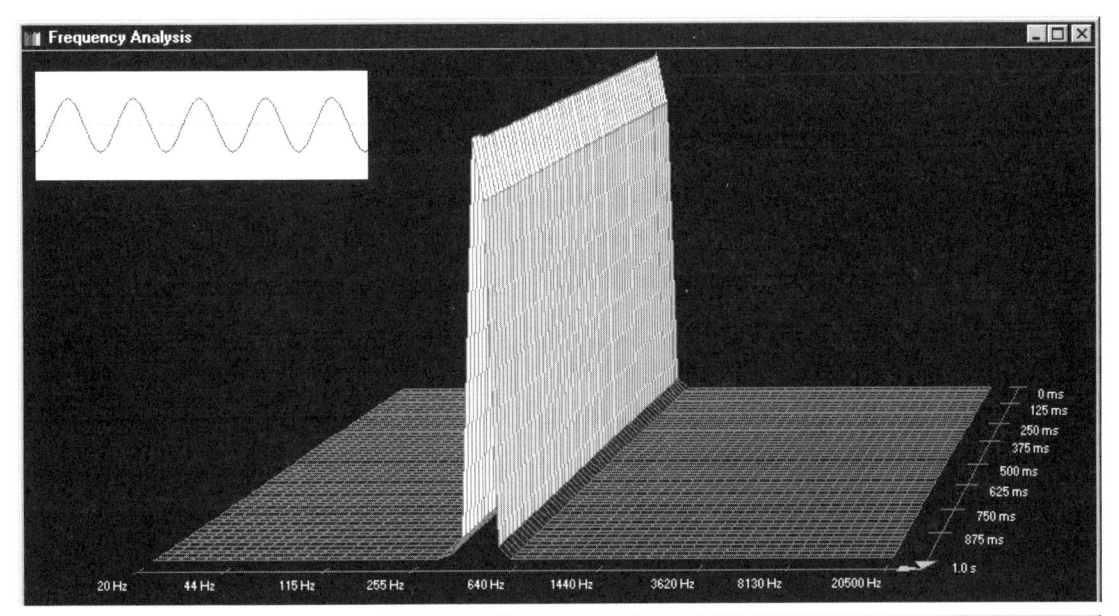

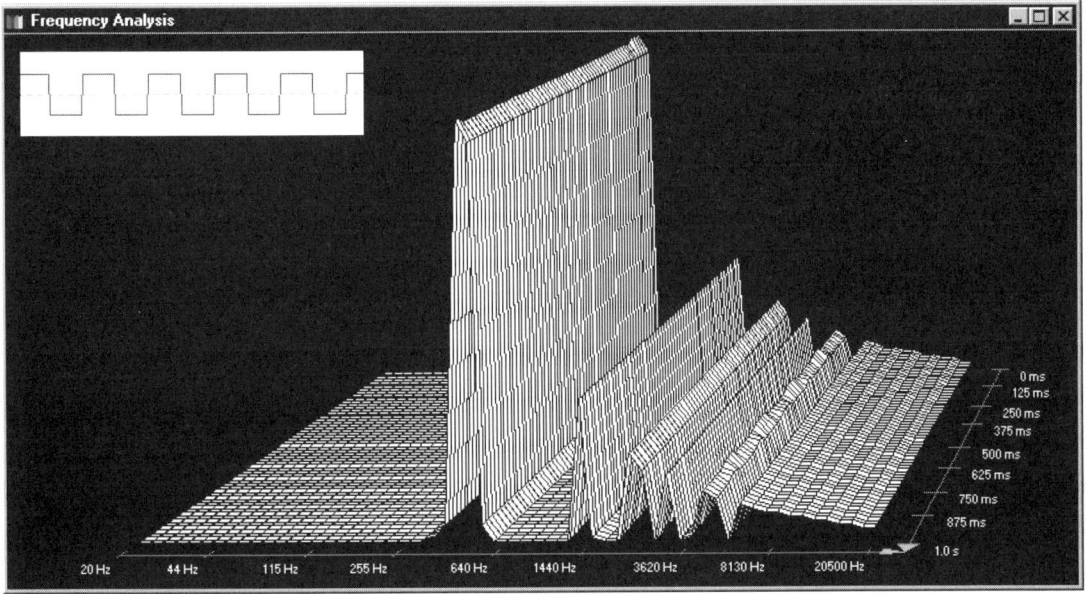

> **INFO**
>
> In the early days of recording, engineers compensated for the frequency loss caused by the rather primitive equipment of the day by running the sound through a tone control to boost the high frequencies. The aim was to make the recorded sound 'equal' to the original, hence the term equalisation. As recording equipment developed, the need for 'equalisation' became less and EQ soon became used a creative effect.

So, frequency analysis software shows which frequencies your recordings contain. It does have a practical application, however, other than producing pretty pictures. One of the most common audio processing functions is EQ which stands for equalisation. It's essentially a sophisticated tone control but modern EQ modules can home in on specific frequencies with great accuracy and cut and boost the exact frequencies in a recording that you want to adjust. It's a useful tool which can fix problem with a mix and improve it, too, as we'll see later in the book.

## The total sound

That, in a nutshell, is sound. It is our raw material and its three parameters – pitch, volume and frequency – are closely linked. When you change one, the chances are one of the others will change or our perception of them will change a little, too.

Knowing a few basics about the physics of sound will help you understand and solve problems such as why it's difficult to get a good bass response at low volume levels, why a sound loses sparkle if you cut the top end, and why it's important to use a system with a good dynamic range.

# 3
# Digital audio basics

Now that we know what sound is, we'll see what happens to it when it enters the digital domain. The first thing to look at is the difference between 'real' sound and digitised sound. Real sound is analogue and varies continuously over time. Digitised sound consists of a series of discrete numeric values. The quality of digital sound hinges upon the way it is converted or digitised so it's very important to understand the process involved. Knowing how it works will also help explain the sort of problems which can occur with digital audio - and how to avoid them. Don't worry, it's easier to understand than decibels.

## Sample rate

What do we mean when we say analogue sound varies continuously over time? Refer back to the sine wave, Figure 2.1, in the last chapter. To convert this into a digital format, we have to turn it into a sequence of numbers. This is fairly easily done by measuring - or sampling - the waveform at regular intervals and recording the values we find there. The more often a sample is taken, the more accurate the digital representation of the sound will be.

Figure 3.1 shows what a digitised version of a sine wave might look like. Compare it with the smooth curves of the example in Figure 2.1 and you'll notice that although both versions are similar in shape, they are hardly identical. The values in a true sine wave vary continuously while those in the digital example move in discrete steps.

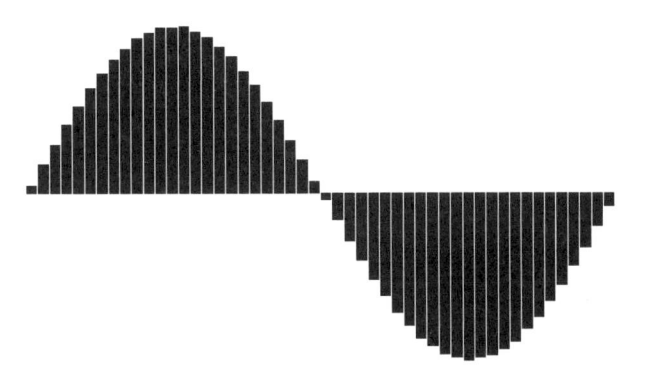

Figure 3.1 A digitised version of a sine wave

We can make the digital representation more accurate by taking more samples and Figure 3.2 shows the result of increasing the sample rate or frequency. Figure 3.3 has an even higher sample rate and is almost indistinguishable from an analogue sine wave. This would sound the most accurate when played back.

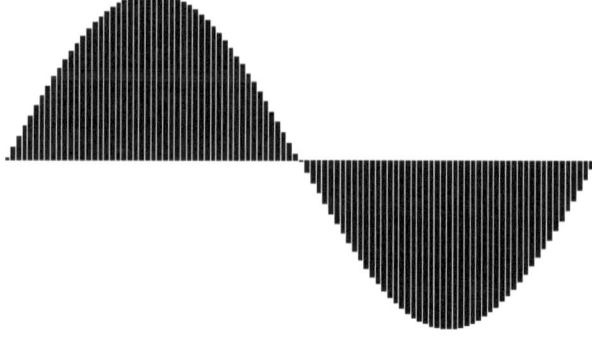

Figure 3.2 Increasing the sample rate produces a more accurate representation of the sine wave

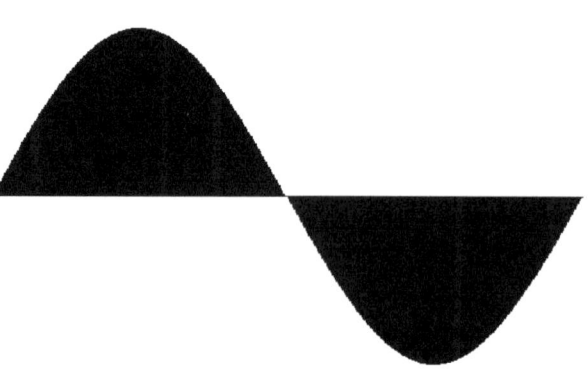

Figure 3.3 A very high sample rate produces a very accurate digital representation of the sine wave

So, the higher the sampling frequency, the more accurate the digital representation of the sound. But just how many samples do we need to take in order to get a truly accurate digital picture of a sound?

## Hooray for Harry Nyquist

Enter mathematician Harry Nyquist who discovered that you can accurately digitise any sound by sampling it at twice its frequency. Isn't that useful?

Let's put this into real world terms. As we saw in Chapter 2, the average range of human hearing is from about 15Hz to 20kHz. Therefore, in order to accurately measure the highest sounds we can hear, we need to use a sampling rate of around 40kHz. It will come as no surprise to learn that audio CDs use a sampling rate a little higher than that – 44.1kHz.

So what happens if we use a lower sampling rate? Well, it will not be able to capture accurately the higher frequencies and there will not be enough information to reconstruct the original waveform.

As we lower the sample rate you can see that the resulting digital

### TECHY BIT

*To be strictly accurate you have to sample a sound at slightly more than twice its frequency but we don't want to get involved with the maths here and "twice the frequency" is a good rule of thumb. But remember the "slightly more" bit in case you get into a discussion with a mathematical theorist or an engineer.*

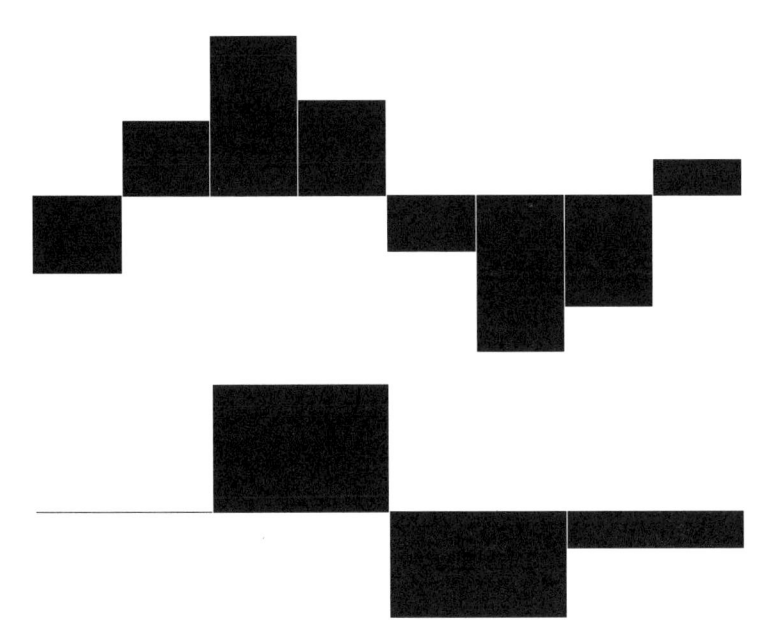

Figure 3.4 The sample rate here is extremely low and the waveform is only just distinguishable as a sine wave

Figure 3.5 The sample rate here is so low that the wave has no discernible shape

image of the sine wave starts to break down. In Figure 3.4 it's looking a little lopsided and in Figure 3.5 the sample rate is so low that's it's even unable to capture the basic sine wave shape.

If a program was given this data and asked to reconstruct the waveform it represented, it could produce something like that in Figure 3.6. If we zoom out on that we might see a waveform similar to the one in Figure 3.7 - a far cry from the original sine wave.

The result of using a sample rate which is too low for the sound being sampled is an effect called aliasing. You can see from Figure 3.7 that the reconverted waveform could include frequencies not in the original (the squarish shape of the waveform indicates square wave-type harmonics) and it's these additional frequencies that produce the aliasing effect.

Figure 3.6 Trying to reconstruct a sine wave from the data in Figure 3.5 could result in a waveform like this

Figure 3.7 Aliasing adds unwanted harmonics to the original data

> **TECHY BIT**
>
> In articles and discussions about sampling, you may come across the term, the Nyquist Limit or Frequency. This is the highest frequency which can be accurately reproduced using a given sampling rate. It's commonly held to be half the rate but it's actually a little less as mentioned earlier.

One way to prevent frequencies higher than the half the sample rate being sampled is simply to remove them and many digital sampling systems include a filter to do just that. It's not usually something you'll have any control over but it's reassuring to know they're working in the background helping to prevent aliasing.

For quality audio work, you will not want to use a sample rate lower than 44.1kHz. Even budget consumer sound cards support this rate so this will not normally a problem. However, budget cards may have poor filters and worse signal-to-noise ratios than cards designed for professional use. Although a card may claim to support 'CD quality' recording, be aware that there are other factors which contribute to the sound quality. There's more about this in Chapter 7.

Most systems support lower sampling rates and some support higher ones, typically 48kHz. This sample rate, sometimes called the 'professional' rate, is used by many audio DAT machines.

Lower sample rates can be useful for certain projects such as multimedia production, but even so, in order to produce the highest sound quality possible you will invariably get better results by working with a higher sample rate and then reducing or downsampling it afterwards.

## Oversampling

So is there anything we can do to improve the quality of the sound during recording? There is, but it's more a feature of the hardware than a process you can invoke yourself. It's called oversampling.

In the early days of digital recording it was all a device could do to sample at a sufficiently high rate to avoid aliasing. Now, with ever more powerful computers and software, we can sample at much higher rates.

But do we need to? According to Nyquist a rate of 44.1kHz should be more than adequate, even for listeners with rabbit-like ears. However, as you know, the higher the sample rate the more accurate the digital representation of the sound will be so if we want the highest quality possible, we ought to use the highest sample rate possible.

The process of oversampling samples the sound at a higher rate than required and averages the results. Oversampling can be anything from 2 to 128 times the usual sample rate. It's usually a feature of the hardware and you will often see an entry in the spec section of a sound card which says something like 64 x oversampling.

## Bits and bytes

We've seen how important a high sample rate is in order to digitise a sound accurately, now let's look at the measuring stick we use. Technically, this is the sample resolution and it's measured in bits. The most common resolutions are 8-bit and 16-bit although some systems use a 20-bit resolution or more.

So what exactly is a bit? You may know that at their lowest level, all computers do is shuffle numbers around. However, they do it so quickly that they have time to translate great long strings of numbers into letters, words, graphics and so on. Unlike humans who use digits in the range of 0 to 9, computers only use two digits – 0 and 1 – which are known as bits or **B**inary dig**IT**s.

In other words, unlike humans who use a numbering system based on the power of 10, computers use a numbering system based on the power of 2. Don't worry if this is starting to sound like a maths course. It's not essential that you understand exactly how it works but knowing a little about the binary system will help you understand the importance of the number of bits in a recording system. And you'll come across bits a lot in digital audio.

When humans count we use the digits from 0 to 9 and when we get to 9 we stick a 1 in the column to the left and start again at 1, a bit like a car mileometer. To find the total value of the number, digits in that column are multiplied by 10. Digits in the third column are multiplied by 100 and so on. Computers do the same but they only have two digits to work with so when they reach 1, they put a 1 in the next column and start counting again from 0.

In our decimal system, each column represents an increasing power of 10. In other words, each column is 10 times bigger than the one to its right:

| $10^3$ | $10^2$ | $10^1$ | $10^0$ |
|---|---|---|---|
| 1000 | 100 | 10 | 1 |

In the binary system, each column represents an increasing power of 2 and each column is 2 times greater than the one on the right:

| $2^7$ | $2^6$ | $2^5$ | $2^4$ | $2^3$ | $2^2$ | $2^1$ | $2^0$ |
|---|---|---|---|---|---|---|---|
| 128 | 64 | 32 | 16 | 8 | 4 | 2 | 1 |

Here are some conversions:

| Decimal | Binary |
|---|---|
| 0 | 0 |
| 1 | 1 |
| 2 | 10 |
| 3 | 11 |
| 4 | 100 |
| 5 | 101 |
| 6 | 110 |
| 7 | 111 |
| 8 | 1000 |
| 9 | 1001 |
| 10 | 1010 |
| 11 | 1011 |
| 12 | 1100 |
| 13 | 1101 |

## TECHY BIT

Unlike humans who usually start counting at 1, computers start counting at 0. Therefore, the total number of different values an 8-bit number can represent is not 255 but 256. By starting the count from 0, we squeeze an extra number out of the system.

In order to make bits more manageable, they are grouped together into words or bytes. A collection of eight bits makes an 8-bit word and a collection of 16 bits makes a 16-bit word. An 8-bit word can represent values from 0 to 255 (128+64+32+16+8+4+2+1) which is a total of 256 different values or $2^8$. A 16-bit number can represent values from 0 to 65535 which is 65536 different values or $2^{16}$.

## Vive la resolution

Now we get to the nitty gritty. The more divisions on our measuring scale – the resolution – the more accurately we can measure the sample. Imagine trying to build a model ship if every item you measured had to cut to the nearest of 256 values. The result may look like a ship – of sorts – and it may even float… but then again, it may not. If the same measure had 65536 divisions, you'd have a far better chance of making the pieces fit. In other words, the ship would be closer to the original plan. So, the higher the resolution, the more the digitised recording will be like the original sound.

Figures 3.8 and 3.9 illustrate the difference. In Figure 3.8 the measuring scale is divided into 11 (including the minus values). If we were to take the value of the waveform where the finger is pointing, it would have to be either 2 or 3 which is a long way from its real value. In Figure 3.9 the measuring scale is divided into 19 and the same position will be stored more accurately as it's virtually on 5. Of course, if the sample we wanted to measure was half way between 5 and 6 we'd have the same problem.

Because analogue signals vary continuously, no matter how many values our measuring stick has, there will always be points in between these values. If a sample hits an in between point, it will be given either the higher or lower value, depending on which it's closest to. The more values in our measure the smaller the 'real' value will have to be adjusted and the more accurate the digital representation of the sample.

For the sake of clarity, these examples have a very coarse measuring stick. Even an 8-bit sample rate has 256 values, not just 19! However, even this is not really enough to give us a truly accurate representation of

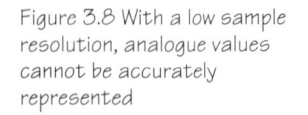

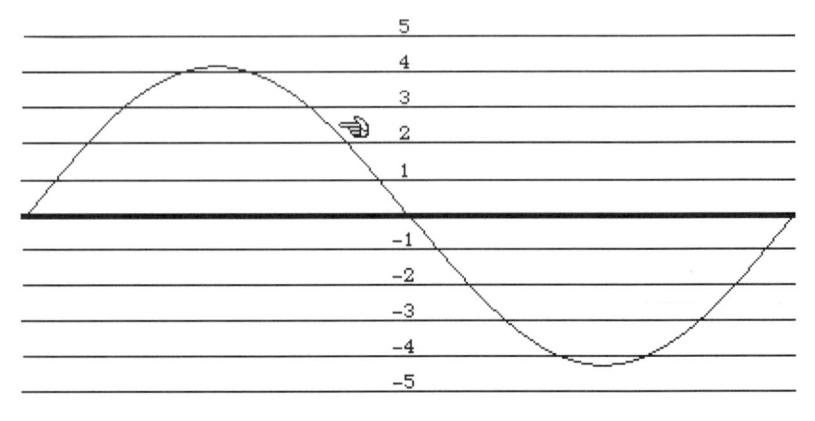

Figure 3.8 With a low sample resolution, analogue values cannot be accurately represented

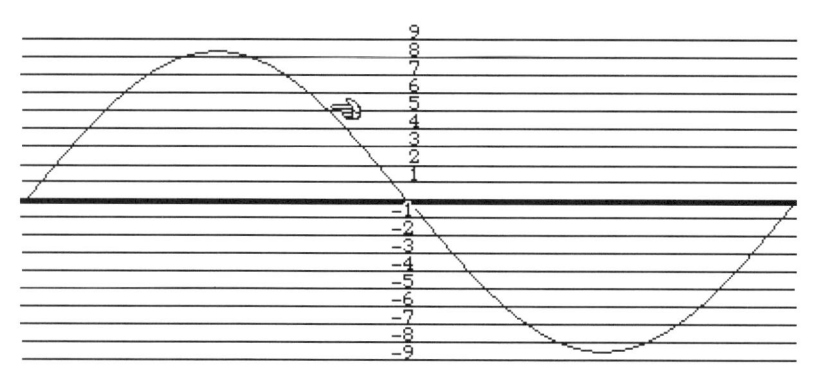

Figure 3.9 Increasing the sample resolution produces a more accurate digital sample

the sound. The 65536 values of a 16-bit sample are much better. It is, after all, 'CD quality' but even that, the audiophiles claim, is not enough for a 'real-life' representation of a sound which is why some pro systems use a 20-bit and 24-bit resolution.

## Resolution and dynamic range

The resolution is closely related to dynamic range which, as you may recall, is the difference between the quietest and loudest parts of the recording. The greater the number of notches on our measuring stick, the greater the number of levels we can record.

Imagine a synthesiser with a volume control with ten notches so the volume could only be set to one of ten levels. Not very subtle. If there was any noise in this system, the lowest it could possibly be would 1/10th of the overall volume!

An 8-bit system with 256 possible levels is obviously a lot better but a 16-bit system with 65536 levels is better still. (MIDI's volume controller, by the way, has 128 values.) An 8-bit system has an 48dB dynamic range and a 16-bit system a 96dB dynamic range.

As mentioned earlier, some high-end systems use a resolution of 20, 24 or even more bits. Real-world sounds and human hearing span a dynamic range of about 140dB so you can see that a system with such high resolutions - giving a dynamic range of 120dB and 144dB respectively - should be able to simulate the sounds we experience in real life extremely accurately.

If you look back over the development of digital sampling, it's interesting to note that the Fairlight 2, which was once a state-of-the-art instrument desired by many but affordable by only a few, was an 8-bit system. Akai's S900 and S950 samplers, long the industry standard, used only 12 bits.

It's quite likely that as technology continues to develop, 20-bit and 24-bit recording will become the norm. There are also a few purists who are holding out for a 32-bit system before they go digital. Imagine - a 192dB dynamic range!

But using a lot of bits in a system is not the whole story and we'll see why in a moment.

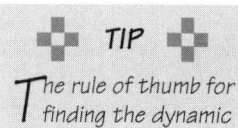

> **TIP**
>
> The rule of thumb for finding the dynamic range of a system is to multiply the bits by 6. So a 16-bit system has a potential dynamic range of 6 x 16 = 96dB.

## Low flying noise

As we have seen, the sampling process converts a sound into a series of numbers and the higher the resolution, the more accurate the conversion will be. However, the result is still a series of stepped numbers and as we lower the resolution, the size of the steps increases. As the steps get larger the output becomes distorted and grainy, an effect known as quantisation noise because it results from an over-rounding - or quantisation - of the data.

The distortion is especially noticeable at the tail end of a sound such as cymbals dying away and at the end of a sound which has had reverb applied to it.

The best way to minimise quantisation noise is to record at the highest possible level without clipping. This is a vitally important aspect of digital recording which is dealt with in more detail in Chapter 9.

Clipping occurs when the input volume is greater than the range of values the sample resolution can handle. It effectively chops off the top and bottom of the waveform, as you can see in Figure 3.10 which is a clipped sine wave. A clipped waveform will be flattened at the top and bottom and the result will be - yes, more noise, akin to a harsh distortion.

Figure 3.10 If a waveform has been clipped it will have flat areas at its highest and lowest peaks

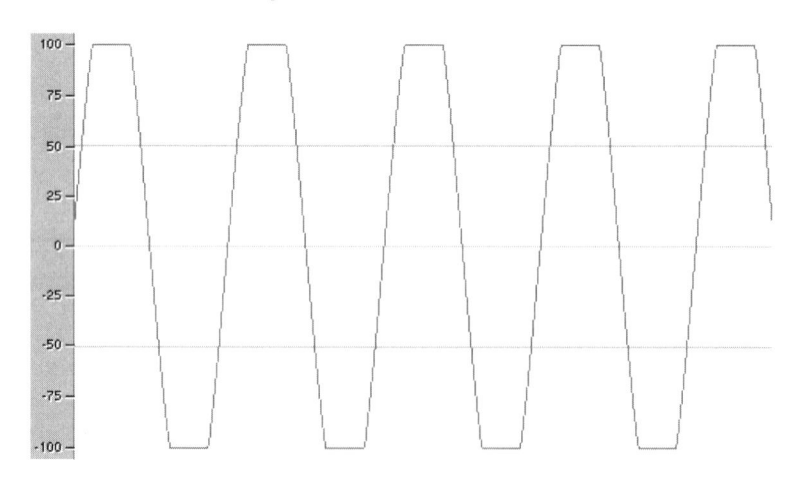

So, if recording at too high a volume can lead to noise, can you play safe by recording at a low volume? Unfortunately, not. Well, okay, you can but the result will be far from ideal. Let's say you're using a resolution of 8 bits (we'll use this as an example simply because it makes the numbers easier to follow) which has 256 values with which to represent the sound. Let's say you record a quiet sound which only needs 100 values to represent. This could be stored in a 7-bit number ($2^7 = 128$) so you've effectively thrown away a 'bit' of storage space and with it lost 6dB dynamic range.

It's worth saying again that if the final format of a recording project only has an 8-bit resolution, you'll get better results working with 16 bits and then downsampling. But, you may ask, will the reduction in the resolution not create the larger steps and the accompanying quantisation noise? Yes, it does. But many pieces of software have sample conversion routines which minimise the noise using a technique known as dithering. This generally produces a better result than recording with 8 bits in the first place.

The point is, the quality of a sound can never get any better than the original. If you start with an 8-bit sound and process it, you'll end up with processed 8-bit sound. If you start with a 16-bit sound, process it and downsample it to 8-bit, you'll still have an 8-bit sound but because it was processed at a higher resolution the quality will generally be better. It won't be as good as the original 16-bit sound, but it will be better than the same recording if it had originally been recorded using 8 bits.

Several systems have an internal processing resolution higher than the output resolution for precisely this reason. They interpolate the values between those produced by the recorded resolution, process the data at a higher resolution and convert it back to the original resolution again. It all helps maintain the quality which is important in all forms of recording.

> **THERE'S MORE**
>
> There's more about 'dithering' in Chapter 11.

## Will the real sample resolution please stand up?

This brings us to another important aspect of digital recording and, yes, another factor to take into consideration during recording. Obvious fact number one - if you exploit the full dynamic range of your system by recording at as high a level as possible, effectively using all the 65536 steps a 16-bit recording supports, you will achieve the best quality audio your system can produce.

However, that's in a ideal world. A tape system can absorb a signal without distortion if it's a little over the top but not a digital system. It has an absolute limit and if you exceed it, the signal will be truncated to the highest value. Not a pretty sight and not a pleasant sound, either.

In order to avoid the risk of clipping most people leave a little headroom so the maximum level is likely to be a little below what the system is theoretically capable of handling. In practice, you'll probably find you're working to a resolution of 14 or 15 bits in a 16-bit system so you've lost some dynamic range before you even start.

However, that's still a dynamic range of around 84dB which beats the heck out of a tape system. If you're old enough to remember the birth of the audio CD, you may recall how bright and clear the sound was compared with records or cassettes. Now you know why - it has a much higher dynamic range.

In the early days of CDs, record companies rushed to put their old recordings onto CD. If the recordings were simply transferred from tape to the CD format as many were, there was no difference in the sound quality at all! A more common practice now when transferring from tape to CD is to digitally enhance the recording to increase its dynamic range.

> **THERE'S MORE**
>
> See Chapter 11 for more about digital enhancing

> **INFO**
>
> Stereo CD-quality digital audio needs around 10Mb of storage space per minute. A five-minute song would require 50Mb and you can do your own sums to work out how much space an entire album requires. Thank goodness for low-cost hard disks!

## DACs and ADCs

We've talked at length about converting analogue sound into digital data but what actually does the job? Naturally enough, a device called an analogue-to-digital converter, often abbreviated to ADC although sometimes A-t-D or A/D converter is used. The conversion from digital to analogue is performed by a DAC.

It's something to be aware of but nothing users usually get involved in unless you start specifying stand-alone DACs and ADCs for high-end systems. DACs are built into virtually all PC sound cards so the first bit of good news is that you don't need any high-end equipment for d-t-d recording.

The card feeds the sound to the computer via a piece of digital audio software, and once the computer has it in its grasp, so to speak, it can do what it likes with it. In d-t-d recording, it saves it to a hard disk. It could, if the software developers had so decreed, store it in memory, but the conversion of sound into digital audio produces quite a lot of data and even if you have 64Mb of RAM in your computer you wouldn't be able to store much sound in it.

## Waveform formats

After the sample rate and resolution has been set and the sound has been analysed and the ADCs have done their work, we're left with a mass of digital data which, in d-t-d recording, must be saved to the hard disk. Some programs allow it to be saved in a number of different formats. The two most common formats are Wave (.WAV) and AIFF (.AIF).

Wave is Windows' native sound file format. Most software will recommend you use this unless there is a specific reason to use another format, which you might do if transferring it to another type of computer such as an Apple Macintosh.

AIFF (Audio Interchange File Format) is a standard defined by Apple computers and commonly used by the Mac and other computer platforms and supported by most audio software.

These two are by far the most common file formats used by PCs but there are dozens of others. Some are generic formats which some PC audio software will be able to read. Others are special formats for specific software or other computer platforms (which some PC software may still be able to read) and some are compressed formats, many of which have been developed to deliver audio over the World Wide Web. In general, stick with the Wave format and, if the final file is to be in another format, convert it when the recording has been completed.

If you use audio files produce by other systems and other computer platforms, you may need the ability to import files in a number of formats. Some software has the ability to import foreign file formats, but most are quite happy with Wave files, AIFF and perhaps some compressed formats. We touch on some of these a little later in the book.

## Summing up

- Use as high a sample rate as possible, preferably 44.1kHz.
- Use as high a sample resolution as possible. Most current systems and sound cards use 16 bits which is fine but be aware that systems with even higher resolutions are coming onto the market and will offer even greater dynamic range and purity of sound.
- If the final product has to be in a lower format such as 22.05kHz or 8-bit resolution which is used in many multimedia applications, you'll get better results if you work with higher rates and resolutions and then downsample the finished result.
- Avoid overdriving the input level during recording as clipping will result which leads to distortion.
- Record using the Windows Wave format unless there's a specific reason to use a different format. Convert it to another format afterwards if necessary.

*Handwritten notes:*

ADC — Analogue to Digital Converter
DAC — Digital to Analogue
d-t-d — direct to disc

# 4

## The PC system

Direct-to-disk recording, digital audio editing and audio processing only became an affordable reality when the hardware powerful enough to do the job became cheap enough for most of us to buy. The PC has been growing more powerful and becoming increasingly cheaper over the years and it's now a consumer item sold in many high street stores.

And most PC systems work well with most applications, including music ones. However, with d-t-d recording, certain parts of the system are particularly important in order to achieve the maximum performance. It's not essential that you have the latest, biggest, fastest PC on the block for d-t-d as long as the most important items are up to speed. With this in mind, let's look at the parts which make up a typical PC system, and see which areas are the most crucial for d-t-d recording.

### Buying a PC

As you probably know, PCs are constructed from lots of interchangeable parts – items like a video graphics card, a hard disk, a monitor, a floppy disk drive and so on can be installed into virtually any PC and it's easy to create your own Frankenstein PC by specifying particular items. However, as with most things in life, everything has a price. For a little more money you can buy a bigger, faster hard drive or a faster video card or add a little more memory... Where do you stop?

The best general advice is to buy the latest, fastest system you can afford. Not only will it run like lightning and impress the heck out of the neighbours, but it will future-proof you as much as it's possible to be future-proofed in the ever-changing PC market.

There are dozens – probably hundreds – of companies constructing and selling PCs. They all have access to the same components but in order to turn out a competitive machine they have to look at areas where they can trim costs. This invariably means some items in a machine from one company will be better or worse than similar items in a machine from another company.

Before buying a PC, it's a good idea to buy a couple of the latest PC magazines and check the adverts from a few large computer suppliers. This will give you a feel for the sort of systems on the market and the amount they cost. Most suppliers have a list of optional extras allowing you to add a larger monitor, a bigger hard disk, more RAM and so on, which gives you the ability to customise your system.

Because of economies of scale, larger companies may not be able to supply parts produced by specific manufacturers although some suppliers, particularly the smaller ones, will build a system from the exact parts you specify. If you want a hard disk by company ABC or a video card by XYZ, they will obtain the parts and build the system for you. If you don't know which item is best, ask.

Most companies have technical staff who should be able to tell you the difference between one hard drive and another, for example, and suggest the best one for the job in hand. But don't get too hung up on this sort of thing – the majority of parts from the majority of companies do a good job.

## Using high street stores

A quick word about buying a computer from a high street shop. Many first-time buyers are nervous about buying a computer from a mail order company (will all the bits be in the box and will the instructions tell you how to put it together?) or from a computer supplier whose offices are filled with techies building PCs in the back room (far too threatening).

And so they troop along to their local high street shop. Invariably, the shop assistants have to learn a little bit about all the items in the shop and some may have scant knowledge of PCs. However, most shops have a number of assistants specially trained in computing so make sure you talk to one of them when asking for advice. You should not have this problem in a dedicated computer shop.

However, as a general rule you will pay more for a computer system from a high street store than from a dedicated computer manufacturer/reseller so before you buy, do check the prices of comparable systems in the latest computer magazines. The difference can be considerable so do your sums carefully. Also, beware of the price of the extras. I have seen RAM on sale in a high street store at four times the price being charged by dedicated computer suppliers!

## The Net Works PC

In order to explain what the various parts of a PC do and the importance they play in a machine to be used for direct-to-disk recording, we'll use a real-life example. But bearing in mind this book is about direct-to-disk recording and not PC hardware, I make no apologies for glossing over some facets of PC design and simplifying others.

The following machine was supplied by Net Works (GB) Ltd, a small but dedicated company specialising in the construction of PCs and Unix systems, network solutions and custom software programming. We'll list the specs first and then go through the items one by one.

*[Handwritten at top: Sound Blaster Live Audio [E300]]*

Making music with digital audio

*[Handwritten in left margin: 992 Mb ← ; 3.00GHz]*

> Intel Pentium MMX 200 Processor
> ABIT IT5H HX Chipset, 512K PB Cache, on-board EIDE & I/O
> 64Mb EDO RAM
> Quantum 3.2Gb EIDE Drive
> ATI 2Mb EDO RAM VideoBoost Graphics card
> ATI TV Tuner Card
> 12 x EIDE CD ROM drive
> 3.5 inch Floppy disk drive
> Full Tower Case with 250W PSU
> Microsoft mouse
> Window 95 Keyboard
> Microsoft Windows 95 OSR2 Release
> 12 months RTB Warranty

### The processor

Regardless of what else you have in your PC, the processor still determines its overall performance. 1996 and 1997 will be remembered as the year of the Pentium and 1997 saw the release of Intel's MMX technology (which had been twiddling its thumbs since 1996 so as not to upset sales of the standard Pentiums on dealers' shelves). But do you need a Pentium and do you need MMX?

Each processor from the 286, 386 and 486 up to the Pentium has offered speed and performance advantages over its predecessor. In 1997 the three major processors included the Pentium, the Pentium Pro and the Pentium MMX. The Pentium is a fast processor offering many performance advantages over the 486, and Windows 95 certainly performs better on a Pentium than it does on a 486.

If you're looking for a new PC and are on a very tight budget – as musicians seem continually to be – this will be your cheapest serious option. It's difficult to recommend a 486 – so I won't! Technology moves so quickly, applications demand an increasing amount of hardware power and the 486 is heading the way of the 386 and 286.

The MMX (Multimedia eXtensions) chip contains 57 additional instructions designed to improve the handing of multimedia functions including graphics, video and sound. It also has 32K of Level 1 Cache (compared with 16K on the standard Pentium chip) which increases the performance of most applications by around 10 percent. However, it really comes into its own when running applications that make use of the additional MMX instructions.

As of writing, few applications have been produced which make use of the additional functions but this will change. As far as anyone can predict the future of computer technology, it looks likely that the MMX will become the standard throughout 1997 and 1998. As prices fall you may think it worth while opting for an MMX chip rather than a standard Pentium just to be there as and when MMX applications come on line.

However, there's also the Pentium Pro. This performs at its best with

---

**INFO**

The processor is often referred to as the CPU – Central Processing Unit. It's essentially the computer 'brain'.

32-bit applications and likes running Windows NT rather than Windows 95. It also needs a Pentium Pro motherboard and these tend to be more expensive. There is probably not enough fully-compatible music software to make this a serious consideration although as the technology develops and becomes cheaper that may change.

There are chip manufacturers other than Intel – Cyrix and AMD are well-known competitors. Although Intel seems to hog most of the limelight thanks to its advertising, chips by the other manufacturers are worth considering. Some of the Cyrix chips, for example, are not only cheaper than the comparable Intel chips but outperform them, too. As Intel is the 'standard', many people prefer to go with the name they know but if you are on a serious budget, check the alternatives.

## Clock speeds

Digital audio requires a lot of processing power – to capture the audio, save it to disk, to process it and play it back – so the faster the processor runs, the better. Pentiums have been available at speeds ranging from 60MHz upwards. The Pentium 200 runs at 200MHz and, as with most things to do with the PC, it pays to buy the fastest you can afford.

It's likely that the Pentium 200 will soon be an entry level machine. However, if budget dictates, go with a Pentium 166 or a 133. However, you'll probably find the price difference between these and faster processors is not very great.

## The motherboard and chipset

The motherboard is the large printed circuit board inside the PC which holds the processor, the RAM, the BIOS, the cache and which has connections for attaching serial and printer ports, and floppy and hard disks. It also has ISA and PCI slots for plugging in cards such as a video card, a modem, a SCSI card and, of course, a sound card.

The chipset controls the movement of data around the computer and although there are several chipset manufacturers, Intel is far and away the most well-known. There are currently three main Intel 'Triton' chipsets – VX, HX and TX. VX uses SDRAM which is optimised for multimedia processing and it has improved EDO RAM timings. It also supports concurrent PCI and the USB.

The HX chipset doesn't support SRAM but has built-in ECC. It has essentially the same features as the VX but uses fewer chips and is aimed at high-end systems. A feature of HX and VX-based systems is that the CPU can use memory or ISA buses while the PCI bus is in use which speeds up multitasking.

The TX chipset supports SDRAM, concurrent PCI and USB. It has fast EDO timings and is optimised for MMX processors. It also has DPMA (Dynamic Power Management Architecture) which includes intelligent power-saving features and is, therefore, well suited to mobile computing.

Few buyers pay much attention to the motherboard and it's probably

> ### INFO
> A bus is simply a route from one part of the computer to another which carries signal. An ISA or PCI expansion slot may often be referred to as an expansion bus or ISA or PCI bus.

> ### INFO
> **USB** – Universal Serial Bus, yet another 'standard' to supplement ISA and PCI. It would have all peripherals connected to one, unified bus although it currently doesn't have the speed for large data transfers.
> **Concurrent PCI** – Intel's update to the PCI system which makes more efficient use of the PCI bus.
> **ECC** – Error Correction Codes, which tell the hard disk if it has read the data correctly.

true to say that the ones in most PCs will be quite adequate for the system. However, there are a few motherboard features worth checking.

**Cache**
Caching systems are essential on a Pentium in order to get the best performance out of the computer. Because the processors are so fast they can handle data far quicker than their surrounding memory subsystems can supply it. If such a situation occurs, the computer sits around twiddling its thumbs and everything slows down.

A cache is a buffer or temporary storage area between two parts of the computer system, one of which operates faster than the other. Data is read from the slower part of the system and stored in the cache. The faster part of the system can access data from the cache quicker than it could from other slower part of the system so it speeds up the computer's operation.

There are two levels of cache called, conveniently, Level 1 and Level 2. L1 cache is resident on the CPU (as described above) and L2 is on the motherboard. There are three primary types of cache – write-back, write-through and pipeline burst and without getting involved in the technicalities, pipeline burst is the fastest and is virtually standard on all fast Pentium motherboards (but check anyway).

Most motherboards offer 256K or 512K of pipeline burst cache and if you go for 256K you can usually upgrade at a later stage. However, the price difference between the two is generally quite small and unless – and here's that phrase again – you're on a seriously tight budget, it's worth spending a few extra quid and going for the 512K. It will certainly enhance performance with faster processors such as the Pentium 166 and above.

**I/O and EIDE controllers**
In order to talk to the outside world – which, for a PC, means disk drives, a printer, keyboard and mouse, MIDI equipment and other serial devices – the computer needs I/O controllers which generally comprise a controller for the disk drives and one for the serial and parallel ports.

With most modern motherboards the controllers are built onto the board itself and you simply connect cables from the on-board connectors to the drives and run leads from the board to the backplane on the computer case for the serial and parallel ports. Some motherboards, particularly older ones, have no or little built-in connectors and require an I/O controller on a plug-in card. Having the I/O controllers built-in obviously simplifies the design and saves a slot.

IDE drives have controller circuitry built into the drive electronics which simplifies the interfacing requirements making it easier – and cheaper – to connect to the motherboard. Strangely enough, EIDE is sometimes referred to simply as IDE although as virtually all modern systems use EIDE, there is rarely any confusion. Honest!

IDE refers to the electronics in the drive, not the interface which is, strictly speaking, called ATA but many people refer to the connection as

> **❖ INFO ❖**
> I/O – Input/Output, the part of the system which controls the floppy and hard drives and the serial and parallel ports.

an IDE interface. But as long as we all know what we're talking about, no serious harm will be done. There's more about ATA and EIDE in the next chapter.

Again, if the interface is built into the motherboard, it saves a slot. It's reasonably easy to add another disk drive if necessary and you can connect a compatible CD ROM drive to the interface, too.

> **INFO**
> IDE – Intelligent (or Integrated) Drive Electronics. EIDE – Enhanced IDE.

## ISA and PCI slots

ISA (Industry Standard Architecture) and PCI (Peripheral Component Interconnect) are expansion slots on the motherboard which allow other devices to be plugged into the computer. These include graphics cards, sound cards, a SCSI card, an internal modem, network cards and so on.

The ISA is the oldest standard. It was originally designed to work with 8 bits of data but it was extended to work with 16 bits of data and cards were called 8-bit and 16-bit ISA cards respectively. 8-bit cards will work in a 16-bit slot but not vice versa. Virtually all ISA slots on modern motherboards are now 16-bit.

The PCI bus provides faster access to the CPU for demanding peripherals such as graphics and sound cards. Most PCI devices are Plug and Play compatible which makes them easier to install. However, there are many ISA PnP devices, too, particularly sound cards.

Most modern motherboards will likely have a combination of PCI and ISA slots. It's essential that you assess what sort of hardware you're going to plug into the PC and get a motherboard with enough suitable slots. With a Pentium system, one PCI slot will be required for the graphics card. Many sound cards still use the ISA bus although a few of the more upmarket ones use PCI.

The IT5H in the Net Works PC has four PCI slots and four ISA slots. However, two of them are shared so you can only use three PCI slots and four ISA slots or four ISA slots and three PCI slots. This is currently a standard arrangement. Be aware that some motherboards have fewer slots.

> **INFO**
> Plug and Play or PnP was designed to make it easy to add new hardware to a PC. The idea is that you plug it in – and it plays straight away. The PC analyses the hardware attached to it and makes all the settings for you. Most of the time. PnP was mainly designed for Windows 95 but PnP drivers enable devices to work under Windows 3.1, too.

## RAM

RAM is the computer's main memory where applications are loaded and run and which is used to perform calculations and manipulate data. To run Windows 95 you need at least 8Mb of RAM. In theory. Practically, settle for no less than 16Mb and preferably 32Mb. Windows 95 likes lots of RAM so don't disappoint it. It needs room to spread out and breath and you'll find programs run faster in 32Mb of RAM than in 16Mb.

If an application does not have enough RAM to run in, it uses the hard disk as a temporary storage area, swapping bits of data between the disk and RAM when required. As you probably know, RAM works infinitely faster than a hard disk so if you have to wait for data swaps, the program will slow down to a crawl. This is something you'd want to avoid when running any program but it must be avoided like the plague when running any real-time program such as direct-to-disk recording.

> ### ✣ INFO ✣
>
> *There are several different types of memory or RAM chips you can plug into your PC including SDRAM (Synchronous DRAM), DRAM (Dynamic RAM), and EDO – Extended Data Out RAM. They all do the same basic job – that of storing computer data – but some do if more efficiently than others. Different PC systems require different types of RAM. In most cases it will pay to use the fastest your system supports.*

Another advantage of having lots of RAM is the ability to run several programs at the same time. You could run a multi-track d-t-d recorder, a waveform editor and a MIDI sequencer, for example. Or you could run your music software and keep an address book open or a wordprocessor for making notes.

To complicate the situation slightly, there are different types of RAM such as SRAM, DRAM and EDO RAM. Most modern Pentium systems use EDO RAM and, again, it makes sense to buy the tools for the job – or the type of RAM which will work best on your computer. The supplier should advise.

If you're buying at a time when RAM is relatively cheap, treat your machine to another 32Mb. The Net Works PC has 64Mb and flies like the wind.

## The hard disk

The hard disk, of course, is one of the most important parts of a d-t-d system and the pertinent aspects of hard disks are discussed in more detail in the next chapter.

There are lots of makes of drives to choose from and even if you weren't using a PC for d-t-d, it makes sense to get a drive which complements the rest of the system. If you have a nippy Pentium, don't buy a slow hard disk or it will slow down your system.

The drive in the Net Works PC is a Quantum Fireball 3.2Gb EIDE drive which, while not the fastest around, was good value-for-money. It has a data transfer rate of around 16Mb/sec and an access time of 10.5ms. We'll look at the significance of these figures in the next chapter.

## Graphics card

The video graphics card is responsible for putting the images on the monitor. Like disk drives, there are lots to choose from. Graphics cards have generally concentrated on putting 2D images on the screen but recently there has been a growing interest in displaying 3D images. 3D is probably of little interest to users of 'serious' applications – although it's probably only a matter of time before the average wordprocessor comes with whizzo 3D menus and buttons – but you may like to consider a card which supports 3D if you also want to play games on your machine.

Video cards have on-board RAM which is used to construct the video image. The more RAM there is, the more colours it will be able to display and the larger the screen image or resolution it can produce.

The screen size you want to use will depend on the size of your monitor. The standard VGA resolution is 640 x 480 pixels and 256 colours. This is fine for a 14 inch monitor but if you have a larger monitor you will almost certainly want to use SVGA which offers resolutions of 800 x 600 and 1024 x 768. Many cards can display even higher resolutions, perhaps up to 1600 x 1200 with thousands or millions of colours.

For most music and d-t-d applications, you probably don't need a lot of colours – 256 will usually suffice, possibly even 16. As you near the limits of the card's capabilities you'll find you have to trade off the number of colours available against the resolution – and vice versa. If you want to combine music with a movie then you may want to ensure that the graphics card supports enough colours at the required resolution.

Most digital audio software and music software cram a lot of information onto the screen. Many use multiple windows and you may want to have half a dozen windows open on screen at the same time. Obviously, the higher the resolution, the more room there is for multi-window displays. Although it may be technically possible to display a resolution of 1024 x 768 or higher on a 14 inch monitor, it would probably be very difficult to read. So, you need to chose your graphics card in conjunction with your monitor.

The ATI VideoBoost Graphics card with 2Mb of RAM includes a customised Display Properties sheet, Figure 4.1, and it can support resolutions up to 1024 x 768 with 256 colours. It's also compatible with the ATI TV Tuner card. Well, you could be working away in your studio and realise that there's a program about your favourite band on the TV. Or you could switch to Teletext to find out who's playing at the local venues...

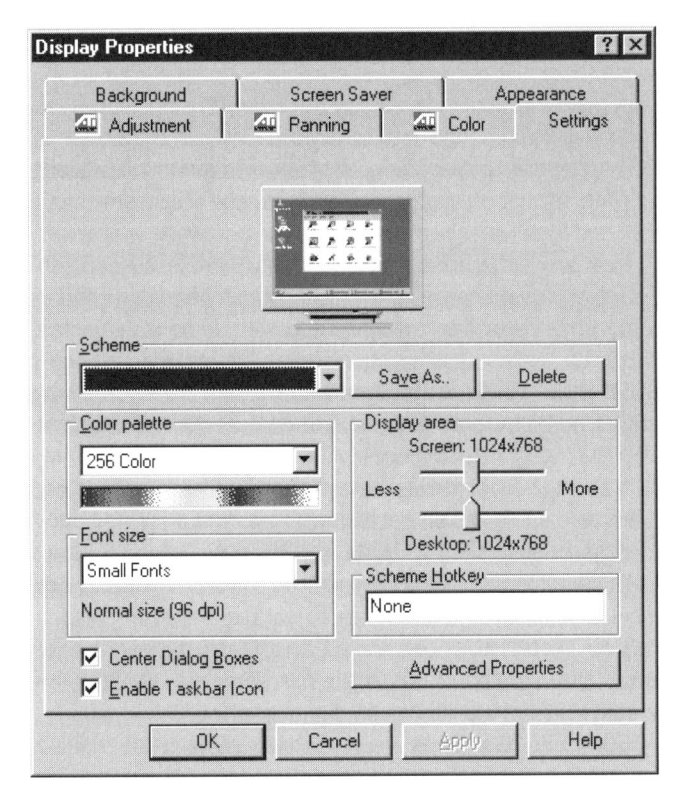

### INFO

*VGA – Video Graphics Array, now a somewhat old display specification. SVGA – Super VGA, still a common standard but most graphics cards are now capable of even high resolutions.*

Figure 4.1 The ATI Display Properties sheet lets you customise your screen size and colours

## INFO

*Single-speed CD ROM drives – which are all but obsolete – read data at round 150Kb/sec. Double speed drives – also virtually obsolete – read data twice as quickly at around 300Kb/sec. Most modern CD ROM drives are 12-speed (1800Kb/sec) and 16-speed (2400Kb/sec) or even faster. However, they don't necessarily transfer data at that speed so don't get mislead by the specs.*

## CD ROM drive

A CD ROM drive is now an essential part of a PC. As applications grow larger and larger, some are only available on CD and even if they are available on floppy disks, the CD version often has lots more files. Installation from CD is far, far quicker than installing from floppies and some software uses the CD as a form of copy protection. CD ROM drives are also so cheap now that it's criminal not to have one!

CD ROM drives were originally intended as mass storage devices and they were very slow compared with hard disks. However, throughout 1996 and 1997, CD ROM drives got faster and 12, 16 and even 24 speed drives are the norm. How much faster they will get is anyone's guess. Pure speed, however, is not the only criterion which determines the data transfer rate.

CD ROM drives can play audio CDs, too, which is useful if you want to give a CD a quick blast without powering up your hi fi. If you connect the audio output from the drive to your sound card (most have an internal connector for precisely this purpose), you'll be able to play CDs through the same sound system as the one you use for your sound card.

Also of interest to digital audio users are sample CDs. There are hundreds, if not thousands, of these containing all sorts of sounds from choirs and ethnic instruments to orchestral instruments and bass and drum loops. Traditionally, sample CDs contain sounds in audio format. They were originally developed for use with samplers – you'd play the CD and record the sound into a sampler. With the increase in popularity of PC-based recording systems, a growing number of CDs are now available in Wave format so you can simply copy the files from the CD to your hard disk and load them into your recording software or wave editor.

However, if you have an audio-only sample CD you can play it on the CD ROM drive, connect the output directly to your sound card, record it using your recording software and save it to disk. In fact the software which comes with many sound cards allows you to incorporate the CD ROM drive's audio output into the audio chain, so if you connect the drive's audio output to the sound card as described above it's usually an easy matter to record from it.

Many CD ROM drives have a digital output connector which enables them to transfer audio data direct to a digital input, removing the audio-to-digital conversion stage in the previous process. Some sound cards have digital connectors but you would need to check both sets of documentation in order to create a compatible connecting lead.

Even better, however, some CD ROM drives have the ability to transfer audio directly from a CD to the hard disk via the drive's interface which should result in a pretty clean digital copy.

But if you have to record via an audio connection, don't worry about it. Before the development of digital transfer, thousands of records were made using samples recorded audio-to-audio.

As storage devices, CD ROM drives do not really need to be super fast. Okay, a slow drive will take a little longer to install a program and copy Wave files to your hard disk but we're talking several seconds longer, not

## THERE'S MORE

*There's more about CD ROMs in general in Chapter 12.*

several minutes. A fast CD ROM drive comes into its own for playing multimedia files, combinations of program, sound and video which must be read, played and displayed in real-time pretty quickly. If you don't want to do this, you can save a little by buying a slower drive. However, the prices of even the fastest drives are continuously falling and it's probably worth paying a little extra to get a drive which is a little bit faster. You never know when you might need it.

An alternative is to buy a CD-R system which lets you create your own CDs and that's covered in the Chapter 12, too.

The CD ROM drive in the Net Works PC is a pretty standard 12-speed drive. It has a digital output on the back, an audio output which can be connected to a sound card, a headphone output on the front and a 'skip to next track' button for use when playing audio CDs. It can transfer digital audio from an audio CD to the hard disk — again, more about this in Chapter 12.

> **INFO**
> CD-R — CD Recordable, a CD ROM drive which can write to CDs as well as read from them.

## Keyboard, mouse and case

The choice of the mouse and keyboard are down to personal preference. Do they feel good to the fingers? The ones in the Net Works PC are standard items but you can spend a lot more on both mouse and keyboard.

The Net Works case is a beaut! It's a solid, full-tower system with a 250W power supply unit (PSU). Full-towers are great if you need to change anything inside the PC often. It gives you more room to work than a mini-tower and certainly more room than a desktop case. However, if you know exactly what you want inside your PC and aren't planning on opening it up very often, the other cases will do fine. Oh, just check the length of any cards you want to install. Some full length cards are rather long and some desktop cases have been known to have rather small insides...

A 250W power supply is more than adequate and could handle a PC full of cards. I'm personally a little wary of smaller PSUs (although I'd be fairly happy with a 230W) but a 200W PSU often used in mini-towers and desktop machines would probably be fine even with several cards. I prefer to err on the side of caution, that's all.

## Windows 95

This book assumes you will be running Windows 95 as it is supplied virtually as standard with all new PCs and the vast majority of software coming onto the market is designed to use it. There are other operating systems, of course, although to remain mainstream we can do little else but ignore them.

Windows 95 is more robust and generally more powerful and flexible than Windows 3.1, its predecessor. Many pieces of music software are being written specifically for Windows 95 and won't run under Windows 3.1 so Windows 3.1 won't figure very highly in the rest of this book. However, the basic processing and editing principles apply, whatever operating system you are using.

> **✥ INFO ✥**
>
> *Multi-tasking – the ability to do two things at the same time such as walk and chew gum, something one of the American Presidents was reputedly unable to do. Computers can't do either, but a good multi-tasking system allows you to process files while performing other edits, load or save data while playing a file and so on.*

Windows NT has many advantages over Windows 95 – it is better at multi-tasking and it has a faster and more reliable file system. Most Windows 95 software should run under Windows NT, too, although you may need special drivers for some applications – and sound cards – and, indeed, possibly a special NT adaptation. If you want to use Windows NT make sure all the hardware and applications you intend to use are fully compatible with it.

Windows 95 was released at the end of 1995 but Microsoft has released some updates for it to correct bugs – sorry, features – and to spruce up a few areas. The OSR2 release in 1996 was initially only supplied to PC distributors although it's probably pretty close to the next commercial release of Windows 95. Its main feature was the ability to handle disk partitions larger than 2Gb.

## The warranty

A 12 month warranty is the norm for computer equipment although some suppliers offer a two or three year warranty. Invariably, though, the additional cost will be reflected in the price.

Most warranties are RTB (Return To Base) where it's the user's responsibility to return faulty equipment to the supplier for repair. This can not only be expensive but troublesome as you really need to keep the original packaging in order to pack the system securely. Also, you may have to return the whole unit even if only one part of it – the floppy disk drive, say – has broken. If you're thinking of accepting a RTB warranty, check. An option here, of course, is to buy from a local supplier.

Some companies offer an on-site warranty where a repair person will visit you in case of a breakdown. Much better and more convenient but, of course, the cost will be reflected in the overall price. You may be able to buy an extended warranty or an on-site warranty from the supplier if you ask them.

Net Works' 12 month RTB warranty is par for the course and helps keep the cost down. The good news is, most PCs are reliable and most parts should last for three years at least. After three or four years, it's usually reckoned that a PC will be so old it's virtually obsolete and needs replacing anyway. Sobering thought.

> **✥ INFO ✥**
>
> *If you have a large disk drive of 2Gb or more, it's often convenient to divide it into smaller sections called partitions. The computer interprets these as individual disk drives which can be useful in helping you organise your files. Also, there is a limit to the size of a single hard disk or partition that most operating systems can read so in some cases you have no option but to partition a large hard disk.*

## Add-ons

To the Net Works PC I added an Adaptec AHA-2940 Ultra Wide SCSI card and a Plasmon SCSI-based CDR4240 CD-R drive. The SCSI card is fast and allows the connection of hard drives and other SCSI peripherals. It was easily installed and, being Wide SCSI, supports up to 16 devices. There's more about SCSI in the next chapter.

The CDR4240 plugged into the Adaptec card and functions as an excellent CD ROM drive, reading at 4x speed which may seem slow but which is quite fast enough for most purposes. There's more about this in Chapter 12.

## All together now

There is no such thing as an 'average' PC. All the items we've discussed here (and there are others) have a bearing on how fast and efficiently a PC operates. When you put all the pieces of a PC together, the resulting machine is only as fast as its weakest link. If you want to make your PC as efficient as possible for d-t-d work, it is, therefore, important that you eliminate any bottlenecks.

The hybrid nature of the PC also helps explain why it is so difficult for manufacturers to; a) write efficient music software in the first place, and b) tell you exactly what sort of performance you will get out a given setup. Software developers do, of course, usually stipulate the minimum system requirements needed to run their software but the actual performance you can get out of two similarly-speced systems can vary enormously.

The Net Works PC is a well-featured, highly speced yet reasonably priced PC. It performed admirably running the various pieces of software mentioned throughout the book. Figure 4.2 shows the results of a speed test which indicates that the system is as fast as it should be! Some

| Score | System |
|---|---|
| 802 | 200 MHz Intel Pentium(R) Pro, 256kb L2 cache |
| 709 | 200 MHz AMD-K6(TM) with Multimedia Extensions, 512kb L2 cache |
| 584 | 200 MHz Intel Pentium(R) with MMX |
| 583 | 200 MHz Intel Pentium(R) with MMX, 512kb L2 cache |
| 491 | 200 MHz Intel Pentium(R), 256kb L2 cache |
| 481 | 150 MHz Cyrix 6x86(TM) P200, 256kb L2 cache |
| 396 | 133 MHz Intel Pentium(R), 256kb L2 cache |
| 158 | 100 MHz Intel DX4(TM), 256kb L2 cache |
| 100 | 66 MHz Intel 486SX |
| 53 | 33 MHz Intel 486SX |

(Your system ==> 584)

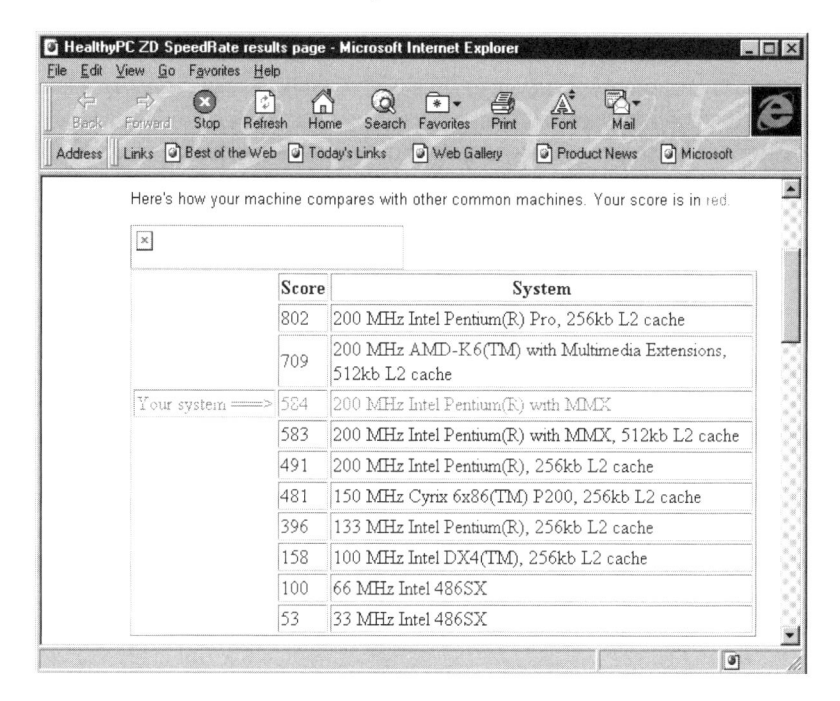

Figure 4.2 Speedrate confirms that the Net Works PC is as fast as it ought to be

aspects of performance, particularly in the area of direct-to-disk recording, were improved by adding a SCSI hard drive but then that will apply to any PC system. It's essential to bear in mind that d-t-d makes specific requirements on a PC and you need to optimise your system to get the maximum performance out of it.

# 5

# The hard disk

Although all areas of computing have their acronyms, hard drive technology seems to have more than its fair share. This chapter was almost called THD! If you're a newcomer, take heart from the fact that, again, many ideas and concepts have been simplified – honestly! The information provided here is there so you can refer to it as and when you decide to upgrade your hard drive or in case you want to specify a PC system to make sure you get the best and most suitable drive for your purpose. Also, bear in mind that if you have an older system, it may not fully support some of the latest hard drives.

If you already have a system you may want to skip the techy bits and go to the section on partitioning. But if you want to know what goes on under the bonnet, read on...

The hard disk stores programs and data. When you switch your PC on and load a program, it's copied from the hard disk into RAM. When you switch the machine off, the contents of the RAM is lost. The hard disk, therefore, is the central storehouse of all your software and should be treated with respect and looked after. But always backup your data, too.

In direct-to-disk recording the hard disk, of course, plays an essential role. However, it's only relatively recently when hard disks became larger, faster and cheaper that affordable d-t-d became a reality. But there's not much point in buying the biggest fastest disk you can get if you're going to put it in a Pentium 75 with 8Mb of RAM.

But assuming that the rest of the PC system is up to scratch what do you need to know when looking for a suitable hard disk? I won't bore you with a complete disk drive anatomy – there are plenty of technical tomes to do that – but you ought to know, roughly, what they are and how they work so here's the abridged version.

## Hard disk basics

A hard disk consists of one or more thin platters of magnetic-coated material which spin typically at speeds from 3,600 (slower than you should find in a modern drive) to 7,200 rpm (revolutions per minute) although faster ones are being developed and you may see drives which rotate at 10,000 rpm or even faster. The faster a drive spins, the louder and hotter it gets and very fast drives may require an extra fan to help keep it cool. Without a fan, its life may be severely shortened.

A head mounted on an actuator arm skims cross the surface of the platters at a distance of two to three micro-inches and reads and writes data from and to it magnetically. Modern drives have a head for both sides of each platter they contain. Although hard disks are relatively sturdy things considering what's going on inside, it's not a good idea to drop, bang or knock a computer while its drive is working as this can serious damage its health.

We won't go into the exact layout of the innards of a drive. You don't need to know exactly how it works in order to use it and if it was ever necessary to investigate its insides, even via software, it would be better done by someone who knows what they're doing. This should never be necessary for the average user. If a drive goes belly up and you can't recover the data on it you really ought to take it to an expert if you desperately need to salvage it.

## The essential specs

So, we're going to slice through the reams of data you may see quoted in disk drive blurb and cut to the quick. For direct-to-disk recording the most important specs are the sustained DTR (Data Transfer Rate) and the access time. The DTR is how quickly the drive can transfer data to or from the disk. The access time is how quickly it takes the drive to find and retrieve a piece of data on the disk.

We need to mention one other spec and that's the seek time. Many people confuse with this the access time but they aren't quite the same. The seek time is the time it takes the drive to move the heads to the correct place in order to access the data. The fastest seek times will be when the head only has to move to the block of data next to where it currently is. The longest is called full stroke and is when the required data is at the opposite end of the disk.

The most useful figure, especially for comparisons between drives, is the average access time. Sometimes hard drive manufacturers play fast and loose with the specs and quote the fastest access time or simply the seek time. You really need to know how long, on average, a drive is going to take to retrieve a piece of data and that's the average access time.

Manufacturers can do lots of juggling with the DTR ratings. A common figure is the burst rate transfer which measures the maximum amount of data a drive can transfer but this is often data coming from the drive's buffer and cannot be sustained. For d-t-d you need to know the sustained DTR because the drive has to supply data for long periods of time, not just in bursts.

The access time is important, too, because if a drive is reading several audio tracks at the same time it will have to skip from one section of the drive to another and the faster it can do this, the better the drive's overall performance will be. Obviously, it cannot read several pieces of data at *exactly* the same time and so it stores the data in a buffer which the computer can read and output virtually simultaneously.

The average seek time on the Quantum Fireball in the Net Works drive is 10.5ms which is a touch on the slow side compared to its contemporaries which could be as fast as 7.5ms. The specs, however, don't quote an access time or a sustained DTR, just a 'data transfer rate' of 16.67Mb/sec which is the theoretical maximum.

## PIO

Which brings us to PIO. It's getting a bit techy now but PIO is an important consideration if you're buying a new drive. It stands for Programmed Input/Output and it's a set of protocols for IDE drives for transferring data at different rates. The highest PIO mode is currently 4 which enables a theoretical transfer rate of 16.6Mb/sec. Some older systems and drives may be mode 3 which supports transfer rates up to 11.1Mb/sec. These are maximum rates, note, and it's unlikely that they will be sustained in real world situations.

The PIO mode is used by the BIOS and stored in the computer's CMOS RAM. When you switch on your computer you will see a message saying something like 'Press DEL to enter SETUP'. This takes you to a series of setup pages where you can change the parameters stored in the CMOS RAM. CMOS RAM stores the parameters the BIOS uses for starting the computer. CMOS: Complementary Metal Oxide Semiconductor – but not many people know that and even fewer worry about it!

The PIO setting in most modern systems can be set to automatic so it automatically detects the PIO mode of the hard disk and configures itself accordingly. On older systems you may have to enter the PIO mode directly. You can't however, simply set it to 4. It must be set to the mode the hard disk supports so you ought to know the mode of any hard disks you install in your PC.

> **Crash alert**
> Do not change any of the parameters in the CMOS RAM unless you know what you are doing. Some are self-explanatory but others require some technical knowledge. At the best you could impair the performance of your PC. At worst, it could fail to boot up correctly when you switch it on.

If you bought a complete PC system, the hard drive should have been set up correctly but if you're replacing or adding a drive, it's important that you a) buy a fast one and b) adjust the CMOS settings so it runs at its optimum speed.

## DMA

DMA or Direct Memory Access is a more recent form of data transfer supported by many drives. Basically, it involves taking over the bus and transferring data directly into memory bypassing the CPU which can get on

---

**INFO**

BIOS - Basic Input/Output System, a set of resident instructions in a chip on the motherboard which performs test routines when the computer is switched on, loads the operating system from disk and enables access to the system's hardware.

with other tasks, a much better arrangement for multi-taking. However, if the operating system is not a true multi-tasking one, the benefits will not be appreciated. DMA is supported by the latest Triton chipsets discussed in the previous chapter.

DMA 2 supports transfers of up to 16.6Mb/sec and DMA 1 rates up to 13.3Mb/sec. DMA 3, when it fully comes on board, will support rates up to 33.3Mb/sec.

## IDE, EIDE and ATA

The hard disk is the main data storage area for the computer. Whenever data is saved and loaded and often while it is being manipulated by the computer, it is being moved back and forth between the hard drive and the PC.

As computers get faster, it's important that the hard drive and the interface which connects it to the computer gets faster, too, otherwise a bottleneck will occur which will slow down the machine. This is especially true for direct-to-disk recording. In most modern computer systems, the interface will be one of two types – EIDE or SCSI.

We'll skip the IDE history lesson and move right along to EIDE (Enhanced IDE) which was developed from the IDE (Intelligent or Integrated Drive Electronics) system. As the name suggests, the controlling circuitry is built into the hard drive's electronics which allows you to plug the drive straight into a bus, simplifying the interface procedure and reducing costs. Such drives are known, naturally enough, as EIDE drives.

The interface specification which connects EIDE drives to the system is called the AT Attachment, the AT coming from IBM's original PC AT specification and which stands for Advanced Technology.

The original ATA specification was used to connect drives to the ISA bus. EIDE usually uses ATA-2 or Fast ATA which adds faster PIO and DMA modes (see above) and allows the software to interrogate the hard drive to determine more accurately how it can perform. ATA-3 includes improved reliability, more sophisticated power management and SMART (Self Monitoring Analysis and Report) which allows the drive to check itself and warn of impending failure. The latest releases of Windows 95 are SMART-aware.

Ultra ATA is a new spec which promises transfer rates up to 33Mb/sec and improved error checking although, as of writing, no current chipset supports it. ATA-4 is already on the drawing board and will likely merge ATA-3 and ATAPI to simplify connection of these devices and it's probable that even faster transfer rates will be discussed.

The original ATA spec only supported two devices. All systems built after 1994 should have an EIDE controller. Most EIDE systems have two channels each of which can support two devices including ATAPI devices such as compatible CD ROM drives. EIDE supports large hard drives (the combination of the older IDE and the BIOS limited the hard drive size) and, of course, it supports the faster transfer rates.

### INFO

Some CD ROM drives can be attached to the ATA bus and these are often called IDE CD ROM drives. There are also tape streamers which can be connected in the same way. Strictly speaking, non-hard disk ATA devices should be called ATAPI (ATA Packet Interface) because although they use the same bus, they don't work in quite the same way.

## SCSI

The main alternative to EIDE is SCSI. It stands for Small Computer System Interface and is pronounced 'scuzzy'. It is common not only with PCs but with other computer platforms, too, such as the Apple Macintosh. It's also used by many devices which need to transfer large amounts of data quickly such as tape streamers, CD ROM drives, scanners, and even musical instruments such as samplers.

Unlike the ATA interface, SCSI is generally not built onto a PC motherboard. It's a separate bus and requires an interface card to connect it to the motherboard. The controllers are built into each SCSI device and the card is, strictly speaking, a host adapter not a controller card. SCSI cards may connect to the ISA or PCI bus and there are several manufacturers and models to choose from.

Although it's not the only manufacturer of SCSI cards, Adaptec is undoubtedly the most well-known name in the field. It produces a wide range of cards supporting various types of SCSI (coming up) and is pretty much a de facto industry standard.

SCSI devices are connected together in a 'daisy chain' fashion. Virtually all SCSI devices have two SCSI sockets and you simply uses these to connect the devices to each other. There are no separate In and Out sockets as there are with MIDI, for example.

All devices receive exactly the same information and so that they know which messages are intended for them, they are each assigned a unique SCSI ID number which is used to ensure that messages go to the correct device. Most SCSI devices have a small push button selector on the back which is used to set the ID number although a few use DIP switches.

Priority is given to devices with the highest ID number. The SCSI card or 'computer' usually has the highest number and the main hard drive in a system often has the lowest – 0. The devices can be assigned ID numbers in any order. It's not necessary to number them in the order in which they appear in the SCSI chain.

The ends of the SCSI chain must be terminated, that is, connected to a set of resistors to prevent the signal being distorted or reflected. Termination can be set in some devices by means of a switch. Others require a small terminator block to be plugged in and these are readily available from computer shops for a few pounds. On other devices termination can be set via software or even sensed and set automatically. The SCSI card is usually terminated or else allows termination to be set by a switch on the card or via software.

SCSI data transmission is quite sensitive to cable length. The best rule of thumb is to us the shortest cables possible and to use good quality cables. Cables should be less than a metre where possible and the maximum total cable length should be no more than seven metres.

Don't skimp on SCSI cable quality, especially if you are using long cable runs or high SCSI data transmission rates. Poor cabling is a common cause of SCSI problems.

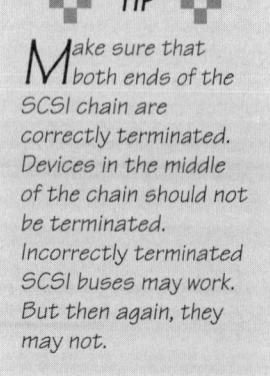

> **TIP**
> 
> Double, double check that each SCSI device has a different ID number otherwise problems will undoubtedly arise.

> **TIP**
> 
> Make sure that both ends of the SCSI chain are correctly terminated. Devices in the middle of the chain should not be terminated. Incorrectly terminated SCSI buses may work. But then again, they may not.

## The SCSI evolution

SCSI is a parallel bus which means it transmits several sets of data at the same time. The original SCSI, now referred to as SCSI 1, was developed in the 1980s and it was an 8-bit system with a 5MHz signalling rate which could transfer 5Mb of data per second. It supported up to eight devices – the host adapter and seven hard disks.

This was superseded by SCSI 2 which added multitasking, command queuing and extended support for other types of device such as scanners, CD ROMs and so on. It also specified two optional modes of data transfer – Fast SCSI with a transfer rate of 10Mb/sec and Wide SCSI which extended the bus width to 16 or even 32 bits and which increased the number of supported SCSI devices to 16. These extensions can be combined in a Fast and Wide SCSI bus.

There's also Ultra SCSI which doubles the signalling rate and allows transfers of up to 20Mb/sec and Ultra 2 SCSI which supports rates up to 40Mb/sec. Again, you can combine Ultra with Wide to get Ultra Wide SCSI with a transfer rate of 40Mb/sec. The SCSI types and the rates are summarised in the table.

*SCSI types and transfer rates*

| SCSI type | Data width (bus) | Signalling rate (MHz) | Maximum data transfer rate (Mb/sec) |
|---|---|---|---|
| SCSI 1 | 8 | 5 | 5 |
| Wide SCSI | 16 | 5 | 10 |
| Fast SCSI | 8 | 10 | 10 |
| Ultra SCSI | 8 | 20 | 20 |
| Ultra 2 SCSI | 8 | 40 | 40 |
| Fast & Wide SCSI | 16 | 10 | 20 |
| Wide Ultra SCSI | 16 | 20 | 40 |
| Wide Ultra 2 SCSI | 16 | 40 | 80 |

And if you think that's starting to look a little complicated, wait until we get to SCSI 3! Although this will support transfer rates up to 80Mb/sec, much of the standard is concerned with improving the management of the system with enhanced caching, better power management and automatic device ID. SCSI 3 also encompasses specifications for serial SCSI systems which we'll look at in a moment.

Like EIDE drives, the performance of SCSI drives vary, too, so you need to check their specifications such as access time and sustained DTR. Just because a drive is Ultra Wide doesn't mean it will be physically able to deliver 40Mb/sec.

When selecting a SCSI card and hard drive, it's important to get compatible equipment. There's no point in getting an Ultra Wide SCSI card

> **TECHY BIT**
>
> A growing number of SCSI devices are starting to support SCAM - SCSI Configured AutoMatically - which enables the host adapter to assign IDs during boot up which should resolve any SCSI ID conflict problems.

and a normal SCSI hard disk as the fast card won't make the drive run any faster. As ever, you pay a premium for faster equipment and Wide and Ultra SCSI drives cost more than their slower counterparts.

The Adaptec AHA-2940UW is an Ultra Wide card which supports speeds of up to 40Mb/sec – providing the connected devices can deliver. It can support up to 15 devices and it works with standard SCSI devices as well as the newer ones.

With the appearance of Mode 4 EIDE hard drives and DMA 3 transfer, only the faster SCSI hard drives offer a speed advantage. However, one of the major reasons for using SCSI is the flexibility of the system and the ease with which additional devices can be added – if you need another hard drive, just stick one onto the SCSI bus. Even a standard SCSI bus can handle seven devices – CD ROM drive, scanner, tape streamer and so on – and it's easier to add these to a SCSI chain than to plug them into an ISA or PCI bus, or the ATA interface and run through the configuration procedure.

SCSI can also be useful, too, if you want to move a large hard drive from one computer to another. Removable media is another option but they tend not to have such large capacities as the largest hard drives.

Although, as of writing, SCSI is the most common and cheapest alternative way to connect a hard drive to a PC, it can sometimes be a little tricky to set up initially although modern Plug 'n' Play cards simplify the process enormously. And it's not the only alternative...

## SSA

SSA or Serial Storage Architecture was developed by Xyratex (which was originally part of IBM) and offers many advantages over SCSI:

- It only uses 6 wires
- It offers up to 80Mb/sec transfer rates
- It supports hot plugging
- It does not require terminators
- It has automatic configuration so no address switches are needed
- It supports up to 127 devices
- There can be up to 20 meter cable lengths between devices

With SCSI, each device listens to the messages running around the SCSI bus until it's told to do something. With SSA, if there were five devices, there could be five 'conversations' going on simultaneously. SSA can work in a loop configuration allowing data to travel along two paths simultaneously as shown in Figure 5.1 which improves reliability.

SSA was primarily developed for networks and works best under Windows NT but a driver for Windows 95 is available. However, currently, a new drive has to be formatted under Windows NT or Windows 95 won't recognise it. This may prompt would-be users who are attracted by SSA's speed and connectivity to investigate using Windows NT rather than 95. If only Microsoft would standardise its OS standards, it would make life a lot easier for users.

> **INFO**
>
> Hot plugging – the ability to add and remove devices from the system without powering down.

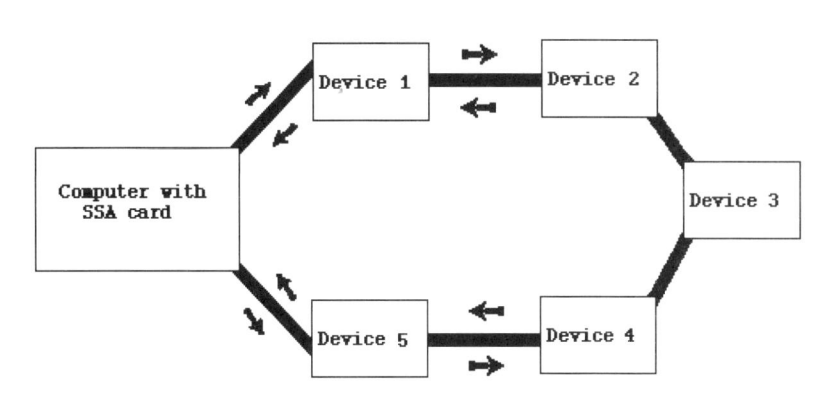

Figure 5.1 An SSA system supports several simultaneous 'conversations' and can work in a loop configuration

Compared with EIDE and SCSI, SSA undoubtedly has a wealth of advantages. But, as with most new developments, the benefits currently carry a price premium although this may fall if the standard is taken up by a lot of developers. However, if you need a lot of storage, it's a viable alternative to SCSI and worth investigating.

## It's a RAID

As you explore the various permutations of hard disk systems you may well come across RAID arrays. This stands for Redundant Array of Inexpensive (or Independent) Disks and it's a way of linking ordinary disks so the user and the system sees them as one storage area.

There are several levels of RAID (just as there are several levels of SCSI) but the basic idea is to spread the storage of data across several disks to increase the data transfer speed and to increase the data security. At more advanced levels, a file is spread across several disks and at higher levels one disk is used for error protection which should help prevent data loss if one of the drives fails.

But, again, the benefits come with a higher price tag. If you're creating a lot of data it may be worth considering and as drives continue to fall in price, RAID arrays may well come more within the consumer budget.

## FireWire and associates

It's worth mentioning some of the other serial data transfer systems which you may see and which are likely to become more popular over the next few years. 1394 (or IEEE-1394) is one, often referred to as FireWire, and several manufacturers have already fitted it to consumer products such as digital camcorders.

Add a suitable 1394 card to your PC and you can transfer video data directly to your computer without passing it through an analogue conversion stage. 1394 promises transfer speeds of 400Mb/sec, 800Mb/sec and higher (although it's likely to be a while before devices offering these transfer rates make it to the consumer market) and it could be used for digital audio, too. It has a built-in isochronous mode which gives preference to devices which need to transmit data in real-time – ideal for video and audio.

Adaptec's AHA-8940 was one of the first FireWire cards to appear and the AHA-8945 FireCard Ultra combines FireWire and Ultra Wide SCSI on one card. The FireWire connections support transfer speeds of up to 25Mb/sec and the UW SCSI supports transfers up to 40Mb/sec.

The Fibre Channel is another data transfer system. It sounds like it uses optical media but it can use copper cable, too. It supports transfer rates of 200Mb/sec and upwards and has already been used in large disk systems by companies such as the aptly-named MegaDrive Systems. Xyratex uses the Fibre Channel in its products, too.

The Fibre Channel is currently a high-end product aimed at the digital video and broadcast markets but it is being touted at the next generation in data transfer and, certainly, it has excellent potential. All we're waiting for is for the price to come down to consumer level – which it probably will do one day.

## AV drives

As we've discussed, one of the most important disk drive specifications is its sustained DTR. Now, while a drive is transferring data to your audio system, you don't want it to sit down and take a coffee break.

But that's just what most drives do. They occasionally need to perform an internal recalibration which involves stopping the data transfer for a short period while it does a few sums. It is only a very short period and you won't notice anything if you're wordprocessing, using a database, editing graphics or the like. However, if an audio stream is interrupted the result could be very noticeable.

One solution is the AV drive which monitors the data throughput and doesn't recalibrate if it would affect the DTR. AV drives have been specially designed for digital audio and digital video use and, of course, come with a price premium. Many AV drives are also a little slower than their contemporaries although if you're getting the sustained DTR you need, that shouldn't be too much of a concern.

So are non-AV drives suitable for digital audio? The answer might seem to be no, but it's not quite as straightforward as that – you knew it would be, didn't you?

Many people are happily using standard EIDE drives for digital audio. In fact, the professional Soundscape Digital Audio Workstation (which we meet later in the book) is based on EIDE drives. The success of an EIDE-based system largely depends on the strain you put on the drive and how well the buffers and caches cope with interrupted data flow. The speed of the overall system plays a part, too.

So, if you already have a system with an EIDE drive, give it a try. If you experience dropouts, which are most likely to occur during sustained playback of large files, you may need to decrease the strain on your drive or you may, indeed, need to investigate an AV system.

## Size counts

Once you've decided on the type of hard drive you're going to use, you need to decide how large a drive or drives you require. As CD quality digital audio (normally assumed to be a stereo 16-bit 44.1kHz recording) requires 10.6Mb of storage space per minute, you can easily calculate the amount of disk space you'll require for a song or an album. Here are a few examples:

*Disk space needed for various stereo track/duration configurations*

| No. of stereo tracks | Duration in minutes | Disk space required in MB |
|---|---|---|
| 1 | 4 | 42.4 |
| 1 | 15 | 159 |
| 4 | 4 | 169.6 |
| 4 | 15 | 636 |
| 8 | 4 | 339.2 |
| 8 | 15 | 127.2 |
| 8 | 30 | 2544 |
| 16 | 4 | 678.4 |
| 16 | 30 | 5088 |
| 16 | 45 | 7632 |

The disk usage may look daunting but the figures do assume that all the tracks are filled with data from beginning to end. There's good news and bad news here. Solo instruments such as the sax or guitar will probably not be playing all the way through a piece and if it hasn't been recorded for half the song, that's half a track's worth of disk space saved.

However, even silence takes up disk space. If you record a minute of nothing at zero volume, it will still consume 10.6Mb of your hard disk. Vocals, for example, usually contain lots of gaps between sections so you won't save any space there although if you stop recording the vocals during the instrumental solo, you will.

So in practice, the actual amount of disk space required for a song could be considerably less that those figures suggest, perhaps even half the amount although the actual requirement is difficult to estimate as it depends entirely on the content of the recording.

But that's not the whole story because you will undoubtedly need a scratch area for storing edits, alternative takes, a collection of samples which you may (or may not) use in the recording and experimental mixes. The working space you require could be as much again as the finished piece so what you gain on the swings you lose on the roundabout. When a piece is complete, you can, of course, delete the unwanted and unused

> **INFO**
>
> What is a megabyte? A megabyte is 1,024Kb or 1,048,576 bytes, yes? Not necessarily. Mega is a prefix meaning million so one million bytes should be 1,000,000. However, computers count in binary and use the nearest power of 2. A kilobyte (Kb), therefore, is not 1,000 bytes but 2^10 = 1,024 bytes. A megabyte is 2^20 = 1,048,576.

files but you will almost surely need more disk space during the project than you may think.

> Question: How big a drive do you need?
> Answer: As big as you can get!

Fortunately, disk drives are getting larger all the time and continue to fall in price. It would be rare to find a PC on sale with a drive smaller than 1Gb. 2-3Gb drives are being fitted as standard and all good suppliers will let you upgrade to an even larger drive.

A lot of software uses the binary interpretation of megabyte and RAM is measured this way, too, but most hard drive manufacturers take the traditional view. If you are more familiar with the binary version, as most computer users are, the other view makes hard drives seem larger! In most circumstances this won't cause major problems but it's something to be aware of.

While on the subject of shrinking megabytes, if you measure the capacity of a formatted drive it will be several megabytes less that the drive's quoted size. Some of the capacity gets swallowed up in the formatting process. It's normal. Odd and weird but that's the way it works.

## Using two or more drives

An option which is worth considering is to buy two or more drives. This has a couple of advantages. First of all, let's take a two-track recording where both tracks are recorded on the same hard disk. The drive's read head has to fly between the two tracks in order to read the data which is supposed to be played simultaneously. Imagine a four-track or eight-track recording – the head has a lot more work to do and this is bound to slow down the actual data transfer rate and possibly cause dropouts if your system isn't quite up to speed.

By recording tracks on two or more drives, you decrease the amount of work the drive heads have to do which will improve efficiency. If you are using a multi-tasking operating system and DMA data transfers (as discussed earlier) this should improve the data throughput even more.

Another reason for using additional drives is to keep your applications and recording data separate. It's mainly a matter of convenience and organisation but if you use your PC for things other than recording you may find it useful to have a drive dedicated to audio data.

Most modern PCs can easily support four EIDE drives but if you're thinking of adding that many to your computer it may be better to consider SCSI, particularly the faster variety. Of course, there's nothing to stop you using EIDE as the main boot drive in your PC and adding additional drives via SCSI.

Most EIDE drives are fitted inside of the computer. In desktop models and mini tower systems, check that there's enough space inside the case to fit another drive. SCSI drives are commonly available in internal and external versions and if you have a small case external drives may be your only option.

## Partitioning

Partitioning is the process of dividing a hard disk into smaller sections. You don't need an axe or a pair of scissors, but you do need a good partition utility.

When a drive has been partitioned it appears to the system as two or more drives. If your hard drive's letter was C and you partition it into three, then you would see what would appear to be three drives on the desktop called C, D, and E.

Why partition? Several reasons. The first is convenience and organisation. If you have a large hard drive you will soon accumulate a lot of programs and data. If you partition the drive you could use one partition for music applications, one for non-music applications and another partition for recording data.

The other reasons are a little more technical but well worth knowing about as they can affect the performance of your system. If you decide not to partition, that's fine, but at least you'll be aware of how efficiently you're using your hard disk.

### FATs and clusters

The FAT or File Allocation Table keeps track of which clusters are used and, most importantly, where files are located. It's the equivalent of the index and contents pages of a book – lose this and you've effectively lost your data. The FAT is so important that it's duplicated to protect your data. When you save a file its details are stored in the FAT including the filename, the size of the file, file attributes (archived, hidden and so on), the date and time and the start cluster.

Now the important point to note is that a cluster is the smallest area of a drive that can be used to store data. So if you save a file which is only 1Kb in size it will still occupy a full cluster!

That means, just to spell it out, that if you saved 100 individual 1Kb files to a hard disk which had 32Kb clusters, you would actually use 3200Kb (32 x 100) of disk space. That's 3.125Mb – 32 times as much disk space as you might think you were using. And if you saved a 33Kb file, 32Kb of it would go in one cluster but another cluster would be required to store the remaining 1Kb. That, of course, is a worst-case scenario but you could easily be losing 10 or 20 percent, possibly up to 40 percent, of your drive space in unfilled clusters.

So, partitioning your hard disk into sizes of 255Kb would create smaller clusters which would result in more efficient storage of your data.

But that's not the whole story. As you will, by now, have gathered, nothing is straightforward in the world of computing. You could not really be advised to partition a drive into such small sections. For direct-to-disk recording, using small clusters has been known to slow down sustained DTR on a drive which is exactly what we don't want.

---

**INFO**

The faster a drive runs, the hotter it gets and some of the faster drives may need additional cooling and come with a large fan. This may be a little noisy. Something to be aware of if it is going to be near the recording area.

**TECHY BIT**

When the format utility formats a hard disk, it divides the drive into small sections called clusters. These are the smallest unit of data storage and the size of the cluster depends on the size of the drive or partition. A 255Mb drive, for example would have a cluster size of 4Kb. On drives up to 511Mb the clusters would be 8Kb. Move up to a 1,024Mb drive and the cluster size becomes 16Kb and on drives up to 2,047Mb they are 32Kb.

However, the storage space lost by saving lots of small files is not generally a major problem with direct-to-disk recording data because most of the files are large and there are not usually a lot of them – compared with the myriad of small files people tend to generate with a wordprocessor, for example. But if you have a separate drive for storing other applications, such as wordprocessing documents, and you do create lots of small files, it may be worthwhile reducing the cluster size on that drive. We'll see how to do this in a moment.

The DOS FAT has a partition limit of 2Gb so if you have ordered a 2.5Gb drive in your new PC, for example, make sure that it's fully formatted, recognisable by your operating system and/or partitioned. The original version of Windows 95 used the DOS FAT and couldn't recognise more than 2Gb of a drive. Any larger drive shipped with this OS should have been partitioned otherwise you would simply lose half a Gigabyte of disk space. It's not unknown for a manufacturer to ship a PC system containing a drive larger than 2Gb but not partitioned so only 2Gb has been available!

As of writing, Windows 95 OSR2 (and presumably later versions of Windows 95) uses a file system called FAT32. It's an enhancement of the FAT system based on 32-bit FATs rather than the 16-bit entries used by the standard FAT. One result of this is the ability to recognise drives up to 2 Terrabytes in size! So, drives larger than 2Gb can be formatted in their entirety and all the space will be accessible from within Windows.

Figure 5.2 shows that Windows 95 OSR2 on the Net Works PC uses FAT32 and confirms that the whole drive is available for use, not just 2Gb.

FAT32 uses smaller clusters than the FAT – 4Kb clusters for large drives, for example – and it has duplicate boot records for added protection. Windows 95 OSR2 which was installed on the Net Works PC had 4Kb clusters. Changing the cluster size to 32Kb significantly improved the DTR, albeit at the expense of losing a little disk space.

### INFO

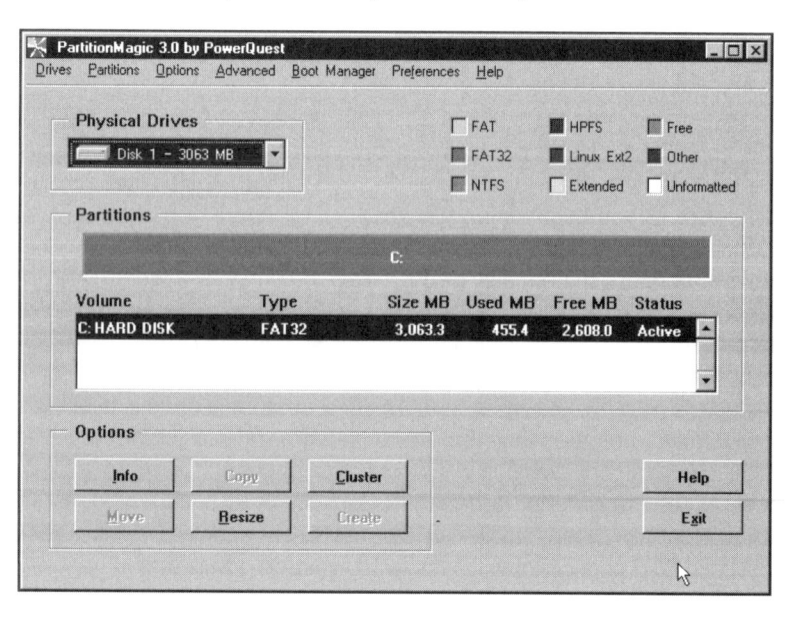

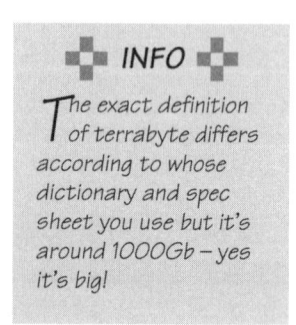

*The exact definition of terrabyte differs according to whose dictionary and spec sheet you use but it's around 1000Gb – yes it's big!*

Figure 5.2 Checking the hard drive's FAT system with Partition Magic

The speed was checked with the Audio Performance Test utility which comes with those Cubase programs which have digital audio capabilities, Norton Utilities (more about this in a moment) and SpeedRate, a simple benchmark program which is freely available from the ZDNet Web site (see the Internet section of the Appendix for more details).

With the original 4Kb clusters created by the original formatting program the Performance Test program only suggested the system would be capable of handling 4 stereo tracks but after changing the cluster size to 16Kb and 32Kb it suggested 7 or 8 stereo tracks would be possible. The difference between cluster sizes of 16Kb and 32Kb didn't seem make much difference. Oddly, after resetting the clusters back to 4Kb, the Performance program showed an improvement up to 6 stereo tracks.

SpeedRate's benchmarks didn't seem to vary much whatever cluster size was used. However, it's likely that it was testing the overall speed of the drive and not the sustained DTR which one assumes the Performance utility was testing.

Norton Utilities includes a benchmark facility which tests a drive's throughput in megabytes/second. The 4Kb cluster size produced slightly slower results than 32Kb clusters.

Some of these tests are rough and ready for our purpose. Running the same test twice often produced slightly different results and running the Performance Test twice in succession usually increases the performance rating due, no doubt, to use of the system's cache. However, the results do indicate how significantly the cluster size can affect the transfer rate.

As of writing, DOS, Windows 3.1, Windows NT and the original version of Windows 95 do not recognise FAT32 volumes and cannot boot from them. However, as all operating systems are in a continual state of development, this may well change.

Windows NT has yet another FAT system called NTFS (New Technology File System). Its clusters are not dependent on the size of the volume and can be as small as 512 bytes. Central to NT is the MFT (Master File Table) and NTFS keeps multiple copies of critical sections of the MFT to protect against data loss. However, other operating systems such as Windows 95 cannot access data on an NTFS partition.

In the original Windows 95, clusters will usually be 16Kb or 32Mb and your hard disk will probably work just fine although you may still like to experiment with other cluster sizes. If you're running a new version of Windows 95 or OSR2, you may have 4Kb clusters in which case, for optimum efficiency you may want to increase their size.

Although a partitioned drive will appear as two or more drives, it still only has one set of heads so the improvements you may get by using two or more physical drives won't apply to partitioned drives.

### It's magic

So how do you re-partition a drive and change the cluster size? You can re-partition a drive using the DOS FDISK command. However, this destroys all the data on a partition and it's a faff to backup your entire drive and restore it or to reinstall all your software.

> **INFO**
>
> *Benchmark – a series of tests used to compare the performance of the components of a computer with those of other computers.*

But with a utility such as PartitionMagic you can re-partition a drive and change the cluster size without losing the data. Of course, you are recommended to backup the drive before performing any such changes – and this is excellent advice, too, which you ignore at your own risk – but assuming the changes go according to plan it means you don't have to reinstall everything.

The program shows how much space you could save on your drive by changing the cluster size. In Figure 5.3, for example, you can see that using 32Kb clusters would waste 11 percent of the space on this drive. However, the disk has very little data on it and the waste would undoubtedly be a lot more if several more applications had been installed.

Figure 5.3 Changing the cluster size can dramatically increase the amount of free disk space

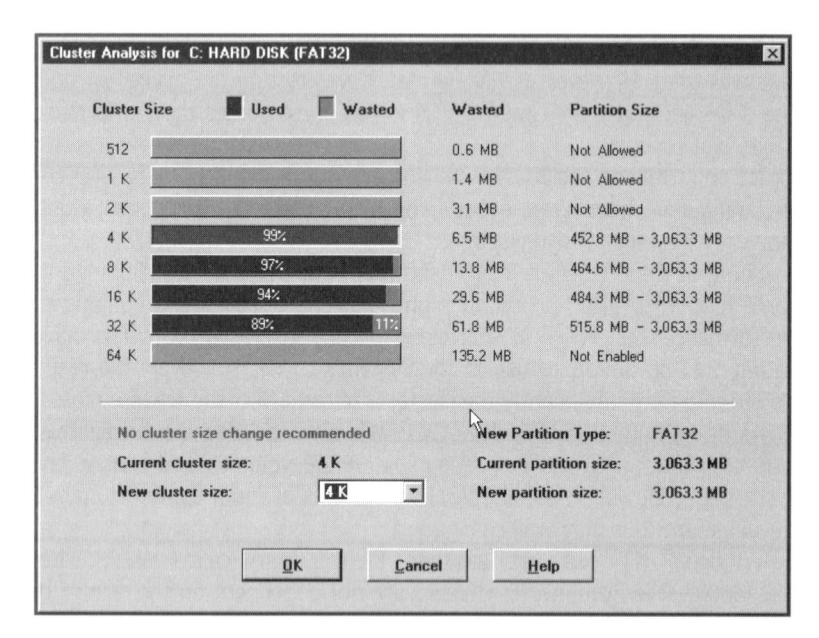

I ran PartitionMagic on the Quantum Fireball drive in the Net Works PC several times, changing partitions and cluster sizes and it worked perfectly. Very impressive.

Another feature of PartitionMagic is the Boot Manager which lets you select different partitions to boot from when you switch on the PC. It enables you to have, say, Windows 95 in one partition, Windows NT in another, IBM's OS/2 in a third and other operating systems in other partitions. The Boot Manger lets you select the one to load. This could be very useful if you need to swap between Windows 95 and Windows NT although you will probably find it better to install these operating systems onto different drives, not just different partitions.

## Zen and the art of hard disk maintenance

As your hard drives are so important in direct-to-disk recording, it makes sense to look after them. This doesn't simply mean not using them as frisbees or pouring beer into them – they aren't real musicians, you know! It means making sure they are working at their optimum efficiency and there are several areas of performance you should check to keep them running at their best and, literally, up to speed.

## Optimisation

Ever wondered how data is actually saved to a hard disk? It would seem to make sense to save files in one chunk in one area of the disk. And that's exactly what the system does. When you save another file that will go in the space next to the first file and so on.

But what happens when you delete a file? The area of the disk the file was occupying becomes free. When you then save a new file the system may try to fit it into the gap left by the one you deleted. If the new file is too large, the system stores what it can in the gap and sticks the rest in the free space following the other blocks of files.

Now, after you've saved and deleted several files and saved some more, the disk ends up with lots of gaps. It tries to keep itself tidy by filling the gaps with new data but this causes files to be split into several sections and saved in several locations over the disk. In other words they become fragmented. You can see this clearly in Figure 5.4 which shows Norton Utilities performing a scan on a disk. The blocks in the middle of the display contain parts of files, the other parts of which could be scattered all over the disk.

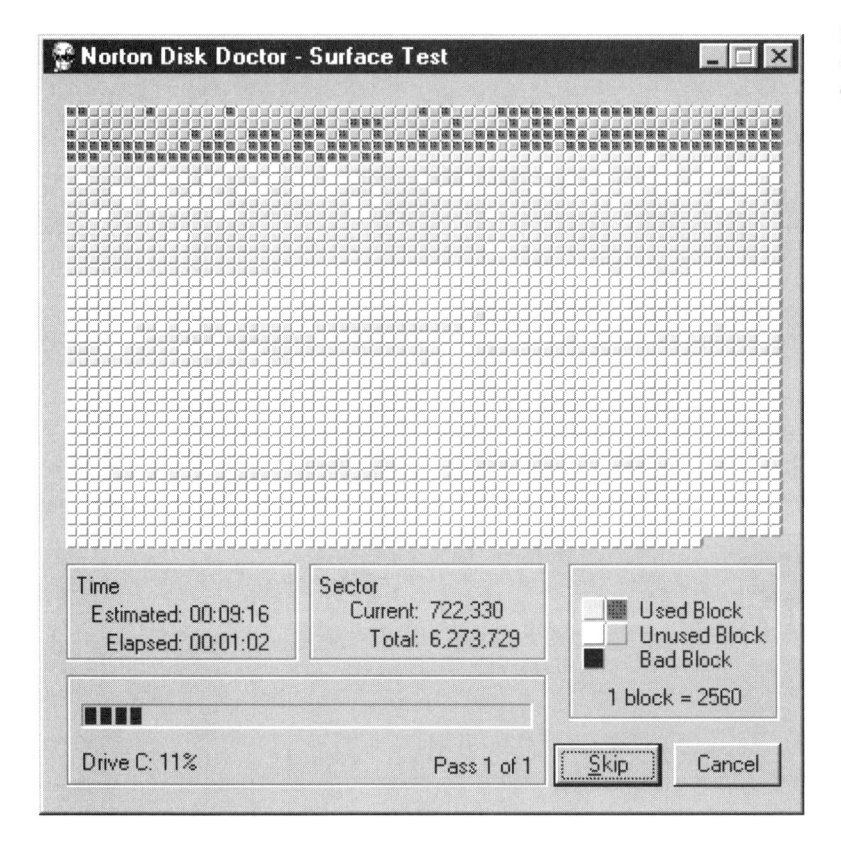

Figure 5.4 Norton Utilities shows that this drive contains fragmented files

As you will realise from earlier discussions about hard disks, if a drive head has to move to several locations on a disk to read a file, it will take longer than if the file has been stored in one contiguous location. This is particularly crucial with direct-to-disk operations when you don't want to give the drive any more work to do than is absolutely necessary. If a digital audio file is severely fragmented it will certainly impair the system's performance.

So the solution is to defragment or optimise your hard disk every so often. Windows 95 has a built-in Disk Defragmenter, see Figure 5.5. In Windows Explorer, put the mouse on a disk icon, right-click, select Properties and click on the Tools tab. Click on the Defragmentation button and the program will tell you how badly the drive is fragmented and give you the option to defragment it.

The analysis in Figure 5.6 indicates that the drive is pretty much optimised but you can still tune it that extra 1 percent if you wish.

Figure 5.5 Windows 95 has a built in Disk Defragmenter

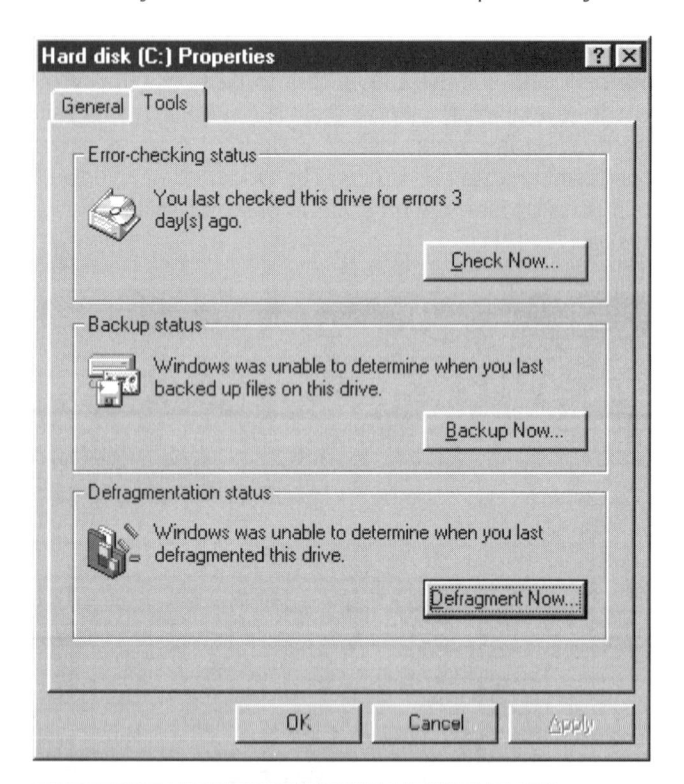

Figure 5.6 This drive is almost free of fragmentation

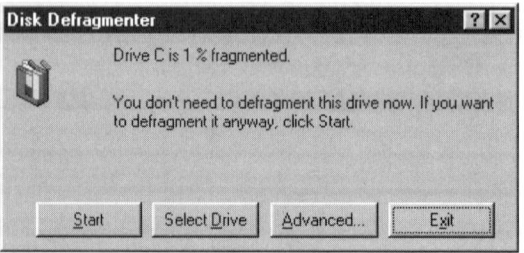

If you select the Advanced Options, Figure 5.7, you can choose whether to defragment the whole drive, just the files or the free space. Unless you're pressed for time there's little point in opting for anything less than a full defrag. You may as well check the box which checks the drive for errors, too.

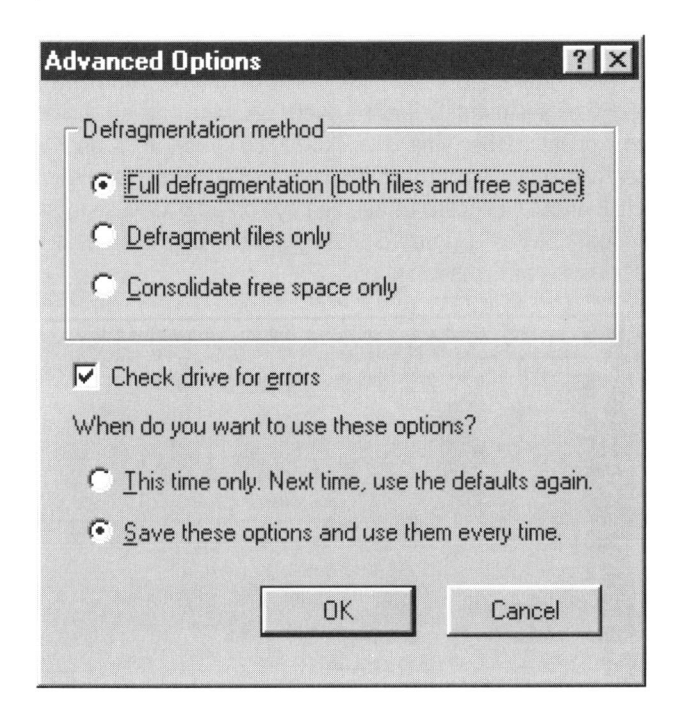

Figure 5.7 Unless you are pressed for time defragment the whole drive

Typical PC users may only need to check a drive for fragmentation every month or so but if you are saving and deleting a lot of large digital audio files, the disk will soon fragment and it will pay to check it regularly and certainly before you start any new project.

## ScanDisk

If a program crashes or if your PC locks up and you have to reset it, this can cause problems with files on the disk. Many programs keep temporary data on the disk and if an application is not closed properly it can forget these files and you may lose data. Sometimes a filename may be corrupted or saved with an incorrect date.

Quite often a crash will create file fragments or cross-linked files. This happens when data from two or more files use the same cluster. As we have already seen, the system doesn't expect more than one file or part of a file to be in a cluster and this is likely to cause problems.

ScanDisk checks for these problems and attempts to correct them. It can also check the disk surface for physical damage. It is accessed from the Tools menu described above by clicking on the Check Now tab in Figure 5.5. It's worth checking your disks every so often to make sure all is well and do check them as a matter of course if you experience a crash or if your PC shuts down in any unnatural way.

### Norton Utilities

Norton Utilities is essential for any computer user and even more essential for anyone who uses their computer for direct-to-disk recording. It began life as a disk checker and maintenance program to check for disk errors, cross-linked files and so on but it has evolved into a much more comprehensive suite of programs.

It can not only optimise (defragment) hard disks and check them for errors, Figure 5.8, it can also check hardware, run benchmark tests, protect files against deletion, recover files which have been accidentally deleted, protect the vital files used by your PC, and monitor system performance. It also includes a SMART sensor (see the section on IDE, EIDE and ATA above) to keep an eye on your drives – assuming the drives support SMART. Figure 5.9 shows some of the areas it can run tests on or provide information about.

Figure 5.8 Norton Utilities is a one-stop solution for hard disk maintenance

Additional functions enable you to modify various aspects of the performance of your system, change the look of Windows, check and edit the Registry and even change system settings.

One thing to be aware of is that many of the utilities lurk in the background, waiting for things to happen. This invariably uses system resources which could slow down your computer, especially when it's under pressure. When using your PC for direct-to-disk recording, best to switch off all the automatic checking functions and run the checks manually. You could leave some automatic functions on but if you experience problems, check that a Norton test hasn't kicked in.

The utilities also include CrashGuard, which monitors your system for crashes, jumps in before they happen and lets you save data before it's lost. Although Windows 95 is far more robust than Windows 3.1, crashes can still occur. Again, CrashGuard runs in the background so be aware that it's there. However, if you are using a program which is prone to crashes, CrashGuard is well worth running until you can trace the source of the problem – or wait for an update which fixes it.

Norton Utilities version 2.0 for Windows 95 supports FAT32 and

> **TECHY BIT**
>
> The Registry is where Windows 95 stores the computer's settings, which programs have been installed and their parameters, and the settings which used to be stored in the .INI files in Windows 3.1. The Registry is a lot cleaner than .INI files – but more complex to edit. DO NOT EDIT THE REGISTRY UNLESS YOU KNOW WHAT YOU ARE DOING.

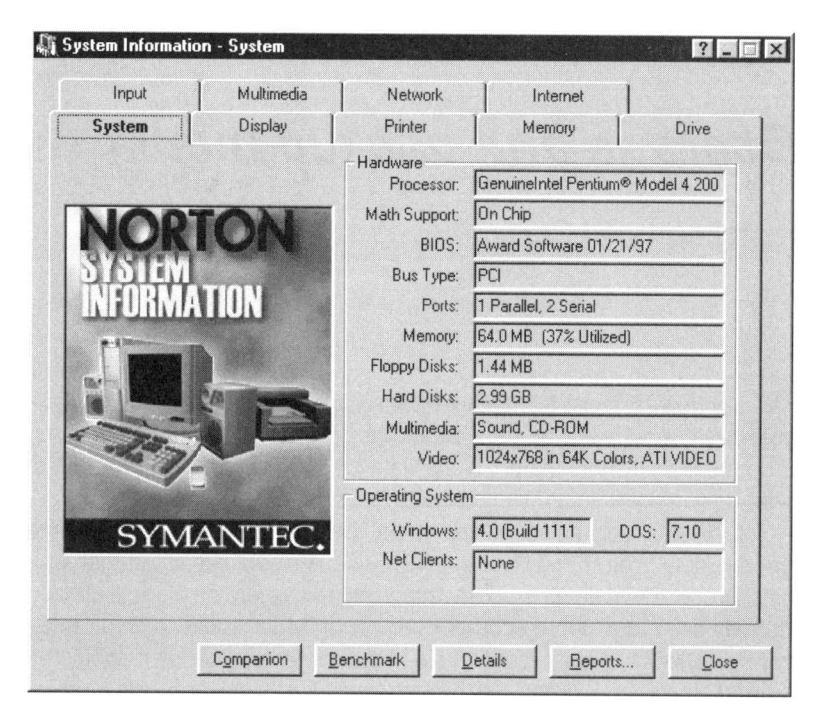

Figure 5.9 Some of the areas of the PC Norton Utilities can check or keep an eye on

although earlier versions may be able to perform most disk checks, it's not advisable to get too involved in editing the disk directly – not that most d-t-d users would want to. However, if you are using OSR2 or an updated version of Windows 95, it makes sense to use Norton 2.0 or later.

## Summing up

As you will now realise, the choice of hard disk is not, perhaps, as straightforward as it might at first appear. If you are building a d-t-d system from scratch you will be able to select the best and fastest data transfer method and hard drives that your projects require and that fit your budget.

If you already have an off-the-shelf computer, don't worry. Most modern PCs, particularly Pentium 133s and upwards, will be well able to handle d-t-d recording even if they haven't been put together with that task specifically in mind. You can always add additional EIDE drives or a SCSI card later on if you want to expand your system.

# 6

## Storage and backup media

Let's say you've spent a month or six recording an album. You've mastered it and now want to start on another project. Your hard disk is full of both the final audio material, alternate takes and various scratch mixes. What do you do?

You could simply delete all the audio material, preparing a clean slate for your new project but I think few musicians would like to do that – all that hard work, deleted ... Something might happen to the master and you may need to produce another one. You may get asked to do a remix. You might listen to the recording six months later and decide it should be remixed. In other words, you probably want to hold onto the original material. How?

In order to free up space on your working hard drive, you need to copy or back up the data you want to keep. There are several ways of doing this.

### Tape streamer

One of the most common methods is to use a tape streamer which is like recording your material onto a DAT tape. The lower-end models are now relatively cheap although you'll pay considerably more for large capacity streamers and fast ones.

Many streamers use SCSI while others plug into the parallel port, and although these may have a 'thru' facility to enable connection to other devices, many will not allow the use of bi-directional printers or dongles. Check before buying.

Data can usually be compressed as it's being saved and most companies quote a compression ratio of about 2:1 although in practice this may be closer to 1.7:1. Another point to note is the transfer rate and, again, the quoted rate is often difficult to achieve. A parallel device ought to be able to throughput about 8-9Mb/min although some may achieve – or quote! – a higher rate. A SCSI drive should be much faster.

Be sure to buy a drive which uses standard tapes. A few drives use proprietary tapes and while they may initially be a little cheaper you need to balance this against a possible restricted supply in the future.

Tape is the cheapest way to backup your data but you have to weigh this against the initial cost of the drive and the slow data transfer rate.

Even if you're backing up at 20Mb/min, that's a couple of hours for a 2.3Gb drive. Not the sort of thing you want to do after a hard day's recording every day, unless you're happy to let it run as you wend your weary way to bed. Another thing to consider is that tape is a linear medium and you can't simply drop into the middle of it to retrieve a single file.

Tape is useful as a 'final' backup at the end of project but do consider both its advantages and disadvantages.

## MO – magneto optical drives

Early MO drives had a small 128Mb capacity but 230Mb drives soon appeared and now 640Mb drives are the norm. Larger drives using larger MO disks have even larger capacities. Xyratex's 3000 MO drive has a 640Mb capacity while the 5000 MO drive has a 2.8Mb capacity.

Data transfer rates are good, too. The 3000 has a sustained write speed of just over 1Mb/sec and a sustained read speed of just over 3Mb/sec. The 5000 is a little faster with a quoted sustained write speed of 1.68Mb/sec and a sustained read speed of 3.37Mb/sec. The drives may be just fast enough, in fact, to use for not-too-demanding d-t-d but their prime use would be for backing up data.

Another advantage of MO is the ability to transfer data from one PC to another. If both computers have MO drives you only need transport the MO cartridge and it can easily be sent by post.

## Removable disks

Yet another option is a removable hard drive. These were popular several years ago when the format became synonymous with the name SyQuest, a manufacturer which lead the market at the time. Again, these are SCSI drives, essentially a hard 'disk' inside a case which you insert into a disk drive 'mechanism' – hence removable disks.

Many of the early SyQuest drives were prone to data errors and the early drives were slow. Now, however, the technology is up to speed and most removable drives are both fast and reliable. Recently, Iomega seems to be becoming the major player with its Jazz and Zip drives – 100Mb and 1Gb storage capacities respectively.

Xyratex has a 540Mb removable drive called the MaxIT which can also read SyQuest 270Mb cartridges. It has an average data transfer rate of around 6.5Mb/sec and can achieve up to 10Mb/sec. Again, the MaxIT could be used for recording but you should still get better performance out of a standard hard disk so it seems more reasonable to use removables for storage.

Removable disks are quite fast, convenient and reasonably priced.

## CD-R

CD-R or CD-recordable drives enable you to record onto CDs. This is a relatively recent development – or rather the technology has been around

> ### INFO
> MO dives have been around for a few years and are proving increasingly popular. They work much like a hard disk – or perhaps it would be more accurate to say a cross between a hard disk and a CD ROM drive. The technology is based on the use of a magnet and laser and MO drives connect to a computer via SCSI.

> **PUZZLE**
>
> *You may like to consider that, as it's cheaper to mass-produce audio CDs than cassettes, why are CDs more expensive...?*

for a number of years but it only really became affordable recently. It combines the large storage capacity of CDs with their cheapness. Blank recordable CDs now cost well under a fiver, which works out at less than 1p per megabyte.

CD-R drives are SCSI devices and can play and read CDs like a normal CD ROM drive, too. However, most CD-R systems are slower than standard drives because the high-power laser which writes the CDs is heavier than the one which reads them. This makes the heads more cumbersome and more difficult to move quickly around the CD.

Some drives read at a faster speed than they write and you may see speeds quoted as 2-write/4-read. Some drives manage to do both at the same speed in which case they may be described as 2-read/2-write or 4-read/4-write.

The latest generation of CD-R systems is CD-E which can write to erasable CDs more than once. Yamaha was one of the first to the market with the 4x2x6 which can write at 4-speed, rewrite at 2-speed and read at 6-speed.

All CD-R systems should include CD mastering software. In fact, most systems are available as a full pack containing all the hardware, software and connections you need. Software is continually being updated, but Adaptec's Easy CD Pro, Figure 6.1, and Corel CD Creator are very usable. With Easy CD Pro, for example, all you do is drag files and folders into the main window.

*Figure 6.1 Adaptec's Easy CD Pro*

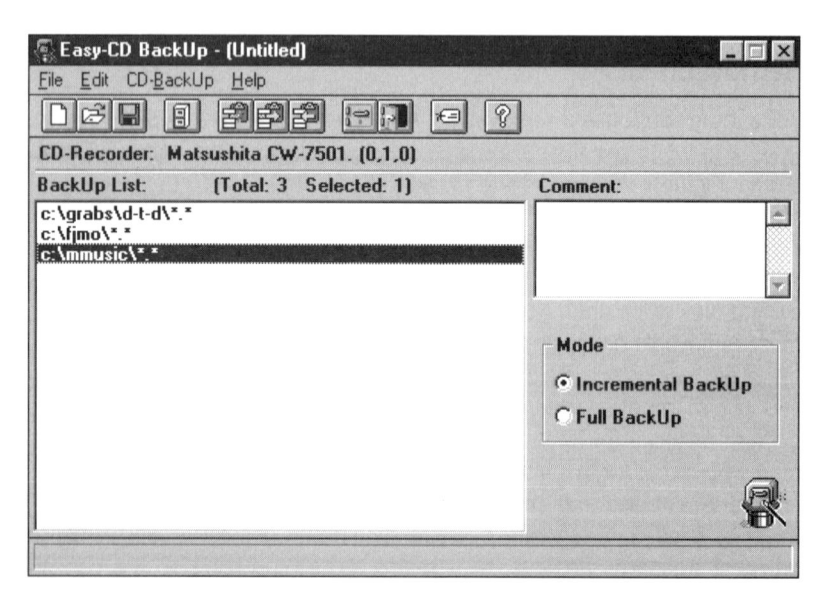

> **THERE'S MORE**
>
> *There's more about recording audio CDs in Chapter 12*

You can also buy mastering software separately if you have special requirements but do check to see what software is bundled with the drive as that ought to do what you need without additional expense.

Note that the CD mastering software discussed here is for copying and backing up normal PC files, not creating audio CDs. This requires different software, although some packs include both types.

## Backing up audio files to DAT

All the methods discussed here can be used to backup programs, data files and audio Wave files. If it appears on a hard disk as a file, it can be backed up.

If you have an audio DAT machine, you may wonder if you can use it to backup just the audio data. You could play each of the sound files on the hard disk through the audio card and save them onto DAT.

It's certainly an option and the process is not totally dissimilar to that of recording a final mix to DAT. However, there are several disadvantages. First, there's the time it will take. How many audio files have you created? 50? 100? More? If you only want the keep the final mixes, fine, otherwise make a mug of coffee and light both ends of the candle.

Another consideration is quality. If your audio card has digital connectors you'll be able to use these to retain the full digital quality of your files, otherwise you'll lose something backing up to DAT and then again restoring from the DAT if you have to rely on analogue connections. There's also the question of recording at the optimum level, and you could spend as long getting this right as you do recording the data.

And then there's the problem of naming the files. You'd need to keep a record of the original file names and the order in which they were recorded onto the DAT. Sounds like a lot of hard work.

However, if all you have is a DAT and you desperately need to clear some disk space, the option is there.

## Good housekeeping

Some people backup all their applications as well as their data. It takes longer but it means you can restore your disk exactly the way it was prior to the backup. However, if you have a lot of applications it can take a long time to do. If you backup regularly, several systems let you perform incremental backups which only save data which has changed since the last backup. This obviously saves time.

Another option is to backup just your data. Providing you keep all your original application software and updates along with any special notes about the installation you will always be able to reinstall your applications if your hard disk goes belly-up. But data is not so easily salvaged so don't backup at your peril.

## Summing up

> There are many backup options to choose from. Select one which can comfortably handle the amount of data you are likely to generate at a speed you are happy with and at a price to suit your budget. As technology develops we can expect to see all forms of storage media increase in size and fall in price, so see what's happening in the market before you make a decision.

# 7

# The soundcard

No matter how up-to-the-minute your PC is, no matter how fast your hard disk is, and no matter how much high-end software you have, the quality of the sound produced by your system ultimately depends on the soundcard. And there's a bit more to quality than simply grabbing the first 16-bit sound card you see.

The majority of soundcards were – and still are – developed for the games market where a touch of hiss here and a dash of crackle there doesn't do much to mar the thunder of cannon fire as you blast your way through another level. But use some cards for quality music production and their shortcomings will show.

As explained in the early chapters, the two most important factors when digitising sound are the sample rate and resolution. CD quality is usually taken to be sound sampled at 44.1kHz and with 16-bit resolution. Virtually all soundcards quote this on the box but there's a little more to it than that.

## Cutting through the tech spec jungle

We'll start by looking at the features you may see in a sound card's specification list. All of these have a bearing on the quality of the sound so it pays to know what the manufacturers are talking about.

*Sample rate*
This has been covered quite thoroughly in Chapter 3. All modern soundcards offer a sampling rate of 44.1kHz and many now also offer the 'professional' rate of 48kHz. This rate was originally proposed in order to permit a degree of compatibility with the varispeed control on analogue tape recorders. However, it has become the norm on many DAT machines and is used for many professional applications. If you want to tweak that extra bit(!) use the higher sampling rate but read the section on recording in Chapter 9 first (you don't get that much more quality from it) and do take into account the card's other features as described below.

Most soundcards can also sampler at lower rates. However, even if you are ultimately producing files to be played at lower rates, you will achieve better results if you sample and work on the files at a high sample rate and downsample them when you've finished editing.

*Frequency response*
This is the range of frequencies the card can handle. You may recall that the human frequency response is from around 15Hz to 20kHz. Ideally, all the frequencies will be reproduced at an equal amplitude – the so-called flat frequency response mentioned in Chapter 2 – so no frequency or lack of frequency will colour the sound.

No device achieves this perfection so it's usual to include a deviation figure or tolerance limit after the response range using our friend the decibel. It indicates how closely the flat signal can be maintained between the response range. Obviously, the smaller the deviation the better, but in most circles values between 0.1dB and 3dB are considered reasonably flat.

*Dynamic range*
This is the difference between the highest and lowest volume levels that can the card can handle, expressed in decibels, and, again, it was discussed in Chapter 2. The more bits a system uses, the greater its potential dynamic range. A good 16-bit system should achieve a dynamic range of 90dB or more although even 80dB is not to be sniffed at.

If a card has a digital output, check its dynamic range as this is likely to be higher than its analogue output and therefore give better results.

*Distortion*
Normally, any sort of distortion in a sound system is unwanted but a little is usually unavoidable. Many soundcards quote a figure for THD – Total Harmonic Distortion – which refers to the creation of unwanted frequencies which are harmonic multiples of the sound's original frequency.

Another form of distortion you may come across is intermodulation distortion which is caused by the sum of and difference between two frequencies (a little like ring modulation for any analogue synth fans) although this is usually associated with power amplifiers. Harmonic distortion, while unwanted, is what gives character to valve-based amps and software which emulates valve-based systems use it to produce the valve effect.

Back to the plot. Our ears can usually detect harmonic distortion when it's between 0.5-1 percent of the sound's total harmonic content. Most modern electronic circuits are good at keeping it down and should quote less than 0.1 percent. Typical figures in a soundcard may range from 0.01 to 0.005 percent. The lower the figure the better.

*Signal-to-noise*
This was also discussed in Chapter 2. It's similar to dynamic range but instead of expressing the range between the highest and lowest possible levels, it's an expression of the range between the highest level and the lowest level before it reaches the residual background noise. Essentially, the S/N ratio describes how quiet a signal is. Typical values may range from 80-93dB, the higher the better. If you think 80dB is low, consider that a high quality cassette multi-tracker with noise reduction will be lucky to have a signal-to-noise ratio of 70dB and it's more likely to be between 40-60dB.

> **TIP**
>
> *The maximum dynamic range possible with a 16-bit system is 96dB – and this, theoretically is also the maximum signal-to-noise ratio – but it is never achieved for reasons discussed in Chapter 3. So be cautious of a card quoting values which are unrealistically high for its resolution!*

### Over weighted

If there's a way to fudge a spec, you can bet someone has latched onto it. Because the human ear does not have the 'ideal' flat frequency response, there is an argument which says that measurements should take this into account.

When measuring noise, for example, which is, by its nature, usually very quiet, a special filter is normally used to equalise the readings. The other argument says that as we don't hear low levels of noise in that way and as our sensitivity to high and low frequencies is lower, levels should be measured in a way more in keeping with our frequency response. And whyever not?

Well, no reason, except it can be baffling when reading specs trying to compare ratings which have been measured in different ways. But that doesn't stop some manufacturers quoting 'A Weighted' figures, particularly in signal-to-noise specs. These have been weighted to follow the normal human frequency response and will be significantly better than flat or 'unweighted' readings. Some helpful manufacturers quote both weighted and unweighted figures.

### *DACs, ADCs and oversampling*

These were covered in Chapter 3. The DACs and ADCs ought to be at least 16-bit although many of the more up-market soundcards are 18-bit or 20-bit. This helps maintain the target 16-bit resolution (or the high dynamic range) which can't really be attained on a 16-bit system.

64x and 128x Oversampling is also common in many sound cards which helps improve the sound quality.

### *Sigma-delta conversion*

There's one more thing you may see in the DAC and ADC section of a spec sheet – sigma-delta conversion. This is a bit technical so I'll spare us all a sleepless night and run through the short version.

Many soundcards, particularly the more professional ones, incorporate a process called noise shaping which is a way of reducing noise in the audible frequencies by increasing the noise in the other frequency bands. It does this by 'shaping' the quantisation noise and spreading it throughout the frequency range. This can be done when oversampling is used because the high sampling rate increases the frequency range over which the noise is spread putting much of it into inaudible frequency bands. The circuits used to do this are sigma-delta converters.

### *Duplex*

Sometimes you may see this mentioned in the specs, sometimes not. If a card is full duplex, it can both record and playback Wave files at the same time. Obviously, if you're doing multi-track recording, it's useful to be able to hear what is on the other tracks while recording. If a card is not full duplex it can probably only record or playback at any one time. Some cards may be able to playback at a lower sample rate while recording at a higher one which is still useful for monitoring purposes.

However, even though a card may be technically capable of full duplex, it still needs suitable drivers in order to do it. Most cards now ship with full duplex drivers but some full duplex cards have been launched without full duplex drivers. So, if you think – or know – that your card is full duplex but it doesn't seem to be working, check that you have the drivers.

In any event, soundcard manufacturers seem to have a predilection for releasing updated drivers (to improve performance and correct 'features') so it's worth checking with the manufacturer that you have the latest drivers. Web sites are particularly good for keeping up to date with these.

*Daughterboard connector*
This is a connection socket built onto some cards to take a smaller daughterboard, piggy-back style. Most daughterboards offer an additional set of sounds such as Creative's WaveBlaster and Yamaha's DB50XG.

## Where the noise comes from

There are two ways in which a soundcard can seem to be poor quality – it can be noisy and have a low-quality output. Most consumer soundcards have an amplified output enabling you to plug them directly into a passive speaker. Because the cards are generally built to a price rather than a spec, the on-board amplifiers tend not be very high quality and can add noise to the output. If a soundcard has an unamplified output, there is less risk of noise from the on-board circuitry. If you have a choice, use the unamplified output.

Do bear in mind, though, that if you are running the output into a pair of computer speakers you will probably lose most of the highs and lows you've been struggling to hang onto during the recording and editing process. Use computer speakers by all means but if you want to know what your recordings really sound like, do also run the output through a decent set of speakers and a pair of studio monitors.

Noise can also be induced into the output by a badly-insulated power supply or even a noisy card which is close to the soundcard. If you think this maybe a problem, put the card in a slot as far away from the PC's power supply and other cards as possible.

## Beware the 'CD quality' promise

So now you know that 'CD quality' is rather more than sampling at 44.1kHz with a resolution of 16 bits. It's quite possible – and legal – to stamp 'CD quality' on the box but if the card's other factors aren't up to scratch, the resulting sound will be anything but CD quality.

Even if a card's output is not noisy, the output could still seem to be low quality. This is likely to be because the card has a narrow frequency response or poor dynamic range, factors which are evident in many low-cost and consumer soundcards designed primarily for games.

So read the spec list carefully and, if you can, listen to the card in action, not just playing shoot-'em-up and blast-'em music but playing quieter passages, too, and music with a large dynamic range and containing a wide range of frequencies.

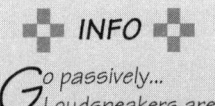

> **INFO**
>
> *Go passively...* Loudspeakers are of two types. Active speakers have built-in circuitry which amplifies the incoming signal. Passive speakers do not and require an amplified signal either from an on-board amp on a soundcard or through an external amp in order to play the sounds at a reasonable volume.

## Sounds on board

A major feature of many soundcards is their on-board sounds, and these have become better and more sophisticated over the past few years. This is really beyond the scope of this book which concentrates on digital audio but it's worth a brief look as many musicians use a card's sounds and its digital audio capabilities together.

The earliest sounds were based on a form of FM (Frequency Modulation) synthesis developed by Yamaha. It's had a good run for its money but the sound is rather thin and users expect better sounds now. However, many cards still incorporate an FM chip mainly, I suspect, for backwards compatibility with games and older programs which were designed for FM.

Most of the better soundcards now use wavetable synthesis which is based on samples of sounds so the realism is much better. Most cards also include effects such as reverb and chorus which can greatly enhance the output.

The next stage was to allow users to sample, load and edit their own sounds and several cards have on-board RAM into which samples can be loaded which can be played from a MIDI sequencer. Among the best-known cards of this kind are Creative's AWE series and Turtle Beach's Pinnacle card although there are others. The Pinnacle is one of the higher-end digital audio cards with built-in sounds but most cards with a 'professional' tag are designed purely with digital audio in mind.

## Digital ins and outs

One of the appealing and attractive concepts behind the 'digital studio' is the ability to do everything within the digital domain. With suitable software, edits and even effects can all be performed in digital land. The first time the sound sees the light of day, so to speak, is when you play it through the soundcard.

If the card has analogue outputs, the sound will be converted into analogue form and can be recorded onto tape, for example. However, the sound quality will be limited by the quality of the analogue outputs and unless you are using a very good quality card, the output may not do justice to the quality of the digital audio inside the computer.

However, if the card has a digital output, you could save the recording directly to a DAT tape and preserve the quality right through to the final master.

The most common digital connections on soundcards are S/PDIF (Sony/Philips Digital InterFace) which manifest themselves as RCA phono-type sockets. Basically, this is an unbalanced version of the more professional AES/EBU digital interface and it's found on many items of semi-professional and domestic digital equipment such as CD players and DAT machines.

Although the S/PDIF only has one wire, it can carry two channels of digital audio (a similar connection could only carry one channel of analogue audio).

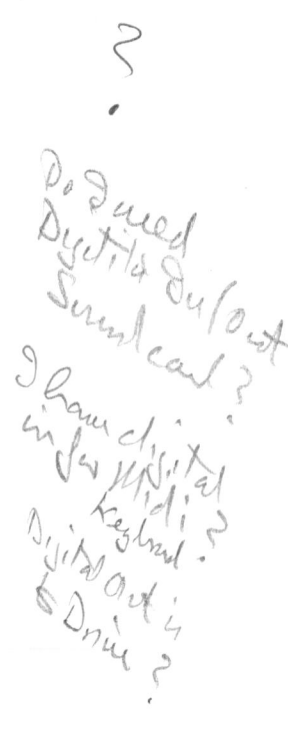

Some cards, including some from Turtle Beach, have an optional digital interface connector, usually on a daughterboard. Others such as Creamware's tripleDAT are available in a version with AES/EBU connections.

Some cards such as Creative Lab's AWE32 have a digital connector on the card's circuit board which can be connected to a digital socket to provide a digital output. This is certainly worth doing if you want a cleaner signal. However, check just exactly what is output through the digital socket. The AWE32 and AWE64, for example, only transmit digital audio through the digital Out, not the on-board sounds.

## Soundcard city

New soundcards arrive on the market every month so it would be pointless trying to produce a definitive roundup here. In any event, this is not the place for lengthy reviews – magazines, Web sites and information sheets can provide more in-depth and up-to-date information.

However, there is merit in looking briefly at a range of cards so you can see the sort of features available and assess the suitability of the types of card for your use. Some of the specs are a little hard to come by, however, and are often not quoted in the manual or on-line documentation. Where no printed specifications were available, the following data has been taken from various Web sites.

### The Creative family

Although there are many consumer sound cards other than those manufactured by Creative Labs, the company produces a wide and excellent range of cards and some of its latest releases are aimed as much at the music market as the games market.

Creative's 'standard' range – and the one most games cards attempt to emulate – is the Sound Blaster range. There are several variations including the Sound Blaster 16, 32, AWE32 and AWE64.

The SB16 and SB32 series are designed primarily for games. They have 20-note and 32-note polyphony respectively, and among their specs you'll find the following:

> Frequency response: 20Hz – 20kHz
> Signal-to-noise ratio: 80dB
> Sampling rate: 5kHz – 44.1kHz

> **INFO**
> *AES/EBU* – Audio Engineering Society/European Broadcast Union, societies which gave their name to a professional digital audio connection standard which uses XLR connectors.

> **INFO**
> *Polyphony* – the number of notes an instrument can play at the same time.

Sound Blaster spec

The signal-to-noise ratio could be better but it's par for the course on a consumer soundcard and better than a tape-based system.

The AWE32 shares many similarities but it has 512Kb on-board RAM for storing samples. It also has a digital output on the card which can be connected to an RCA socket fitted onto a backplane slot so you can plug it into a DAT or DCC. However, only the output from the on-board synthesiser is routed to the digital output, not digital audio.

Although the AWE64 seems to be an extension of the AWE32, it is actually based on new architecture. It has 512Kb of on-board RAM and is

64-voice polyphonic – 32 voices come from the on-board synth and 32 come from software.

*AWE 64 spec*

> Frequency response: 20Hz – 20kHz (line out)
> Signal-to-noise ratio: 80dB (amp out)
> Sampling rate: 5kHz – 44.1kHz
> AD/DA resolution: 16 bits

The AWE64 Gold was the first major Creative card to be aimed as much at the musician as the games player. It has 4Mb of on-board RAM for user samples and this can be expanded to 8Mb or 12Mb. However, expansion requires a special RAM module. Unlike the previous cards, you can't simply plug in off-the-shelf SIMMs, although the price of the modules is not extortionate compared with the price of standard RAM.

*AWE64 Gold spec*

> Frequency response: 15Hz – 50kHz (+0/–1dB)
> Signal-to-noise ratio: 90dB
> THD: 0.005%
> S/PDIF output: 20-bit, 120dB dynamic range
> Sampling rate: 5kHz – 44.1kHz
> AD/DA resolution: 16 bits

The AWE64 Gold has been designed to optimise the quality of the audio output. It has no on-board amplifier which helps keep the noise level down and the digital Ins and Outs maintain the quality. It has a much wider frequency response than the other cards, a better signal-to-noise ratio, good THD and a high dynamic range on the digital output.

### Life's a Beach

Turtle Beach was one of the first companies to produce high quality sound cards for the PC, although the company's range also includes cards more suitable for games. Many have distinctive Hawaiian names such as Maui, Tropez and Tahiti. We'll take a quick look at two of them.

The Tahiti was designed primarily for digital audio recording and its specs reflect that:

*Turtle Beach Tahiti spec*

> Sample rates: 11.025kHz, 22.05kHz, 44.1kHz
> Resolution: 8-bit and 16-bit
> ADC: 64x oversampled sigma-delta, 16-bit
> DAC: 8x interpolating filter, 64x oversampled sigma-delta, 18-bit
> Signal-to-noise: –89dB (A weighted), –85dB (unweighted)
> THD: < 0.01% (A weighted), < 0.02% (unweighted)
> Frequency response: 10Hz – 20kHz

Two main features of the Turtle Beach cards are the Hurricane Architecture which increases the data throughput and the built-in Motorola 56001 DSP chip which handles the digital audio processing.

The card has no digital output and on-board sounds but it does have a daughterboard connector which can take a wavetable plug-in daughterboard.

The Pinnacle is one of Turtle Beach's high-end cards with an on-board Kurzweil synth chip and it can take up to 48Mb RAM for user samples. It has a daughterboard connector and an optional digital I/O connector is also available.

> **INFO**
>
> *DSP (digital signal processing) chip – a chip dedicated to processing digital signals (not necessarily restricted to audio data) to take some of the load off the computer's CPU.*

---

Signal-to-noise: > –97dB
THD: < 0.00.5% (A weighted)
Frequency response: 10Hz – 22kHz (+0/–1dB)
Sample rates: 5kHz – 48kHz
ADC: 20-bit delta-sigma modulation with 128x oversampling
DAC: 20-bit delta-sigma with 128x interpolation filters

*Turtle Beach Pinnacle spec*

---

The specs are even better than those on the Tahiti and ought to ensure high quality audio, especially with the digital output.

## Back at the Digital Audio Lab

DAL has also specialised in quality digital audio cards and offers three main options to the PC musician.

---

*The CardDplus:*
ADC: 16-bit delta-sigma 64x oversampling
DAC: 18-bit 8x oversampling
Frequency response: 20Hz – 20kHz (+/–5dB)
THD: 0.003% typical
Sample rates: 22.05kHz, 32kHz, 44.1kHz, 48kHz
Dynamic range: 92dB typical

*DAL CardDplus spec*

---

Another good set of specifications which ought to deliver quality audio. You can add the optional I/O CardD to the CardDplus which provides a digital In and Out via a S/PDIF interface. It fits in an adjacent 8-bit ISA slot and connects to the CardDplus with an internal ribbon cable.

DAL also produces the Digital Only CardD, a stand-alone card for direct digital transfer of data to and from a DAT or other digital source. Having no analogue connections, this may seem to be of little use to anyone wanting to record live sound but if you have a digital source such as a DAT, you could record through that and probably get better quality than the analogue Ins on many soundcards offer. And if you never record audio but construct pieces using samples from sample CDs, for example, you wouldn't need an analogue In.

### Ready to Creamware

Creamware – or Creamw@re as the company likes to spell its name – is a German company which specialises in quality digital audio hardware and software. The tripleDAT system includes a high quality card plus high quality complementary recording software. The card is extremely well specified.

*Creamw@re triple DAT spec*

| Inputs | Outputs |
|---|---|
| 1 analogue stereo | 1 analogue stereo |
| 1 optical (S/PDIF) | 1 optical (S/PDIF) |
| 2 x coax stereo (S/PDIF) | 2 x coax stereo (S/PDIF) |
| 1 MIDI | 1 MIDI |

AES/EBU connections are available as an option.

Sample rates: 32kHz, 44.1kHz and 48kHz
**ADC**
Frequency response: 20Hz – 20kHz (< +/–0.015dB)
THD: < -87dB (A weighted)
Dynamic range: > 90dB

**DAC**
Frequency response: 20Hz – 20kHz (< +/–0.01dB)
THD: < –90dB (A weighted)
Dynamic range: > 96dB

Both the ADC and the DAC are 18-bit and use 128x oversampling.

This is a high spec card with enough variety of connections to interest the professional user and other musicians serious about their audio quality. The card and software go together although it is possible to use the card with other software (but check with the supplier before you try this). We look at the software in the next chapter.

Creamware also produces the MasterPort package which contains exactly the same hardware but with a cut-down version of the software – also mentioned in Chapter 8.

### Digi by design

Digidesign made its name producing high-end digital audio systems such as Sound Tools and Pro Tools for the Apple Macintosh. Those who couldn't afford the biggies could maybe just possibly stretch to an Audiomedia card which was one of the first dedicated, quality digital audio cards for a popular computer platform. In 1996, the Audiomedia card reached version III, acquired a PCI interface and became available, with software, for the PC.

> Digital ins and outs: S/PDIF 24-bit
> ADC: 18-bit delta-sigma, 128x oversampling
> DAC: 18-bit (software in Windows 95 writes 16-bit files, Windows NT supports 16-bit and 24-bit files)
> THD: 0.008%
> Signal-to-noise ratio: 88dB
> Frequency response: 20Hz – 20kHz
> Sample rates: 11.025kHz, 22.05kHz, 44.1lkHz, 48kHz

*Digidesign Audiomedia III spec*

High quality specs as you would expect. Perhaps the signal-to-noise ratio is, surprisingly, just a fraction lower than you might imagine but the other specifications make up for it.

The software available with the Audiomedia III card is Digidesign's Session Software. It offers up to four tracks of simultaneous recording (using analogue and digital inputs simultaneously) and eight-track playback. It has eight bands of parametric EQ, user-definable crossfades and automated mixing. It links to several popular MIDI sequencers including Cakewalk Pro Audio, Steinberg's Cubase and Passport's Master Tracks Pro.

### It's Emagic

Emagic, creator of the Logic sequencer and Logic Audio sequencer/digital recording software, moved into the hardware market with AudioWerk8, a PCI-based digital audio card. It offers 8 analogue outs, 2 analogue ins and a pair of digital stereo S/PDIF in/out connections.

> Dynamic range: > 90dB (A-weighted)
> THD: < 0.006%
> Frequency response: 20Hz – 20kHz (+/–0.5dB)
> ADC: 18-bit
> DAC: 18-bit
> Oversampling: 128x
> Sample rates: 38.5kHz – 50kHz

*Emagic AudioWerk8 spec*

It can playback eight channels at once and record on two. On release it would only work with Logic Audio 2.6.5 or Logic Audio Discovery 1.1 (the updates were included with the package). It doesn't have an on-board DSP but relies on the PC's processor and versions of Logic Audio from 3.0 onwards will support DSP functions such as EQ, reverb, chorus and so on.

## External d-t-d systems

While most direct-to-disk recording software uses what it's given – the host PC, EIDE or SCSI disk drives and so on – some manufacturers have produced dedicated d-t-d hardware which either uses its own proprietary software or else can integrate with established digital recording programs. Because the hardware in the system is standard and specifically designed for the purpose, systems using it ought to be able to guarantee a certain level of performance and a certain sound quality.

Because these systems are based on dedicated hardware they are more expensive than software/plug-in card solutions. If you need certain features or levels of performance which you think plug-in cards may not be able to deliver then it may be worth looking at a dedicated hardware system. There are several systems on the market, here's a brief look at just two.

### Soundscape

The Soundscape SSHDR1 consists of a 19 inch rack unit containing the audio processing hardware plus front-end software which runs under Windows on the PC. A plug-in card connects the hardware to the computer. The unit can play back up to 8 tracks simultaneously and several units can be linked to give up to 128-track playback. Here are a few specs:

*Soundscape SSHDR1 spec*

> ADC: 16-bit sigma-delta 64x oversampled
> DAC: 18-bit sigma-delta 64x oversampled
> Input signal-to-noise ratio: > 93dB (unweighted)
> Output signal-to-noise ratio: > 113dB (unweighted)
> Internal signal processing: 24-bit
> Sample rates: 11.05kHz, 32kHz, 44.056kHz, 44.1kHz, 47.952kHz, 48kHz.

The system uses standard EIDE hard drives (the company has a list of recommended drives) and as it achieves professional results the drives are obviously up to the job. The hardware handles most of the processing which takes the strain off the computer and the company reckons you could run the system on a 386DX with 4Mb of RAM.

Users with Windows 95 can run software version 2 which offers 12-track playback per unit plus many other enhancements which take advantage of Windows 95's 32-bit operating system. It supports several real-time effects including EQ, compression and reverb and you can define as many mixer channels as you need. There is also a CD writer option allowing users to burn their own audio CDs.

By the time you read this, Emagic has probably released an extension for Logic Audio for Windows to enable it to support the SSHDR1. Other developers may follow suit.

The SSHDR1 is a highly professional system used by studios, in broadcasting and by many musicians around the world. The standard system costs just a little more than a reasonably-specified PC.

### Yamaha CBX-D5

Yamaha was one of the first companies to release dedicated hardware for direct-to-disk recording. The CBX-D5 offers two-channel simultaneous recording and four-channel playback, a little limited by today's standards but the system has built-in EQ and reverb effects which can be controlled in real-time.

*Yamaha CBX-D5 spec*

> ADC: 16-bit 8x oversampling
> DAC: 18-bit 8x oversampling
> Sample rate: 22.05kHz (analogue input only), 32kHz, 44.1kHz, 48kHz
> EQ: 4-band parametric
> DSP: 82 reverb and modulation effects

As well as the D5, there was the D3, a less expensive version without the EQ and effects although this was never really marketed in the UK. The CBX-D5 is supported by some digital recording software including Cubase Audio XT.

## Summing up

> There are lots of digital audio cards and dedicated digital recording systems to choose from. The main consideration for most users is the quality of the audio output, tempered with price but, of course, the hardware and software need to be compatible. This is not usually a problem with standard soundcards as they have Windows drivers but not all software supports dedicated hardware.
> So, before you buy, make sure the collars and cuffs match...

# 8

## The software

As with analogue recording, digital recording can be used for several purposes. Its two main uses are multi-track recording, and stereo mixing and mastering. Digital audio software comes in five flavours:

- Multi-track recording software. This can record and playback several tracks of digital audio. It's similar to analogue multi-track reel-to-reel recording but editing and processing is much more flexible!
- Stereo recording and editing software, sometimes called Wave editors. These programs are designed to edit and process stereo (and mono) files. One of their main uses is to master recordings before they go off to be copied.
- Combined digital audio and MIDI sequencing software. For anyone who uses MIDI and also wants to record acoustic sounds or use sample loops, these programs offer the best of both worlds. In most software, MIDI and audio patterns appear on the same arrange screen and can be manipulated and edited in similar ways.
- Plug-ins. These are add-on modules for the above three types of software which allow you to increase the functionality of the program. They integrate with the main program and are accessed from a menu. Most plug-ins offer additional processing functions such as reverb, noise reduction, EQ and so on.
- Utility software. This category includes programs which convert between sample rates and resolutions, software which generates digital audio samples (software-based synthesis) and specialised software for manipulating samples such as Steinberg's ReCycle.

The first three categories all have a set of basic common functions such as the ability to record, edit and playback digital audio. Any additional processing or flexibility they offer is more down to the individual programs themselves than the category they fall into although because the purpose of a wave editor is to edit and process sound files, you will often find that these have a particularly good range of features.

## How digital recording software works

Let's see how digital audio recording works and why it's so powerful. Say you've recorded a saxophone solo. It will appear on a track in the recording software as a block or pattern, often showing the waveform inside it as in Figure 8.1.

Figure 8.1 An audio recording in Cubase Audio

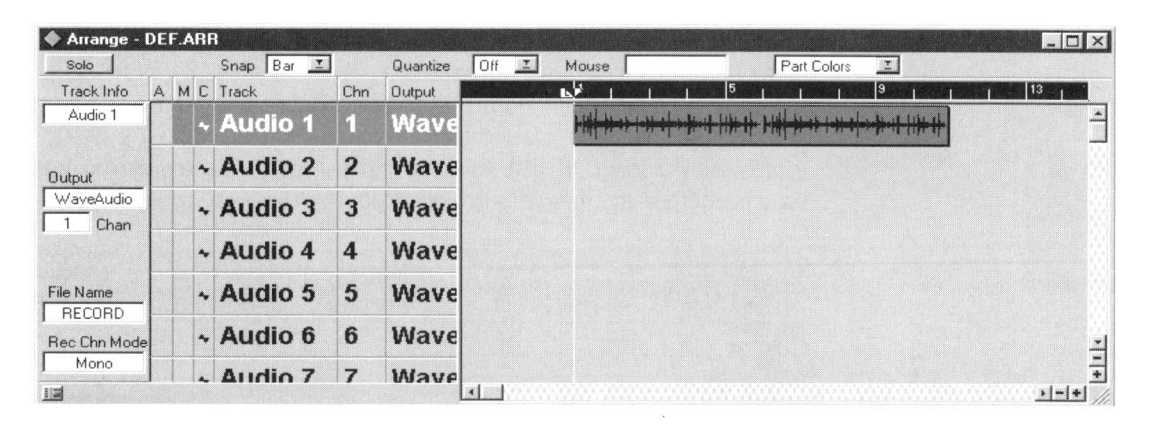

However, as the actual data is stored on the hard disk, the program simply references it using a system of pointers whenever it's told to play it. If you drag the pattern further towards the end of the song, the program will play it a little later. Drag it towards the start of the song and the program will play it earlier. This is simply impossible to do with analogue tape. Most pattern-based MIDI sequencing software works in a similar way.

And again, it's an easy matter to use the same recording more than once. If you copy the pattern to another part of the track, the program will simply play it twice. And here is an important feature of digital recording – copying a pattern in this way doesn't physically copy the data on the disk. All it does is to instruct the program to play the same recording again starting at a different point.

You can, in fact, copy the pattern onto another track and play the same recording two or more times simultaneously! You could offset one a little to create an echo effect (although echo and reverb effects are available for most software and offers more flexibility).

> **INFO**
>
> The pointers referred to here are used internally by the program. All the user does is place the pattern on the track at the point where it should play and the program does the rest. These 'pointers' are not to be confused with Markers which are placeholders designed to help users find their way around large recordings.

## Non-destructive editing

Now let's say that the sax solo you've just recorded is too long and you want to cut out four bars in the middle. So that's what you do – cut it out. It is, of course, possible to physically remove unwanted data from a file on disk but you never know when it may be required. Instead, the program changes its pointers so on playback it skips the bit in the middle. This is known as non-destructive editing and is used by all good digital audio software.

Using the same principle, it's possible to take a recording, cut it up into sections and reassemble it. You could swap the positions of the first and second verses, for example, double the four-bar intro, extend the guitar solo and so on. And if you decide you don't like the changes, the original material is still on disk so you can revert to your first arrangement.

## Audio file storage

Many programs have a window called a playlist or filepool which lists all the audio files associated with a song as in Figure 8.2. You can import pre-recorded files into the list and then transfer them onto the tracks, usually by dragging. This enables you to use material recorded in one song in another and to add recordings from sample CDs.

Figure 8.2 A list of audio files in session

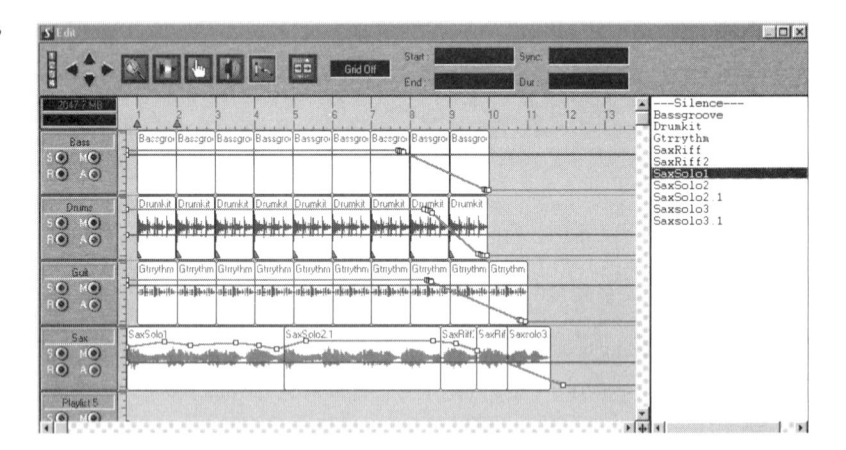

If you cut a recording into smaller sections, these often appear below the main recording as in Figure 8.3 so it's easy to see where each audio item comes from.

Figure 8.3 Logic Audio shows how recordings have been 'cut up' within the program

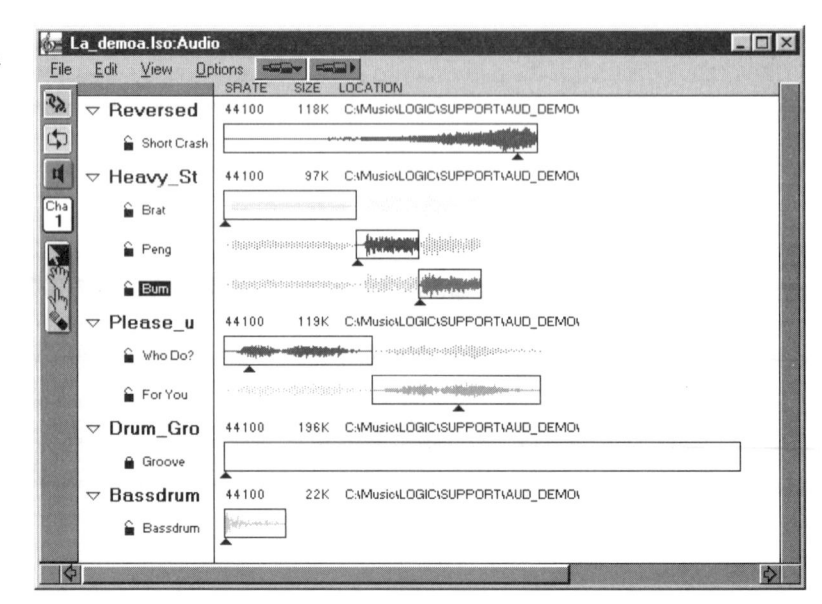

## Flying edits

Virtually all digital audio software has a mixer where you can set the playback level and pan position of the parts. If fact you will probably want to tweak a recording in many ways without actually altering the data – perhaps boost a frequency with a dash of EQ, mute and unmute tracks, and if two recordings overlap you may want to create a crossfade.

Whatever you do, you will almost certainly want to do it on the fly during playback. You won't want to wait while the program does some sums before it plays the amended recording.

Most software can now perform changes such as the ones mentioned above during playback. However, all changes require some processing power and if you try to do too much there may be a glitch or small delay. This is particularly true of processing functions. You can, of course, write edits to a file before playback and on a slow system or with software which has limited 'on-the-fly' functions you may have to do this.

There are some functions which are particularly useful to be able to change on the fly. Imagine tweaking the EQ, for example, if you can't hear the result of a new setting until it's been processed! Some functions may require too much processing power to perform on the fly but if the software has an Undo and Redo function, after processing you will be able to flip between the 'before' and 'after' versions to compare them.

## Of tracks and channels

Before we look at the main features of the different types of software in more detail, there's one more aspect of digital recording that needs explaining – the difference between tracks and audio channels. It's more relevant to multi-track systems than stereo editors but it highlights an important difference between digital and analogue recording.

On an analogue system, tracks and audio channels are the same. Take a 16-track analogue reel-to-reel system. Each track can hold a mono recording which could last the entire length of the tape. A track could, in fact, hold several recordings scattered along its length but the important thing is that in contrast to a digital multi-track system, each recording is fixed at a certain position on the tape. It cannot be moved to another position on that track and it cannot be moved onto another track.

The output from each track is usually routed to its own channel in a mixer so each track's volume level can be set independently. Thus a 16-track system would feed to 16 audio channels which would probably be summed to a two-channel stereo output.

The number of tracks a digital multi-track system can playback at once is limited by a combination of the speed of the PC, the amount of RAM it has, the speed of the hard disk and the capability of the digital audio card.

Let's take an 8-track system. This would be capable of playing back – yes, you guessed! – 8 tracks or channels of audio. If the system used a consumer-type sound card, the 8 tracks would probably feed a software mixer which would combine the tracks into a stereo signal routed to the card's audio output. We'd say such a system has eight audio channels.

> **INFO**
>
> *Crossfade* - a function which fades out one track while fading in another in order to create a smooth transition between the two.

However, many pieces of software offer more than eight tracks. In fact, you may have 100 or 128 audio tracks to play with. But, if you put a recording on each track, the system would still only play eight audio channels at once because that is its limit. In such a system, the additional tracks are known as virtual tracks because they do not have a physical output.

It's a very flexible and powerful system as it allows you to create lots of alternative takes and arrangements. You decide which ones will play by assigning them to the audio channels. The way in which you do this varies from system to system.

## Audio channel assignment by part

Let's use as an example the Soundscape SSHDR1 which has 64 virtual tracks. Recordings can be placed on any track at any position. None of the tracks have a permanent physical output. Instead, individual recordings are assigned to one of the eight audio channels. This means that eight recordings on one track could each be assigned to a different one of the eight outputs. Different colours are used for each of the eight channels so you can see at a glance which parts are assigned to which channel. The tracks are like holding places for the recordings.

As there are only eight outputs, you cannot assign two recordings which are at the same vertical position – and which would, therefore, play at the same time – to the same audio channel. If you try to assign a part to an audio channel which is already being used by another vertically-aligned part, the new part will be assigned to the channel and the previous part will be muted.

The system gives the user a lot of flexibility and it works extremely well although it's rather different to the concept of tape recorder tracks and to the track arrangement used by most MIDI sequencers. Users familiar with these systems may take a while to become familiar with it.

## Audio channel assignment by track – method 1

Another method of assigning audio channels, and one which is rather more common, is to assign them by track. This may seem similar to the tape recorder arrangement and in some systems it is.

Evolution Sound Studio Gold, for example, supports up to 16 audio tracks on 16 audio channels. Any recordings placed on a track always playback on the audio channel the track uses. You can add and remove audio tracks at will but the first 16 tracks are always set to audio channels 1 through 16 in order.

If there are 16 audio tracks, they will be assigned to audio channels 1 to 16 as in Figure 8.4. Delete, say, track 10 and all the following tracks will be assigned to a lower audio channel as in Figure 8.5. You cannot change the audio channel assigned to any particular audio track.

The program supports an unlimited number of virtual audio tracks where you can place audio parts but these tracks cannot be assigned to an audio channel and are best thought of as storage areas.

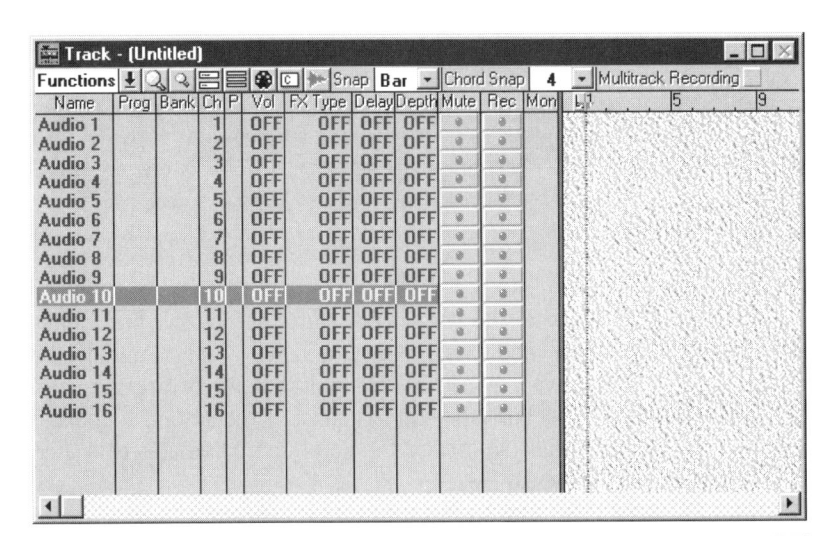

Figure 8.4 Sound Studio Gold supports up to 16 audio channels

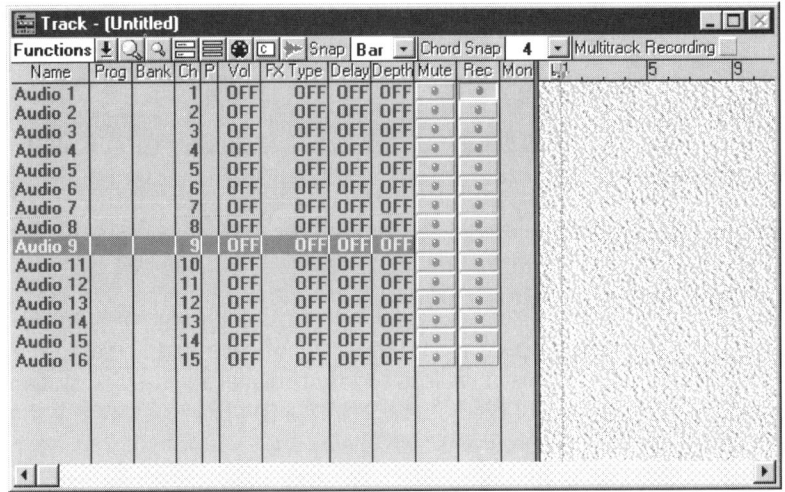

Figure 8.5 If you delete an audio track the audio channel assignments are automatically adjusted

## Audio channel assignment by track – method 2

Programs such as Logic Audio and Cubase Audio also use audio tracks with each track assigned to an audio channel. However, unlike the previous example, you can specify which audio channel each track uses. For example, the second audio track could use audio channel 1, the third audio track could use audio channel 7 and so on. Whatever recordings are placed on a track playback on that track's audio channel.

In addition, more than one track can be assigned to the same audio channel. But each audio channel can only play one part at a time so if two tracks are set to the same audio channel, they cannot both play at once. The usual method for determining which track plays is for the latest track to steal the audio channel.

In Figure 8.6, for example, the Guitar and Vocal tracks are assigned to the same audio channel – 2. However, as the two parts don't overlap and don't play at the same time, that's fine. They aren't fighting for the audio channel so they will both play.

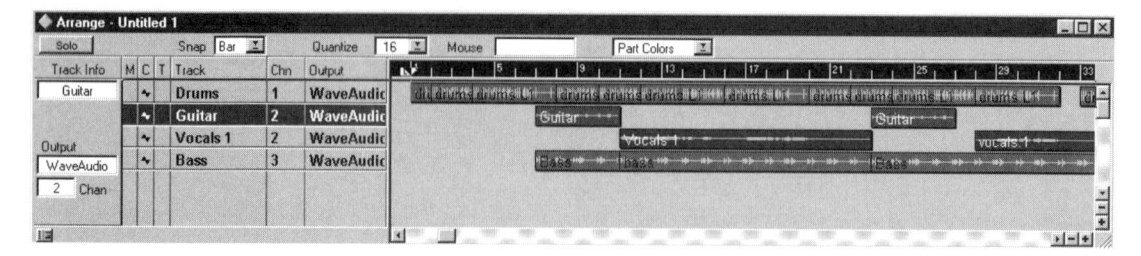

Figure 8.6 Guitar and vocal tracks are assigned to the same audio channel and both will play correctly

In Figure 8.7, however, the vocal track starts before the first guitar part has finished playing and it will 'steal' the audio channel, muting the guitar at bar 10. However, at bar 21, the guitar starts before the vocal has finished and will steal back the audio channel. If the system supported four audio channels, you could change the Vocal Chn parameter to 4 then both guitar and vocals would play.

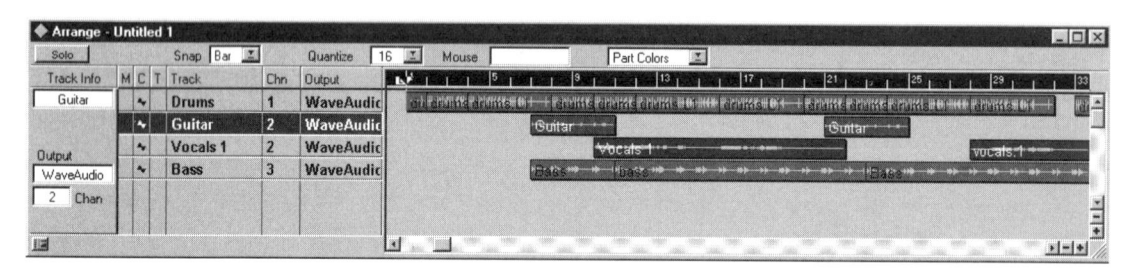

Figure 8.7 Vocal track starts before the first guitar part has finished playing and 'steals' the audio channel

## Multi-track recording software

For many musicians, particularly those who have used reel-to-reel recorders or cassette-based multi-trackers, a digital multi-track system will be the cornerstone of their studio. Here's a few brief glances at just a handful of some of the programs available.

### SEK'D Samplitude Studio

From version 4 onwards, Samplitude, Figure 8.8, was designed with Windows 95 in mind in order to use 32-bit code. It supports multiple soundcards to increase the number of tracks it can playback and it has an unlimited number of virtual tracks although a very fast Pentium or Pentium Pro processor are recommended if you want to play 16 tracks or more.

With a Pentium 90 and a fast SCSI hard disk the program should be able to play 16 mono 44.1kHz tracks. A Pentium 200 with a SCSI AV drive should manage 32 tracks. Playing stereo tracks instead of two mono tracks will increase performance.

The on-screen mixer, Figure 8.9, has 8 channels with volume, pan, EQ, compression and echo/delay on each channel. The effects are calculated in real-time. The mixer scrolls through projects with more than 8 channels so real-time effects can be used on all virtual tracks. You can draw volume and pan curves directly onto the waveform which is often easier than trying to create real-time changes with the mixer.

Figure 8.8 Samplitude was designed with Windows 95 in mind

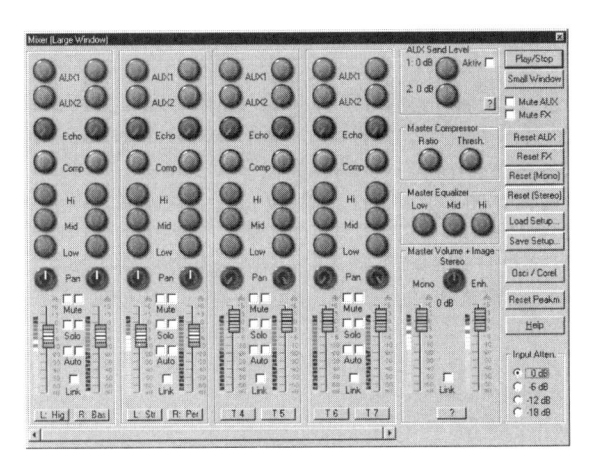

Figure 8.9 Samplitude's on-screen mixer has 8 channels with volume, pan, EQ, compression and echo/delay on each channel

It has several processing tools including FFT, noise-reduction, declipping, time stretching and a CD audio transfer function for SCSI CD ROM drives under Windows 95. It supports the MIDI Sample Dump so sampler users can utilise the program to edit samples before transferring them to their sampler, and it supports the playback of MPEG and AVI files. It can run in multitasking mode with a MIDI sequencer and if you want to sync it to other systems, it supports external synchronization via SMPTE, MTC and MIDI Clock as both master and slave.

## Session

Session, Figure 8.10, is available with Digidesign's Audiomedia III card and, in fact, will only work with the Audiomedia III card. As the developers know exactly what hardware is being used, it enables them to be more exact about the performance of the software. You can appreciate

Figure 8.10 Session software offers four tracks of simultaneous recording

the problems faced by software designers if they don't know exactly what system their software is going to be used on.

Session offers four tracks of simultaneous recording using both the card's analogue and digital inputs, 8 bands of real-time parametric EQ (up to four per channel), automated mixing and you can draw volume and pan curves onto the waveform.

Session will sync to most popular MIDI sequencers including Steinberg's Cubase, Cakewalk's Cakewalk Pro Audio and Passport's MasterTracks Pro. It acts as the master and controls the playback of the sequencer. It can also import AVI files and allows frame-accurate synchronisation with the video.

**Soundscape SSHDR1**
Soundscape SSHDR1 is a dedicated system with its own external hardware connected via a plug in card, Figure 8.11, and software. The standard hardware pack supports 8 digital audio tracks which can be expanded by the addition of other hardware units. The software expands to suit. It supports 64 virtual tracks and edits can be performed on the fly during playback.

Figure 8.11 Soundscape SSHDR1 card

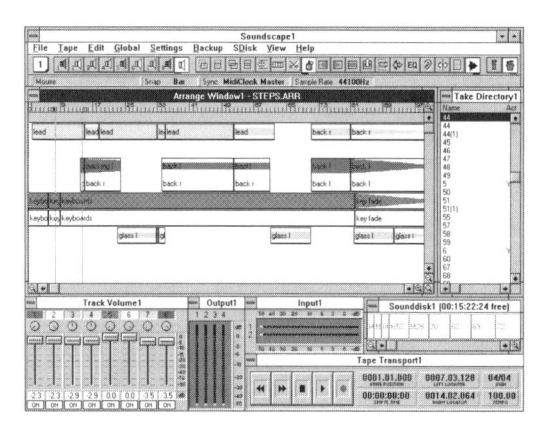

Figure 8.12 Soundscape's recording software

Up to eight parametric EQs can be applied to a track, split across several tracks or linked as stereo pairs. Processes include a noise gate and varispeed (+/–10%). It also supports all SMPTE formats and AVI files.

The software, Figure 8.12, runs under Window 3.1 and Windows 95 but from version 2 onwards it requires Windows 95 to make use of 32-bit technology. The SSAC-1 Accelerator card is also required to run this version of the software and it increases the number of playback tracks to 12 per unit.

The new mixer page has a completely user-definable routing/channel structure. Each channel can run any number of real-time processes such as EQ, compression, reverb and so on, limited only by the available DSP processing power.

There is an optional Time Module plug-in which offers time stretching, pitch shifting and sample rate conversion. The Reverb Module offers a wide range of reverb and delay effects. There are also Music Recording and CD Mastering, and Video Editing Modules.

## tripleDAT

The tripleDAT software is designed for use with the tripleDAT digital audio card, Figure 8.13, and will not work with any other card. Creamware's MasterPort system includes the same card but has slightly cut-down software. The card includes a host of cables, a stereo digital link, and a remote control for DAT machines. It supports up to 16 stereo tracks, real-time 4-band parametric EQ and real-time fades. It also has a host of off-line effects including a sample rate converter, compressor, limiter, de-esser, noise gate, expander, delay, room simulator and pitch shifting.

Figure 8.13 The tripleDAT digital audio card

The full tripleDAT software, Figure 8.14, which MasterPort users can upgrade to, supports up to 256 stereo tracks (although this is unlikely to be achievable for a while given the current state of affordable PC technology), off-line time stretching and pitch shifting. All the other effects can be used in real-time and include pan and volume fades with fade curves, spectrum analyser, room simulator, compressor, limiter, de-esser, noise gate, expander and delay.

It also has a Warp mode which allows the PC to be used as an external effects processor using the system's real-time effects. Signals entering the card's in sockets are processed and passed thorough to the out sockets.

Figure 8.14 tripleDAT
software

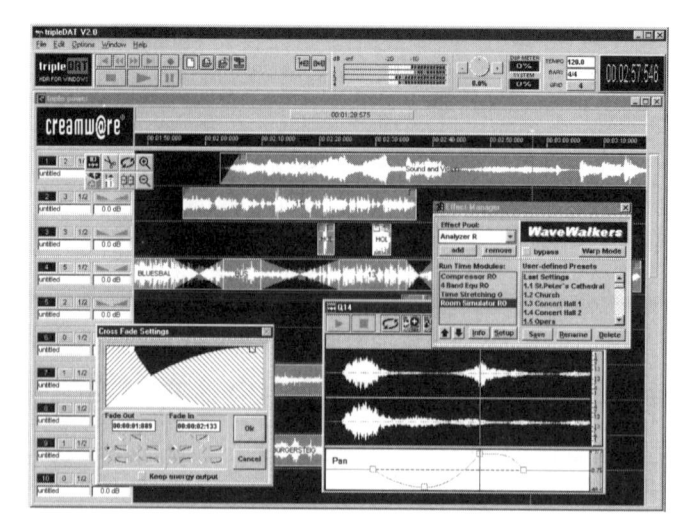

Version 2.3 includes a complete CD mastering system allowing users to create their own audio CDs. It also features archiving software which can automatically save all PC files to a DAT machine. Very handy for backing up.

There is also an optional set of plug-in modules called FireWalkers which work in real-time. They include an 8-band parametric EQ, graphic FFT analyser, chorus, stereo flanger, pan modulation, signal generator, dynamic transposing and a VU meter.

## Stereo recording and editing software

Before a multi-track recording can be distributed to a wider audience, it must be mixed down to a stereo (or sometimes a mono) format. This is known, naturally enough, as 'mixing down' or sometimes just mixing. If the object is to produce the final mix from which CDs or cassettes will be made, the process is commonly known as mastering and the mix known as the master or stereo master.

After a recording has been mixed into a stereo format, it is still sometimes necessary to perform other edits or apply additional processing. You may want to change the order of the songs in an album, for example, or increase or reduce the gaps between the songs. You might want to tweak the mix by applying a little EQ, compression or reverb in certain places.

To create a stereo mix from a multi-track recording you need, of course, a multi-track system. However, if you are only working in stereo or if you want to re-edit or tweak a stereo master mix, you only need stereo recording software. Programs which work with just two tracks of digital audio don't have the concerns of multi-track recorders in the way they assign tracks to the audio channels and they can apply the system's freed-up processing power to real-time processing.

### WaveLab

Steinberg's WaveLab, Figure 8.15, was one of the first wave editors to be written especially for Windows 95 and Windows NT to take advantage of

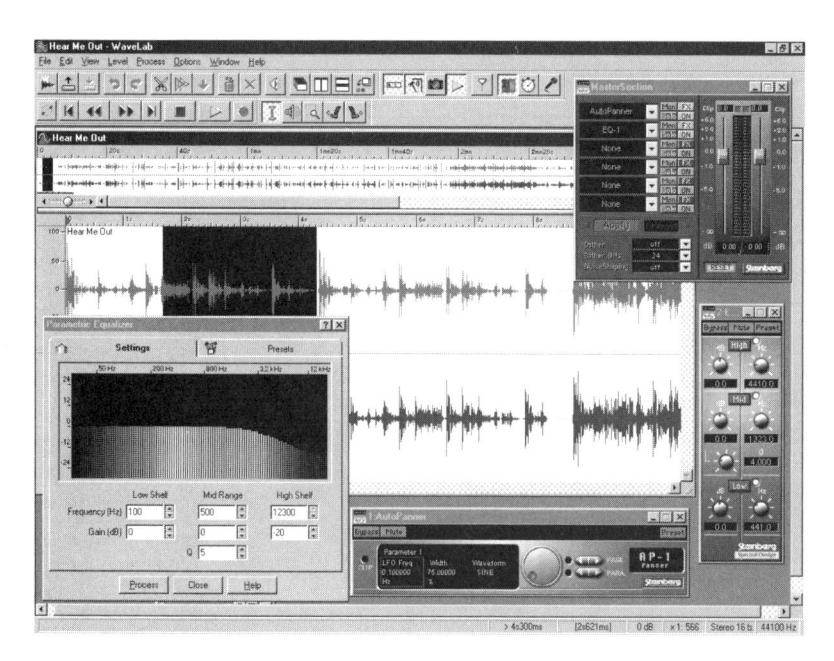

Figure 8.15 Steinberg's WaveLab – one of the first wave editors to be written especially for Windows 95 and Windows NT to take advantage of 32-bit code

32-bit code. It uses internal 64-bit processing and supports 20-bit and 24-bit files (providing the audio card does).

Most functions and processes can be applied in real-time – although a fast Pentium helps – and it supports an unlimited number of Undos and Redos. The main processing functions include normalise, change gain, invert phase, eliminate DC offset, fade in and out, crossfade, reverse, time stretch, pitch correction, harmoniser, chorus, EQ, dynamic processing and there's a FFT display.

Version 1.6 onwards supports plug-ins which appear in the MasterSection mixer. It has six slots into which you can load the effects which include autopanner, chorus, echo, EQ, Leveller (reduces or boosts the signal), resampler, reverb, stereo imager and a grungelizer. Steinberg expects third-party developers to add to the range.

WaveLab also supports DirectX effects. This is an open standard for audio and video plug-ins which lets you use any DirectX plug-in with any DirectX-compatible program.

The program can transfer audio from an audio CD in a SCSI CD ROM drive to your hard disk and it can create audio CDs if you have a CD-R. It includes the code for creating Red Book CDs. It also includes an audio file database which lets you categorise your files and search for them using keywords.

## Sound Forge

Sound Forge, Figure 8.16, was one of the first major wave editors to appear on the PC and it has grown into a truly comprehensive and feature-packed program. It supports a wide range of audio files as well as Wave files including Internet audio and video file formats, RealAudio 3.0 and ASF (ActiveX Streaming Format) used by Microsoft's NetShow On-Demand. It handles sample rates up to 96kHz.

### INFO

When DirectX was announced, Microsoft used the terms ActiveMovie and ActiveX to refer to this plug-in technology. You may see references to them in software manuals and readme files. However, these terms are now being used by Microsoft to describe specific player controls in Internet Explorer, the company's Web browser. The DirectX technology and principles are the some, only the name has been changed.

Figure 8.16 Sound Forge supports a wide range of audio files as well as Wave files, including Internet audio and video file formats

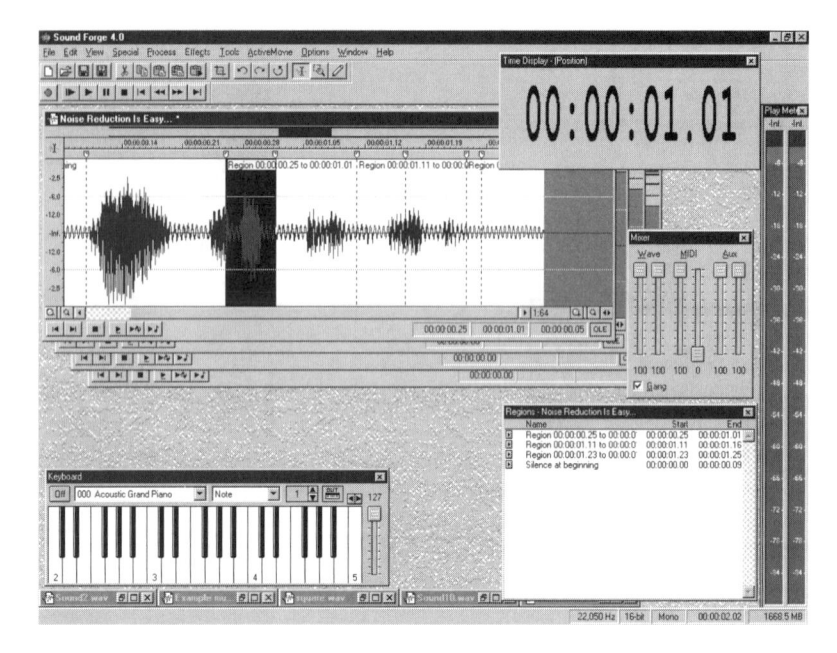

Built-in effects include amplitude modulation, chorus, delay and echo, distortion, dynamics, envelopes, flange and wah-wah, grapper/snipper (cuts chunks from the sample at regular intervals), noise gate, pitch bend and shift, reverb and vibrato. The dynamics effect has presets for reducing plosives and sibilants (a de-esser).

Other processes include auto trim/crop which removes silence, a channel converter which converts between mono and stereo files, a crossfade loop function to help with loop creation, DC offset, EQ, fade envelopes, invert/flip, normalise, pan/expand to create pan and stereo expansion effects, reverse, smooth/enhance which adds or removes high frequencies, and time compress/expand. Playback is almost in real-time – the program has to build a preview file but on a fast PC this only takes a couple of seconds. Like WaveLab, it also supports DirectX plug-ins.

It can generate simple waveforms such as sine, square, saw, triangle and noise and it has a four-operator FM synth. It supports the MIDI Sample Dump Standard and the SCSI MIDI Device Interface, a relatively new standard which enables sample transfers via SCSI which is much faster than MIDI. It outputs MTC (MIDI Time Code) so it can synchronise externally and it has a Virtual MIDI Router which can synchronise it to a sequencer running on the same PC.

## Combined digital audio and MIDI sequencing software

Combining a MIDI sequencer with digital audio software was a natural step for developers. Many musicians use MIDI to create backing tracks but want to add vocals or solo acoustic instruments to the arrangement, too. For them, a combined system is ideal.

The general approach has been to incorporate audio tracks in the same window as the MIDI tracks so you can see at a glance how the audio parts line up against the MIDI parts. You can usually edit the audio parts much as you edit the MIDI parts – copying, dragging, cutting, pasting and so on.

An alternative to the combined approach is to use separate digital audio and MIDI sequencer programs and sync them internally (see Chapter 14). This is an option worth exploring, especially if you like the features in a particular program or only occasionally need to combine MIDI and digital audio material. As combined programs grow in sophistication, they are starting to offer facilities to rival stand-alone software.

## Cubase

With the release of version 3, all versions of Cubase for the PC, Figure 8.17, include digital audio facilities. The three programs are Cubase (the standard edition), Cubase Score and Cubase Audio XT. The first two can use any compatible sound card and the Audio XT edition is for use with dedicated hardware such as Yamaha's CBX-D5. In all versions, audio patterns appear in the Arrange page like MIDI patterns and you can edit them in similar ways, too.

Audio patterns are stored in a Pool and you can drag them from the Pool window to the Arrange window. Processing functions include pitch shifting, time stretching, normalise, reverse and varispeed.

All versions include WaveLab Lite, a cut-down version of WaveLab. It launches automatically when you want to edit an audio file although you can choose to launch any wave editor.

WaveLab Lite includes normalise, change gain, invert phase, eliminate DC offset, fade in and out, crossfade, reverse, EQ and convert sample rate functions. It has a Dynamics window but this only functions as a Compressor. It doesn't have WaveLab's Expander, Limiter and Noise Gate functions in the Dynamics window and it can't create Dynamics Presets. There are a few other WaveLab functions missing but it still handles basic editing well.

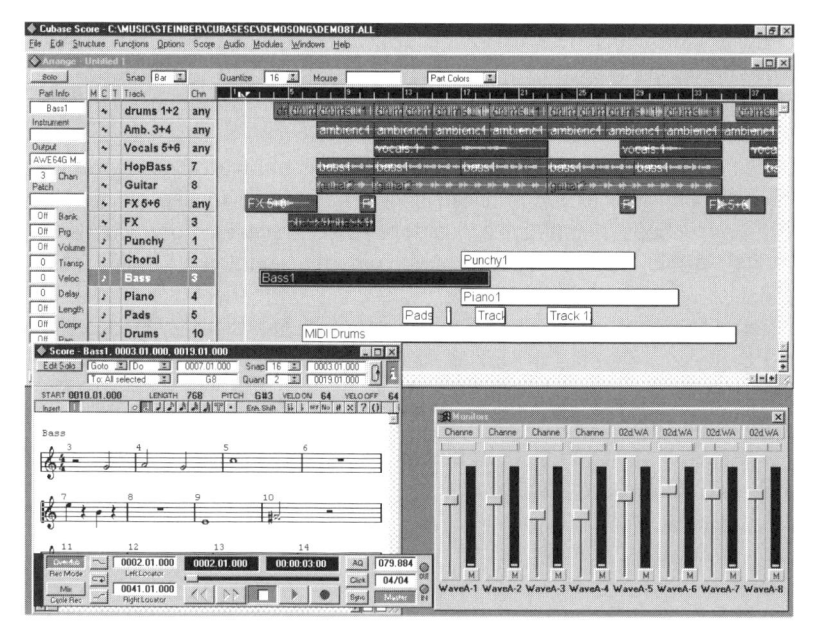

> **INFO**
>
> As you might expect, handling both MIDI and audio data requires more processing power than handling just one type of recording, but today's fast machines are quite up to it. You need to ensure that the software and digital audio card are compatible and it's important to check the performance you can expect to make sure it meets your requirements.

Figure 8.17 Cubase for the PC includes digital audio facilities

### Cubase VST

Cubase VST, Figure 8.18, was originally developed for Apple's range of PowerMacs. It uses the Mac's built-in DSP to handle the audio and perform real-time processing functions. Steinberg ported it to the PC under Windows 95 where it runs with a standard audio card and uses the PC's processing power to do its stuff, although you need a fairly nippy Pentium to get the most from it.

Figure 8.18 Cubase VST offers up to 32 tracks of digital audio

Its full potential includes playing 32 tracks of digital audio with up to 128 real-time EQs. It has all the main Cubase features but lots of extra digital audio processing functions, too. The main ones are the effects modules which look like hardware effects units and which have rotary controls and 'push buttons', not totally unlike the effects in WaveLab.

### Logic Audio

Emagic's Logic MIDI sequencer is one of the most powerful sequencers on any platform and, although it can take a little while to become familiar with its functions, it contains a wealth of edit and processing functions.

Logic Audio, Figure 8.19, is Logic with the addition of digital audio facilities. The audio integrates very smoothly with the MIDI tracks and patterns appear on the main Arrange page much like their MIDI equivalent and they can be edited in similar ways. You can play as many tracks as your system supports, typically 4, 8 or 16, and the program supports unlimited virtual tracks.

Volume and pan settings can be adjusted in the mixer. They respond to MIDI data (Controller 7 for volume and 10 for pan) so you can create control tracks to automate changes. Data in this format is easy to edit, too. You can also draw volume and pan envelopes onto the waveform display.

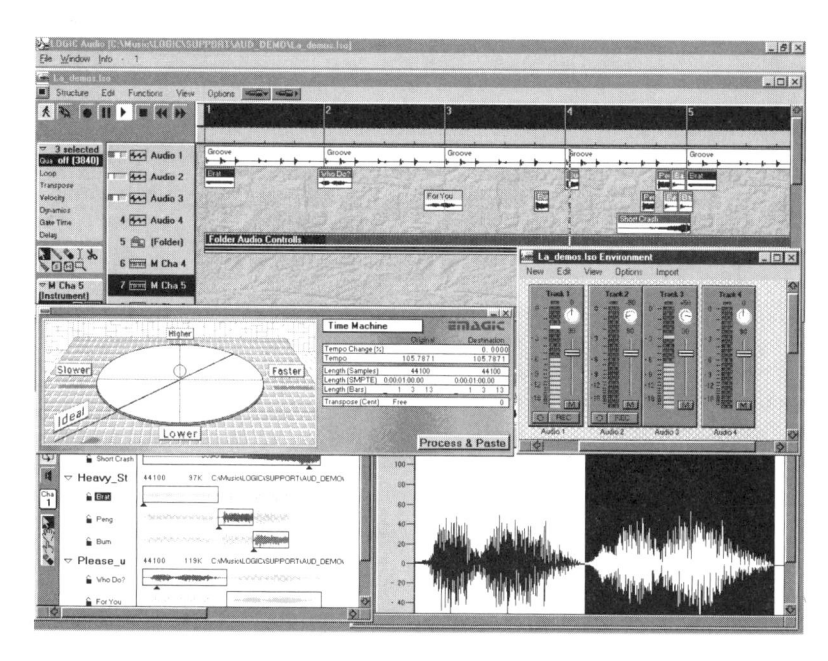

Figure 8.19 Logic Audio allows an unlimited number of virtual audio tracks

Recordings are listed in the Audio window and they can be dragged from the window into the arrangement. Double-click on a waveform to open the sample editor for even finer editing control. Here you'll find the processes and effects. The Functions menu includes normalise, change gain, fade in and out, silence, invert, reverse, trim and search for peak options.

The Factory menu houses the Time and Pitch Machine which adjusts duration and pitch. The Groove Machine quantises audio, much as the MIDI quantise function quantises MIDI (although the quality of the results depends on the rhythm of the source material). The Audio to MIDI Groove Template creates groove templates you can apply to MIDI data while the Quantise Engine lets you apply a MIDI groove to an audio file.

The Audio to Score Streamer converts an audio recording into notation although this only works with mono recordings and the results depend on the quality or purity of the audio data. The Audio Energiser boosts the perceived volume of the sound without changing the audio material while the Silencer has noise reduction and spike reduction which can be used separately or together.

## CakeWalk Pro Audio

Cakewalk Pro Audio, Figure 8.20, is one of the most popular sequencers in America although it doesn't quite have that honour in the UK and Europe. It's a solid, feature-packed program which supports 256 tracks. It started life as a linear-based sequencer following traditional tape recording techniques and it appeals to many users who come from that background. However, it does allow you to work in a pattern-based way, too.

It supports the CardD+, Audiomedia III and the Scoundscape system as well as standard Windows soundcards. Audio tracks sit alongside MIDI

Figure 8.20 Cakewalk Pro Audio supports up to 256 tracks

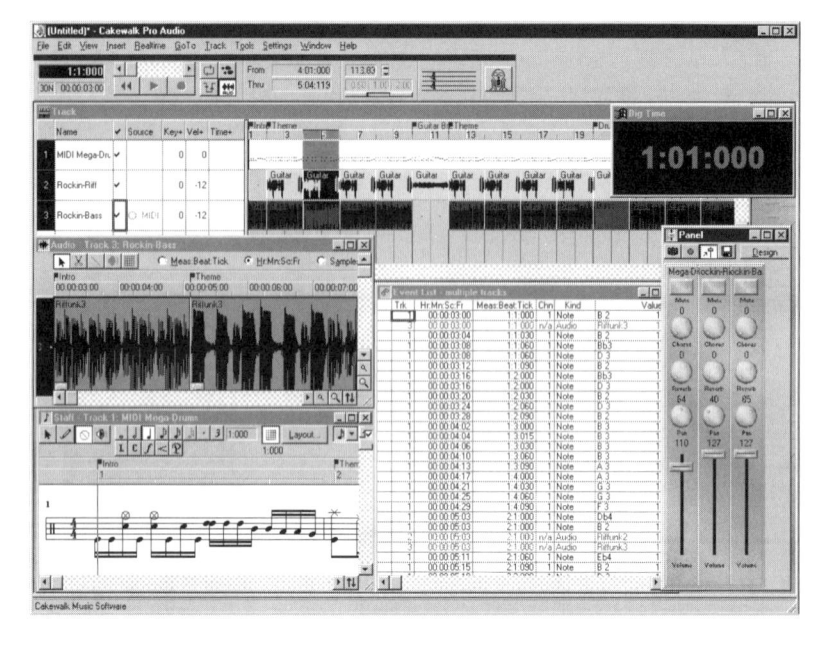

tracks and can be imported although there is no audio file pool. You can perform the usual cut, copy and paste functions on the audio patterns, draw in linear fades, set the output volume, and apply fade in and out envelopes and crossfades.

Extract Timing enables you to extract timing information from audio tracks and create grooves which you can apply to MIDI tracks. This works best with rhythmic material. The Groove Quantise function can quantise short digital audio events.

The program has a range of digital effects including chorus, delay/echo, flanger, reverb, and time/pitch stretch which work in real-time. There are both graphic and parametric EQs which are adjusted by sliders.

> **INFO**
>
> Plug-ins usually install in a special folder. Sometimes the parent program checks the folder when loading and displays the plug-ins it finds in a menu. In other cases the required plug-in is selected from a dialogue box. In all cases they integrate with the program as it they were a part of it.

## Plug-ins

With an increasing number of programs supporting plug-ins and with the take-off of Microsoft's DirectX technology, we can expect to see more companies developing digital audio plug-ins. Support for DirectX in a program is important because it means developers have a larger market to sell into. Rather than develop several plug-ins for each of a number of products, one DirectX plug-in will do for all which should encourage developments and, hopefully, help reduce costs – and the selling price – due to economies of scale.

This doesn't prevent companies from producing dedicated plug-ins for individual products. Steinberg has an open standard for VST plug-ins and they run considerably faster than DirectX plug-ins. So if you need performance, go for the dedicated plug-in.

## Sound Forge Plug-in Pack

The Sound Forge Plug-in Pack contains a set of three dedicated plug-ins for Sonic Foundry's Sound Forge editor – Noise Reduction, Spectrum Analyser and Batch Converter.

The Noise Reduction plug-in, Figure 8.21, analyses and removes background noise such as tape hiss, electrical hum and machinery rumble, usually without removing any of the source material. It does this by separating the audio into its frequency components and creating a noiseprint of the unwanted material. This is derived from a part of the recording which does not contain any source material – theoretically silence, but it will contain the background noise. The noiseprint is then used as a guide to determine what parts and how much of the noise should be removed.

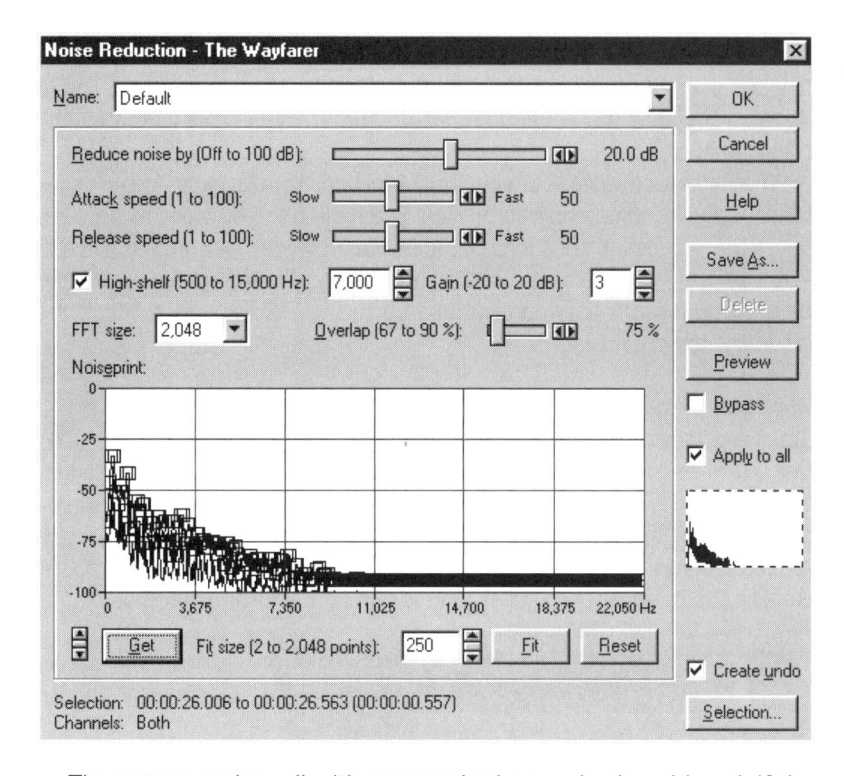

Figure 8.21 Sound Forge's noise reduction plug-in

The system works well with constant background noise, although if the level is very high it's almost impossible to remove the noise without affecting the source material.

There's also contain a Click Removal function. Clicks and glitches appear in the waveform display as spikes. The routine can automatically search for clicks in a selected region or you can select glitches manually. There are several options for removal – interpolating the click using data immediately before and after it, replacing it with data from the opposite channel, and manually redrawing the waveform.

The Vinyl Restoration tool, as its name suggests, is designed to remove pops and click and broadband surface noise from old recordings.

Figure 8.22 The graphic display of Sound Forge's Spectrum Analyser

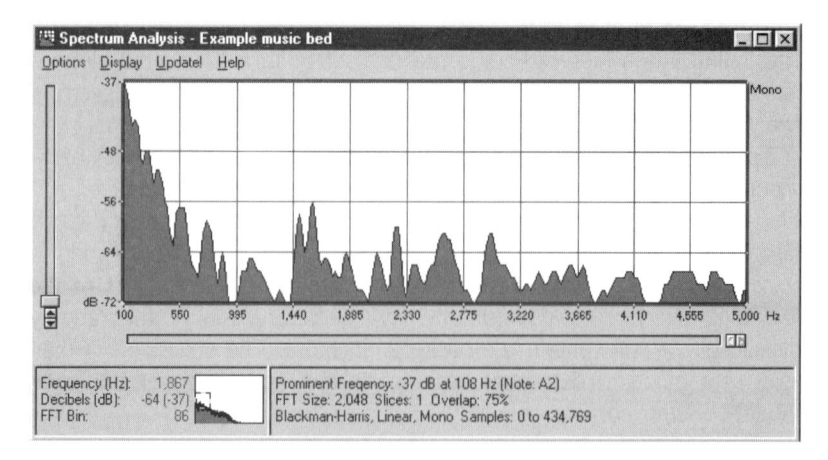

The Spectrum Analyser, Figure 8.22, produces a graphic display of the frequency content of a recording. It offers a Spectrum graph and a Sonogram where the amplitude of each frequency is represented by the colour intensity.

The Batch Converter lets you apply functions to hundreds – even thousands – of files in one operation. You select the files you want to process, select the processing functions and destination folder, and press Convert. You can use any of the processes and tools installed in Sound Forge. Before running a batch you can build up to five Previews to monitor the results of the processing.

### WaveLab plug-ins

Steinberg is leading the way with plug-ins for its WaveLab editor. The DeNoiser removes broadband noise in real-time. Unlike most noise reduction systems, it does not use a noiseprint. Instead it uses an adaptive process whereby noise changing in either character or level is automatically reduced. It has an Ambience parameter to ensure that the natural room ambience is not destroyed. Operation is fairly intuitive and automatic.

Figure 8.23 The Steinberg De-clicker for Wavelab

The DeClicker, Figure 8.23, removes pops and clicks in real-time although it can be used off-line, too. It analyses the audio using a Threshold parameter to determine what amplitude a click needs to be in order to get detected. The Mode setting is used for different types of material – Old for 'antique' recordings with limited high frequencies, Modern for contemporary recordings with a wide frequency range, and Standard which is the one to try first.

The Loudness Maximiser, Figure 8.24, is essentially a dynamics processor, but it's designed to increase the perceived loudness of the material even if it has been set to its maximum level. It does this by increasing the density of the audio material (basically by increasing the amount of compression), by limiting the transients and simultaneously raising the overall level. By definition, it alters the audio data but it does so in a way consistent with the data. However, the effectiveness of the results depending upon the source material and some material responds better than others.

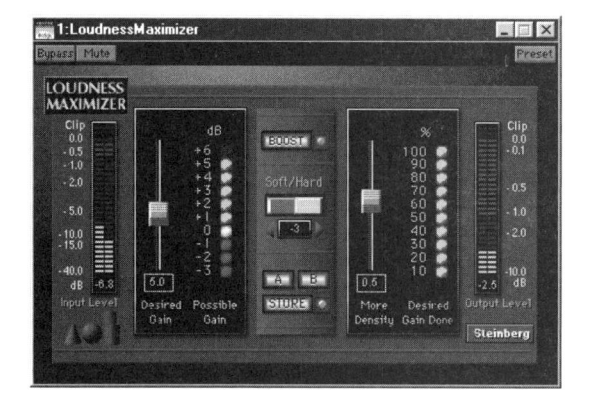

Figure 8.24 Steinberg's Loudness Maximiser for Wavelab

Although plug-ins can use any interface, these three plug-ins look similar and work in a similar way. Each plug-in has its own dongle which plugs into the parallel port so if you use all three plus Cubase, for example, you would have a chain of four dongles sticking out the back of your PC!

**Waves Native Power Pack**
Waves came to prominence as a developer of high quality digital audio plug-ins for Digidesign's top-flight systems such as Pro Tools on the Apple Mac. The company has since ported many of its products to the PC and the Native Power Pack consists of six plug-ins plus WaveConvert, a standard alone program. The plug-ins work with any DirectX-compatible software including Sound Forge 4.0a or later, CakeWalk Pro Audio 6.0 or later and WaveLab 1.6 or later.

The interface is similar throughout the collection and you can create and save presets in all of them. The Preview button lets you hear changes you make to settings in real-time although on a slow system real-time operation may not be possible.

IDR (Increased Digital Resolution) is Waves' custom dither system which increases the perceived resolution of a file.

*THERE'S MORE*

*There's more about Increased Digital Resolution in Chapter 11.*

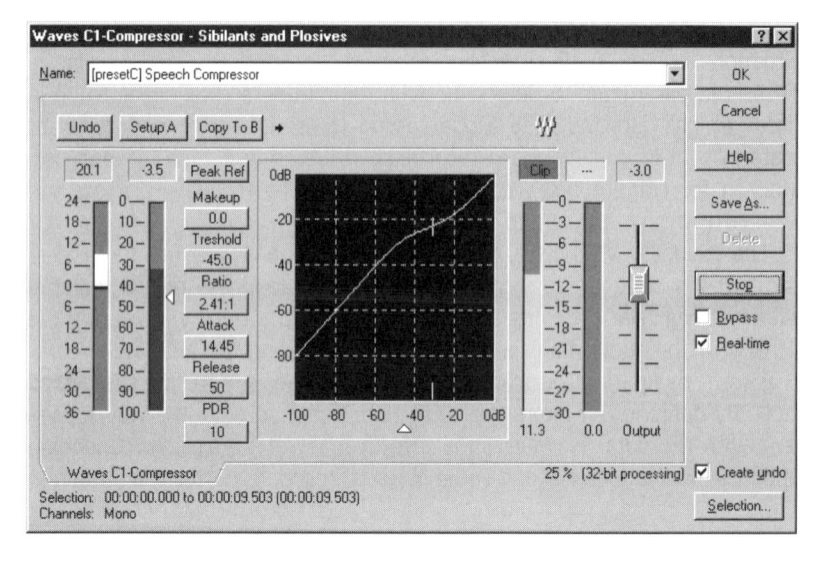

Figure 8.25 The display of the C1 compressor/gate

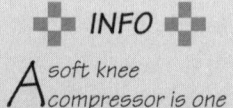

> **INFO**
>
> A soft knee compressor is one which smoothes the transition of the compression curve to make the sound more natural that an abrupt transition. There's more about 'knees' and dynamics processing in Chapter 11.

The L1 Ultramaximiser maximises the level and resolution of the file using a combination of a peak limiter, a level maximiser and a high performance requantiser. It effectively increases the perceived clarity of a 16-bit file to that of a 19-bit file and an 8-bit multimedia file would have a perceived clarity of 11 bits.

The C1 Compressor/gate is a soft knee variable-ratio processor. The C1 display is shown in Figure 8.25. It has a 'cancellation' mode whereby very high signals well above the threshold can be cancelled out completely. The Gate/Expander can be switched between gate and expander modes. It works as a soft knee low level expander to reduce low level signals and as a traditional gate. It can also produce a gain increase to 'compress up' low level signals. The effects have similar sets of controls and a graphic display shows how the signal will be affected as the signal is compressed or gated.

The Q10 Paragraphic EQ, Figure 8.26, has ten bands of EQ which can be configured as two mono equalisers or a stereo equaliser. Each band can be configured as a parametric, shelving or pass filter. The graphic display shows which frequencies have been cut or boost and you can pick up points on the curve and adjust them with the mouse.

The S1 Stereo Imager works with stereo files and lets you adjust various aspects of the stereo image. The Width control alters the width of the stereo 'stage' and you can increase this to place the sound beyond the speakers! Rotation moves the whole field left or right and Asymmetry adjusts the relative levels of the left and right parts but keeps the central sounds in the middle of the stage. Using the Rotation and Asymmetry controls together effectively gives you a traditional balance control.

The Shuffling control increases the stereo width at bass frequencies to help compensate for the fact that the ear hears stereo effects more narrowly at bass frequencies than treble frequencies. The graphic displays shows the width and positions of the left and right channels.

TrueVerb, Figure 8.27, is a high-quality reverb module which is particularly geared towards simulating room environments. The Time Response

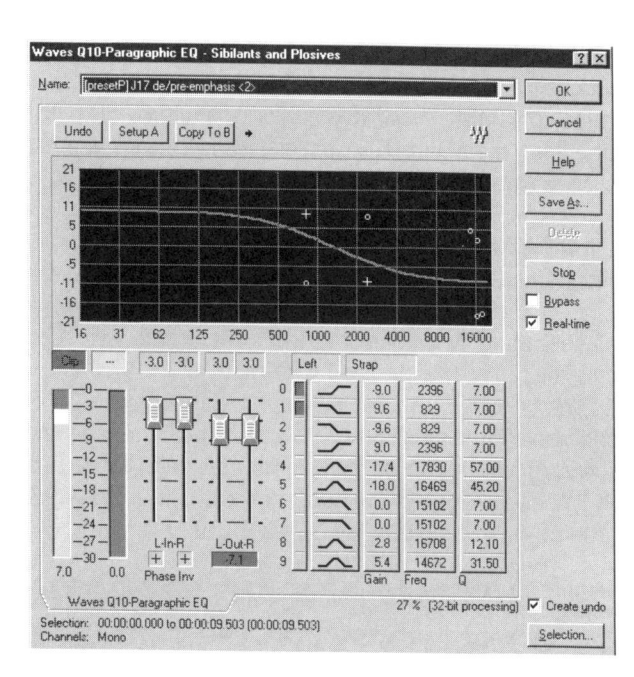

Figure 8.26 The Q10 Paragraphic EQ

graph on the upper graphic display shows the room size, distance to source, early reflections, pre-delay, reverb tail and relative levels. You can change settings by dragging. The lower Frequency Response graph shows the reverb's frequency contour, the RevShelf (a filter which acts on the input) and the RoomAbsorb factor which simulates the absorption characteristics of the room. TrueVerb can create a pseudo stereo file from a mono file but that's not its main function.

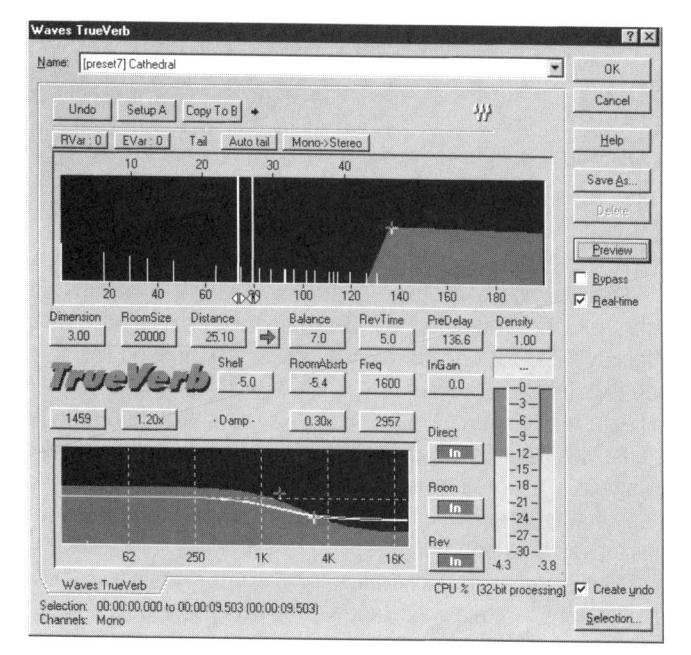

Figure 8.27 TrueVerb is a high-quality reverb module which is particularly geared towards simulating room environments

> **❖ INFO ❖**
>
> *H*TML - Hypertext Mark-up Language, a scripting language used to design pages for the World Wide We

WaveConvert converts between sampling rates, 8-bit and 16-bit resolutions, stereo and mono files and audio file formats. It supports sample rates up to 48kHz and it can process multiple files. The only documentation is on the CD in HTML format which means you need a Web browser such as Netscape or Microsoft Explorer to read it.

### tripleDAT FireWalkers

FireWalkers is a range of eight DSP effects for Creamware's tripleDAT and MasterPort digital audio systems. They can be used in real-time and all have a highly graphic interface. They come with a collection of presets and you can create and save your own.

They include a flexible 8-band parametric EQ, Figure 8.28, with adjustable filter modes (bell, low pass, high pass, notch, and high and low shelving) which can be dynamically assigned to each band. The Graphic FFT Analyser displays the audio spectrum in up to 8096 bands and can be used to view changes made by the 8-band EQ.

Figure 8.28 The FireWalker's 8-band EQ

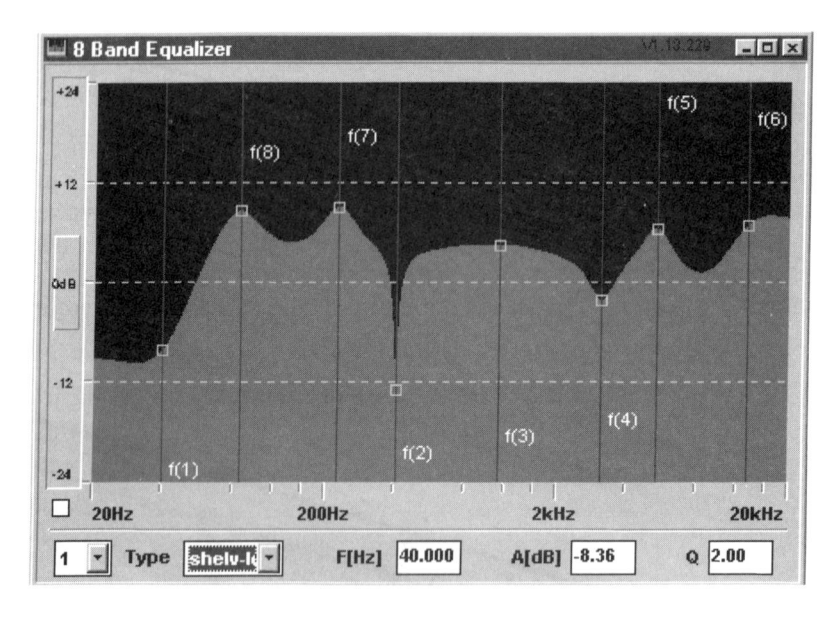

> **❖ INFO ❖**
>
> *A* 'tap' is a sort of mini version of the effect which can be given its own set of parameters. The term is generally used in relation to 'multi-tap' effects modules where the taps can produce a series of different effects throughout the duration of the main effect.

The Chorus has six taps, each allowing independent modulation parameters for pitch, volume, pan, depth and width. The Stereo Flanger/Phaser, Figure 8.29, has 2 taps with a similar set of modulation parameters as the Chorus plus feedback.

Pan Modulation, Figure 8.30, is an auto pan module with many adjustable parameters including rate, depth, width and waveform. The Dynamic Transposing module, Figure 8.31, offers pitch correction facilities of +/-12 semitones, while the VU Meter is completely resizable and has a peak hold option.

Finally, the Signal Generator creates test signals for measuring purposes. It can generate a wide range of test tones including sine, triangle, rectangle, noise and sweeps on frequency, volume and DC offset. You can also pass a sample through it for real-time resynthesis.

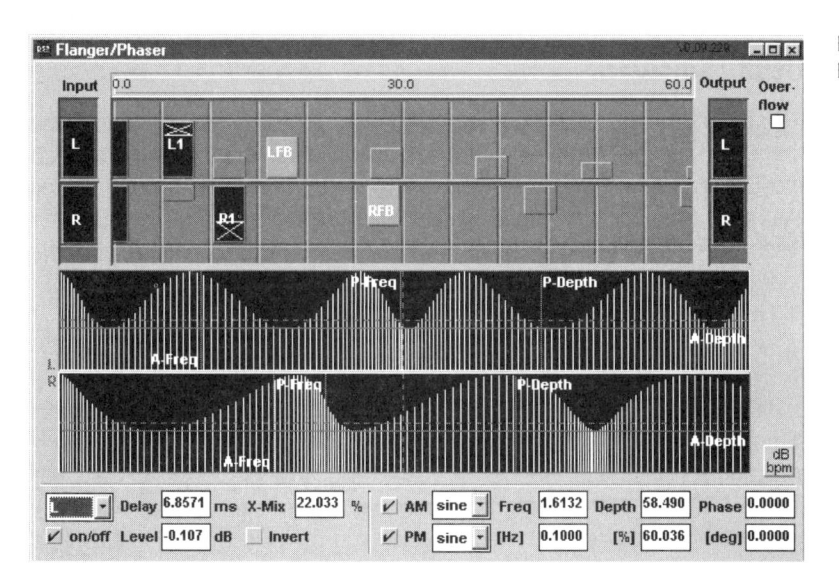

Figure 8.29 The Stereo Flanger/Phaser

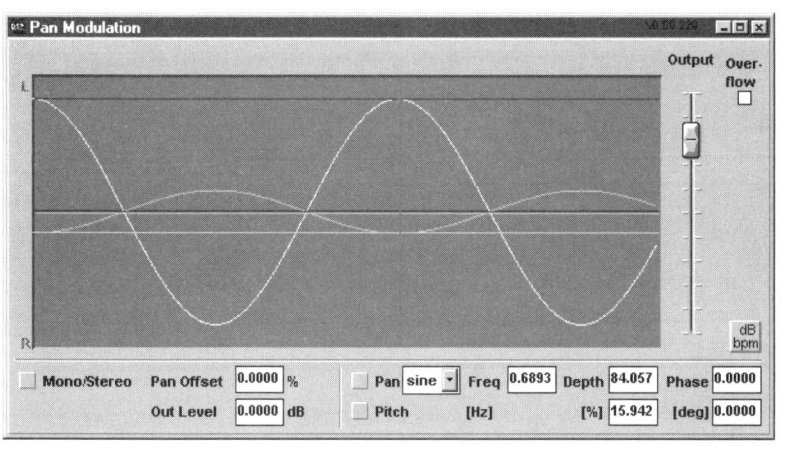

Figure 8.30 Pan Modulation is an auto pan module

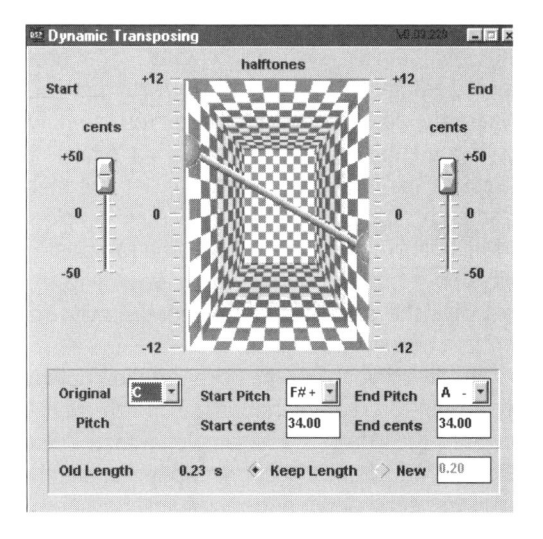

Figure 8.31 The Dynamic Transposing module offers pitch correction facilities of +/-12 semitones

## Utility software

As interest in digital audio and direct-to-disk recording grows, so does the range and number of ancillary utilities, and programs are starting to span the divide between classifications. Many digital recording programs, for example, now include digital audio file format converters, once the reserve of dedicated utilities. Sound Forge has built-in sound synthesis and many programs write audio CDs.

Here's a brief look at some of the utility software currently available.

### ReCycle

Steinberg's ReCycle, Figure 8.32, is designed for anyone working with sample loops and grooves. It lets you change the tempo of a loop without affecting its pitch and vice versa. It can also quantise loops, extract the timing from a loop to create a groove map which you can apply to other loops or MIDI recordings, and it enables you to replace individual sounds in a loop with other samples.

Figure 8.32 Steinberg's ReCycle allows the tempo of a loop to be changed without affecting its pitch

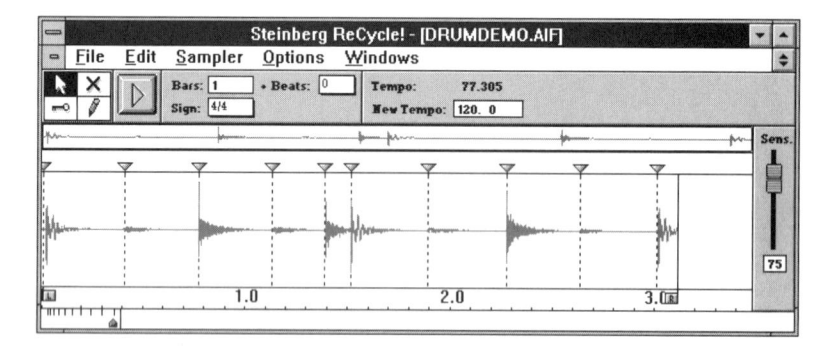

How's it done? Well, if you load a sample you'll see the waveform in the main window. Raise the Sensitivity slider and triangular markers appear at the volume peaks. These are called slices and divide the recording into smaller sections or 'hits'. The process will work with most recordings but it works best with rhythmic material such as drum loops where the peaks are well defined. You can now do a number of things.

If you enter the number of bars and beats the loop spans, ReCycle will calculate the tempo. You can transfer the material to a sampler in which case each slice is sent as an individual sample. The process also generates a MIDI file which is used to play the samples – individual notes trigger the slices so it plays in perfect time. Now, if you slow down the MIDI file, it will play the same slices but more slowly, thus slowing down the loop without changing the pitch.

As the original loop has been broken down into slices, you can change the order to create variations. You can even use samples from different loops or recordings – any sample, in fact! You can also transpose samples, even individual ones, again, without changing the tempo.

If you slow down a loop too much, there will be a gap between hits. The Stretch function helps prevent this by elongating the release part of the slices to fill the gap.

ReCycle is ostensibly for use with a sampler but you can also use it with Wave files and load the result into a digital audio program. The program currently supports Digidesign's SampleCell, Akai's S1000, S1100, S2800, S3000, S3200 and CD3000, and samplers by Kurzweil, Roland, Emu and Ensoniq samplers. Support for other instruments will doubtless be added.

## ReSample Pro

If you work with other musicians, are involved in multimedia, use other computer platforms, collect sound samples from the Net or use samplers, the chances are you will have to handle digital audio in formats other than Wave. KCCM's ReSample Pro, Figure 8.33, is a sample format converter which can convert almost any sound file format into any other. In fact, it supports around two dozen formats including those used by many popular samplers including instruments by Akai, Roland and Ensoniq.

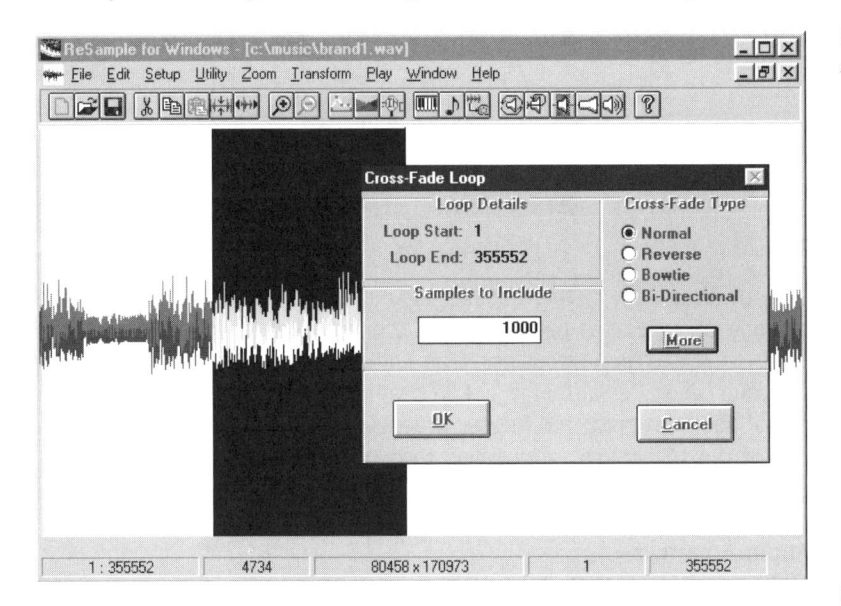

Figure 8.33 ReSample Pro is a sample format converter

It has a range of edit facilities including cut, copy, paste, insert silence, reverse and crossfade, and an Envelope Shaper lets you draw a volume envelope over the waveform. The Loopfinder General butts the end of a loop to the beginning to help you find good loop points. It supports the MIDI Sample Dump Standard so you can download a sample from a sampler, edit it, set loop points and upload it.

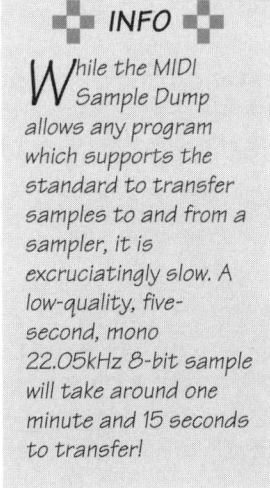

## WaveCraft

Audiovirtual's WaveCraft, Figure 8.34, is an analogue synthesiser realised in software. It has a host of 'analogue synth' modules which you place on a grid and connect using virtual patch chords. There are 17 types of module including oscillators, LFOs, VCAs, noise generators, filters, envelope generators, sample and hold modules, amplitude modulators and mixers. If you're not familiar with analogue synthesis some of this may seem a little strange but essentially the modules are used to generate and modify waveforms.

### INFO

While the MIDI Sample Dump allows any program which supports the standard to transfer samples to and from a sampler, it is excruciatingly slow. A low-quality, five-second, mono 22.05kHz 8-bit sample will take around one minute and 15 seconds to transfer!

Figure 8.34 Audiovirtual's WaveCraft is a software based analogue synthesiser. It has a host of 'analogue synth' modules

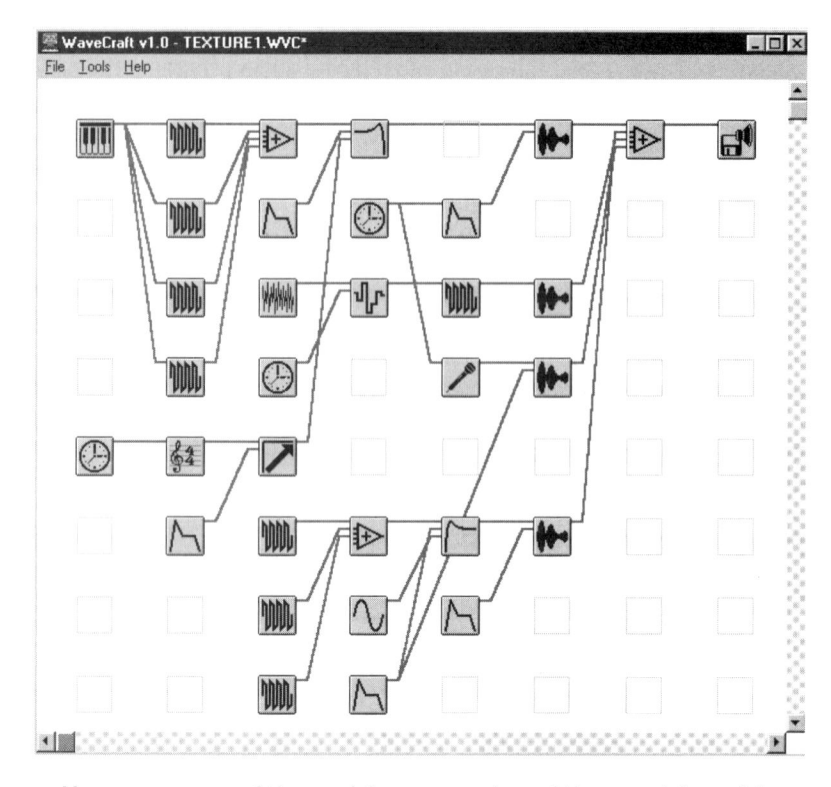

You can use any of the modules any number of times and they all have a range of adjustable parameters so the potential is there to construct some truly gargantuan patches. The end result is a Wave file which the program generates although not in real-time. This can be loaded into a digital audio program for further processing or into a soundcard such as one of the AWE family and played through a sequencer. As the sound is generated in software it is extremely high quality.

**Audio Architect**

Audio Architect, Figure 8.35, from Karnataka is another software-based analogue synthesiser, very similar to WaveCraft. It has a similar collection of modules – although they're not exactly the same – which are connected with virtual patch chords. The output is a Wave file written to disk.

One of the program's most powerful modules is the sequencer which is based on a three-channel, 16-step analogue sequencer. It can produce all manner of rhythmic patterns, bass lines, melodic riffs and so on. Operation is a little numeric but it functions well.

The company is currently developing the program to enable it to generate sounds in real-time. This will make it more immediate, more fun and more accessible, even to users who have no background in analogue synthesis. But you can expect to need a pretty powerful PC to run it.

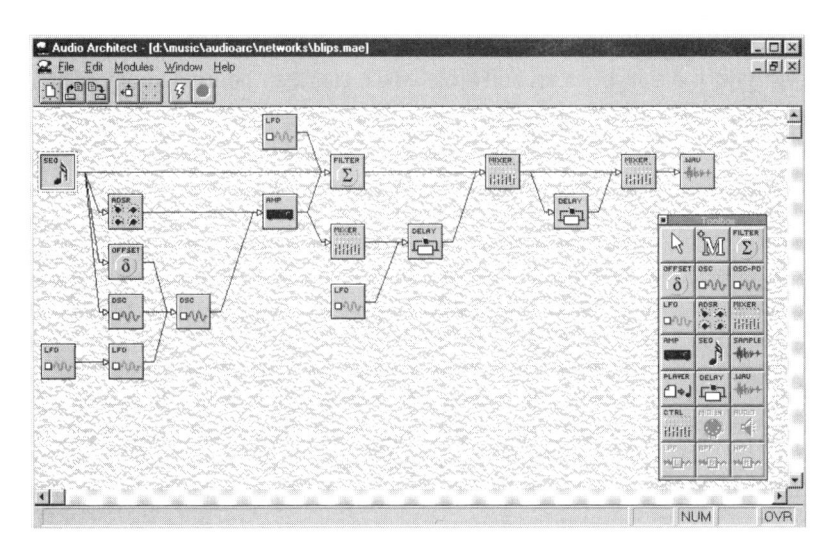

Figure 8.35 Audio Architect, is another software-based analogue synthesiser

## ReBirth RB-338

Steinberg's ReBirth RB-338, Figure 8.36, is a combination of three pieces of analogue – vintage! – equipment. It's based on two Roland TB-303 Bass Synths and a TR-808 Rhythm Composer. It looks like the originals and it works like them although, unlike the originals, it has also decay and distortion effects.

It lets you create up to 32 patterns for each module and link them together to form a song. You can then play the song while recording knob twiddles into it. The favourite twiddle is to adjust the resonance and cut-off frequency controls to produce those famous filter sweep effects.

It generates sounds in real-time so you can twiddle the dials and construct patterns as it's running. It's great for techno, dance, ambient, rave and all that sort of music and it's good fun to pay with, too.

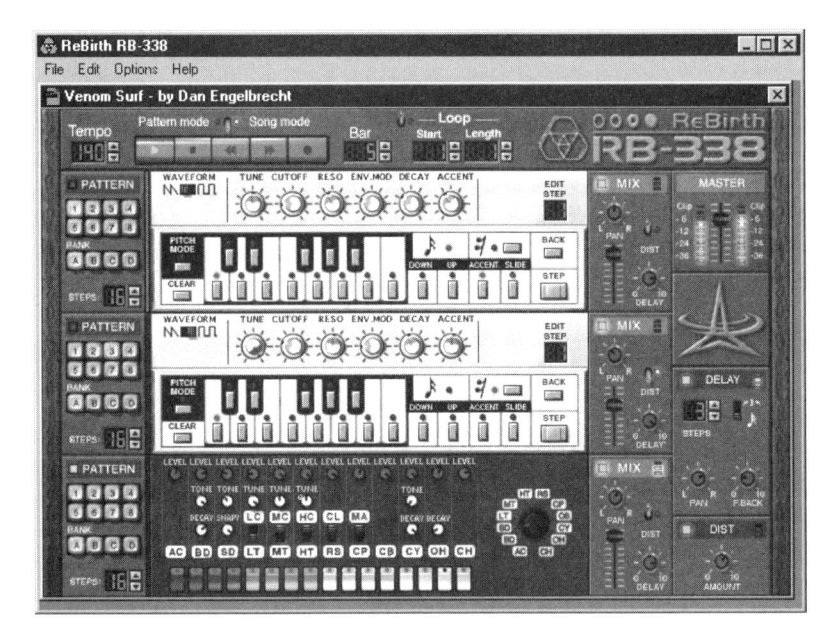

Figure 8.36 Steinberg's ReBirth RB-338

You can sync it internally to a sequencer such as Cubase and you can also save the output to an audio file which can then be used in any digital audio program.

## Summing up

For those interested in digital audio, the range of software is really opening up – multi-track recorders, wave editors, digital FX processors, conversion utilities, synthesis generators... the list goes on. As digital audio becomes increasingly popular we can expect the list to grow.

The software mentioned here is only a sample of what is available. Already there are too many programs to write about individually in a book of this nature. However, the ones we have mentioned will give you a flavour of what's out there.

# 9

# Recording and playback

You've probably heard the term GIGO: garbage in = garbage out. It was originally used in connection with data fed into a computer. If the data was meaningless rubbish, the computer would turn a few tricks and churn out more meaningless rubbish. The term, however, could have been coined with digital audio in mind – or any type of audio recording, come to that.

If there's one rule to bear in mind when recording it's this – it never gets any better than the original recording. This is especially true of analogue recording where you can't even make a copy, tape to tape, without seriously degrading the sound.

Digital recording fares significantly better and you can do a lot to spruce it up – remove noise and clicks, maximise the volume level and so on – but it will never be quite as good as a recording made without any noise and recorded at a good level in the first place. To take an extreme example, if you convert a sound which has been recorded using 8-bit resolution to 16-bit resolution, all you're doing is using twice as much space to store the same 8-bit information. Software may be able to interpolate between the bits but you can never fully recapture what was not there in the first place.

So, if you're using a 16-bit system and don't make full use of all the bits (bearing in mind that with optimum performance you may still only achieve a resolution of 14 or 15 bits – see Chapter 3) the quality of the sound will suffer.

All of which is simply a way of saying how important it is to pay very close attention to the recording process – which you ought to do in any form of recording anyway, analogue or digital. And although you can 'improve' a digital recording if necessary, far more easily than you can a tape recording, it's far better to take care over the initial recording in the first place.

## Basic recording techniques

The same basic recording principles apply whether you're recording to tape or digitally. There are many books and articles on recording technique, and the principles described generally apply to both analogue and digital recording. That means that if you are recording live (as opposed to transferring data from a sample CD or a DAT machine) you need to take all the usual precautions to minimise background noise, leakage from microphones, attend to soundproofing and so on.

We won't go over this ground again here as such information is readily available. Instead we'll concentrate on the main difference between the two methods – what happens to the sound when it reaches the computer. However, even before it gets into a digital format there are other aspects of recording to consider.

## Mic and line level

Let's start by seeing how the sound gets into the system in the first place. It's via the sound card, of course, but many sound cards have both line and mic inputs. Which one should you use? In case their names aren't a dead give-away, here's a bit more information.

The output from all sound-generating equipment is a voltage, usually a low voltage, and this is what determines the volume or level of the output. Mics have a low voltage output and equipment such as synthesisers have a higher output. Mic inputs expect low voltage inputs and line inputs expect a higher level input. So far so good.

If you connect a mic to a line level input, the signal will not be strong enough to record as cleanly and as loudly as we would like. You can increase the volume level after recording, of course, but that will increase the noise which is not what we want. So, if you want to record with a mic, use the mic input. You can, however, connect a mic to a line level input if you boost the signal first and running the signal through an audio mixer is a good way of doing this.

If you connect a line level output to a mic input, the signal will be too high and you risk overload and distortion. You could trim back the input but it's not a totally satisfactory solution and you'll probably find the levels difficult to control.

Just to confuse matters slightly, there are actually two line level standards. Line level in domestic equipment is usually –10dB and in professional equipment it's +4dB. A good guide to telling which is which (although it's not infallible) is look at the connections. A phono connection usually means domestic line level. An XLR connection usually means pro line level or mic level.

> **INFO**
>
> *Most sound cards have phono connections although some of the higher-end systems including Soundscape and tripleDAT have optional XLR connections.*

## Balancing tricks

There are two types of cable used to carry audio signals from one piece of equipment to another – balanced and unbalanced. Unbalanced connections use two wires and this is the norm with most domestic equipment and most sound cards, too.

Balanced connections – the pro standard – use three wires. Two carry the signal and the third acts as a screen to cut down on interference such as hum which may be generated by nearby equipment. Unbalanced lines act like a radio aerial and can pick up interference from power supplies – and computers!

Because balanced cables are good at keeping down noise they are often used for low level signals such as the output from microphones. They can also carry signals for several hundred feet whereas an unbalanced cable should not run for more than about 25 feet.

You can tell a balanced cable by its three-pin connector. They are commonly referred to as XLR connectors and often called Cannons after the designer.

## Impedance

A lot could be said about impedance but we'll only pay it lip service here. It's to do with the resistance a device has to the signal flowing through it and you'll generally be told that it's important to match a device to the input – a high impedance device should be connected to a high impedance input. Line inputs usually have a high impedance.

However, most modern equipment is quite tolerant on this score and you can usually plug just about anything into anything else, providing the levels match.

Many cheap microphones are high impedance and although the more discerning audiophile may shun them, if you have to use one you'll get better results if the input impedance is also high. Or you could run it through a DI box.

Remember – there's little point in using state-of-the-art recording equipment with a cheap microphone. All you'll succeed in doing is recording a poor signal and cheap noise...

## Noise – know your enemy

In any recording process the number one enemy is noise. This is any unwanted signal which has been added to the recording. It could be a sound introduced during the recording process such as hum, hiss, background noise and so on, or it could be distortion caused by a digital process. For example, if a sound is not sampled at a high enough frequency aliasing can occur (see Chapter 3) and if you try to record the signal at too high a level it will be clipped and you'll lose part of it.

If you use a tape system you're stuck with noise because it's an inherent part of the system. Noise is not an inherent part of a digital recording system but it can creep into it in several ways.

There is noise in virtually every electronic device including cables, microphones, mixers and synthesisers. The more noise you can eliminate at the recording stage the better – prevention is better than cure.

Before recording in your studio, sit down and listen to the sounds which are happening around you, particularly ambient sounds. These can be partially eliminated by using a cardioid or uni-directional microphone which only picks up sounds from a particular direction.

There are two sources of potential noise you ought to be aware of which can be caused by the computer. The first is the sound of the moving parts inside the computer. This will most likely be the fan which keeps

---

**TECHY BIT**

*Balanced cables do a little more than shield the signal. The inner wires in a balanced cable carry identical signals but one is positive and the other negative. When the signals reach their destination they are combined. If the cable collects any interference on the trip it is cancelled out leaving only the original signals.*

**TIP**

*You can plug a guitar into a mic level input and it may work fine but you'll get better results if you use a DI (direct injection) box. This matches the impedance of the guitar (which is usually high) to the impedance of the input (which is usually low).*

> **TIP**
>
> Whatever you do – DO NOT COVER the vents in the computer in an effort to blanket the sound. This is asking for trouble and could cause a part of the computer to overheat. In a worse-case scenario it could catch fire (yes, it has happened!) and in an only slightly less worse-case it could destroy the power supply, CPU chip or disk drive.

the CPU chip cool and the fan in the power supply. Many disk drives, particularly fast ones, also make a whirring sound which can seem very loud in a quiet studio.

Some users have built a sound-proof enclosure for the computer although this solution won't be possible for everyone. Take care not to block the vents and do leave enough space around the computer for ventilation. Other users put the computer in a desk drawer during recording.

If you have a noisy external disk drive, you could put just the drive in a drawer but the computer and drive will probably need to be fairly close together. The most common method of connecting an external drive is SCSI and SCSI cables ought to be as short as possible, preferably less than a meter.

Another solution is to place the computer outside the room completely. You would need extension cables for the monitor, mouse, keyboard and audio connections but this is certainly a viable way of cutting down on noise particularly for users working in a small area.

The other potential problem is a resonating computer case. It's not unknown for a case to vibrate in sympathy with a part of the computer such as the power supply. Certain sounds, particularly low-pitched ones such as those produced by bass instruments can also make it resonate.

If your computer does resonate, there are a couple of quick fixes to try. Sometimes tilting it slightly by putting a sheet of cardboard under an edge can stop the vibration. If one of the items inside the computer such as a CD ROM drive is vibrating, loosen the mounting screws, move it a little and tighten the screws again. If this doesn't stop a fixture vibrating, try adding thin rubber washers between the fixture and the frame.

## Clipping

One of the most important procedures in digital recording that you must get right is the recording level. When recording to tape, engineers try to keep the level to around 0dB on the meter. This is the optimum recording level and it gets as much signal – that is, the signal is as loud as possible – onto the tape without it distorting.

However, with tape, you can push the levels a little so the meter can flick over the 0dB mark occasionally without causing any problems.

But – and this cannot be overemphasised – this is something you cannot do with digital recording. You cannot overdrive the recording level. Why? Well, it's all to do with the bits.

If you refer back to Chapter 3 you'll recall that the more bits the system uses the more numbers there are to store the digital data. Every digital sample taken must be assigned a number in the allotted range. In an 8-bit system the numbers range from 0 to 257. In a 16-bit system they range from 0 to 65535.

So what happens if a signal is so loud that it needs a value of 65536 or higher in order to be stored accurately? Tough! There simply aren't enough numbers – bits – to store it so it gets truncated or clipped back to the highest value. It's as simple as that. A digital system doesn't squeeze

> **INFO**
>
> It's a relatively common practice among some engineers to overdrive the recording level. This squeezes or compresses the sound as it goes over the top and creates a 'warm' sound. Certain brands of tape are able to take more level than others and you'll find that engineers who use this technique have their own favourite brands of tape.

the signal as tape does so don't try pushing the levels to get a warmer sound – use a software compressor instead (see Chapter 11).

Refer back to Chapter 3 and Figure 3.10 to see what happens to a clipped waveform. You may get away with a small amount of clipping but that's usually because the signal is only truncated by a small amount and the distortion is lost in the main signal. Digital distortion is particularly unpleasant and needs to be avoided.

## Setting the recording level

But, as in tape recording, we still want to get as much signal into the system as possible. Most digital recording software has a meter which shows the level of the incoming signal. These are normally calibrated in dB and 0dB is usually taken as the maximum recording level above which no signal ought to go.

Most meters also have a peak or clip indicator which lights or flashes if the signal passes the 0dB mark. A peak hold meter will stay lit so you don't have to sit with your eyes glued to the screen watching for an errant spike.

The meters in Sound Forge, Figure 9.1, also show the maximum level reached during a recording and the percentage by which the input level can be increased before clipping occurs. Jolly helpful indeed.

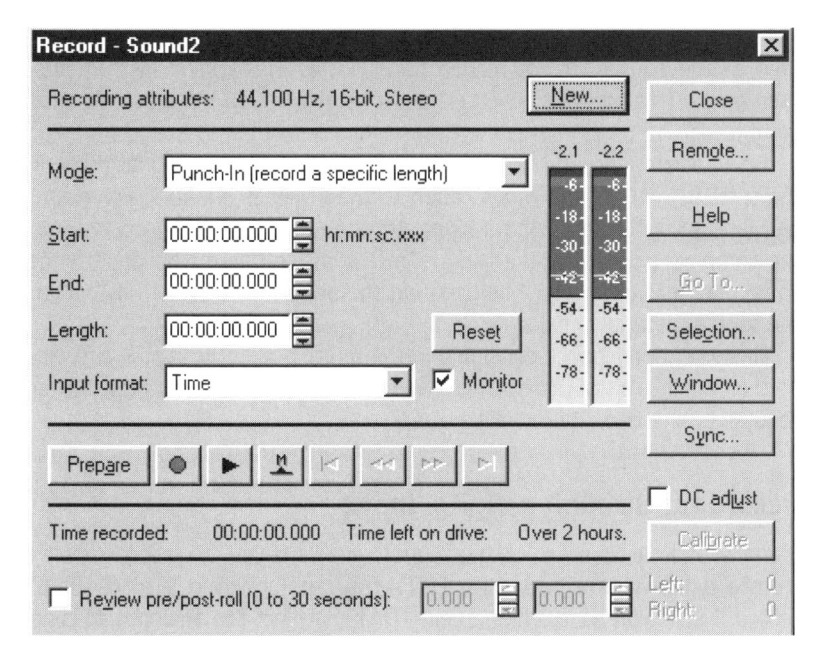

Figure 9.1 The meters in Sound Forge show the maximum level reached during a recording and the percentage by which the input level can be increased before clipping occurs

Most meters use coloured bands as a further visual aid to help you get the level right. Green is usually the norm, followed by yellow and then red. You ought to aim to keep the signal in the yellow. If it hits red it's probably in the distortion range. However, check the software manual to see what the limits and tolerances of the system are.

One problem you will invariably come across if you are recording live sound is that the volume of each take can vary. You ask the singer to run through a song and you set up the recording levels so it's just short of clipping. You do a take, the singer gets carried away and the signal bursts into the red.

In an analogue system the engineer would sit at the mixing desk riding the faders to keep the volume at the right level. Some software has an input volume control but not all, and the effectiveness of a monitor or mixer window depends on the audio card you are using and the compatibility of its drivers. Figure 9.2 shows Steinberg's WaveLab and an associated mixer which lets you adjust the levels from several different sources.

Figure 9.2 Steinberg's WaveLab and an associated mixer which lets you adjust the levels from several different sources

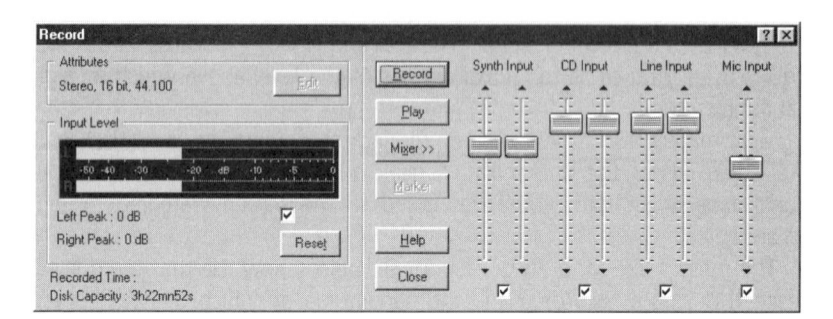

In some cases you may only be able to monitor the incoming volume level, not control it in the software, and you will have to adjust the volume at the source. If you're recording vocals or acoustic instruments, then you ought to have an external mixer which you can use to adjust input levels.

When setting volume levels, you should aim to pass a signal through the system with as little modification to the levels as possible. For example, let's say you're running a signal through an external mixer and into the computer, don't cut the level from the mixer only to boost it in the computer. If you do, you'll be boosting the noise in the system as well as the source material.

Likewise, don't boost the signal in the mixer and cut it in the software as this, again, raises the noise as well as the source and cutting it later reduces everything, not just the noise.

## Recording through a digital input

Some sound cards have a digital input, enabling you to record directly from a digital source such as a DAT. You can, however, also use it to record live. If you have a high quality DAT machine, the analogue-to-digital converter may well be of higher quality than the ADC in the soundcard. If that is the case, plug the recording source into the DAT's analogue input and connect the DAT's digital output to the card's digital input. Control the recording level with the DAT's volume control.

## Selecting a sample rate and resolution

Most digital recording systems let you select the recording sample rate and resolution. The resolution is usually 8-bit or 16-bit but, of course, if a system supports higher resolutions, they will be available, too. Sample rates typically vary from 5kHz up to 48kHz although some systems don't support 48kHz and others may not offer some of the lower rates.

The higher the rate and resolution, the higher the quality of the audio – but the more disk space the data will require for storage and the more processing power you'll need to do the recording. A system which struggles to handle four stereo tracks at 44.1kHz may quite comfortably handle six stereo tracks at 22.05kHz.

It is, therefore, sometimes tempting to work with lower rates or resolutions in order to squeeze extra performance out of a system or if the final file format is for multimedia use and doesn't have to be the highest quality. And in some cases the results may be adequate for the job in hand.

However, bearing in mind everything which has previously been said about digital recording, you will achieve better results – yes we say it again – if you record and work with the highest quality samples possible and then downsample the finished material to the required format. And don't forget the Nyquist limit – you may have to use a high frequency simply to capture the range of sound you want to record.

## 44.1kHz or 48kHz?

Some systems don't support a sample rate higher than 44.1kHz and for most purposes, including music production, this is quite adequate and, in most cases, the best rate to use. It is the rate at which the final recording, say to a CD, is likely to be made and the rate which should capture all the frequencies the human ear can hear.

There is, however, an argument which says that although we may not be able to hear sounds higher than, say 20kHz, higher frequencies do affect our perception of sound quality and contribute towards our tonal perception of the sound. There seems to be little consistent and conclusive evidence for this so, although it's a fascinating area of exploration, it's probably not something you would want to build a recording career around.

The sample rate of 48kHz doesn't offer a marked improvement over that of 44.1kHz. However, it wasn't developed to improve the sound quality but to offer scope to implement a varispeed control. Varispeed is common on tape machines. It simply speeds up or slows down the speed at which the tape runs thereby raising or lowering the pitch.

Varispeed on some digital recorders is implemented by changing the sample rate, that is, the rate at which the recording is played back. However, this can cause aliasing if the speed is varied too far. In most modern systems this problem has been solved through the use of low pass filters which vary with the playback rate.

Some DAT machines will only work at 48kHz when recording through their analogue inputs.

If you are mastering to a DAT at 48kHz, you may prefer to record at 48kHz rather than 44.1kHz. But bear in mind that most material will eventually be converted to 44.1kHz and, notwithstanding the comments made earlier about the benefits of recording at a high rate and downsampling later, the difference between the two rates is not very great.

## Playback

A chain is only as strong as its weakest link. Having taken every precaution to ensure that you have recorded the cleanest sound at the maximum level, your efforts may not be fully appreciated if you playback through a low-quality amplifier and speakers.

Ideally, you should use the line out from the sound card and run it into your usual studio amp and speakers. Many sound cards, particularly consumer models, have a speaker out socket carrying the output from a built-in amplifier which can be plugged directly into a set of 'computer multimedia' speakers. This may be fine for games and listening to the output from a CD ROM encyclopedia but such speakers are generally not designed with quality music reproduction in mind.

However, it's also worth remembering that the digital data on the hard disk remains the same whatever you play it back through. You can use any system and any sound card to monitor the results of edits, for example, without compromising the sound quality. This is useful if you've been working at a studio using a high quality digital system and you want to take the material home to do some editing. You can do the edits on a low-quality system and take the result back to the studio for playback and mastering.

Many pieces of digital audio software let you set the playback rate and resolution so if your work will eventually be converted to a 8-bit 22.05kHz multimedia format, you can play it back using those settings before doing a conversion so you know roughly what it will sound like. A point to note here, however, is that many conversion routines include features such as dither and filtering which help retain quality after conversion. These features may not be applied during normal playback so you may get better quality than this leads you to expect.

> **THERE'S MORE**
>
> There's more about sample rate conversion in Chapter 11

## Playing back through a digital output

The remarks made about recording through a digital input apply to playing back through a digital output. The digital-to-analogue converters in a quality DAT may be better than those in your soundcard so you could route the card's digital out to the DAT's digital in and play the recording through the DAT.

Even if you have a quality card, you may like to try this as an experiment to see if you can tell any difference between the two outputs.

## Hi fi in the studio

Many home users start out by pressing their hi fi system into use for their music-making and wonder whether it's all right to do this. There are a couple of issues to consider – the amp and the speakers.

What's the difference between hi fi speakers and monitors? Hi fi speakers are usually designed to make the music sound 'better'. Listen to speakers in a hi fi shop and the salesman will remark on the excellent bass end or the clarity of the highs. You may even find a set of cheap speakers which make the music sound good. They often deliberately colour the sound to make up for shortcomings in the speaker design.

The aim of monitor speakers is to tell it like it is. They should give a flat frequency response without colouration so what you hear is what you've actually got. If you can create an interesting and exciting mix on 'flat' speakers, it should sound good on almost anything. Mix on a pair of speakers which accentuate the bass, for example, and you're likely to cut the bass to compensate. Play this mix on a different pair of speakers and the bass may be almost non-existent.

So, you can use hi fi speakers for monitoring but you need to be aware that they may not be painting a true picture of the sound.

A reasonably good quality hi fi amplifier will usually do a good job. If you have a home studio you may be restricted to how loud you can play your music but don't think you only need a low power amp. It's better to use a powerful amp and less-powerful speakers. Watch the volume dial. It really shouldn't go above three-quarters maximum, preferably below half way. If you crank it up higher – of if you have to turn it up to get a good volume – you risk damaging the speakers.

Most pre-recorded music has been compressed. Music you're in the process of creating will not be and it's not difficult to whack a bass line or some fast transients such as percussive sounds and drum parts through the system and burn out a speaker coil or damage the cone. So take it easy.

But alongside your recording equipment, you ought to budget for a pair of monitor speakers. They will play your music more accurately and help you become aware of the differences between systems and the colouration added by some hi fi speakers.

> **TIP**
>
> It can be useful to play a track or an album on a few systems – the walkman, the ghetto blaster, in the car, on your mate's hi fi – and try to spot to the differences. Is it flatter, more bassy, too toppy or does it sound okay? How does it compare with the sound delivered by your hi fi system?

# 10

## Editing

The flexible and powerful editing functions found in most digital audio software are some of the many attractive aspects of direct-to-disk recording.

Editing can be split into two types of function – re-ordering the playback order of the recording or parts of the recording which we look at here, and processing such as adding reverb, normalising, sample conversion and so on which we look at in the next chapter.

### Non-destructive editing

We mentioned non-destructive editing in Chapter 8 and this is the very heart of d-t-d editing. It essentially allows us to play fast and loose with the material we have recorded without altering the original data in any way. It's a bit like having your cake and eating it and the flexibility it offers is way beyond anything a tape-based system can offer.

When you make a recording and save it to disk, the software logs the start position and the end position of the file. During playback, it tells the drive to read the data between those points. It is, therefore, a relatively easy matter for the software to tell the drive to read and play the data at a point a little way into the file, thus cutting out the first part of the recording during which the singer coughed.

It's also easy to point to the places in a recording where the verse starts and ends and to tell the system to play it several times to create repeat verses at the end of the song. This does not involve adding several copies of the verse data to the end of the file. The original data on the disk stays exactly where it is – when the program reaches the end of the song the playback routine simply points to the start of the verse again.

As you only need to change the pointers to the section of the audio you want to play, it follows that operations such as cut, copy and paste can be performed non-destructively. You can chop up a recording in a digital audio program, move sections of it onto other tracks and paste a different recording into the middle of it on the screen, but none of this physically changes the data on the hard disk, it only changes the pointers the program uses during playback.

Likewise, If you delete a recording from the arrange window, it is not deleted from disk – the program simply ignores it. You can, of course, delete files and perform destructive edits on audio data and you may want to do this when finalising a mix, but you don't have to, and this keeps your original recordings safe.

## Pools and regions

Different pieces of software have different names for the sections of audio you create when you 'cut up' a recording. They may be called parts, sections or regions, for example. If you are performing many edits and there are several recordings in the piece you are working on, you could easily end up with several dozen regions.

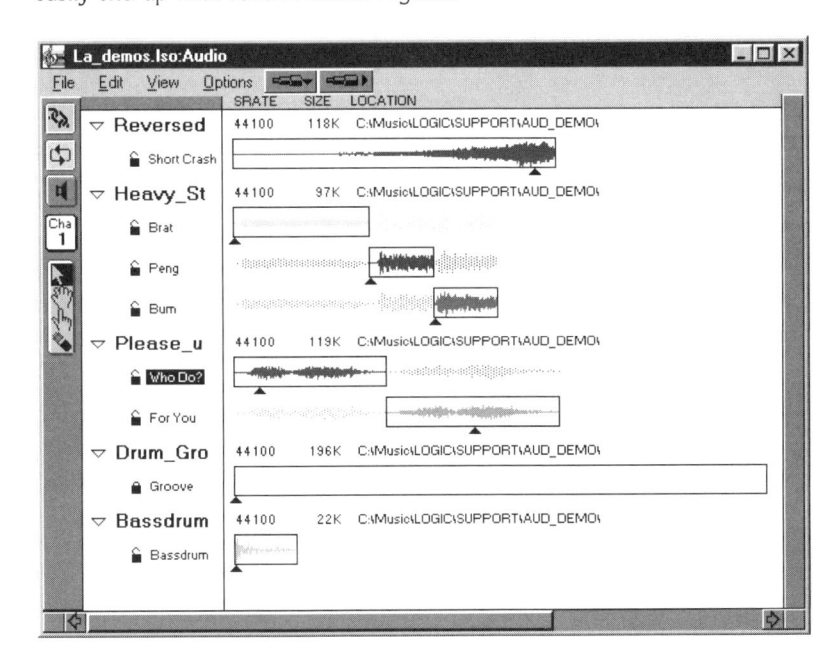

Figure 10.1 The audio window in Logic Audio

Most software has a regions list or a filepool which keeps track of the recordings and the bits you cut them into. Figure 10.1 shows the Audio window in Logic Audio and you can see that three regions have been created from the file called Heavy_St and the Please_u file has been cut into two regions. In Logic and many other programs, you can drag a region from the pool window into the arrange window, making it easy to create new arrangements from existing recordings.

Sound Forge has a regions window, Figure 10.2, which lists sections of a recording. To add a region you simply define it in the main window and drag it to the Regions window. You can change the size of the region by dragging the markers at the top of the window or by changing the start and end point numerically as in Figure 10.3.

Most programs let you import files into the audio pool so you can easily incorporate earlier recordings into your present work. It's also ideal if you use sample CDs as you can import lots of samples and try them in context with the piece.

Figure 10.2 The regions window in Sound Forge

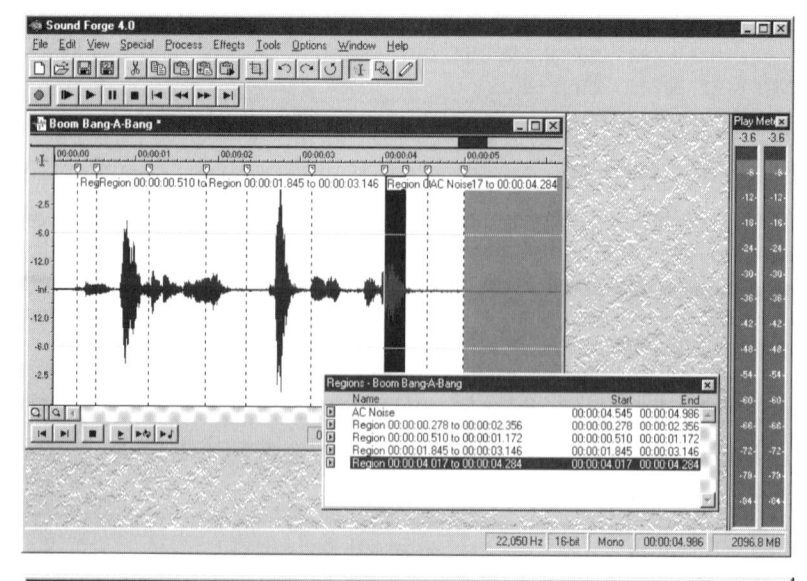

Figure 10.3 Changing the start and end point numerically in Sound Forge

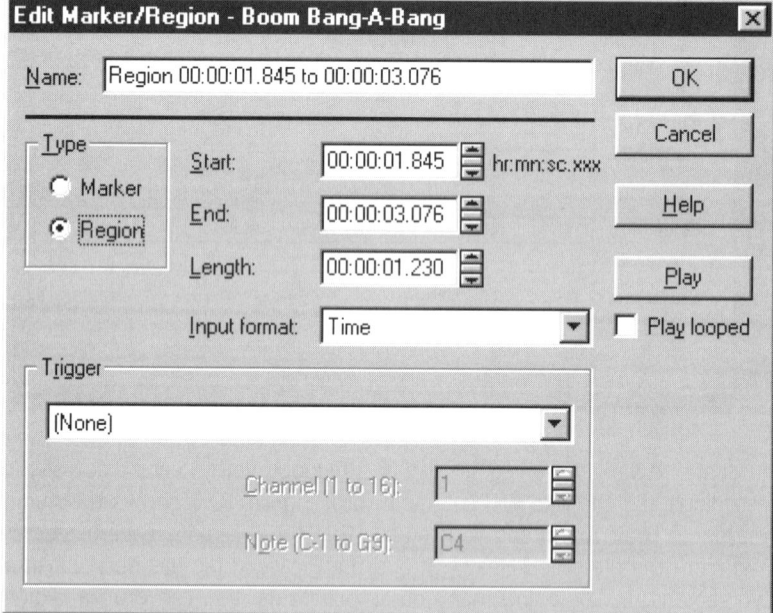

## Real-time control changes

Most software has a mixer where you can set the volume levels and pan positions of the audio tracks. These take effect on playback only and, in keeping with the non-destructive editing ethos, the settings are not written into the files.

Some software also lets you draw volume and pan envelopes onto the audio tracks. If your background is in recording rather than computing this may seem a little strange – and it is more a function derived from computer software than music hardware – but it is extremely useful and powerful.

Figure 10.4 Envelopes drawn onto the recordings in Samplitude

Figure 10.4 shows envelopes drawn onto the recordings in Samplitude and Figure 10.5 shows a volume envelope drawn onto an audio part in Logic Audio. In Logic the data you create is stored as MIDI data which can be edited in the usual way so you can create the exact changes at the exact points in the piece that you want.

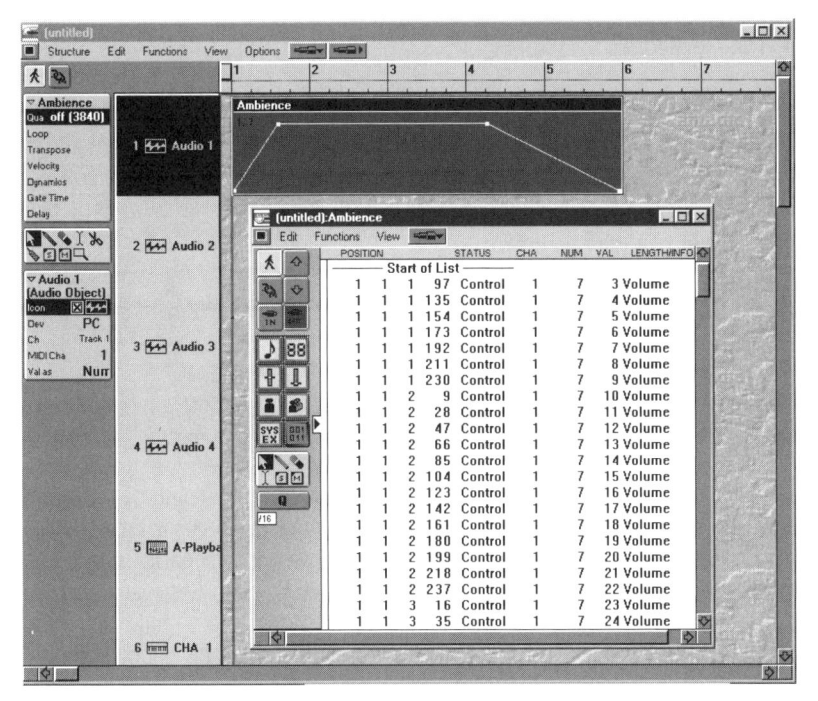

Figure 10.5 A volume envelope drawn onto an audio part in Logic Audio

Again, these changes are applied in real-time. Some software gives you the option of disabling real-time changes which may be necessary if your system is under powered and struggling with real-time playback.

## Markers and handles

In multi-track systems, regions appear as blocks in an arrange page. In waveform editors, a recording usually occupies a full window. Whatever the system, you can usually cut, copy and paste sections of audio to change their position and create new arrangements. In multi-track software you can probably drag regions around the tracks much like patterns in a MIDI sequencer.

Many systems have a 'snap to' function which ensures that when you move the audio it sits squarely on a beat or onto a certain time position. Other systems tell you the time position of the cursor as you move it so if you paste a block by dragging you know exactly where it's going to go.

To help you navigate your way around a recording, many programs let you insert markers throughout the piece. You can usually name markers and 'go to' any particular marker, which is particularly useful if you are working with large chunks of audio.

Figure 10.6 shows the marker list in Logic Audio. Setting markers in this program is particularly flexible as you can enter them with the mouse, from a menu or with a keyboard command, and you can create markers automatically for all currently selected objects. Each marker also has a text window, large enough for copious notes about the position you've marked.

Figure 10.6 The marker list in Logic Audio

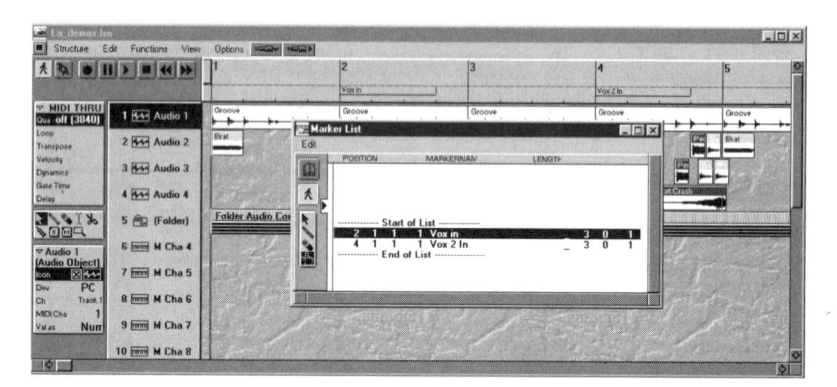

Quite often you will only want to play a part of a recording or a region, omitting the start or end of it. One way to do this is to cut it into smaller regions and play only the ones you want. However, an easier way is to mask the part of the recording you don't want to play. Software such as Cubase Audio has start and end handles which you drag to hide or reveal parts of a recording. The full waveform is still there, the handles simply determine which part of the recording is played.

The four regions in Figure 10.7 are identical. This illustration shows how handles have been used to make the top left region start playing half way into the waveform and the top right region stop playing half way through.

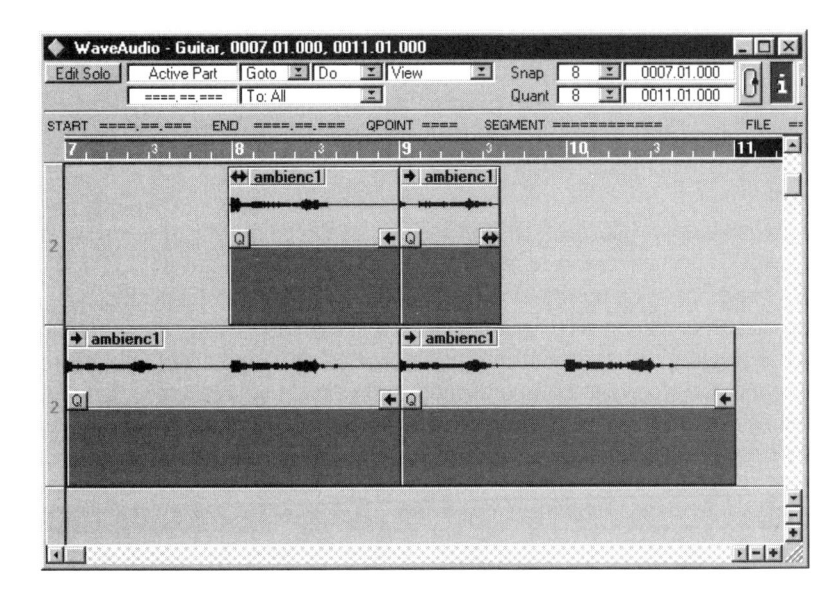

Figure 10.7 Using handles to mask parts of a recording

## Anchors and Q points

One of the problems with positioning an audio region is knowing exactly where any particular point in it is. In a MIDI recording you can see the notes in a piano roll editor, in a list or as notation on the stave. Most audio programs can show the recording as a waveform but you won't be able to look at it and hum the tune!

What you can do, however, is spot the 'hits' – peaks in the recording where the sound is loudest. In most rhythmic pieces of music these will correspond to the main beats. This is most evident in drum patterns, for example, as you can see in Figure 10.8.

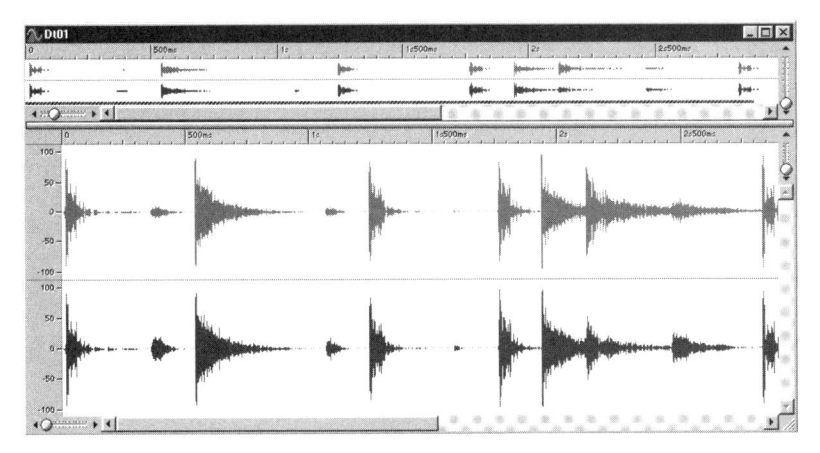

Figure 10.8 'Hits' showing up in a drum pattern

However, you may want to line up an audio section where the start of the event does not correspond to a musical position. Perhaps there's a short silence before the sound begins or perhaps a drum hit occurs just before the main beat.

Enter anchors and Q points. These are types of markers which you can place anywhere in a region to identify a particular point in it. They both perform essentially the same function but the two names are used by different programs. Figure 10.9 shows an anchor – the triangle below the waveform – in Logic Audio. Figure 10.10 shows a Q Point in Cubase Audio.

When a point has been set it is used as a snap point when the region is moved. This enables you to identify a section which is musically significant in a region and line up that point with other patterns or time positions.

These points are also useful when working with video. Many digital audio programs support Video for Windows movies and allow you create a soundtrack for them. Using anchors or Q points you can easily line up recordings to audio or visual cues in the movie. They really come into their own when adding sound effects which have no musical cue points.

Figure 10.9 An anchor in Logic Audio

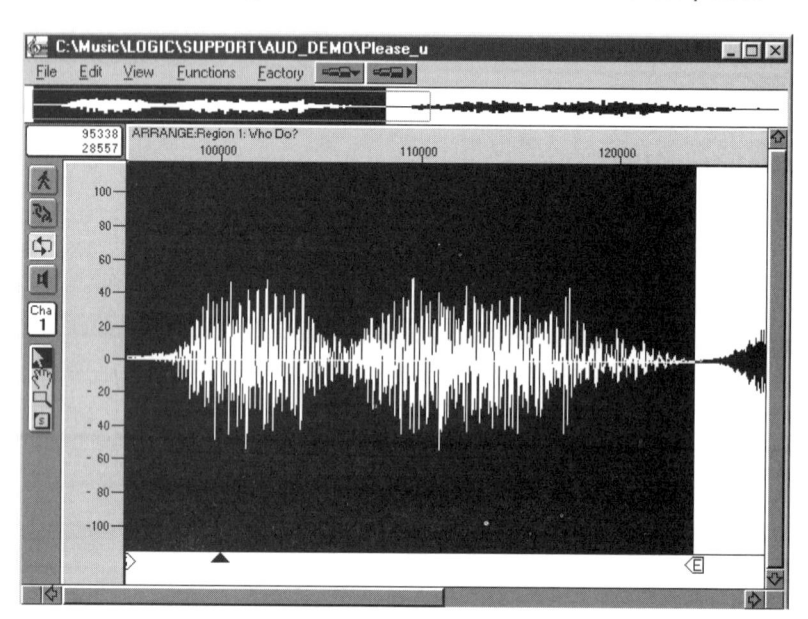

Figure 10.10 A Q point in Cubase Audio

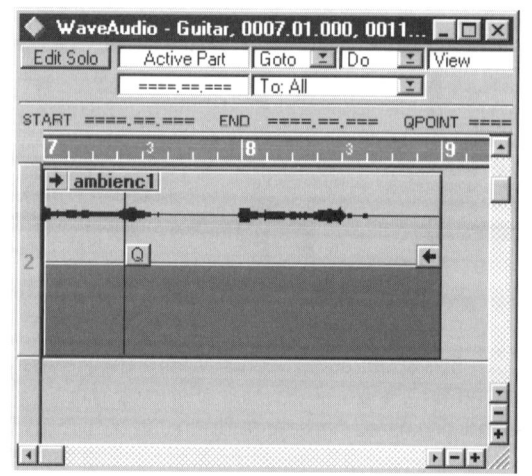

## Mixing it

Mixing is a common feature in all digital audio programs and it can take two forms. In multi-track programs, the mix function lets you mix two or more tracks into one track. As in audio recording, this frees-up tracks which you can record on again. If you have reached the limit of the number of tracks your system can play, then it may be time to do a mixdown. But before you do the deed, make sure that you are not going to destroy your original data. Logic Audio, for example, retains the original files and creates a new file of the mixdown.

## Zero crossing points

When you're cutting and pasting audio, you can't simply cut off an audio region and stick it onto another region as you can often do with MIDI data. Well you can, but the result may contain a few clicks and glitches. Audio doesn't work in quite the same way as MIDI.

If you zoom in closely on a section of audio data you will see a display similar to that in Figure 10.11. The central line represents a zero volume level and the waves above and below represent positive and negative voltages which generate the sound.

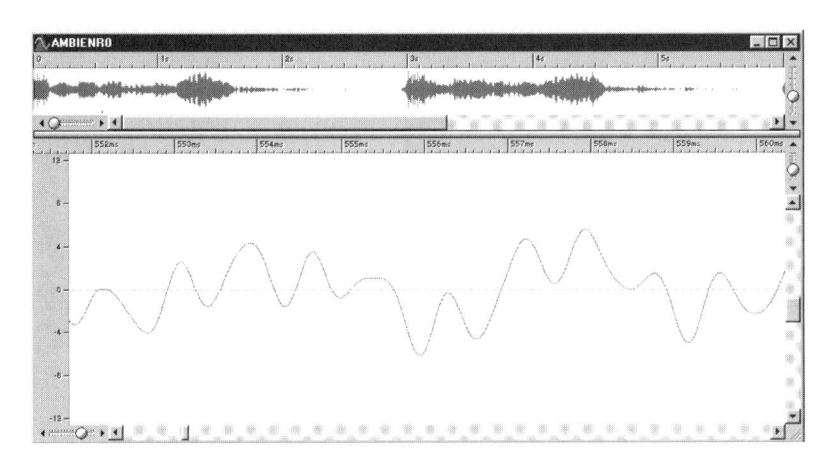

> **INFO**
>
> Wave editors, programs which only have a mono or stereo track, may not have a mixdown function as such but they invariably have a mix or blend function which allows you to mix two waveforms together. The function may mix the contents of the clipboard with that of the current window, for example, although the exact details vary from program to program.

Figure 10.11 A close-up view of a typical audio waveform

There's no need to go into any more detail here, but for the purposes of editing digital audio, it means that when the waveform is on the central line it is generating a zero volume level – that is, silence! An edit made to the audio at a point where it crosses the line – at the zero crossing point – will minimise the chance of a click at the join.

If you cut audio at a point where the waveform is positive or negative, the volume will change abruptly from that value to zero and produce a click or glitch. If you need to butt one end of an audio region to another or create a fast cut from one section to another, then the edit should be performed on a zero crossing point.

There are other ways to avoid glitches such as using crossfades (three sections on) or by applying the same principles used in creating loops...

## Going loopy

If you need to butt the end of one region to the start of another, you ought to pick zero crossing points to minimise the volume at the changeover point. However, you should also try to pick points where the waveform at the end of the first region flows into the waveform at the start of the second. This is particularly important when you're constructing loops as the repeat point will be heard continuously but the same principles apply when joining any sections of audio together.

Figure 10.12 Sound Forge's Loop Tuner. Creating a loop at this point would produce a click

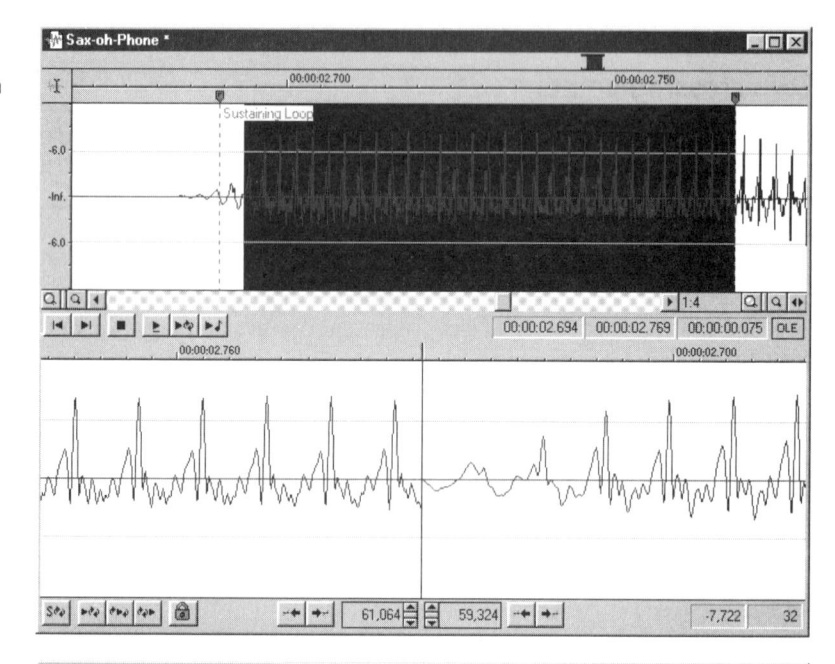

Figure 10.13 This join makes the looped waveform seem continuous

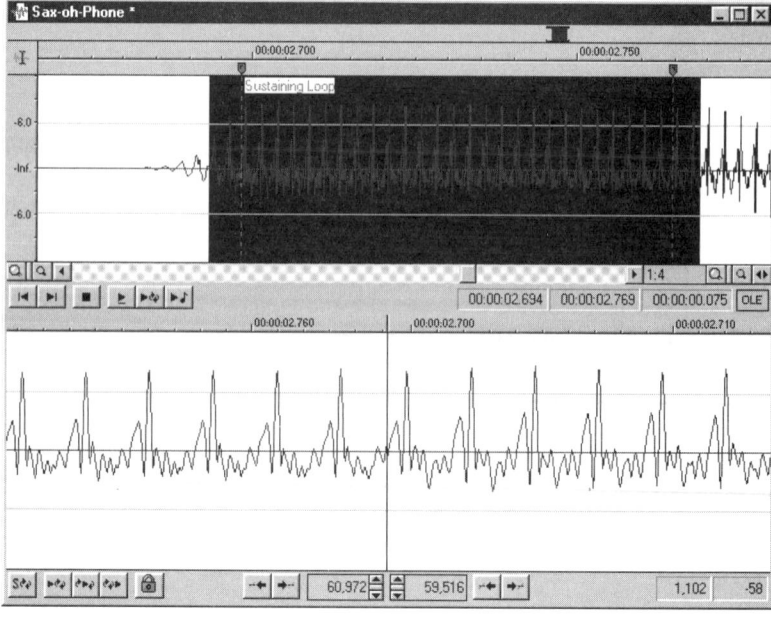

### ✥ INFO ✥

Some software has a loop maker function which shows the end of the loop butted against the start of it (got that?). In other words, it's the point at which the end of the sample loops back to the beginning.

In Sound Forge's Loop Tuner, Figure 10.12, the lower area shows the loop point. As you can see, the end of the first section is below the zero crossing point although even if it was on the line, the following waveform does not match it so a glitch would still result. A little judicious twiddling of the controls produces the join in Figure 10.13 which makes the looped waveform seem continuous.

Another point to bear in mind is the tone or timbre of the two audio sections. Trying to join two different tones by a splice may not meet with much success as there will still be a jar from one tone to another even if the waveforms do join at a zero crossing point. Creating good loops and splices is still regarded as a black art by many although it's not as difficult as some practitioners would have you believe.

The Soundscape software automatically creates a little crossfade when two samples butt against each other to minimise the risk of glitches.

## Fades

A fade is a change in volume over time. Fading a section in or out are the two most common fade functions. Once upon a time an engineer would create a fade by physically moving the faders on a mixer. If he got it wrong the mix would have to be done again.

Most audio software includes automatic fade functions and they usually offer a choice of fade curves. You can often design your own curves, too. The choice is usually between linear fades as in Figure 10.14 and exponential or logarithmic as in Figure 10.15. You can see that with the logarithmic curve, the volume stays higher for longer and then drops more quickly than it does with the linear curve.

> **TIP**
>
> Loop tip 1. If you can, record the section you want to loop twice and use the second recording for the loop. This ensures that any frequencies at the end of the recording are present in the loop. For example, let's say the loop ends with a sound which contains reverb. In the first recording, the reverb won't be present because it hasn't occurred yet so if the first recording is looped the reverb will cut off abruptly when playback goes to the beginning of the loop. If you use the second recording there will already be some reverb at the start of the loop and the transition should be smoother.

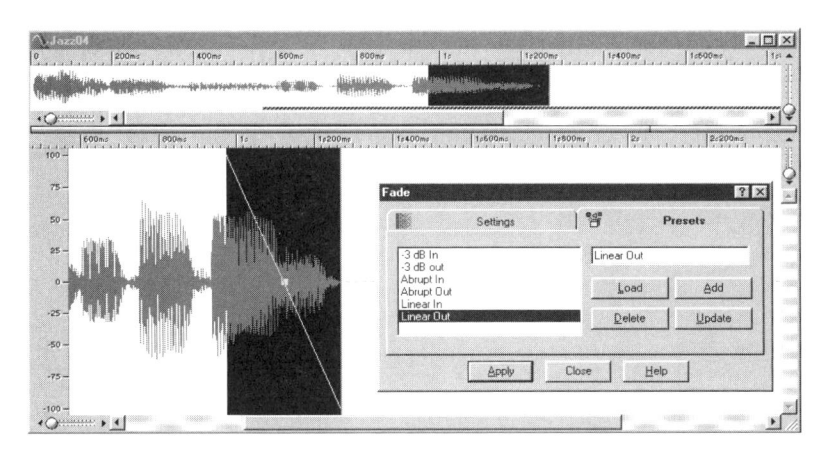

Figure 10.14 Linear fade

The type of curve to use depends on the material being processed and the length of the fade. One point to be aware of is that if the fade is long and the sound is playing at a low volume for a long time (the term 'long' here is subjective), then the reduced volume may add noise to the output. This may be apparent on a short fade of a couple of seconds as well as on longer fades. It will be more noticeable if the recording uses an 8-bit resolution.

Figure 10.15 Exponential or logarithmic fade

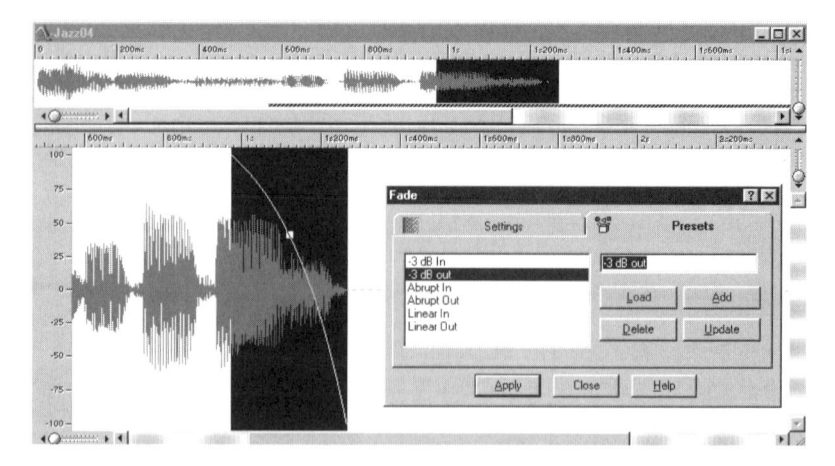

In such circumstances, a logarithmic curve will help minimise the noise as it keeps the volume higher for longer but as always, your ears and the demands of the project must be the judge. Check Chapter 15, too, before you apply fades to a recording if it's to be part of a larger collection, say on an album.

## Crossfades

A crossfade is when one section fades out while another fades in. It provides a smooth transition between two recordings which may not share any tonal similarities. It can also be used to create loops from material which is proving particularly obstinate to loop.

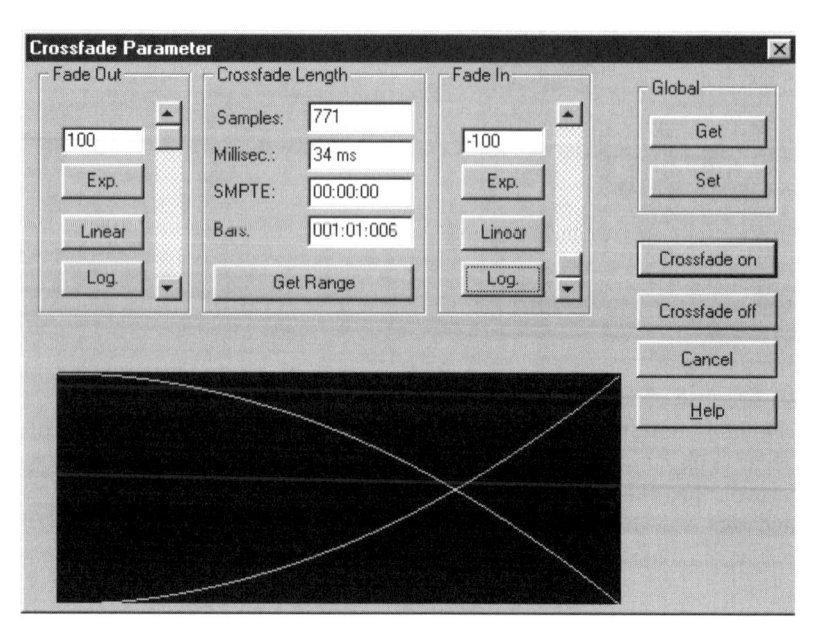

As with fades, most software offers a choice of crossfade curves. You can design your own crossfades in Logic Audio, Figure 10.16, and Samplitude, Figure 10.17.

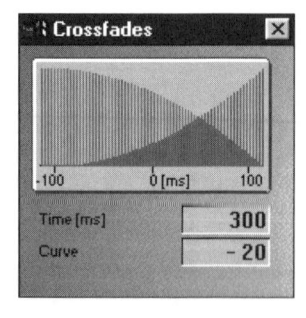

Figure 10.16 Designing your own fades in Logic Audio ...

Figure 10.17 ... and in Samplitude

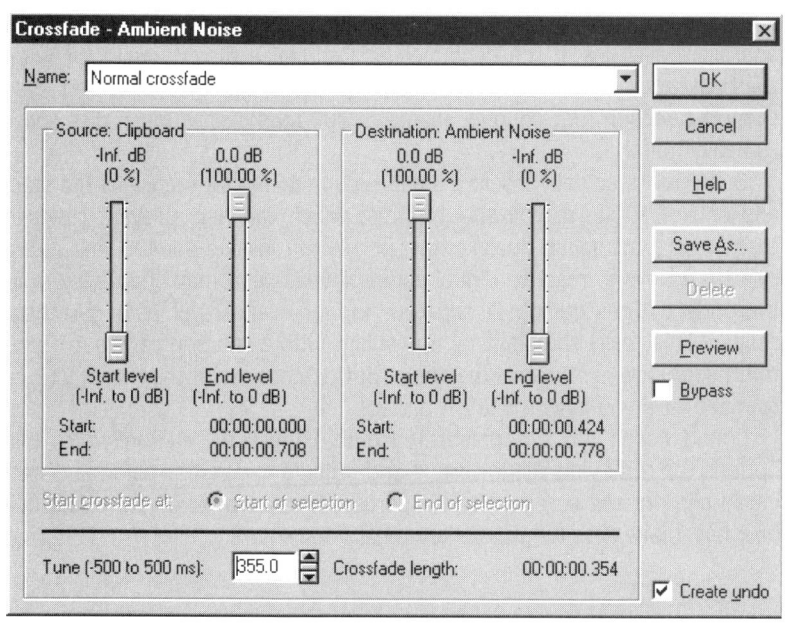

Figure 10.18 Sound Forge offers a choice of crossfades

If your software doesn't have a specific crossfade function, you can use a fade in and a fade out. In multi-track software, overlap the end of the first section with the start of the second and apply a fade out to the first and a fade in to the second.

Most wave editing software lets you paste or mix the contents of the clipboard with an existing audio section and this function can also be used to create crossfades. When you do this in Sound Forge, Figure 10.18, it offers a choice of crossfades and lets you create your own curves.

## The sound of silence

There are two types of silence – natural and digital. A digital silence is the absence of any sound whatsoever. It's what you get if you use a program's 'insert silence' function or if you delete all data from a section of a recording.

Natural silence is the background ambience or noise you get when the system is set to record but there's no signal. Actually, there is a signal. There's always a signal, if only the noise in the cable leading to the input. If you zoom in on a section of 'natural' silence you will almost certainly find some low-level data there.

The difference is important, particularly if the natural noise is fairly high. To take an example, let's say you've recorded some speech and there are gaps between the words which sound a little noisy. Okay, you delete the gaps replacing them with digital silence. But now it sounds even worse. The perfect silence accentuates the noise in the recording. Oops!

The best way to deal with noise like this is to use a noise reduction effect or a noise gate. The best way to minimise recording noise is at the source by using good, clean equipment and record at as high a level as possible without clipping

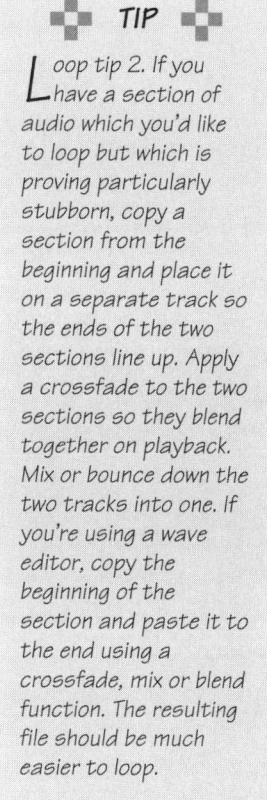

### TIP

Loop tip 2. If you have a section of audio which you'd like to loop but which is proving particularly stubborn, copy a section from the beginning and place it on a separate track so the ends of the two sections line up. Apply a crossfade to the two sections so they blend together on playback. Mix or bounce down the two tracks into one. If you're using a wave editor, copy the beginning of the section and paste it to the end using a crossfade, mix or blend function. The resulting file should be much easier to loop.

### THERE'S MORE

See Chapter 11 for more on noise reduction effects and noise gates

It's usually a good idea to trim recordings to remove unwanted sounds and silent sections at the beginning and end of a file. If you don't want these sections to play, remove them. It keeps the files trim and even though a section may contain 'silence' it still uses just as much disk space as heavy metal!

Some users actually insert a small section of digital silence at the start and end of a file, maybe about 50ms, which can help prevent clicks in cases where the sound doesn't start at a zero crossing point. Some sound cards are slow to react to digital audio playback and may need a few milliseconds to 'get going'. A short period of silence will help get them rolling. This really shouldn't be a problem with a modern card but if you think your card is slow this may help. But do check with the manufacturer to make sure you have the latest drivers.

Sound Forge has a sophisticated auto trim/crop function which has options for removing silence inside and outside a marked region and fading in and out the end points of a phrase. It takes a lot of the effort out of it but, make sure the results are what you require.

# 11

# Processing and FX

For many musicians, the ability to process audio and apply effects to sounds within the computer is the most exciting aspect of digital recording. You don't have to route the sound through a bank of outboard FX racks, converting it into analogue and back into digital data again. Corrections, alterations and a whole range of processing functions can be applied to the audio with the click of a button.

As the sound stays within the digital domain at all times, the quality is maintained. Some high quality effects convert the audio to 24 bits, process it and convert it back to 16 bits in order to retain as much of the signal's original quality as possible.

And most digital audio software comes with loads of effects. If you had to buy a rack unit for each one it would cost thousands! Specialised plug-in effects can still be expensive, however, even software ones, although the prices seem to be coming down. If DirectX technology catches on we should see more effects and cheaper ones, too.

Many effects were originally designed to correct a sound, not enhance it, but they have now become part of the creative process. In this chapter we'll look at all the common effects, see what they do, how they work and when and why you should apply them.

> **INFO**
>
> *There must be well over two dozen effects categories and sometimes the choice is bewildering. Many users, particularly newcomers to digital recording, are tempted to use lots of effects simply because they're there. This can lead to overkill and effect saturation so do keep a check on this desire if you feel it coming over you.*

## EQ

We'll start with the most popular effect of all – EQ or equalisation. This was originally a corrective process used to compensate for the loss of frequencies during recording caused by the equipment being used. It took the form of a tone control and was used to boost the high frequencies which, as you may recall from earlier discussions about sample rates and the Nyquist limit, are the most susceptible to loss. The idea was to use the control to make the recorded sound 'equal' to the original, hence its name. With today's equipment, such compensation is rarely necessary and EQ is now used more as a creative effect.

There are several types of EQ but they all perform the same function which is to cut or boost certain frequencies in a recording. Modern EQ is simply a more sophisticated version of the original 'corrective' EQ tone control.

## Terms of EQ

There are several terms used in EQ processing so we'll look at these first.

**Cutoff frequency/point** When we're filtering a sound we home in on a certain frequency or group of frequencies and cut or boost them. The frequency at which the filter comes into effect is the cutoff frequency or cutoff point. Frequencies before, after or around the cutoff point may also be cut or boosted, depending on the type of filter being used.

**Attenuation** The opposite of amplification. It's a term often used in filtering and means reducing the level of a certain frequency.

**Roll-off** This is the rate at which the attenuation increases as the filtering moves further from the cutoff frequency. It is sometimes called the slope. The steeper the roll-off, the more severely the attenuation is applied and the greater the filter effect. The roll-off is usually measured in dB and the distance or interval from the cutoff point is measured in octaves.

A fairly gentle filter, therefore, might have a roll-off of 6dB/octave which means that for every octave away from the cutoff frequency, the signal is attenuated by 6dB. A filter with a 12dB/octave roll-off would be twice as strong and attenuate the signal by 12dB every octave.

In analogue synthesis there are components within the filter circuits called poles which apply an attenuation of around 6dB per octave. Some synthesisers use several poles and you may hear synthesists or engineers refer to a 1-pole, 2-pole, 3-pole or 4-pole filter. These would have a roll-off of 6dB/octave, 12dB/octave, 18dB/octave and 24dB/octave respectively. In other words, the more poles a filter has, the steeper the roll-off and the fewer frequencies will pass beyond the cutoff point.

Software filters tend not to use the term 'pole' (although you may hear it used in certain studios and if you mix with certain synthesists).

Unfortunately, not all filters tell you what the roll-off is or allow you to adjust it – which ought to be easy in software – although the other controls are usually sufficiently flexible to compensate. If the roll-off is fixed, most tend to be about 12dB/octave.

Some examples are in order. Figure 11.1 shows the effect three roll-offs have on the frequencies they are attenuating. You may think that the best filters are the ones with a high roll-off rate and that a perfect filter would have a very steep, almost vertical curve. In theory that may be so, but musically you will rarely want to chop a band of frequencies dead so severely because it sounds very unnatural.

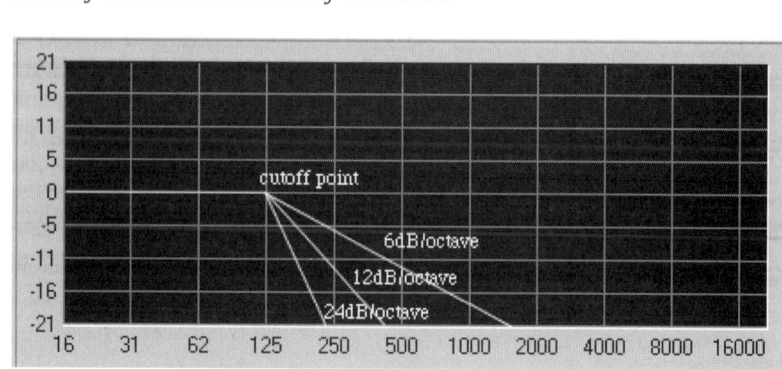

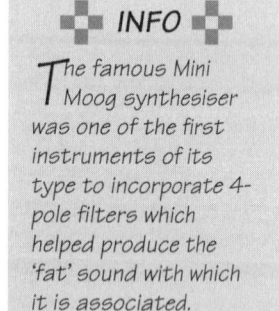

> **INFO**
>
> The famous Mini Moog synthesiser was one of the first instruments of its type to incorporate 4-pole filters which helped produce the 'fat' sound with which it is associated.

Figure 11.1 Three typical roll-off slopes

**Bandwidth/Q/resonance/emphasis/peak** The bandwidth is the range of frequencies the filter will affect either side of the cutoff point. It ought to be measured in octaves but hertz seems more popular. Figure 11.2 shows a frequency boost around 3000Hz. In Figure 11.3 the bandwidth has been reduced and you'll notice that although the central frequency has still been boosted, those around it have been affected far less.

Bandwidth is often referred to as Q which is an abbreviation for 'quality' or 'figure of quality' although these terms are no longer used. It's also sometimes called resonance. In synthesisers, turning up the Q or resonance control and feeding the signal back into itself often causes the signal to resonate or go into self-oscillation. And if you hear the terms emphasis or peak – yes, it's bandwidth by other names.

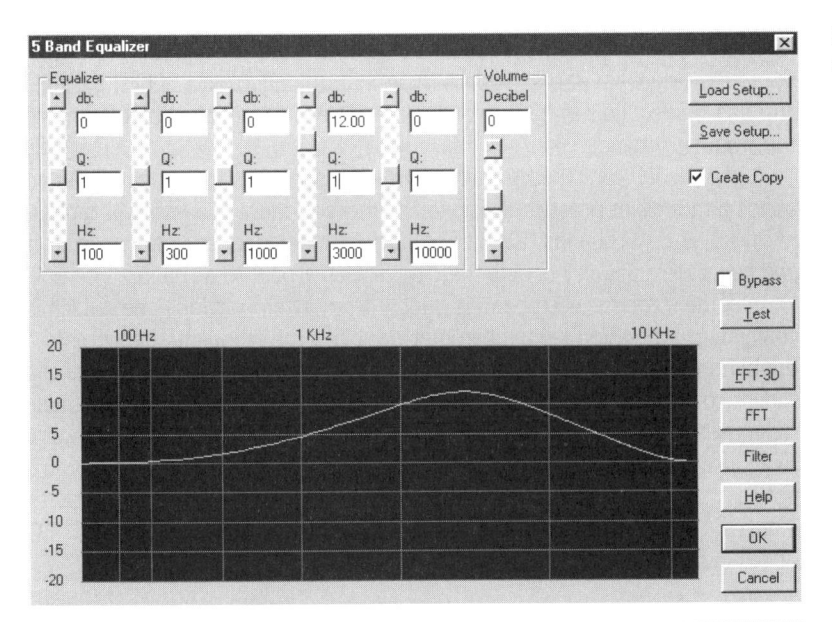

Figure 11.2 A frequency boost around 3000Hz

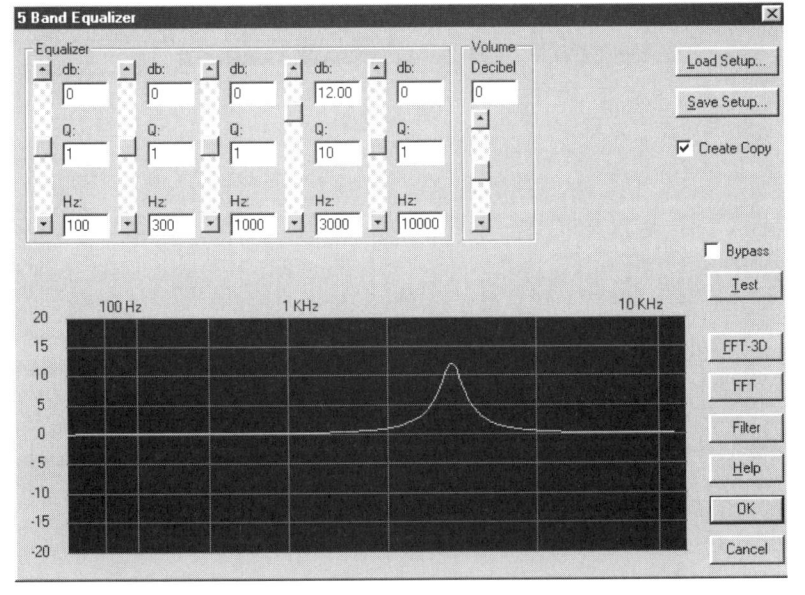

Figure 11.3 Reducing the bandwidth reduces the effect the filter has on surrounding frequencies

**Level/gain** This determines the amount by which the signal is cut or boost. Sometimes a control may be labelled cut/boost which is rather helpful.

### Types of EQ

There are several types of filter which are useful for different purposes. The two main types are graphic and parametric although there are other variations as we shall see.

Traditionally, there are passive and active filters. Passive filters can only remove frequencies, while active filters can also boost them. In practice it's unlikely that you'll come across a passive software filter.

### Graphic EQ

A graphic EQ divides the frequency range into bands which you can cut or boost individually. Graphic equalisers are commonly found in hi fi systems and can be recognised by a line of sliders, each of which controls one of the frequency bands.

A graphic EQ can, theoretically, divide the spectrum into any number of bands although in practice divisions are more modest and you will typically find 5, 8 or 10 bands. Each band has a central frequency assigned to it and the slider cuts and boosts the frequencies around that band.

In some systems, each band is double that of the previous one, which is convenient when you remember that doubling the frequency represents a doubling of the octave. Other systems let you specify the frequencies the sliders control which is starting to verge into the territory of the parametric equaliser.

Figure 11.4 shows the 10-band graphic EQ in Sound Forge, and you'll notice that each band to the right doubles in frequency. Refer back to Figures 11.2 and 11.3 and you'll see Samplitude's 5-band graphic EQ which lets you change the frequency of each band.

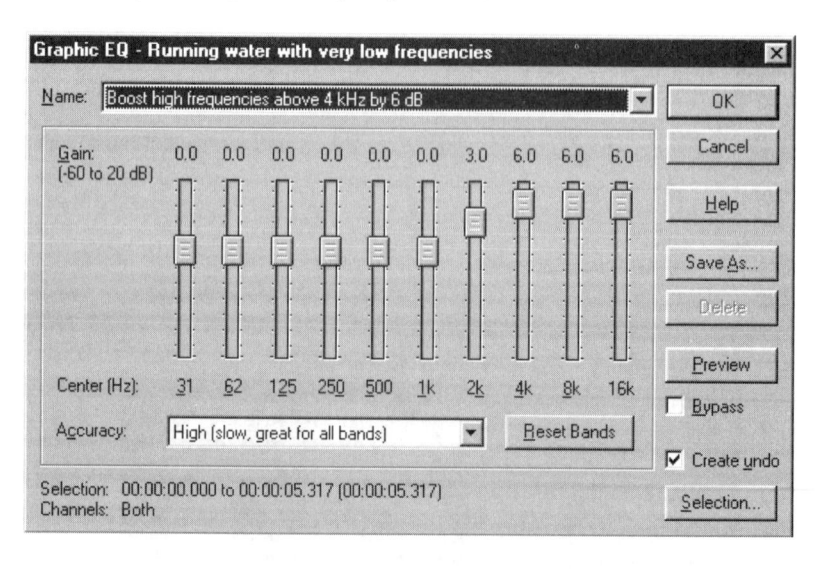

Figure 11.4 The 10-band graphic EQ in Sound Forge – each band to the right doubles in frequency

Graphic EQs are used to shape the entire sound. They were originally designed to compensate for frequency anomalies within a listening environment. For example, if you like to listen to music in your bedroom, you may find the curtains and coverings kill the high frequencies, so you could use a graphic equaliser to boost them. If you listen to music by the side of your indoor swimming pool you may find the reflective surfaces amplify the high frequencies in which case you could use a graphic EQ to reduce them.

## Parametric EQ

A parametric EQ offers greater precision and control over specific frequencies than a graphic EQ. Essentially, it lets the user select the cutoff frequency of each filter band. Traditionally there are three controls – the cutoff frequency, the bandwidth and the level. However, as EQ software has become more sophisticated, some systems offer additional options.

Whereas a graphic EQ is designed to be applied across the whole frequency spectrum, the parametric equaliser is a trouble-shooting tool for homing in on problem frequencies.

Figure 11.5 shows the EQ-1 plug-in for Steinberg's WaveLab. It has three bands – high, mid and low – and each band has a cut/boost control marked dB and a control for selecting the frequency marked Hz. The mid band also has a Q control: the higher the value, the narrower the band of frequencies the control affects.

Figure 11.6 shows the parametric EQ built into WaveLab. It has similar controls but the graph also shows how the settings will affect a signal.

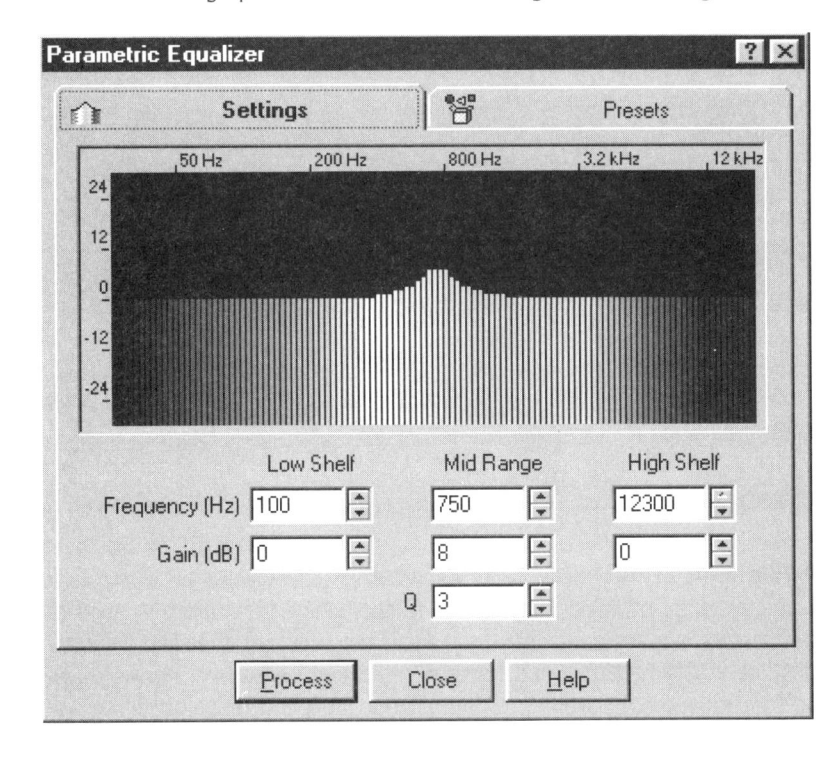

(Above) Figure 11.5 The EQ-1 plug-in for WaveLab

(Left) Figure 11.6 The parametric EQ built into WaveLab

Figure 11.7 Samplitude's parametric EQ has three bands and the same set of controls as WaveLab

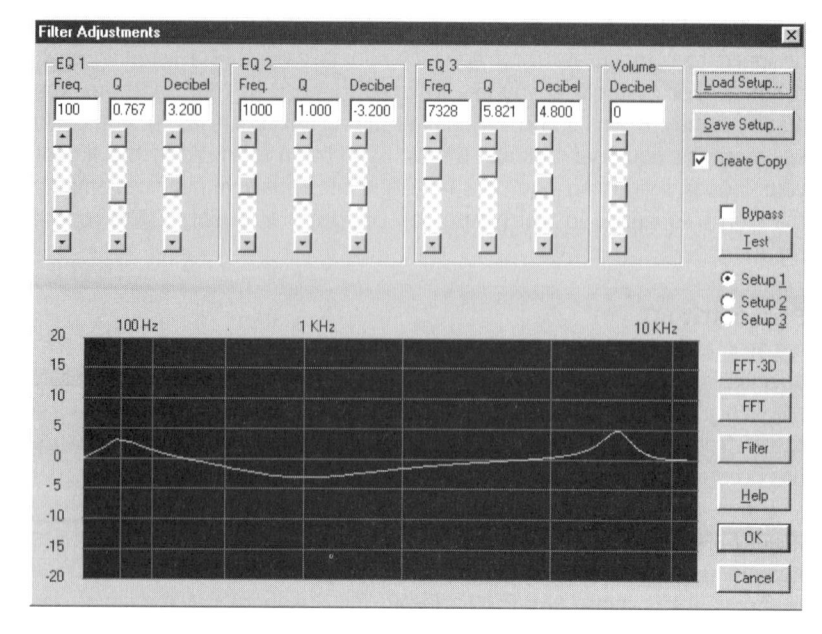

Figure 11.7 shows Samplitude's parametric EQ which, again, has three bands and the same set of controls.

tripleDAT's 4-band parametric EQ, Figure 11.8, has frequency, amplitude and Q settings for each of the four bands. It's highly graphic, and you can pick up the nodes and drag them around the display, listening to the changes in the sound during playback in real-time.

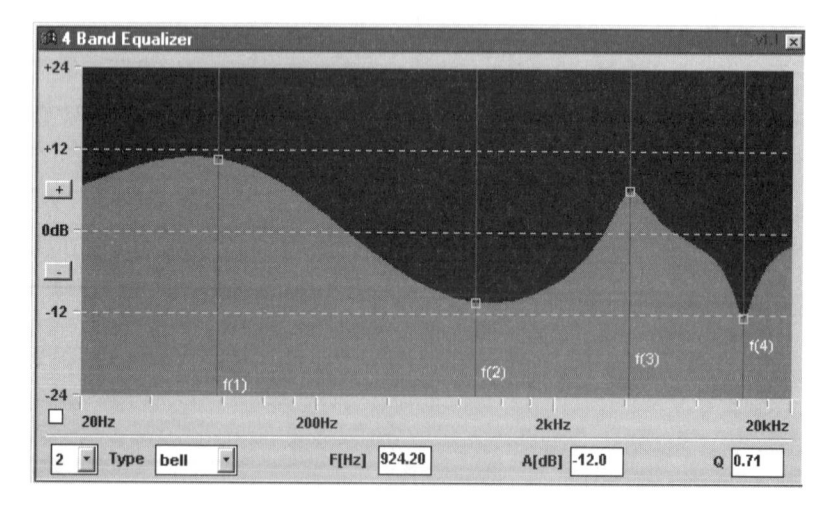

Figure 11.8 tripleDAT's 4-band parametric EQ

## Paragraphic EQ

Some systems, however, go a stage further and offer multiple bands of frequencies like a graphic, but they allow the user to define the frequencies like a parametric. Sound Forge's Paragraphic equaliser, Figure 11.9, offers six bands of parametric filters. Four independent bands allow you to cut or boost specific frequencies while two other filters let you control the overall balance of high and low frequencies in the recording.

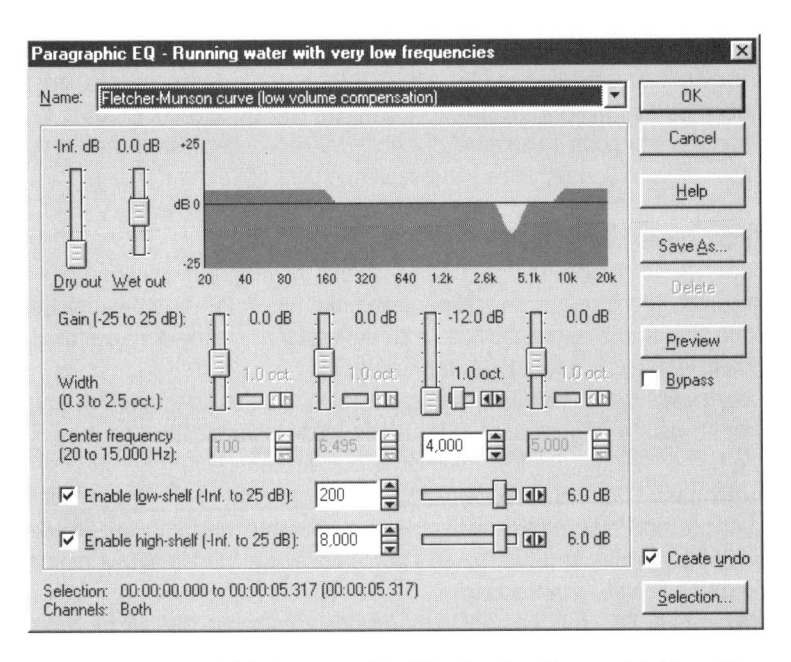

Figure 11.9 Sound Forge's Paragraphic equaliser has six bands of parametric filters

However, Waves' Q10 Paragraphic EQ plug-in, Figure 11.10, offers 10 bands of EQ, each of which can be configured as one of five types – band pass, low shelf, high shelf, low pass and high pass. The individual bands are identical apart from the default frequencies which are spread

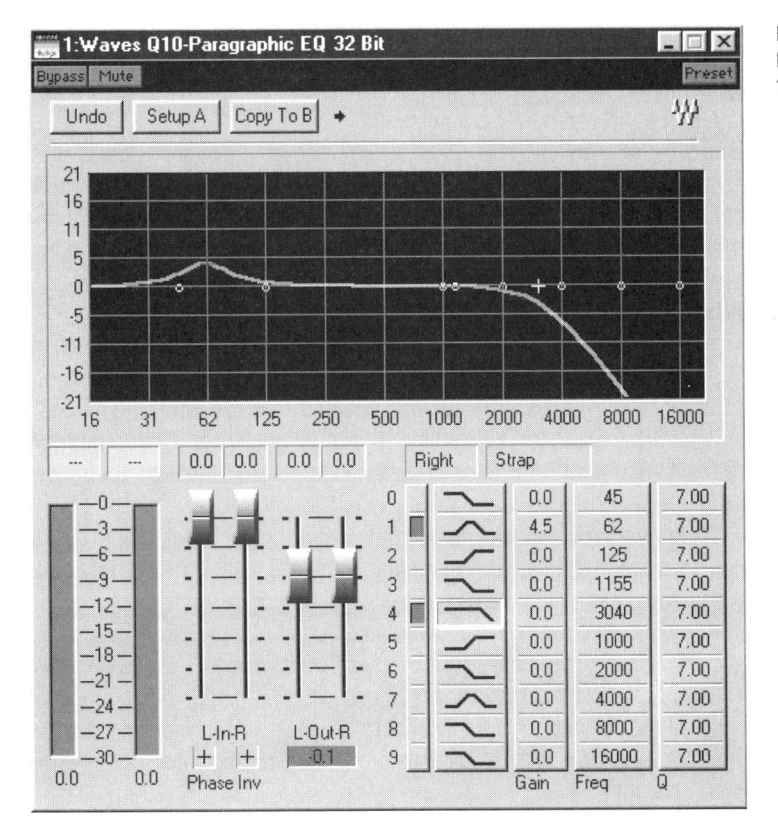

Figure 11.10 Waves' Q10 Paragraphic EQ plug-in has 10 bands of EQ

across the frequency spectrum, but you can easily alter these. Individual bands can be switched in and out at the click of a button, and there's an option to apply different filters to the left and right channels of a sound. For total control it's extremely flexible, but don't get lost in the wealth of possibilities if you only need to tweak one part of your recording.

### Filter types

Somewhere within the gamut of filters hovering between paras and graphics, there reside several popular filter types. Initially, they may seem confusing but they are fairly easy to understand as they only perform one function. We can divide them into six types.

**Low pass** This passes low frequencies at and below the cutoff frequency and attenuates higher ones. This is the most 'natural' filter as it removes the higher frequencies lost in absorbent environments.

**High pass** This is the opposite of the low pass filter – it passes high frequencies and attenuates lower ones. It is useful for removing unwanted bass frequencies and heavy use can remove the fundamentals of a tone resulting in a very thin sound.

**High shelf** This cuts or boosts the frequencies above the cutoff point. Its main use is as a tone control to shape the upper section of the frequency spectrum.

**Low shelf** This is the opposite of the high shelf filter and is useful for controlling the overall tone of the lower frequencies.

**Band pass/peak/bell** As its name suggests, this passes a band of frequencies leaving those either side of it untouched. It's particularly useful for homing in on a specific frequency, such as tones produced by solo instruments, or for tackling problem areas in the mix such as hum and noise. It is, in effect, a parametric EQ.

**Band reject/notch** This is the opposite of the band pass filter and removes frequencies within a certain range. Quite often the band pass and band reject are combined into one filter which can either boost or cut at the specified frequency.

### When to use EQ

There's an old saying – 'we'll fix it in the mix' – which usually refers to the application of judicious amounts of EQ in order to make the best of a bad recording. EQ has become so sophisticated that it's tempting to use it as a universal panacea for everything that's wrong with a recording. And at times it may well do the job. However, the results will be far more natural if the recording is made properly in the first place.

There's so much advice about EQ floating around out there, it's difficult knowing what to believe. Personally, I use EQ very little, mainly to tidy up highs and lows which have gone astray during recording and processing. The only rule you should follow is what your ears tell you. Listen to advice and try it out by all means, but ultimately let your ears be the judge.

Having said that, on many modern recordings EQ has been used as a creative effect and there's no harm in that as long as you know what you're doing and why you're using it. Learn the rules first before you break them.

> **INFO**
>
> *B*eware of ear fatigue. Yes, this is an acknowledged phenomenon. If you've been listening to the same frequencies – or, indeed, the same song – for several hours, your ears will become less sensitive to it. Your brain, too! After a hard day's mixing, put the piece away and listen to it the next day with fresh ears. If you can afford the luxury of leaving if for a few weeks – and you have the patience – it will be fresh and you'll be better able to analyse it.

## EQ tips
So here are a few EQ tips you can totally ignore:

- Only use EQ if you have to. Try to get the recording right in the first place. If you can't then use EQ to fix it but don't rely on it like a crutch.
- The band pass and band reject filters are perfect for homing in on specific frequencies. Use them to add some punch to a snare or bass drum, or to add sparkle in the higher frequencies of an instrument.
- If you have ambient low-frequency background noise in a recording try cutting the lower register with a low shelf filter.
- Use the high shelf filter to increase the sparkle across the higher frequencies of a recording.
- Guitars can create problematic bands of low frequencies, especially if recorded through an amplifier. These are best removed with a band reject filter.
- If you need to EQ a bass guitar, try the 2-4kHz area for the mid frequencies and 80-120Hz for the lower end.
- If you want to make a section stand out, accentuate the frequencies in the 1kHz to 5kHz range. This is the area into which speech falls and our ears are naturally attuned to it. But don't try to put everything into that range or the recording will lack depth.
- As a general rule, cut the frequencies you don't want rather than boosting the frequencies you do want. Boosting increases noise as well as content. It's not unknown for a newcomer to boost a frequency and then boost another one because it's too low and then boost a third... and end up boosting the entire frequency spectrum of the mix!
- Boosting EQ generally raises the volume level of the recording which could well cause clipping. Before applying an EQ effect, check that it's not going to clip the waveform and make it distort. If it is, reduce the effect or the levels to compensate.

## Dynamics

If EQ is one of the most common effects, dynamics processing is one of the most useful, particularly with the dynamic range constraints of digital audio.

There are several types of dynamics processing and many dynamics FX routines in software cater for them all which can sometimes seem confusing. Different processes seem to do the same thing and it's mainly the degree to which they do it that causes them to be called by different names.

Dynamics processing reduces (compression) or increases (expansion) the dynamic range of a signal. In other words, compression reduces the difference in volume between the loudest and quietest parts of the recording. Expansion does the opposite and increases the dynamic range.

> **INFO**
>
> *The large dynamic range of vocals can be controlled considerably if the singer has a good microphone technique. This involves using a mic stand to minimise hand noise, moving away from the mic during the loud bits – making the vocalist a human compressor! – and using a cover or pop filter on the mic to minimise plosives like 'p' and 'b'.*

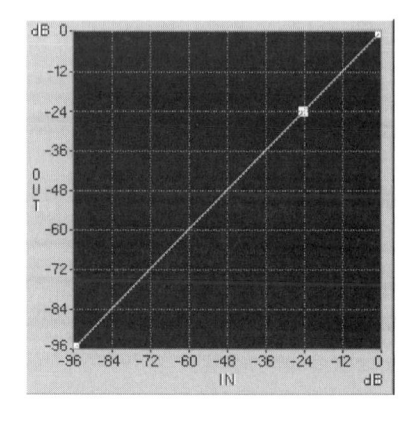

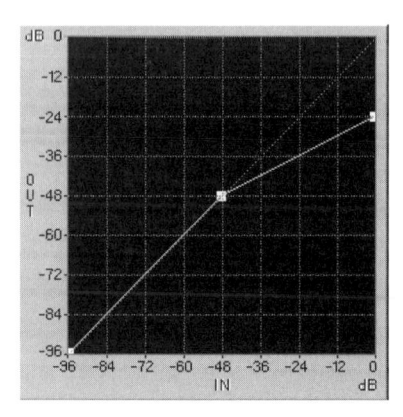

Quiet sections become quieter, louder sections become louder. Compression in its various forms is the more common and popular effect.

Why do we need dynamics control? Several reasons. Let's say you're producing a song with a MIDI backing track and you're using d-t-d to record the vocals. The human voice has a very large dynamic range and there could be sections where the voice is far too loud for the backing and other points where it's too quiet. If you run the vocals through a compressor, it will even out the volume making the quiet sections louder and the loud sections more quiet.

A similar compression technique can be used with any sound or instrument with a large dynamic range which has to sit alongside other sounds with a smaller dynamic range. This includes brass, some percussive sounds and sound effects.

Compression is often used on the final mix to squeeze more sound or 'warmth' into a recording, a little like pushing the levels on a tape recording. It increases the apparent loudness of a recording.

Compression is used a lot in radio broadcasting. Listen to a piece of classical music (which has a much larger dynamic range than pop music) on the radio and then play the CD. You'll soon notice the difference.

Dynamics processing involves monitoring the level of a recording and then changing it when it reaches a certain point. Most processors display the changes on a grid which makes it very easy to see exactly how the sound is being affected. Figure 11.11 shows what happens when no effect is being applied. The X axis (horizontal) plots the incoming volume of the source material and the Y axis (vertical) shows the outgoing level. In this example, all the Out levels are exactly the same as the In levels so the signal is passing through unchanged.

The average dynamics processor has four main parameters:

**Threshold** This is the point at which the effect comes into play. In Figure 11.11 the threshold is set to -24dB but as no effect is being applied there is no change in the output.

**Ratio** The ratio, sometimes called the compression ratio, is the amount by which the incoming signal is reduced. Figure 11.12 shows a 2:1 compression ratio which means that for every 2dB increase in the incoming volume level, the output level is only increased by 1dB. In this example, the incoming level at -24dB is only output at -36dB.

(Left) Figure 11.11 No effect applied so the output levels are exactly the same as the input levels. (Threshold set at –24dB)

(Right) Figure 11.12 A 2:1 compression ratio

(Left) Figure 11.13 3:1 compression ratio

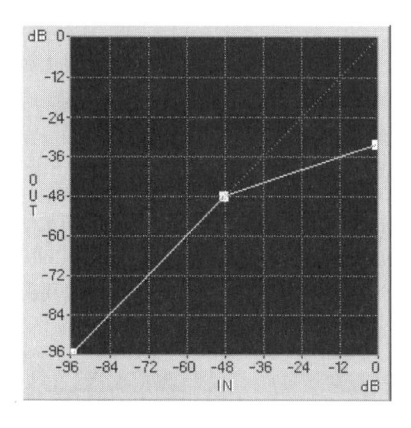

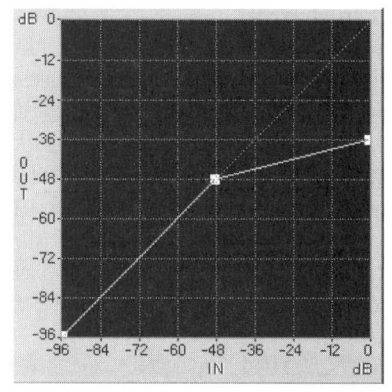

(Right) Figure 11.14 4:1 compression ratio

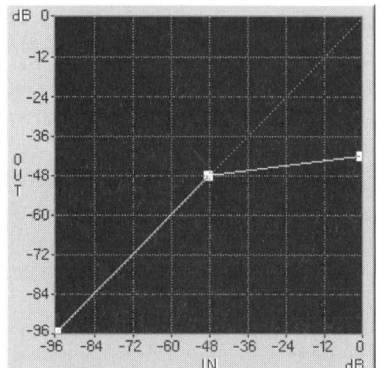

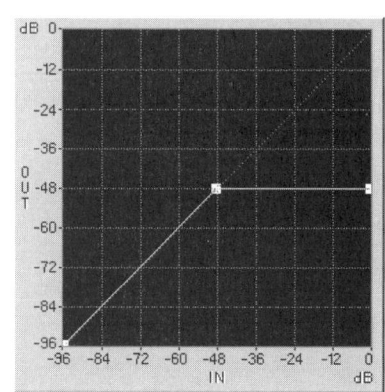

(Left) Figure 11.15 8:1 compression ratio

(Right) Figure 11.16 infinity:1 compression ratio

In Figure 11.13 the ratio is 3:1 and the incoming level at -12dB is output at -36dB. Figures 11.14 and 11.15 show ratios of 4:1 and 8:1 respectively. And finally, Figure 11.16 shows a ratio of infinity:1 – no matter how loud the incoming signal is above the threshold, it will never get any louder than -48dB.

**Attack time** The attack time is how long it takes the compressor to react to the incoming signal once it has reached the threshold. For those familiar with synthesis, it works in a similar way to the attack phase in a volume envelope. Attack times typically range from 0 to 100 or 500ms.

With a fast attack time, the effect will kick in straight away but this may not always be desirable. Consider a percussive sound such as a guitar or xylophone. If the attack is fast, it will reduce the initial transient of the sound creating a dull or muddy effect. By increasing the attack time, the percussive transient passes through the effect before compression begins, retaining the percussive effect and, in some cases, accenting it. This can be useful for adding punch to drum sounds.

**Release time** This determines how quickly the effect relinquishes control over the signal when it drops below the threshold. A fast release could cause the sound to swell up in volume very quickly and create an effect called pumping or breathing. It's a little like someone moving a volume fader up and down very quickly. If the release time is too slow, the system may not react to subsequent volume changes and keep the level compressed when it ought not to be.

## Gain controls

Most dynamics processors also have some sort of gain control. Because compression, by its nature, reduces the volume of the signal, you will generally want to increase it after compression.

WaveLab, Figure 11.17 has options to normalise (maximise the volume level of the signal – coming up in a moment) the signal before and after processing. Sound Forge, Figure 11.18 has an output gain control which lets you adjust the volume level after processing. It also has an 'auto gain compensate' function, which applies gain during processing in an attempt to keep the maximum input and output levels constant.

Figure 11.17 WaveLab can normalise a signal before and after compression

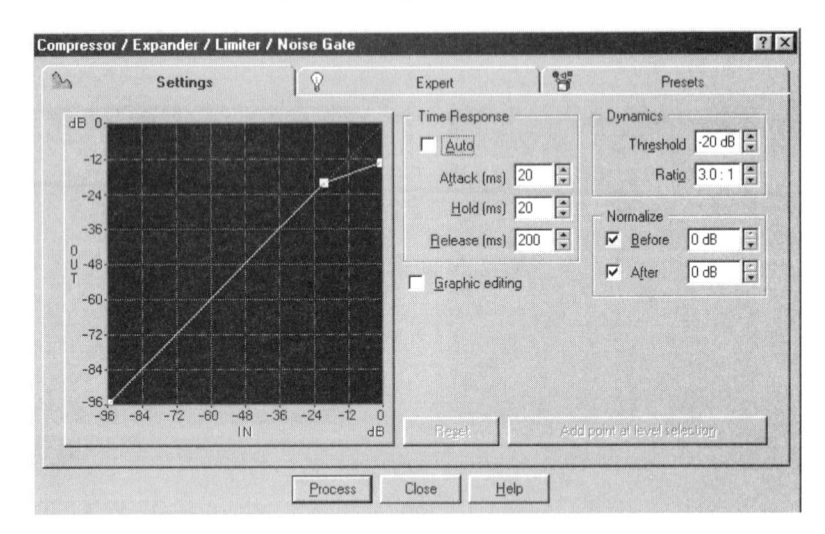

Figure 11.18 Sound Forge's output gain control

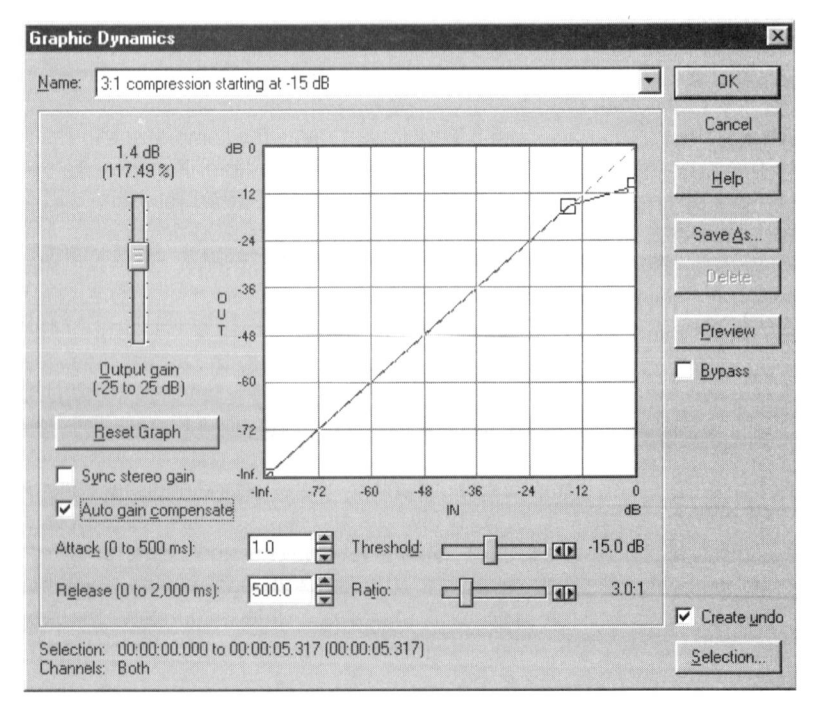

## Hard and soft knees

All the examples we've used so far are described as 'hard knees' – which is what they look like! – and the changes applied to the signal come into effect abruptly as soon as the signal passes the threshold. This can cause unwanted side effects such as the pumping described above.

However, you can create a smoother change by applying the effect gradually, in which case the curve becomes rounder and the effect is known as a 'soft knee'. This is shown in Figure 11.19.

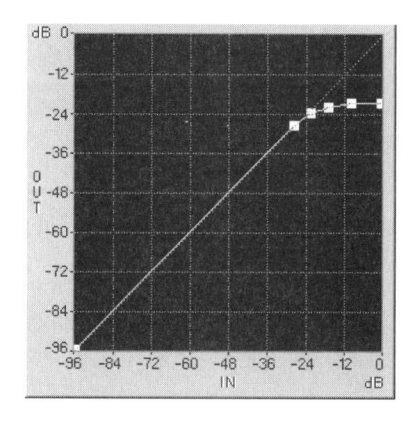

*Figure 11.19 Soft knee compression*

tripleDAT's compressor, Figure 11.20, is highly graphic and includes a Softknee setting to automatically smooth out the curve. The ratio is also displayed on the graph so you can see how this is affecting the compression.

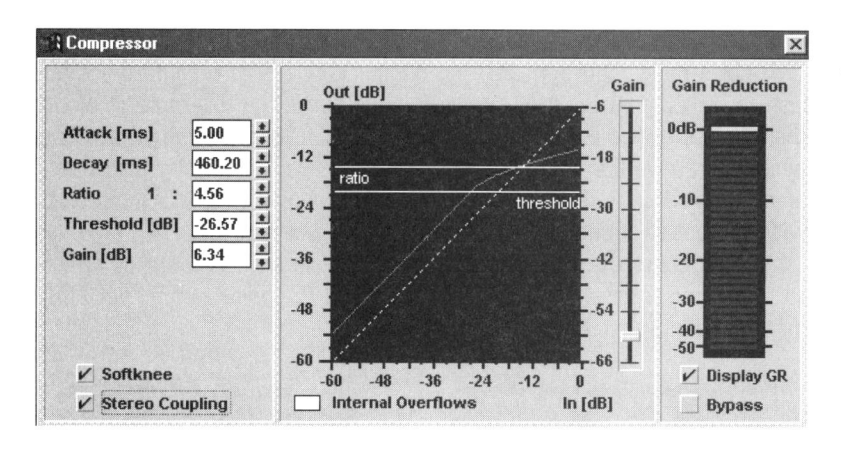

*Figure 11.20 tripleDAT's compressor*

## Compression and limiting

So, let us see what sort of effects dynamics processing can produce. Most of the examples we've used illustrate compression where the louder incoming signals are 'compressed down' to a lower level.

Limiting works in a similar way but it's much more severe. In fact, the traditional limiter sets a limit on the output volume which will never be exceeded no matter how loud the incoming signal becomes. Refer back to Figure 11.16 which is a limiter. You'll notice that the output volume will never rise above the threshold level of -48dB.

(Left) Figure 11.21 Most limiters have a high threshold setting

(Right) Figure 11.22 Soft knee version of Figure 11.21

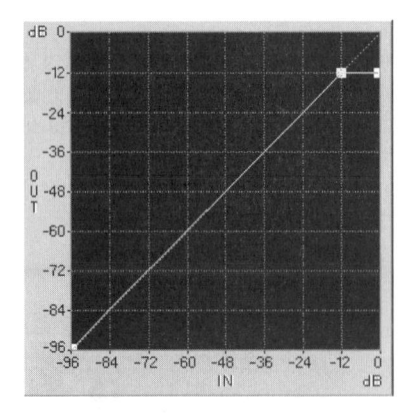

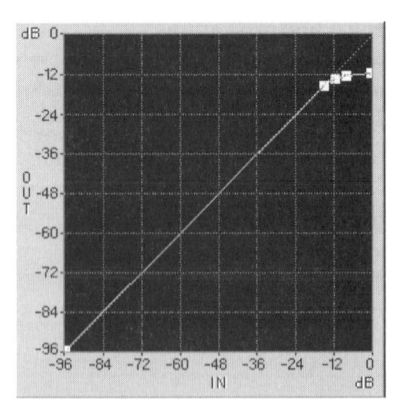

The threshold in this example is extremely low and in practice, the average limiter is likely to look more like Figure 11.21 which just stops the signal going 'over the top'. Figure 11.22 shows a soft knee version of the same effect.

Limiting is often used to pull very loud peaks back into line. It needs to be used with care because it can cause unwanted side effects. Beware of setting the threshold too low as this will probably cause distortion.

### Noise gate

Noise gates were devised to keep low level noise out of a recording. You probably know that many electronic instruments generate noise even when they aren't playing. Plug a guitar into an amp and you'll probably hear some background noise or hum. Many synthesisers, particularly older ones, were prone to generating noise, too.

A noise gate, Figure 11.23, has similar controls to a compressor but instead of compressing levels when they go above the threshold, it blocks them unless they are above it. In other words, it lets through only signals which are above the threshold. If you want to record a noisy instrument or are recording an acoustic sound in a noisy environment, a noise gate will keep out all sound until the signal reaches a certain level.

As with compression, severe gating can produce unwanted side effects so to minimise these, most systems allow you to create a soft knee noise gate as in Figure 11.24.

(Left) Figure 11.23 Noise gate

(Right) Figure 11.24 Soft knee noise gate

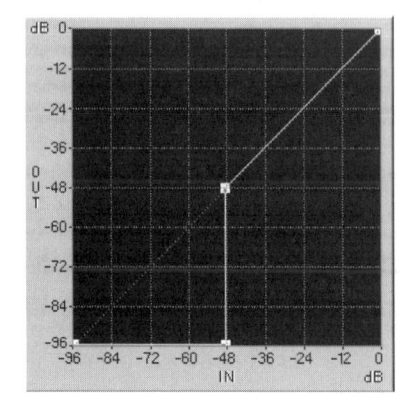

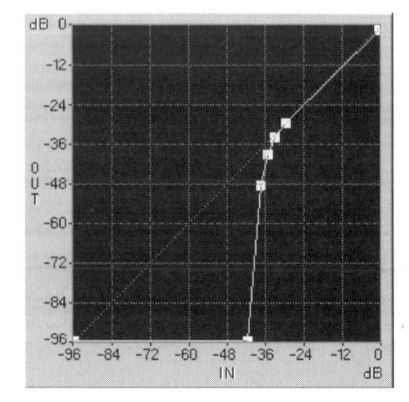

## Expander

Expansion is the opposite of compression. When a signal reaches the threshold, its level is increased instead of being reduced as in Figure 11.25. It can also work on signals below the threshold as in Figure 11.26, where you'll see that, as the input signals become increasingly quiet, the expansion effect makes it quieter still! If the effect is increased sufficiently it will make the signals so quiet they will become inaudible and the effect will have become a noise gate.

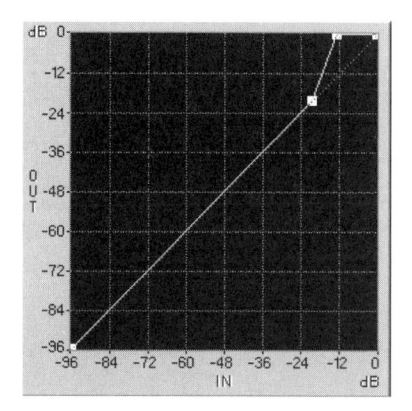

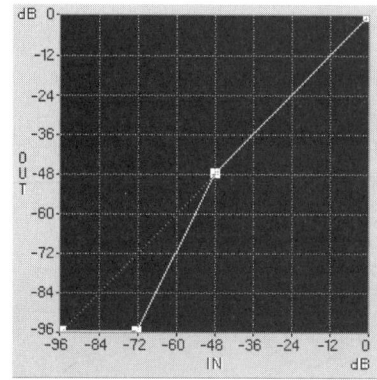

(Left) Figure 11.25 Expansion is the opposite of compression. When a signal reaches the threshold, its level is increased instead of reduced

(Right) Figure 11.26 The quieter a signal becomes, the more quiet this effect makes it

Expansion can be hard or soft knee and it is often used in conjunction with other effects. Figure 11.27 is a combination of an expander, limiter and noise gate. The noise gate is the lower vertical line. It's not quite vertical so the effect is more gradual than instant. The expansion area is the curve in the middle and the limiter is the horizontal line at the top.

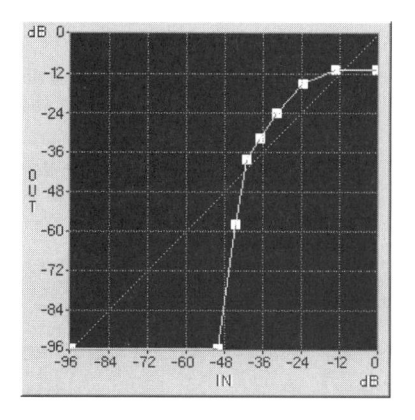

Figure 11.27 A combination of an expander, limiter and noise gate

## Multi-band dynamics

You may come across a multi-band dynamics processor, a very interesting device which compresses only selected frequencies. It's particularly useful for removing sibilants such as 's' and plosives. A sibilant remover is often called a de-esser ('cause it removes the Ss). By setting the multi-band to around 5kHz which is where sibilants usually occur and compressing them, they can be reduced.

Figure 11.28 shows Sound Forge's multi-band dynamics processor de-essing the Ss at the high end of the frequency range and de-plosing the plosives at the lower end.

Figure 11.28 De-essing the Ss at the high end of the frequency range and de-plosing the plosives at the lower end

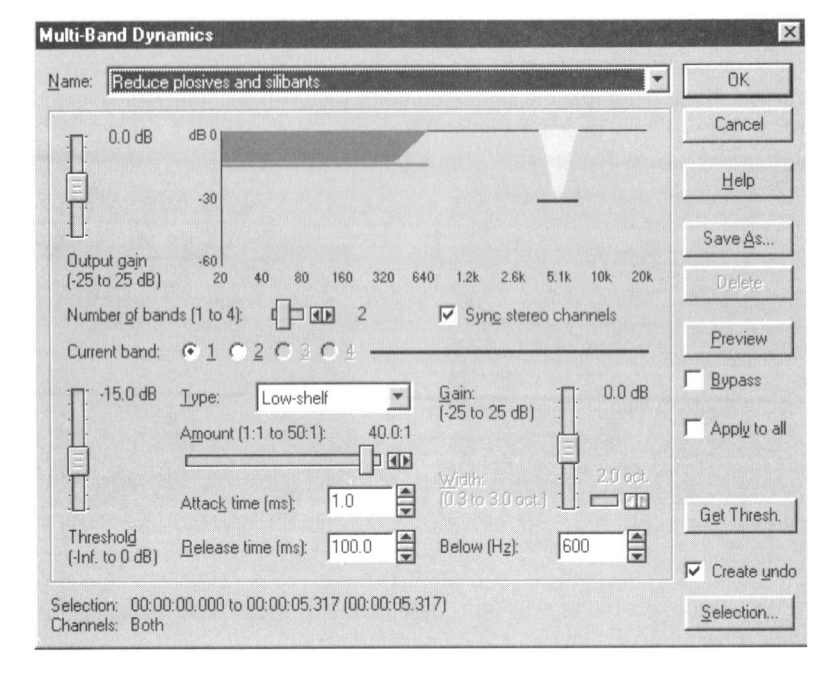

## De-esser

Sibilants are the S, T, CH and SH sounds produced during speaking and singing. When recorded they are quite often louder than the rest of the voice and can produce a hissing effect which is annoying. Figure 11.29 shows the peak caused by the letter S in the middle of the word 'sibilant'.

Sibilants can be removed – or certainly reduced – by compressing only the sibilants, a task performed using a combination of filtering and compression. Although a multi-band dynamics processor can be used to do

Figure 11.29 The peak caused by the letter S in the middle of the word 'sibilant'

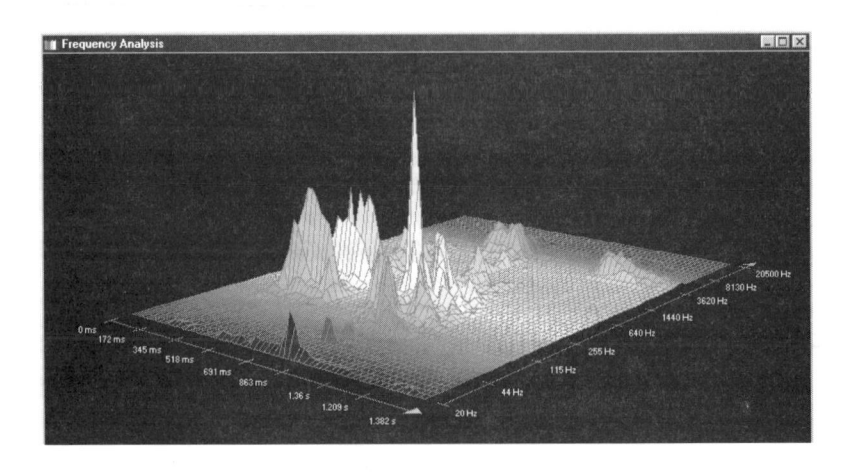

this, there are dedicated de-essers which do a better job. They use a similar set of tools with controls such as threshold and frequency although most do the de-essing using a processing algorithm rather than relying purely on compression and filtering.

## Change gain

This is usually a simple function used to change the overall volume level of the recording making it either louder or quieter. Ideally, there ought to be a check on the increased level otherwise you could increase it to the point where the waveform clips and distorts. WaveLab, Figure 11.30 and Logic Audio, Figure 11.31, for example, have options to find the highest level in the recording. It's then up to you how much change you apply.

There's one point to bear in mind if the recording contains any particularly high peaks. If you use a function to get the level of the highest peak, this could well be almost as high as the level can go. You would not, therefore, be able to increase the gain by very much before the peak clipped. The solution is to run the recording through a compressor to lower the peak and then increase the gain. In fact, this very function is included in many compressors and described earlier in the dynamics section.

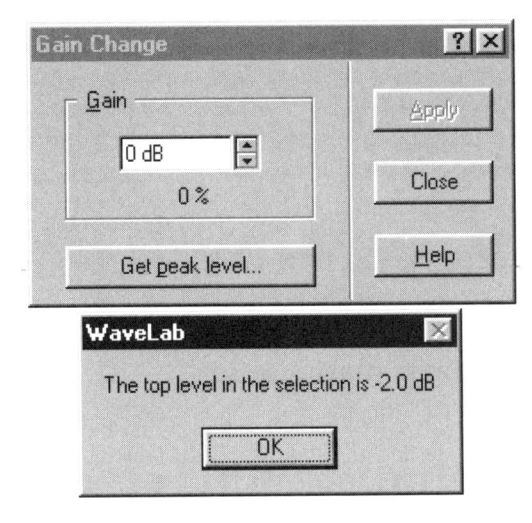

Figure 11.30 Finding the highest level in the recording with Wavelab ...

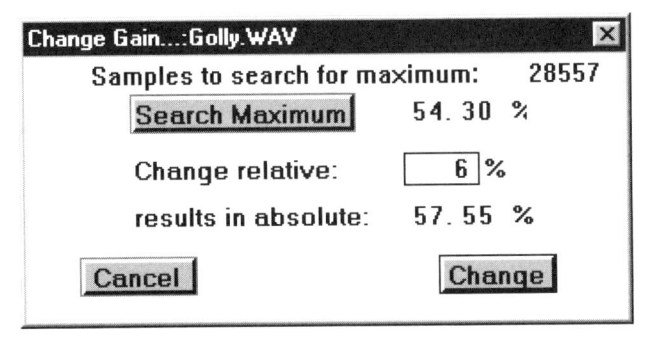

Figure 11.31 ... and with Logic Audio

## Normalise

This increases the level of the selected section to the maximum it can possibly be without distorting. Most software performs this function automatically without further input from the user although WaveLab will maximise up to a level set by the user.

Sound Forge, Figure 11.32, has several more options including the ability to normalise by RMS power, which is useful for maximising the apparent loudness of different recordings. It can also automatically compress a file if clipping occurs. and it has attack and release parameters which determine how quickly the process responds to peaks.

Figure 11.32 Sound Forge has the ability to normalise by RMS power

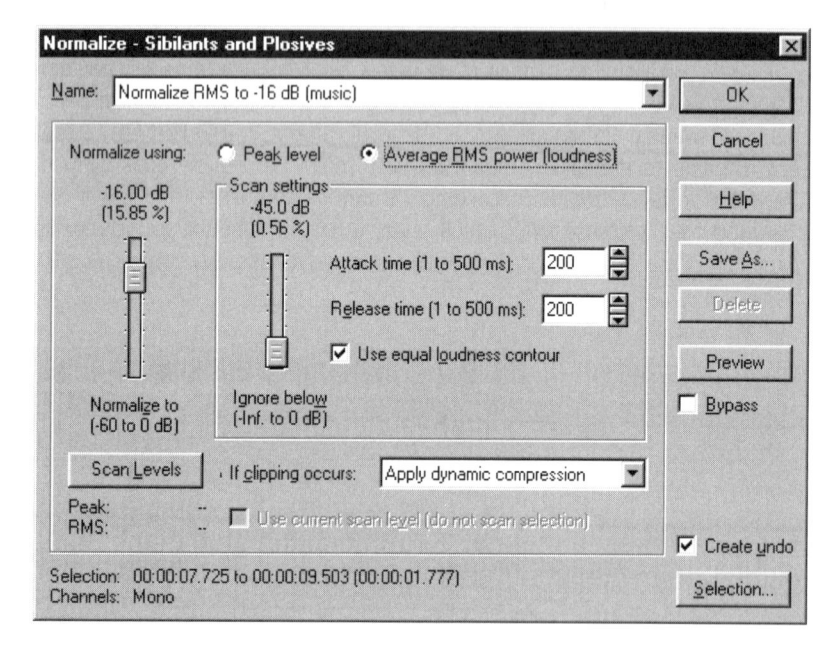

## Loudness maximisation

If you have the impression that a major part of digital audio processing is about getting the biggest sound and the highest volume levels out of a recording, you'd be right! Just as tape recording engineers strive to get as much level onto tape as possible, so digital audio producers want to maximise the levels, quality and dynamic range of their recordings. The potential dynamic range of 16-bit digital audio (96dB, although not readily achievable in practice) is impressive but it doesn't satisfy everyone (it'll probably take 32-bit audio to do that!), and there's always the challenge of going that extra mile.

The processing functions discussed so far, such as compression and normalisation, can do a lot to maximise the apparent volume level of a recording, so it should come as no surprise that developers have produced software dedicated to the task. Most use a combination of compression, limiting and resampling.

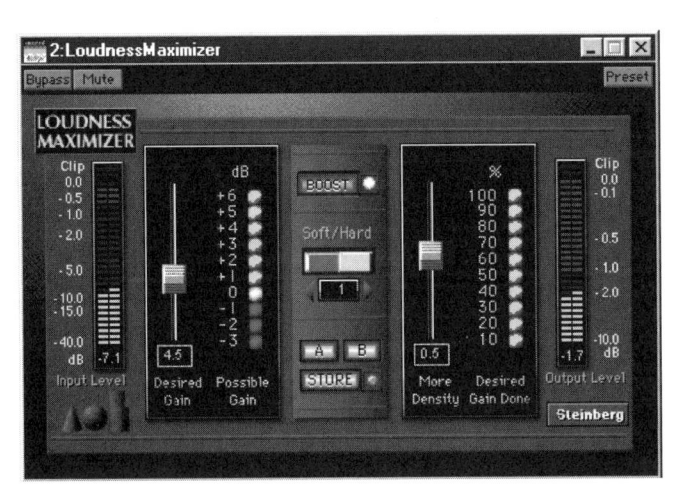

Figure 11.33 Steinberg's Loudness Maximiser plug-in for WaveLab

Steinberg's Loudness Maximiser, Figure 11.33, is a plug-in for WaveLab. It uses adaptive algorithms which are controlled by the source material itself. It can even increase the perceived volume of a recording which has been normalised, a feat it accomplishes by judicious compression and limiting. The density slider adjusts the balance between the two, and there's a boost button to give the audio a final kick, which increases its level by another 2dB!

Its efficiency depends on the source material – uncomplicated modern dance music can be maximised very well, although more sonically complex material may not be able to be maximised to the same degree. The routine, by its nature, does modify the audio data but the result is natural and very effective.

Waves' L1 Ultramaximiser, Figure 11.34, can be used with any DirectX-compatible program. It performs a similar function to the Loudness Maximiser and combines similar processes, along with a requantiser which can change the sample resolution. It has threshold, output and release sliders, which you can juggle in real-time, and three noise shaping settings

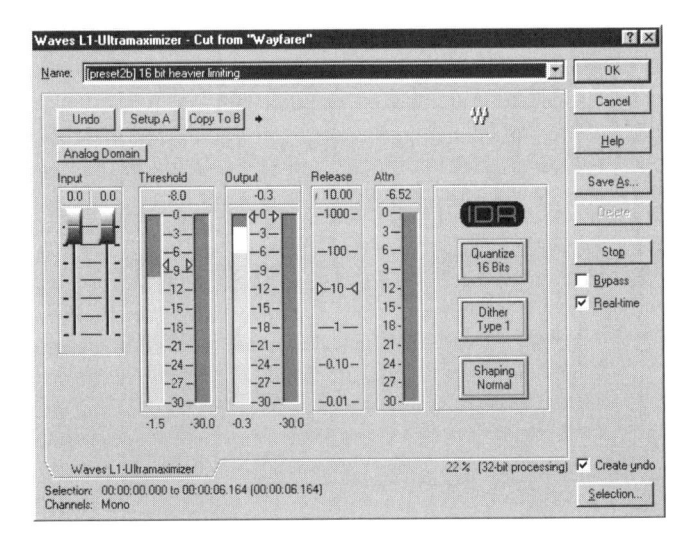

### TECHY BIT

Noise shaping is a process in which noise in the most audible parts of a recording is reduced and increased or shifted to the less-audible parts. To put it another way, the noise's frequency content is 'shaped' so there is more of it in the frequency range we hear least. There's a teeny bit more about this in the sigma-delta conversion section in Chapter 7 but you don't need to know how it works in order to use it. Some systems which use noise shaping do so without even telling the user and those which do stamp it on the front panel generally only give you the option of switching it on or off, or selecting one of a couple of shaping options.

Figure 11.34 Waves' L1 Ultramaximiser

*Figure 11.35 An unprocessed reading from a file*

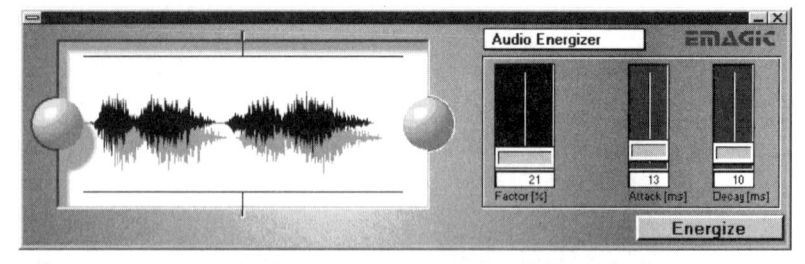

*Figure 11.36 When it passes 100 the peaks start heading towards the upper limits*

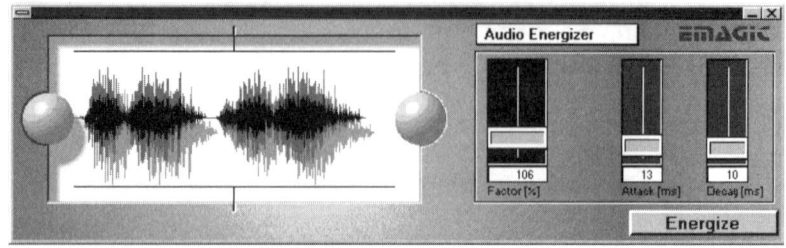

Logic Audio's Audio Energiser has one main control, factor, which adjusts the 'energy' level. Figure 11.35 shows an unprocessed reading from a file. It's suggested that the factor value be somewhere between 40 and 100.

Figure 11.36 shows that when it passes 100 the peaks start heading towards the upper limits. Push it too far and they will be clipped causing distortion. The function also has attack and release controls which determine how quickly the effect comes in and drops out.

## Enhancers

Enhancers are very popular outboard effects units. They add sparkle, presence, brilliance, depth, lift, density, boost, shine and pizzazz to a sound, depending on whose literature you read! Different enhancers apply different processes to the sound, although the aim of them all is to 'enhance' the sound one way or another.

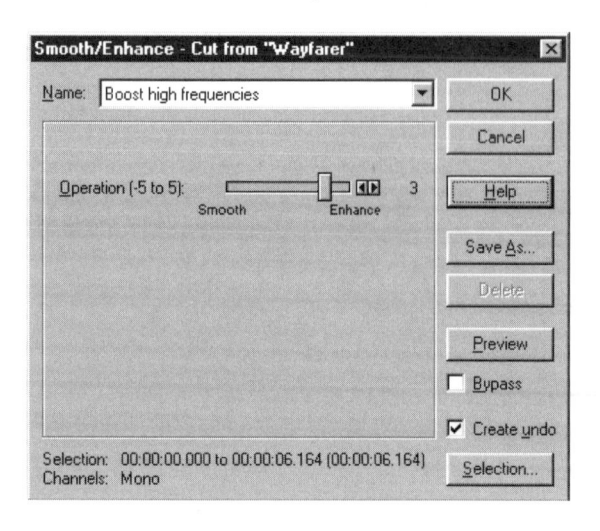

*Figure 11.37 Sound Forge's Smooth/Enhance function*

There are rather fewer software enhancers, although the maximisers described above could possible fall into the enhancer class, and you can do a bit of enhancing on your own by tweaking the high frequencies with the EQ section and applying a little compression.

Sound Forge's Smooth/Enhance function, Figure 11.37, doesn't pretend to do much other than add or remove high frequency content. You have to set the balance between smoothing, which reduces fast-changing transients (useful for reducing glitches), and enhancing, which boosts the very highest frequencies (those close to the Nyquist limit). Perhaps it's not the ideal software enhancer but it's a start.

## DC offset

When you look at a waveform display in an editor, the zero line should run directly through the centre of it. Sometimes, due to a mismatch in recording equipment such as the microphone or the soundcard, the waveform may be offset so its centre is a little higher or lower than the zero line as in Figure 11.38. This is a DC offset caused because there is too large a DC (Direct Current) component in the signal.

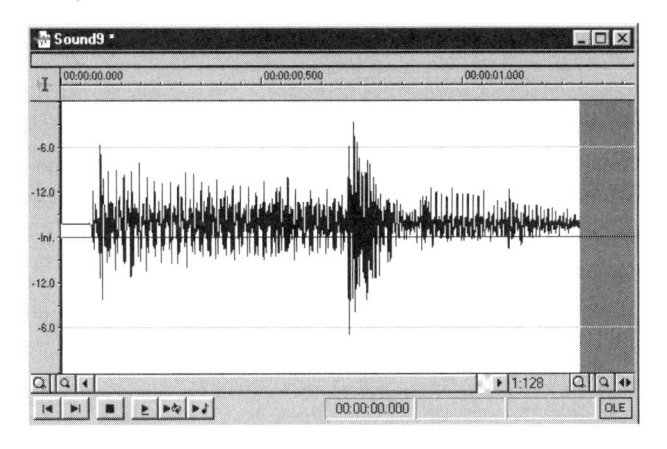

Figure 11.38 DC offset occurs when the centre of the waveform is not on the central 'zero volume' line

This can cause clicks and glitches on playback and create problems if you try to edit or process the file. For example, as the zero volume (the centre) part of the recording is not on the zero line, trying to find a zero crossing point would be difficult.

The example in Figure 11.38 is extreme and indicates a severe equipment mismatch but it's not uncommon to have a small DC offset which may not be readily visible in the editor. However, if you zoom in on a part of the file which contains silence you may be able to see a small offset in the waveform as in Figure 11.39. Before performing a DC offset adjustment, WaveLab scans the file and reports the severity of the offset as in Figure 11.40.

Before you apply an edit function to a recording, and particularly before creating a loop, check for a DC offset and, if one is present, correct it.

Figure 11.39 A small offset in the waveform

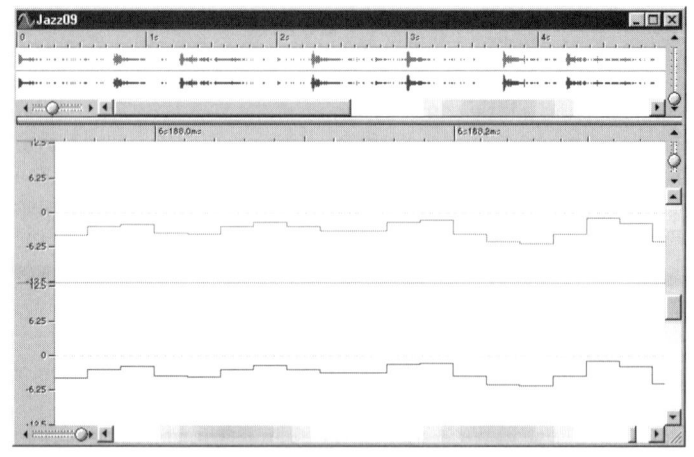

Figure 11.40 WaveLab reports the severity of a DC offset

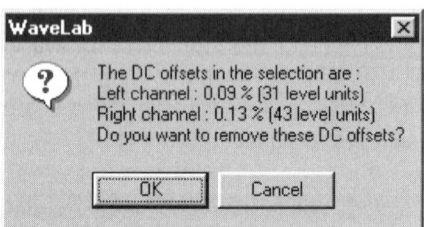

## Invert phase/flip

This reverses the phase of a waveform. That is, the parts of the wave which were above the zero line (those with a positive amplitude) are made negative so they appear below the zero line and vice versa. Figure 11.41 shows what happens when a waveform is flipped or inverted.

Figure 11.41 Inverting the upper waveform produces the lower one

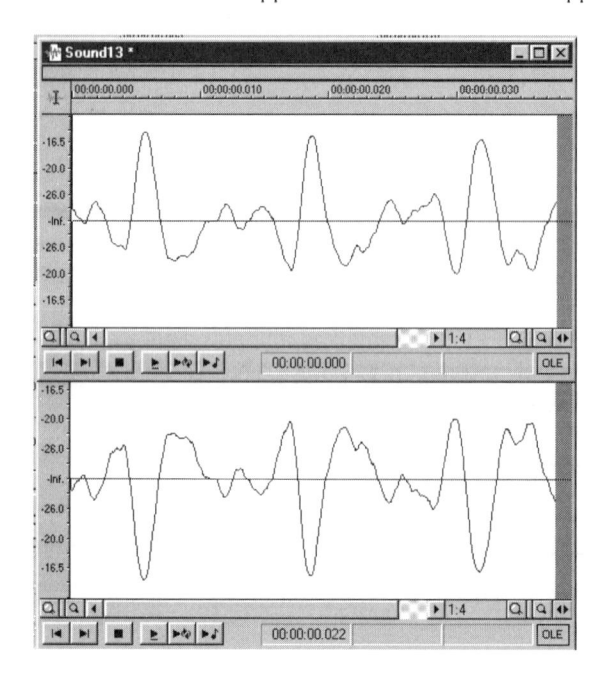

This doesn't make any difference to the sound at all but it can help correct phase cancellation errors. If one channel in a stereo recording is out of phase with the other, this can result in a blurred stereo image and a loss of bass frequencies. It's particularly important that recordings are 'in phase' when mixing down to mono.

## Reverse

This simply reverses the selection so it plays backwards. Apart from using it to create satanic messages to put at the end of your song (old heavy metal joke), its practical uses may seem limited. However, one popular reverse effect is the reversed cymbal which starts with the fade out and builds up to the crash. Try it! Reverse is also a useful tool for musicians generating new sounds, particularly for ambient and industrial music.

## Pitch shifting and time stretching

In tape recording, pitch and duration are inexorably linked. If you want the recording to play back faster, you have to speed up the passage of the tape across the tape heads and this, as you probably know, also causes the pitch to rise. Slow down the speed and the pitch falls. That's the way it is with tape.

But with digital audio data, we can change the speed without changing the pitch and vice versa. However, the two processes are linked and many programs use one window to handle the pitch shifting and time stretching functions.

The simplest pitch shift control lets you transpose the audio by a certain amount. The shift may be in semitones or in cents. Because traditionally, pitch shifting and time stretching went hand in hand, some software has an option for adjusting the duration, too – á là tape recorder.

WaveLab has separate windows for the two functions. Figure 11.42 shows the pitch correction function which is fairly simple and allows you to set the shift factor in semitones and cents. Figure 11.43 shows the time stretch function which lets you specify the new duration by tempo, duration or as a ratio.

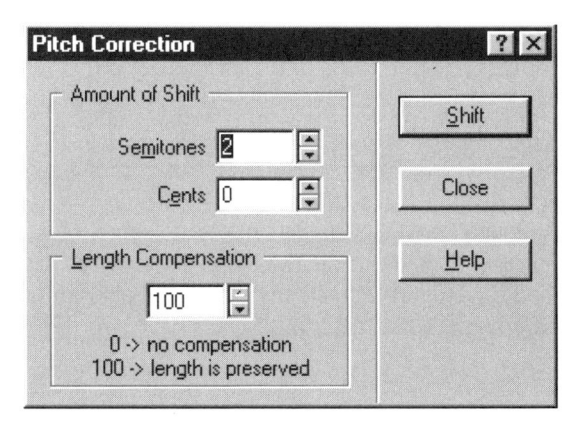

> **INFO**
> There are 100 cents in a semitone.

Figure 11.42 WaveLab's pitch correction function

Figure 11.43 The time stretch function in WaveLab

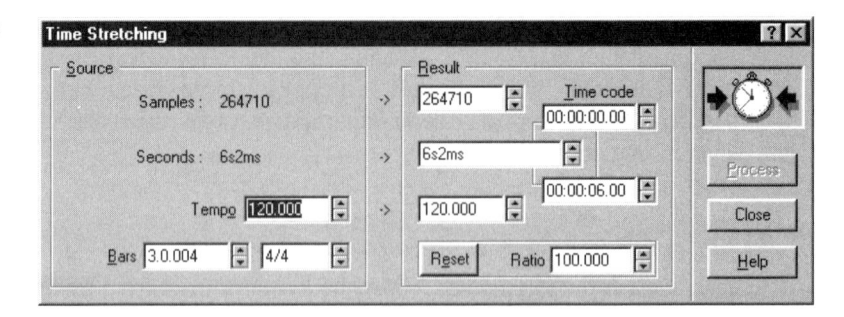

Cubase, Figure 11.44, combines pitch shifting and time stretching in one window. It also has a varispeed function, Figure 11.45, which uses an almost identical window. The only difference is that as you change the pitch or the speed in the varispeed window, the other parameter automatically changes, too.

Figure 11.44 Cubase combines pitch shifting and time stretching in one window

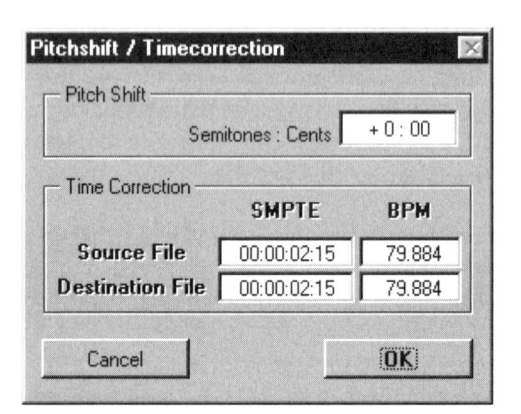

Figure 11.45 The Cubase varispeed function

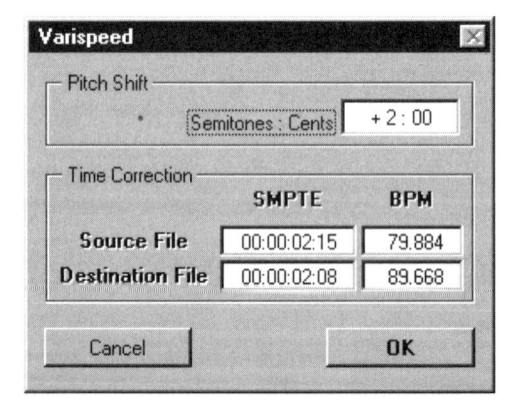

Sound Forge's pitch shift function, Figure 11.46, includes several additional options including the ability to apply an anti-alias filter and three modes which are actually three different algorithms used for pitch shifting different types of material.

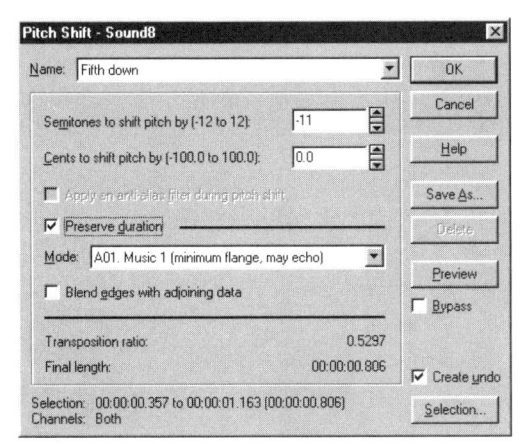

Figure 11.46 Sound Forge's pitch shift function

### TIP

*Because changing the pitch of a sample involves a form of resampling it can cause aliasing, so the application of an anti-alias filter can help prevent this. Check that your software uses a filter or, if you're not sure, listen carefully to the output for signs of aliasing.*

Logic Audio's Time Machine, Figure 11.47, combines pitch shifting and time stretching and uses a 3D display to show the relationship between pitch and time changes. Notice the Ideal line. This is the 'traditional' or tape-recorder relationship between pitch and duration and moving the ball along this line will produce exactly the same result as speeding up or slowing down a tape machine. The closer to this line a change is, the better the sound quality of the processed file will be.

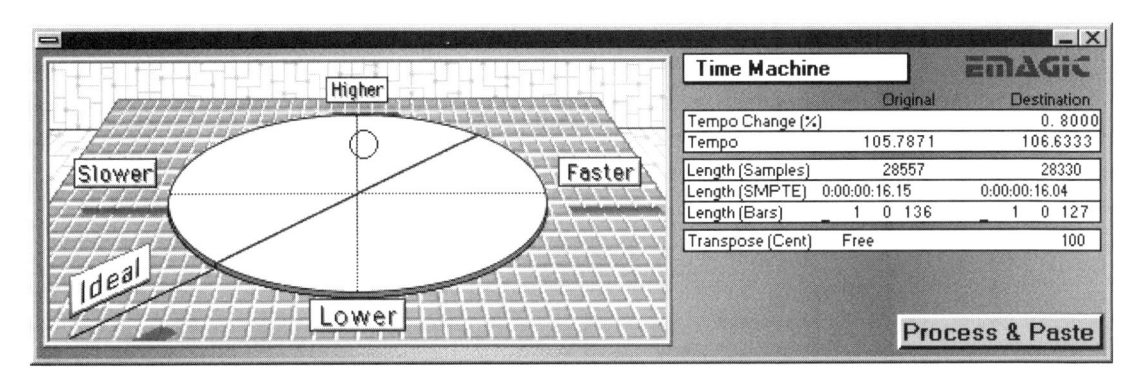

Time for a brief excursion into the world of...

Figure 11.47 Logic Audio's Time Machine combines pitch shifting and time stretching

## Formants and harmonic correction

Formants are groups of partials or frequencies which are evident in many sounds but particularly in speech. They are responsible for the sound's tonal characteristics. If they are changed during a pitch shift function, for example, the timbre of the speech will change, too.

The higher you shift a voice up in pitch, the more it takes on a Mickey Mouse-like character – cute, perhaps, but rather unnatural. A similar but opposite harmonic and timbral change occurs when you pitch shift a voice downwards. In fact, you'll find that you can't shift a vocal very far away from its natural pitch without it taking on an unnatural quality.

The solution is to correct the formats in a recording after a pitch shift. Several programs on the Apple Mac take formants into consideration dur-

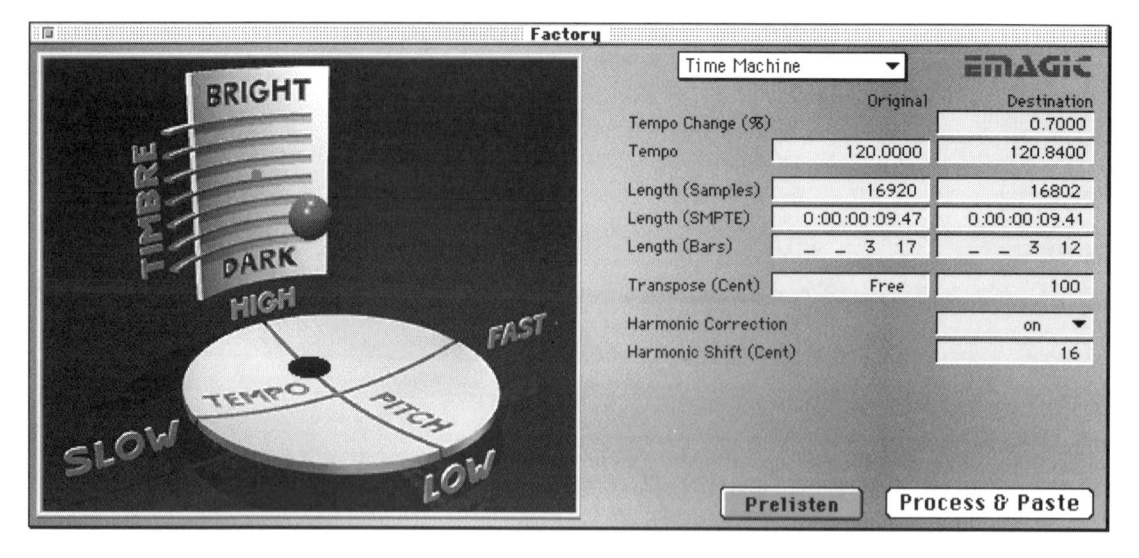

Figure 11.48 Logic Audio's Time Machine on the Mac

ing transposition but they are slow in making their way to the PC. Logic Audio's Time Machine on the Mac, Figure 11.48 has a harmonic correction function and this will likely soon be in the PC version, too.

## Harmoniser

If you can change the pitch of a sound without changing the duration, it's but a small step to think of creating several pitch shifted versions of a recording to produce instant harmonies. And with a little application you can do just that using any audio software with a pitch shift function.

WaveLab, however, has a built-in harmoniser, Figure 11.49. It generates a file containing up to 16 voices, each with their own transposition, level and pan setting.

Figure 11.49 WaveLab's has a built-in harmoniser

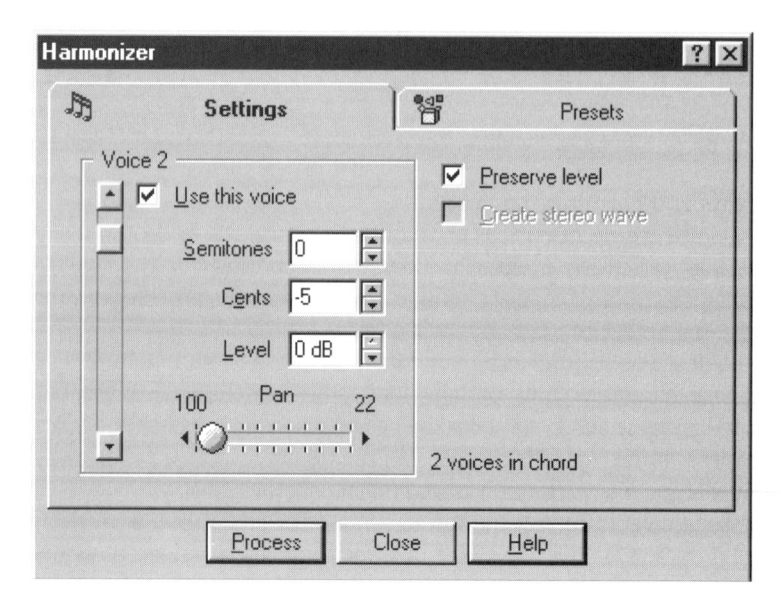

## Reverb

Of all the processing effects, reverb – or reverberation to give it its full name – is the most popular, enduring and arguably the most useful. It's also a very complex effect, and modern reverb units have a vast number of parameters which all have a bearing on some aspect of the sound.

Natural reverb is most evident in large buildings with hard, irregular surfaces, such as halls and churches. It is generated by the sound bouncing around the surfaces and, as you can imagine, the variety of the resulting signals is truly complex. This is what makes reverb so appealing.

Early reverb units consisted of large springs and metal plates. Now, sophisticated computer algorithms allow us to simulate virtually any environment which can be created both in the real world and in imaginary environments as well as the reverb effects produced by early reverb units.

Basically, reverb consists of a vast number of echoes or reflections that occur so quickly we hear the result as one continuing sound. Reverb occurs in virtually every environment, although areas such as furnished houses and small rooms absorb most of the reflections. Large open areas such as fields, where there are few surfaces for reflections to bounce off, can seem to lack reverb, too.

In such places we are generally unaware of any reverb, particularly when we compare it with a concert hall or even a large, tiled bathroom. However, even in places where there are few reflections, our ears are still aware of them, and we use this information to form an acoustic image of our environment. So, as well as adding depth and 'wetness' to a sound, reverb can also be used to make us believe a singer, band or orchestra is playing in anything from a garden shed to the Grand Canyon.

Here are some of the parameters you might find on a reverb unit:

**Pre-delay** This is the time it takes the reverb to 'kick in' and it contributes to our perception of the size of the environment. Longer pre-delay times suggest a larger room.

**Early reflections** These are first echoes or reflections from the environment, and these, too, contribute to our aural perception of the environment. What we hear after these are the reflections of the reflections – the reverberation.

**Reverb/decay time** The amount of time it takes the reverb to die away as the reflections decrease in volume. Usually, the larger the environment, the longer the reverb time.

**Diffusion** This controls how widely spread-out the reflections are. With very low values you may be able to hear distinct echoes. With higher values, the reflections are closer together and are heard as reverb rather than discrete echoes.

**Density/width** The time between the early reflections and the rest of the reverb. The shorter the time the more dense the reverb appears to be. High density values are useful with percussive sounds.

**Damping/frequency attenuation/frequency decay** As the reflections bounce around the environment, the surfaces absorb various frequencies in the sound. This varies according to the reflective surface but the high frequencies are usually the first to go. In a highly reflective environment, the high frequencies take longer to decay and the space will seem to have more 'life'.

Reverb units also have controls for adjusting the amount of the original signal sent to the reverb effect and the amount of effect mixed back into the output. Most reverb units, both hardware and software, have many other parameters, too, but most are based on the above parameters.

Sound Forge's reverb, Figure 11.50, has pre-delay, decay time and early out, which determines the amount of early reflections mixed into the output. It has several preset reverb modes ranging from plate effects to caverns, and 10 preset early reflections styles ranging from 6ms to 36ms some with pan options. It also enables you to attenuate the high and low frequencies.

Figure 11.50 Sound Forge's reverb

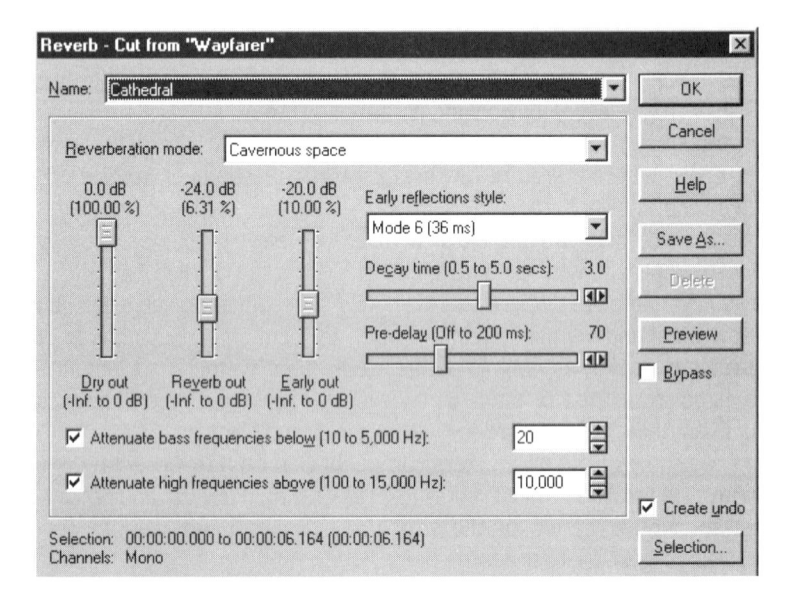

## Room simulators

Some of the latest new-generation reverb effects don't so much attempt to generate reverb as simulate an acoustic environment. Samplitude doesn't have a 'reverb' effect but a Room Simulator, Figure 11.51. It uses the 'impulse response' of a room – the reflections and reverb created by a loud percussive sound – which it applies to the recording.

Controls let you change the impulse response envelope by adjusting the early reflections, late reverb (volume of the main reverb echoes), and the length (reverb time). You can also set the high and low frequency damping and adjust the mix between the reverb and the original signal.

WaveLab's reverb, Figure 11.52 combines traditional reverb and room simulation. There are controls to adjust the size and width of the room plus early reflection start, width, gain, decay and output.

Waves' DirectX TrueVerb plug-in, Figure 11.53, is a very sophisticated room simulator. RoomSize governs the overall size of the acoustic area, Dimension is the character of the early reflections and distance is how far

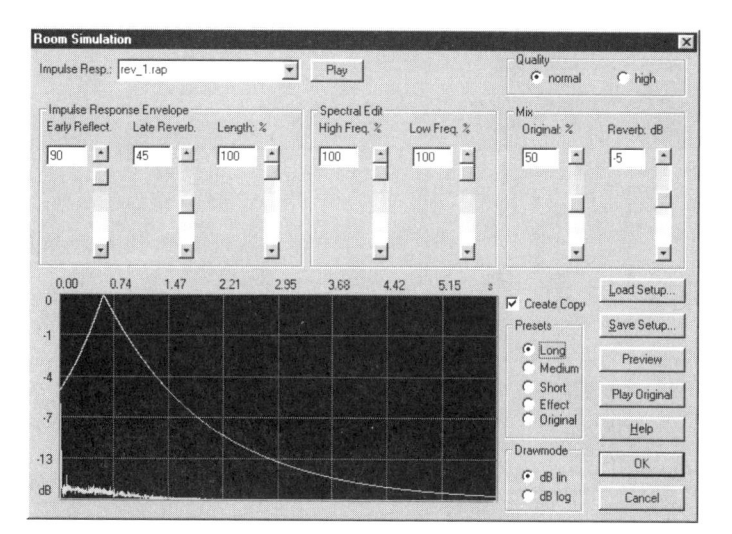

Figure 11.51 Samplitude's Room Simulator

Figure 11.52 WaveLab's reverb

away the listener is from the input source. It also has reverb time, pre-delay and density controls. Another parameter controls the absorbency factor of the room, and there are frequency and damping controls. It has two graphic displays, one showing the time response and the other the frequency response, which help when setting up the parameters.

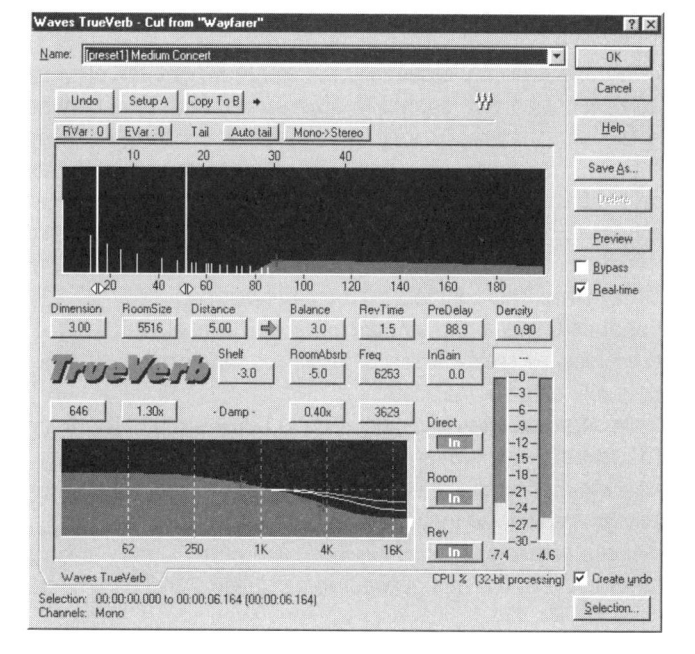

Figure 11.53 Waves' DirectX TrueVerb plug-in

Figure 11.54 tripleDAT's Room Simulator has settings for room size, room type, pre-delay, high frequency decay and liveliness

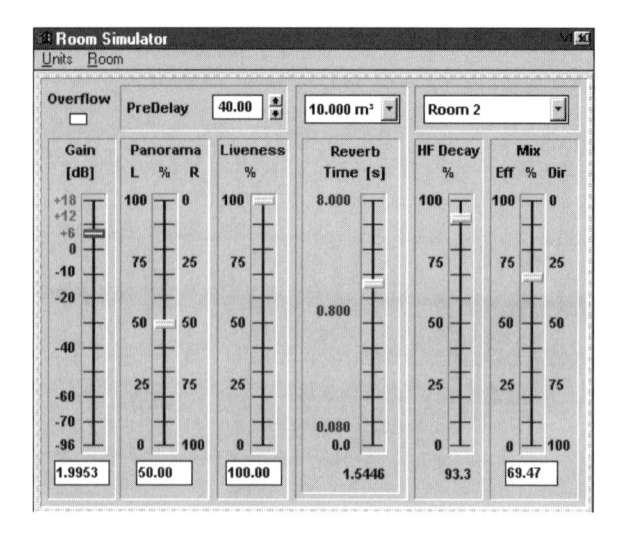

tripleDAT's Room Simulator, Figure 11.54, has settings for room size, room type, pre-delay, high frequency decay and liveliness. It also has a panorama control which lets you specify how much the left and right stereo channels will be used in generating the reverb.

#### Tip
There are three rules to bear in mind when using reverb:

1 Don't use too much reverb
2 Don't use too much reverb
3 Don't use too much reverb

### Delay and echo

Delay and echo are essentially the same. Strictly, an echo is a distinguishable repetition of a sound. In other words, the time between the original sound and the echo is long enough for us to perceive them as two separate sounds, as opposed to reverb, for example, where the reverb effect seems part of original sound. However, many echo systems can generate echoes so close together than the result is very like reverb.

There are two main echo parameters:
**Delay time** This controls the time between echoes.
**Feedback** This is the amount of delayed signal which is fed back into the echo loop to create a series of echoes. With this switched off there will probably only be one echo.

In some systems, including Sound Forge's Multi-Tap Delay, it's possible to crank this up so high that the sound feeds back on itself and goes into oscillation. You can see this in the graph in Figure 11.55 where the later echoes are so loud they are clipping causing distortion.

Echo controls also include input and output, and a mix or balance control to govern the mix between the original signal and the echoes.

> **TECHY BIT**
>
> In order for a sound to be heard as a separate echo, it must follow the original by at least 100ms. That means that if the sound is bouncing off a surface, it needs to be about 16.5 metres away, otherwise the echo will seem to be part of the original sound.

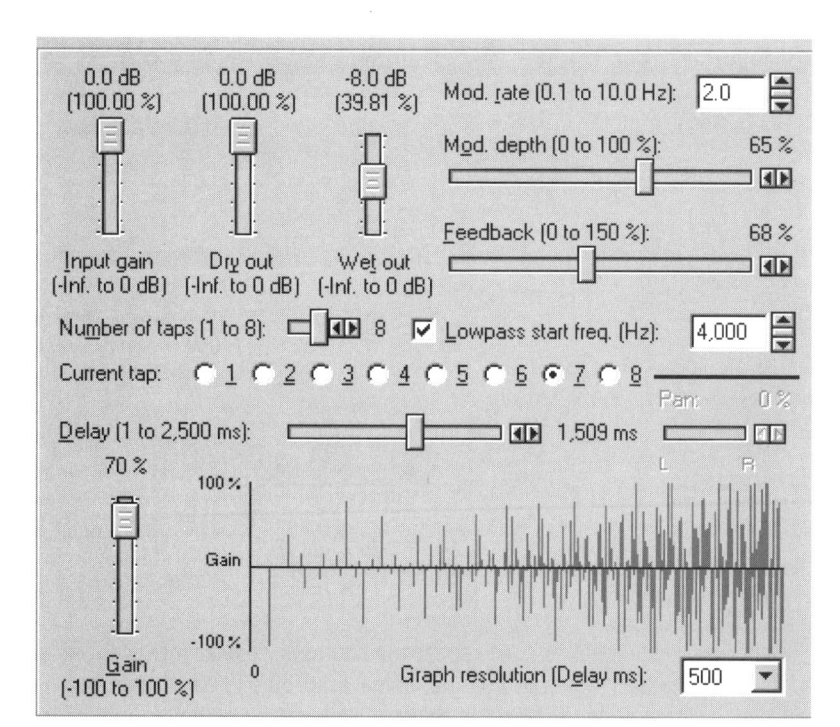

Figure 11.55 Increasing the feedback level can cause an echo effect to go into self-oscillation which quickly results in distortion

Samplitude's Echo/Delay effect, Figure 11.56, contains a graph which shows how quickly the echoes die away. Sound Forge's Delay/Echo, Figure 11.57, has a decay time parameter which determines how long it takes the echoes to die away. It also has an interesting pre-delay/echo option which adds the delayed copy *before* the sound.

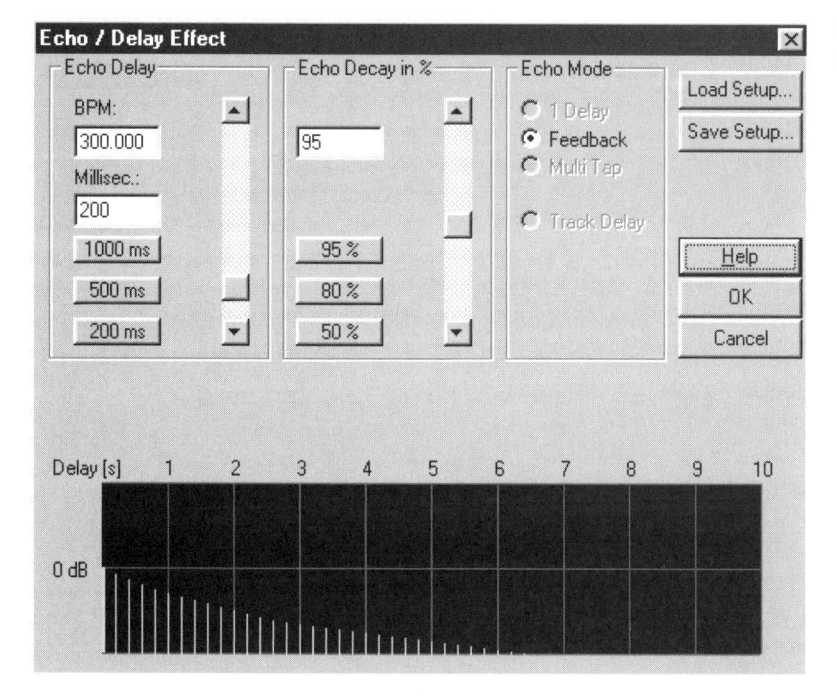

Figure 11.56 Samplitude's echo/delay effect

Figure 11.57 Sound Forge's delay/echo

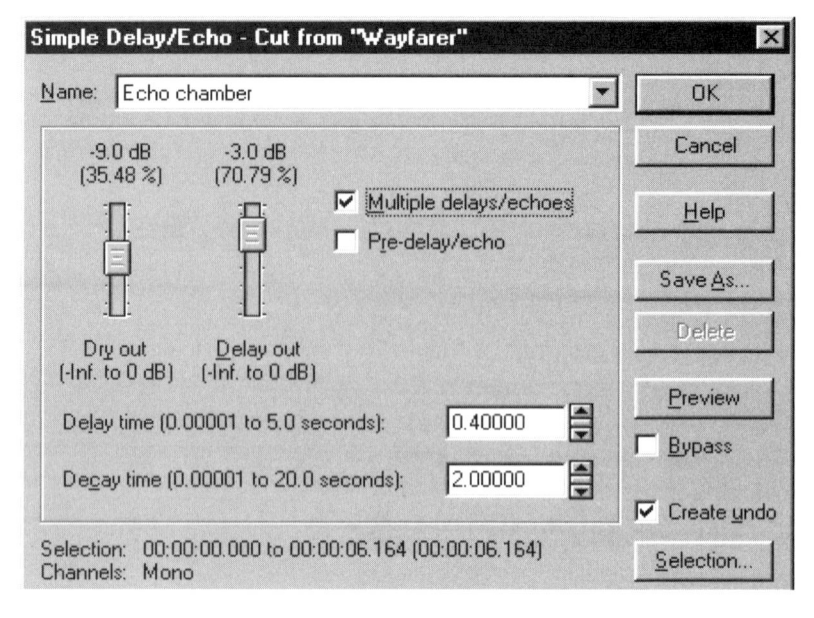

Whereas 'traditional' echoes repeat the sound at regular intervals, each echo gradually decreasing in volume, some echo effects can create multiple echoes each with different settings. These are known as multi-tap delays. Sound Forge's Multi-Tap echo, Figure 11.58, has eight 'taps' which can be given their own delay time and gain setting, making it possible to create some complex – and unnatural – echo effects. It also has modulation rate and depth controls which enable it to add modulation effects to the echoes.

Figure 11.58 Sound Forge's Multi-Tap echo

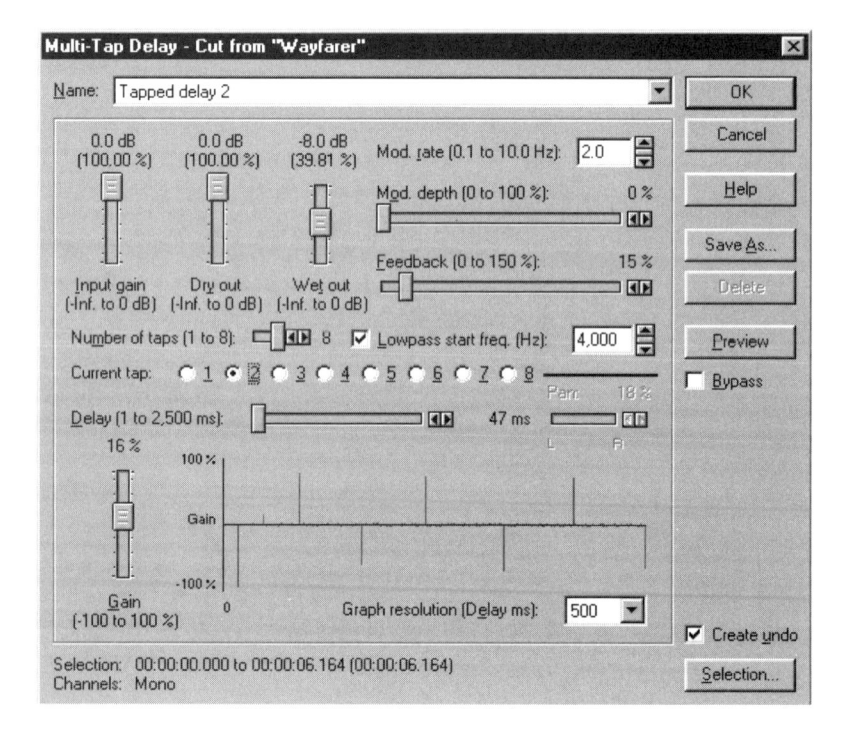

## Creating a stereo mix from a mono file

There's a simple trick you can perform to create a pseudo stereo file from a mono recording. Try it with echo but it can also work with reverb, too. Copy a mono file to both the left and right channels of a stereo file and generate a very short echo on one of the channels. This makes our left and right ears hear the sounds at different times which is how stereo works.

## Chorus

Chorus gives the impression that a sound is being made by more than one instrument. It can be used with almost any sound, including vocals, and is often applied as a 'sweetener'. Traditional chorus is created by delaying a sound, applying a small pitch change and mixing it with the original sound. The idea behind this is that no two musicians play in perfect time and no two instruments are exactly in tune.

WaveLab's Hi-fi Chorus, Figure 11.59, takes this idea a stage further and lets you create up to 100 voices! The Dispersion parameter determines how close to the original pitch the chorus voices are and the Intensity sets their volume.

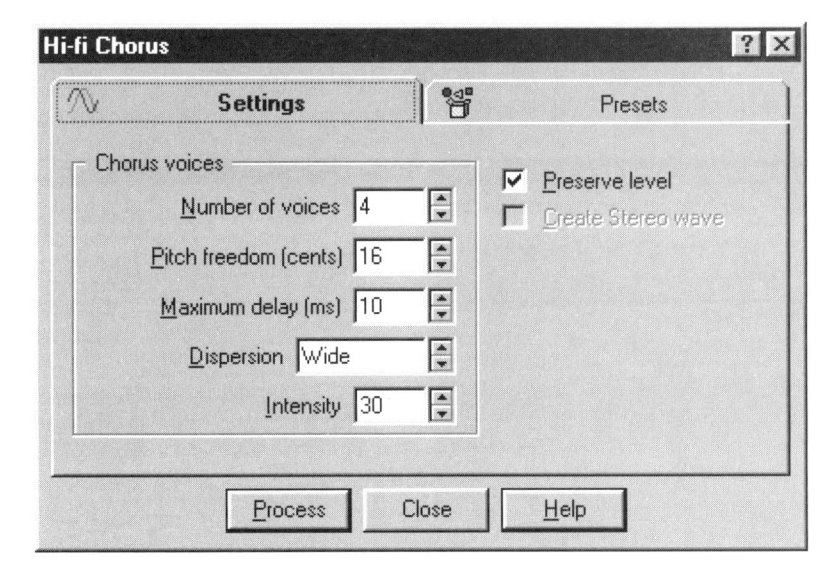

Figure 11.59 WaveLab's Hi-fi Chorus

WaveLab's plug-in chorus, Figure 11.60, can produce a sweeping effect. The width control determines how much the delay time varies with the modulation, and the frequency control sets the speed of the sweep. You can adjust the level of the feedback and pan the chorus signal around the stereo image.

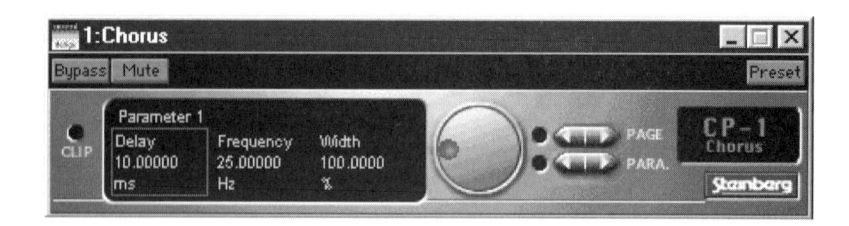

Figure 11.60 WaveLab's plug-in chorus

## Flanging, phasing and wah

According to tradition, flanging was created by playing two tape decks containing the same material simultaneously and slowing one down by pressing a hand on the flange of the tape reel. The result is two signals which drift out of phase with each other creating a sweeping, swooshing, swirling sound.

Phasing is similar but instead of a simple delay, frequencies are phase shifted. Wah wah is a very popular effect with guitarists – it's superb for creating funky effects – and uses a band pass filter which attenuates low and high frequencies over time.

These effects are relatively easy to generate electronically. Flanging, for example, can be produced with a delay effect by changing the delay of a signal and mixing it with the original sound. Effects which produce delay can often perform flanging, including both WaveLab's and Sound Forge's Chorus effects. Sound Forge also has a Flange/Wah-wah effect, Figure 11.61, with frequency and resonance controls.

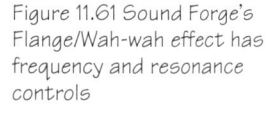

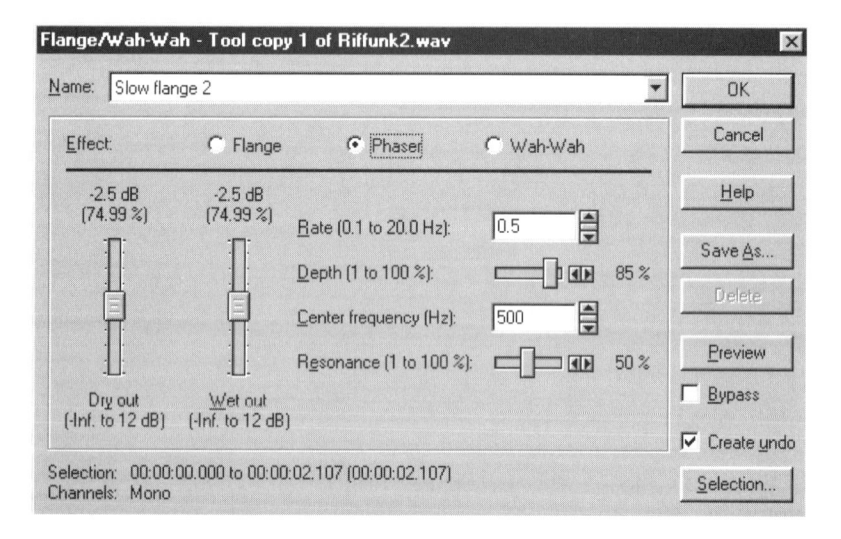

Figure 11.61 Sound Forge's Flange/Wah-wah effect has frequency and resonance controls

## Vibrato

Vibrato is pitch modulation used by singers and many instrumentalists, particularly string players. Musical vibrato is usually a small, even modulation in pitch but you can apply severe degrees of vibrato to a sound to produce unusual effects. Sound Forge's Vibrato, Figure 11.62, can produce both.

Figure 11.62 Sound Forge's Vibrato

> **INFO**
>
> *The tremolo arm on a guitar, much used by The Shadows, is actually incorrectly named because it produces vibrato, not tremolo*

## Tremolo

As vibrato is pitch modulation, tremolo is amplitude modulation. Sound Forge has a dedicated amplitude modulation effect, Figure 11.63, offering sine and square wave modulations. It can also create panning effects by applying modulating to the two channels in a stereo recording so they are out of phase which creates the effect of the sound panning left and right.

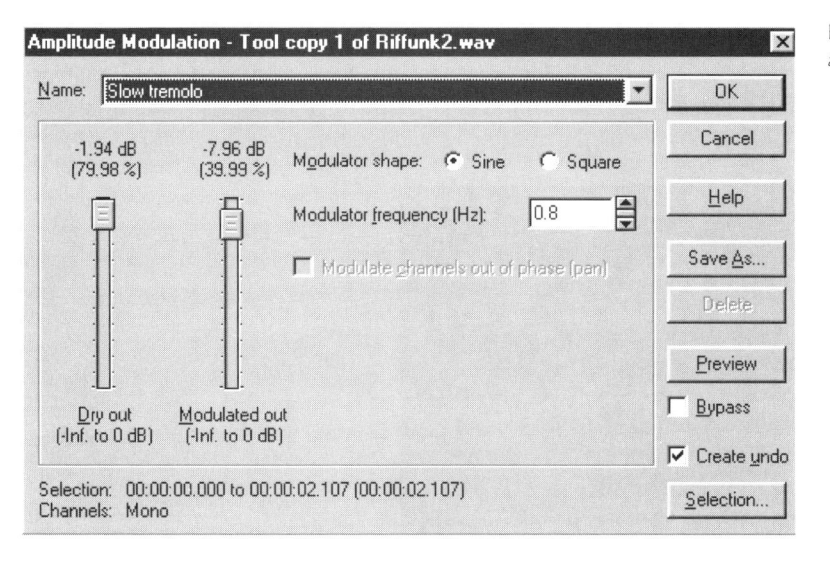

Figure 11.63 Sound Forge's amplitude modulation effect

## Distortion

Several of the effects already discussed can produce a distorted sound – if you're not careful! However, in some circumstances you may actually want a distortion effect. It's often used with guitar to simulate the effect of an amplifier overloading. Sound Forge's Distortion effect, Figure 11.64, lets you set the level above which the signal will be distorted. As distortion inevitably adds volume to a signal, there's also a Clamp control which limits the signal when it passes the threshold level.

Figure 11.64 Sound Forge's Distortion effect lets you set the level above which the signal will be distorted

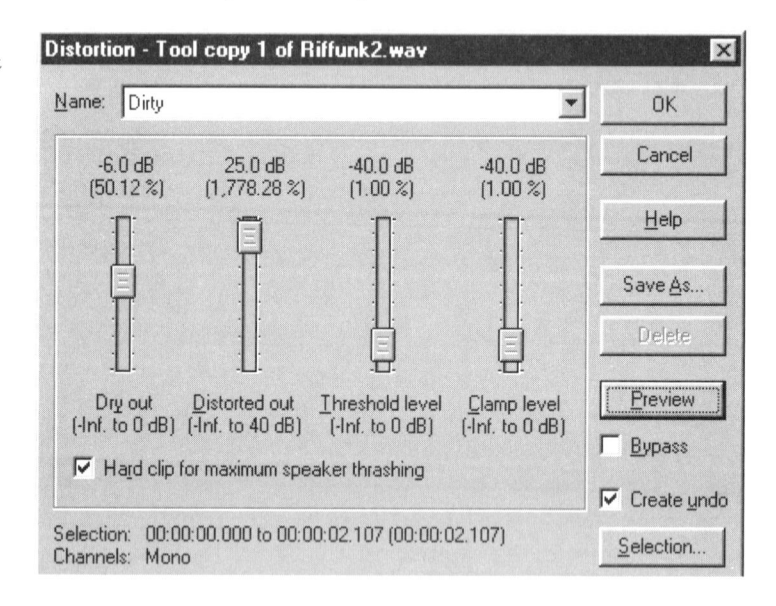

WaveLab's Grungelizer, Figure 11.65, is designed to add all those elements of a bad recording you try to keep out! It includes settings for crackle, noise, distortion, AC hum (ho! ho!), and a filter to reduce the signal's frequency range. The timeline control moves all the knobs simultaneously simulating recording standards from today's clean sound back to 1900 which has all the effects in copious amounts.

Figure 11.65 WaveLab's Grungelizer

## Noise reduction and other correctional facilities

However much care you take in making a recording, it's still possible for some undesirable elements to creep into it somewhere along the line. It could happen that a problem goes unnoticed until it's too late to correct it or the original material was not perfect – many of the effects and processes described in this section were designed specifically for cleaning up vinyl recordings.

There are several possible problems but the most common ones are noise in its various insidious forms, pops, clicks and spikes. Most noise reduction systems work by taking a noise print of the noise you want to remove. The routine then tries to remove the material in the noise print from the source material. The noise print needs to be a section of the recording where there is no other signal. It works best with continuous noise such as hums, fans and hiss rather than intermittent noise such as passing traffic.

The effectiveness of the process depends, as you would expect, on the source material and on the type of noise you're trying to remove. In some cases, it's not possible to remove the noise completely without affecting the source material, but quite often the routine will do a surprisingly good job. You need to be aware that if the level of the noise is very high the process could add artefacts to the material, often characterised by a metallic sound.

Samplitude's noise reduction function, Figure 11.66, shows a spectrum of the noise and above it, the spectrum of the corrected signal. It has several presets and if none of them is exactly what you need they provide a good starting point for setting your own parameters. It also has a set of controls to reduce artefacts.

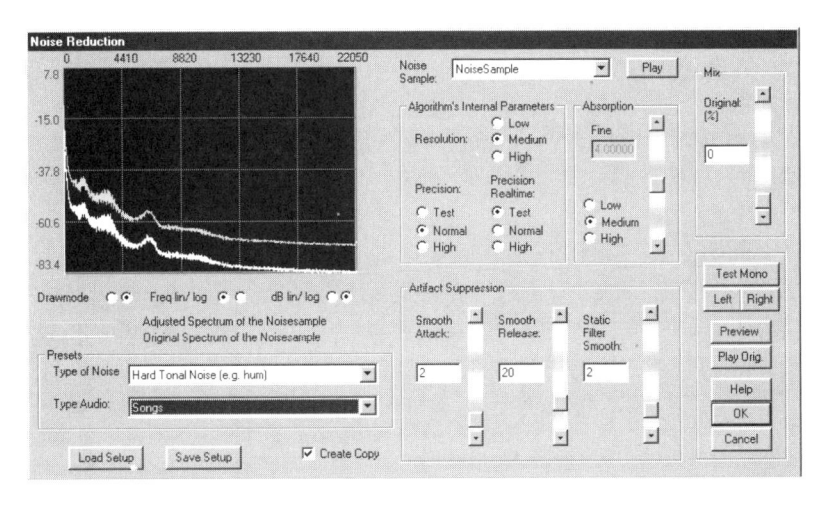

Figure 11.66 Samplitude's noise reduction function shows a spectrum of the noise and above it the spectrum of the corrected signal

Sound Forge's Noise Reduction plug-in, Figure 11.67, contains three tools – Noise Reduction, Click Removal and Vinyl Restoration, each of which functions independently.

The noise reduction tool uses a noise print which it shows on a graph.

Figure 11.67 Sound Forge's Noise Reduction plug-in contains Noise Reduction, Click Removal and Vinyl Restoration

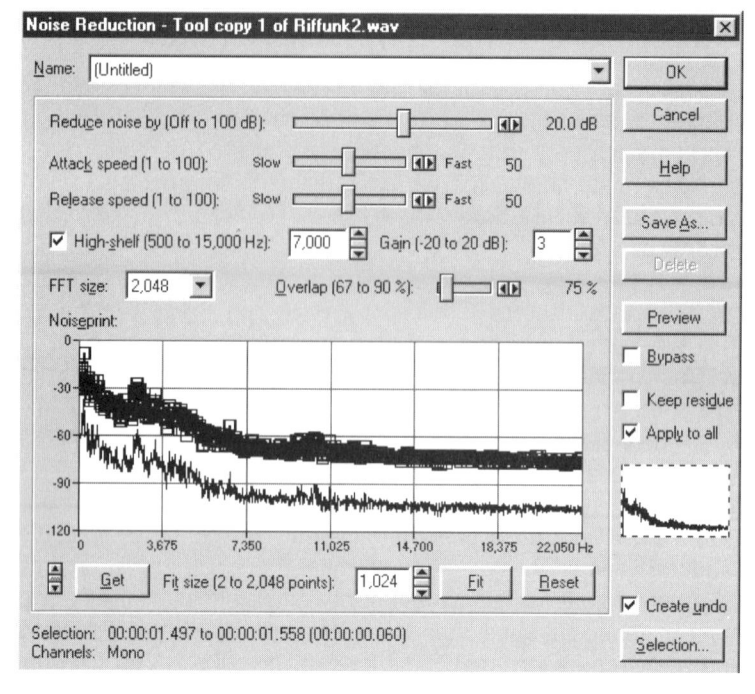

Above it are a number of envelope points which define the level of the frequencies which will be removed. The program sets these a little way above the noise print frequencies helped by a Best Fit function. There can be up to 2048 envelope points so you can zoom in on an area to create a better fit around a frequency spike, for example, by dragging the enve-

Figure 11.68 Close-up of the noise print with the envelope nodes above it

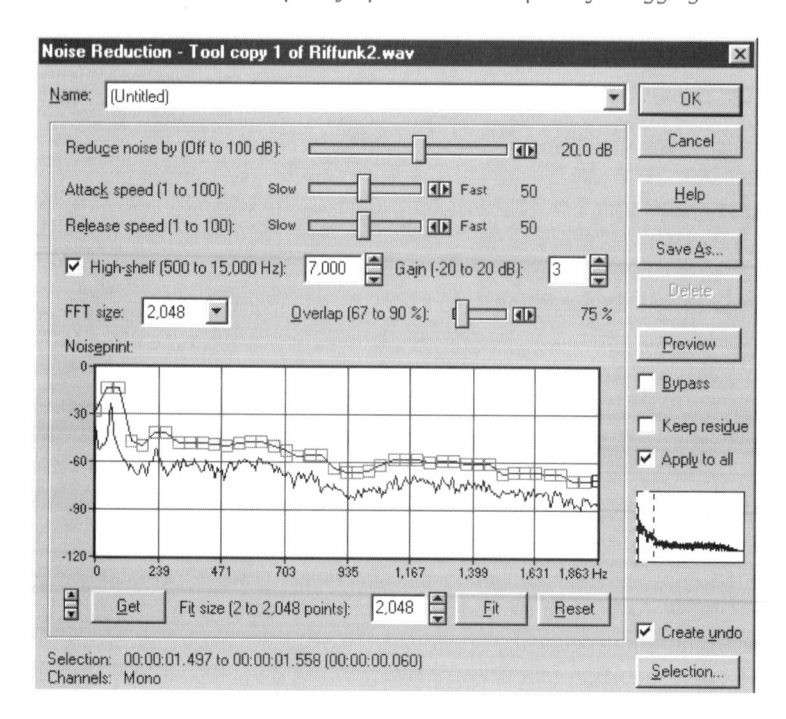

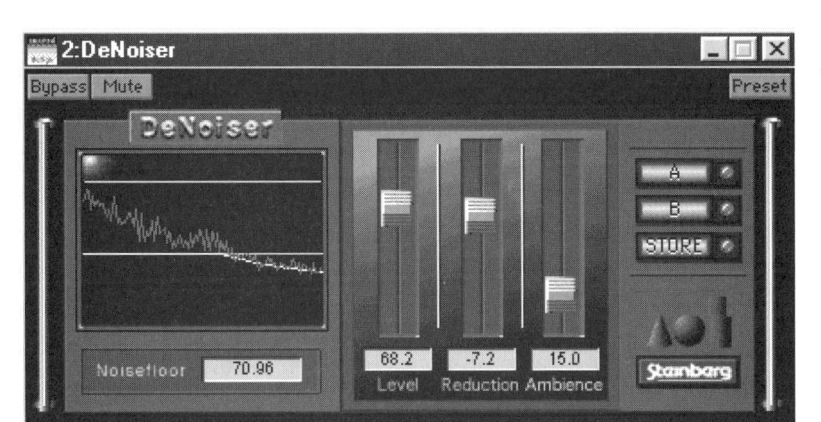

Figure 11.69 WaveLab's DeNoiser

lope points closer to the noise display. Figure 11.68 shows a close-up of the noise print with the envelope nodes above it.

WaveLab's DeNoiser, Figure 11.69, doesn't use a noise print. It's primarily designed to remove broadband noise and it uses an adaptive process whereby noise changing in either character or level is automatically reduced.

WaveLab's DeClicker, Figure 11.70, has a threshold control to determine how loud the clicks are before they're detected. You can set the quality of the restoration process. Use low quality when experimenting with the effect in real-time on a slow machine. DePlop is a high pass filter which works on signals below 150Hz which should help minimise 'plop' noises.

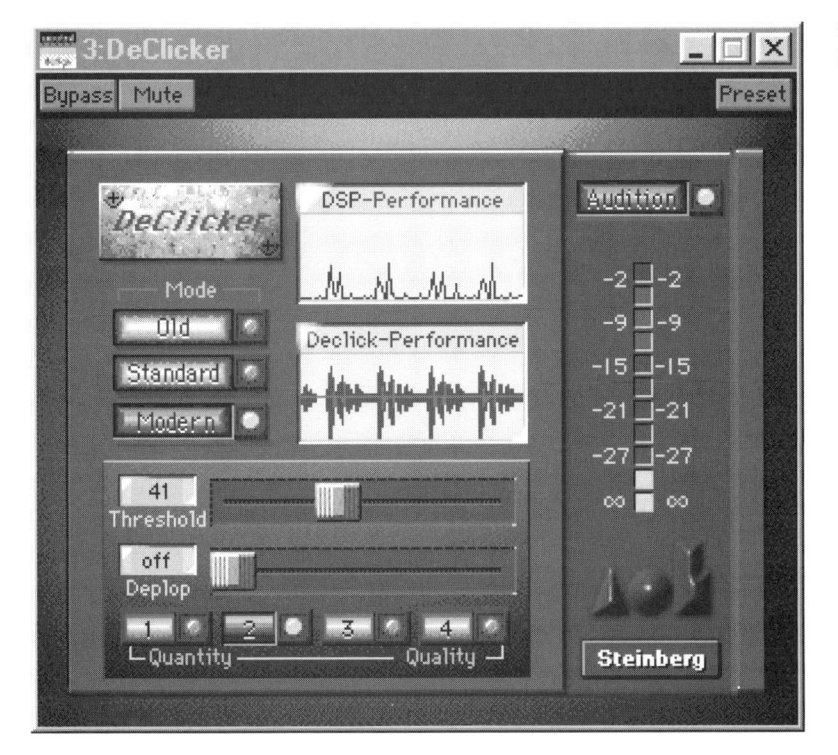

Figure 11.70 WaveLab's DeClicker

It also has three mode settings – antique, suitable for recordings with limited high frequency content; modern, suitable for contemporary recordings with a wide frequency range; and standard which is suitable for a range of material. As well as removing clicks, the program can also help reduce the hardness created by clipped signals.

Sound Forge's Click Removal function is designed to remove the sort of clicks you're likely to find in a vinyl recording. Select a region in a file and the routine will locate and fix the clicks automatically although you can also do searches and fixes manually. It has four options to replace clicks – Replace replaces it with other sound data; Interpolate removes it and interpolates the data either side; you can redraw the data with a pencil tool; and in a stereo recording you can replace a click with the other channel's audio.

The Vinyl Restoration function, Figure 11.71, combines most of the noise reduction and click removal functions into one window. Filtering detects and removes fast transients produce by dirt and scratches, and noise reduction reduces the surface noise.

Logic Audio's Silencer, Figure 11.72, combines noise reduction and spike reduction which can be used separately or together. The Noise Reduction section only has one control and that determines the intensity of the effect. The Spike Reduction has a sensitivity setting which controls how large the spikes have to be before they are recognised, and a Method

Figure 11.71 Sound Forge's Vinyl Restoration function

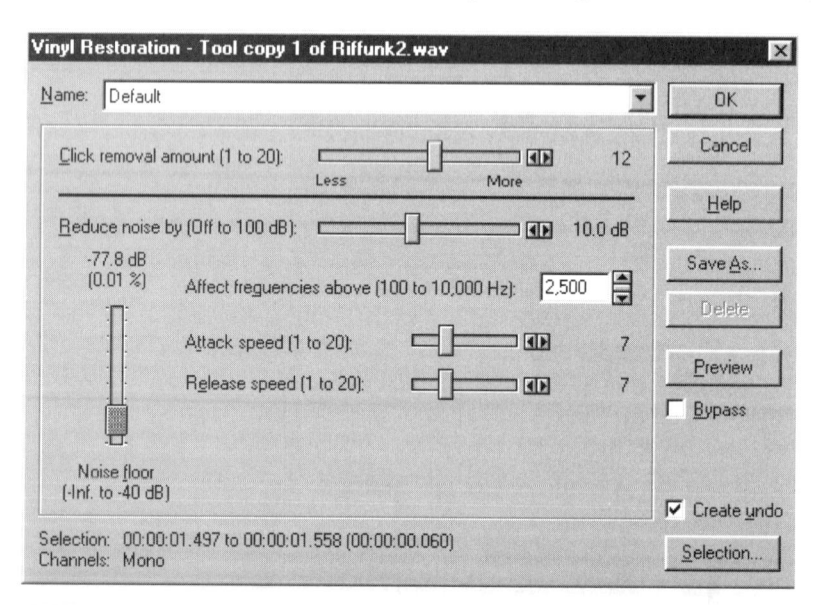

Figure 11.72 Logic Audio's Silencer combines noise reduction and spike reduction

control which determines how aggressively the function goes about its business. The lower the setting the more gentle the routine is with spikes. The Re-build setting completely replaces unusable material with plausible synthetic signals.

Samplitude's Declipping process, Figure 11.73, tries to remove the distortion produced by clipping. It may require a little experimentation to get the settings right, but it's worth trying if you have a clipped file.

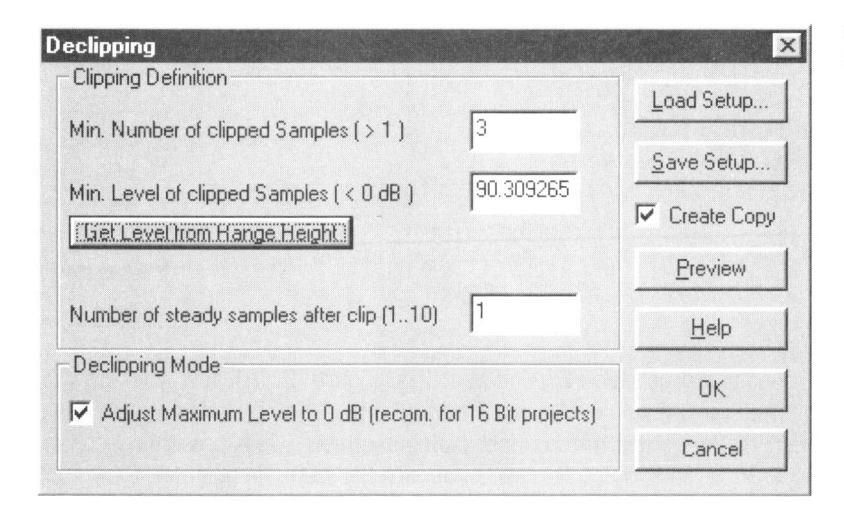

Figure 11.73 Samplitude's Declipping process

## Stereo expansion

Relatively new to the market is a range of effects which let you mess around with the stereo image. The simplest is probably a panning effect such as WaveLab's Auto Panner, Figure 11.74, which moves a signal around in the stereo field. You can adjust the width of the field, the speed of the movement and select the waveform which controls the panning.

With only one control, WaveLab's Stereo Expander, Figure 11.75, is easy to use. It can enlarge or reduce the stereo field of a signal and it can create a stereo signal from a mono one.

Figure 11.74 WaveLab's Auto Panner

Figure 11.75 WaveLab's Stereo Expander

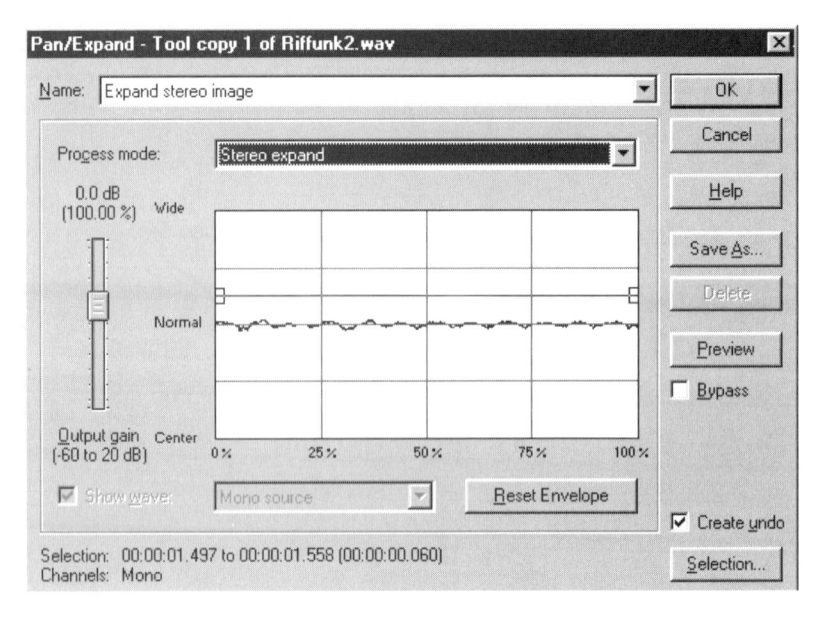

Figure 11.76 Sound Forge's Pan/Expand function

> **INFO**
>
> MS or Mid Side recording is a two-microphone technique where one mic faces the source and the other points 90 degrees away from it. It usually has to be converted into a standard left/right (sometimes called AB) track to play correctly on most systems.

Sound Forge's Pan/Expand function, Figure 11.76, lets you draw a pan, stereo image or MS mix envelope into a graphic window. You can perform left and right channel panning effects while preserving stereo separation, and you can expand or reduce the stereo image

Waves' Stereo Imager plug-in, Figure 11.77, works with stereo files and allows you to move the whole stereo image left or right while maintaining the balance of the mix. You can adjust the relative levels of the left and right channels while keeping the central sounds in the middle of the image, and you can increase and decrease the stereo width. You can even move them beyond the speakers!

Stereo appears narrower when we listen to lower frequencies so there's a control to increase the stereo width at lower frequencies. The central display provides a very graphic illustration of what the stereo image is doing which helps make adjustments easy.

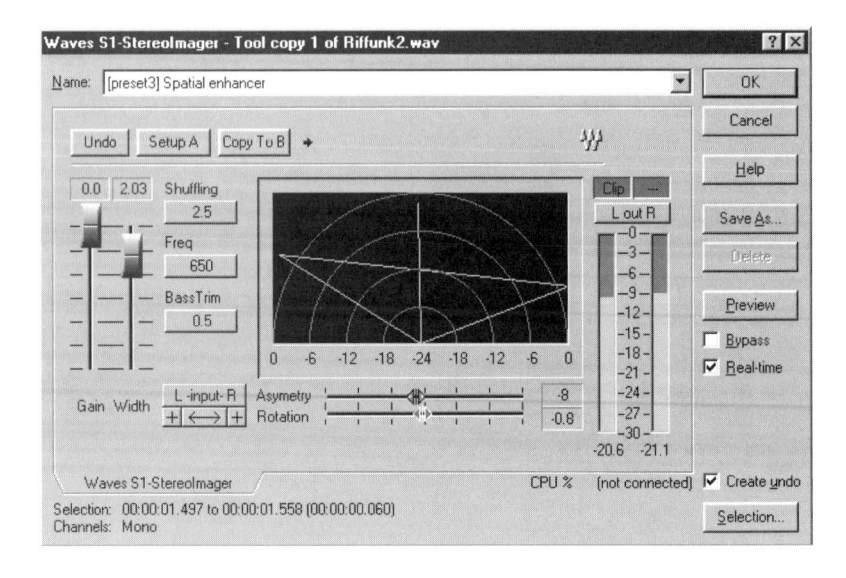

Figure 11.77 Waves' Stereo Imager plug-in

## Spectrum analysis and FFT

A short lesson in synthesis. Most early synthesisers used a form of subtractive synthesis which simply involved starting with a waveform such as a square wave or triangle wave and removing bits of it with a filter. The opposite of this is additive synthesis (sometimes called resynthesis) which involves constructing sounds by adding together waveforms of different frequencies and amplitudes. Any sound can, theoretically, be generated by additive synthesis and all sounds can be broken down into their individual partials which is essentially a list of sine waves.

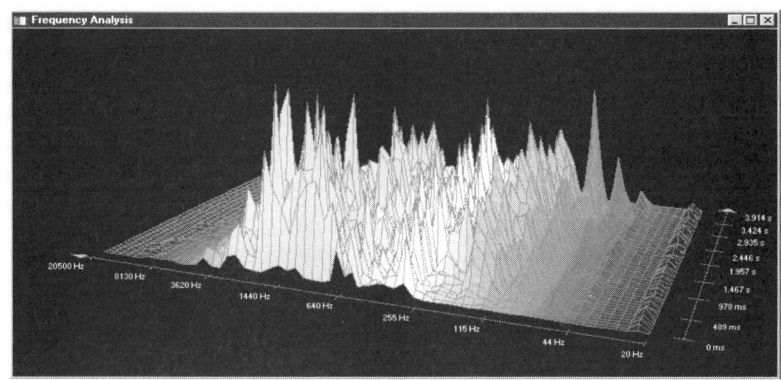

Figure 11.78 An FFT analysis of a vocal passage

Spectrum analysis is the process of analysing and displaying the individual components of a sound – an ideal task for a computer. FFT – Fast Fourier Transform is a method of doing this and produces the famous 'mountains' display. The example in Figure 11.78 was produced by WaveLab and it's an analysis of a vocal passage. The X axis is hertz and the Y axis is time so you can see how the frequencies change over time.

Sound Forge's Spectrum Analyser plug-in can display the analysis in a 'mountain' format, Figure 11.79, or as a sonogram, Figure 11.80, where

**INFO**

*Baron Jean Baptiste Joseph Fourier (1768-1830) developed the formula (a rather complex one) for analysing the frequency components of a sound and lent his name to the process.*

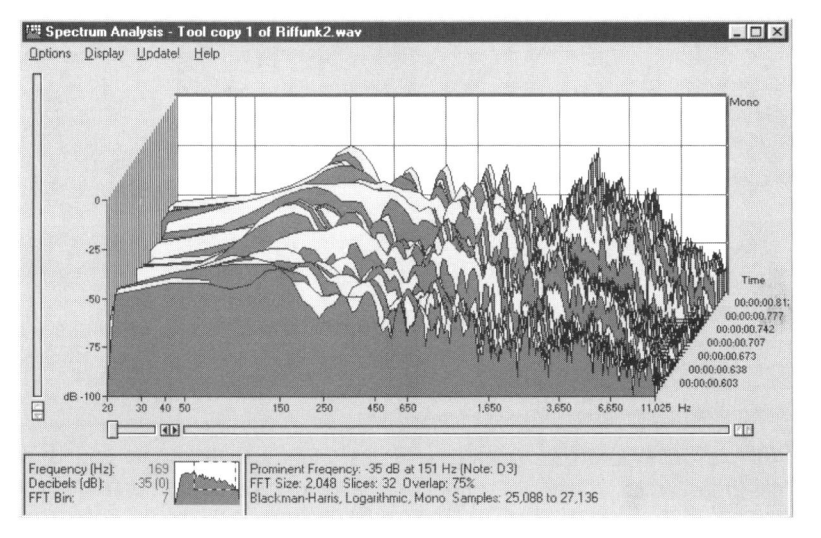

Figure 11.79 Sound Forge's Spectrum Analyser

Figure 11.80 A Sonogram display in Sound Forge

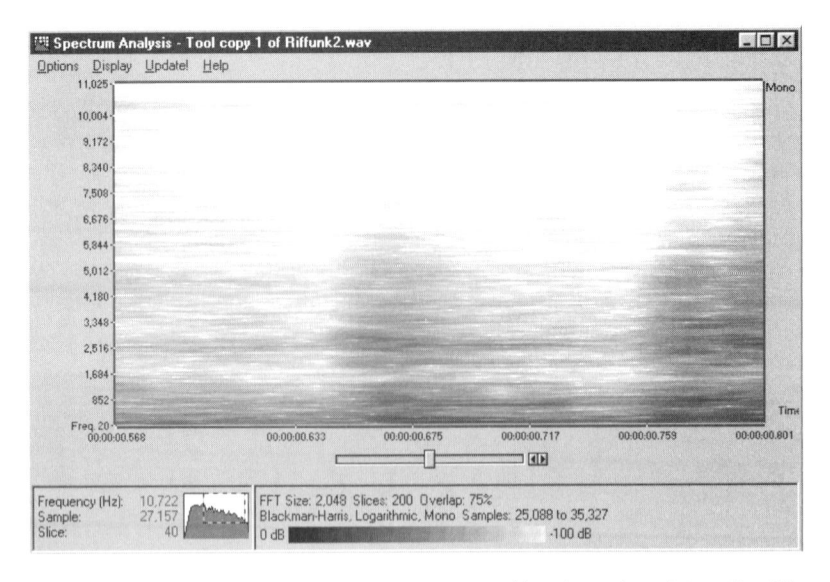

the amplitude of each frequency is represented by the colour intensity. It's useful for identifying distinctive spectral patterns created by sounds such as speech and certain musical instruments. The system provides a lot of information and is a good tool for anyone requiring detailed information about the frequency content of a recording.

Samplitude's Draw Filter/Spectrum, Figure 11.81, is also designed for serious work. It combines an FFT analyser and FFT filter, allowing you to draw a new frequency response curve onto the graph and apply it to the audio. It also allows you to transfer the frequency response of one sample to another.

Figure 11.81 Samplitude's Draw Filter/Spectrum

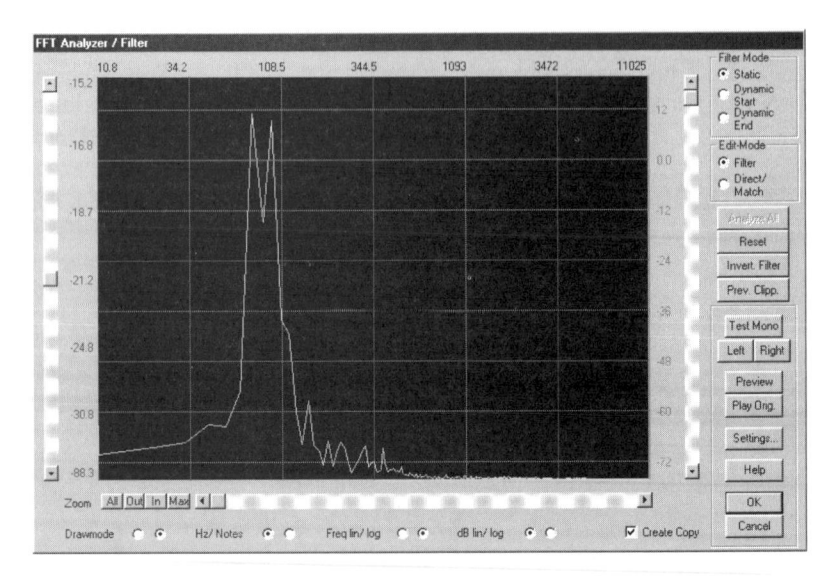

tripleDAT's Spectrum Analyser, Figure 11.82, analyses the sound in real-time and produces a continually changing display of the frequency content of the sound. You can specify the number of bands you want to

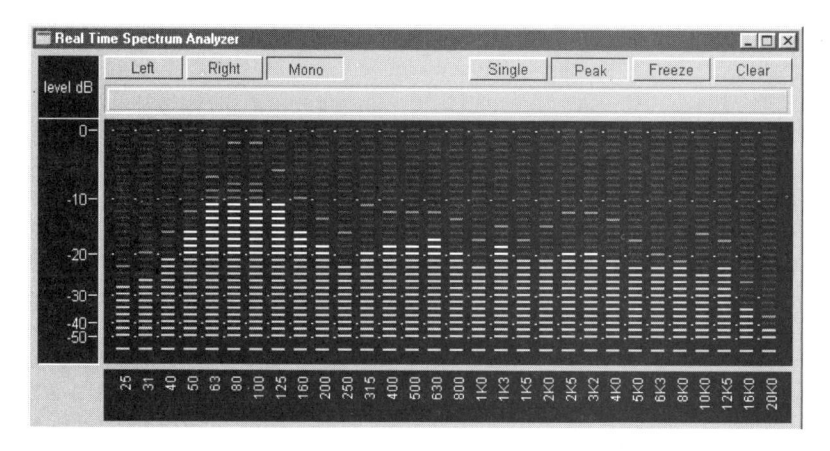

Figure 11.82 tripleDAT's Spectrum Analyser

see (you may have to reduce this on a slow computer) and you can home in on any band with an accuracy of 1Hz.

## Sample conversion

Whenever you process digital audio you lower the quality of the recording. It's usually not much, rarely noticeable in fact, and most people would be unaware of any deterioration. It's nowhere near as bad as copying tape tracks, for example, but it's something to be aware of if you're planning on running a sample through umpteen effects. The deterioration depends on exactly what you do to it.

However, if you have to change the sample rate or resolution to create 8-bit files for multimedia use, for example, or if you're working with 20-bit audio and have to reduce it to 16-bit for CD mastering, then the quality of such reductions is much more likely to be noticed. Various processes have been developed to minimise the problems caused by processing and sample conversion, and many digital audio programs use one or two of these, although sometimes they tend to work in the background rather than offering a set of parameters you can adjust.

### Truncation, rounding and dithering

So what exactly is the problem in converting a 16-bit file into an 8-bit file? Quite simply, there are not enough values in an 8-bit system (which can only store 256 different values) to store the 65536 values used by a 16-bit system. Bearing in mind that digital values must be a whole number – that is, there are no fractions – how can we accurately represent the contents of a 16-bit value in 8 bits?

Let's consider a 16-bit number as being constructed from two sets of 8-bit numbers. Translated into decimal, the digits in a 16-bit number have the following values:

32768 16384 8192 4096 2048 1024 512 256 128 64 32 16 8 4 2 1

You can see that the most important digits are those on the left as they contribute the most 'value' to the number. If we were to use only the eight left-most numbers, they would give us a rough approximation of the waveform. So one way to do the conversion is simply to cut off the lower eight bits. This is known as truncation.

However, this discards important information. If the value of the discarded digits is over 128 (more than half the possible value of an 8-bit digit), it would make sense to round the converted number up by one. This conversion method is called rounding.

Then there's dithering. This involves adding noise to the signal in order to compensate for quantisation errors (for more information about quantisation noise, see Chapter 3). Add noise, after everything you've done to produce a noise-free recording! Let's see how it works.

Say you've recorded some music which contains quiet passages. The levels are low so they don't need all 16 bits for storage. If these bits are discarded during truncation or rounding, a lot of the information will be lost. However, if we add a small amount of noise, effectively increasing the number of bits the signal uses for storage, and then we truncate the data, we lose far less information. A small amount of noise is preferable to the distortion which would otherwise result.

When some systems process a recording with effects, they increase the bits to 20 or 24, perform the processing and then convert the result back to 16 bits. They probably use a dithering system on the conversion to retain the maximum amount of important information.

**Resampling**

Most software has an option to convert the sample rate or change the sample resolution. This is easily done on a purely mathematical basis, but for quality results you ought to look for routines which take into account the losses which occur during these processes.

Logic Audio has a simple sample rate converter, Figure 11.83, and Samplitude has a similar one-parameter option. Sound Forge has an 8-bit converter, Figure 11.84, with truncate, round and dither options, and a Resample function, Figure 11.85, with an anti-alias filter. It also has several conversion options in its Save As ... dialog, Figure 11.86.

WaveLab also has a sample rate conversion function, Figure 11.87, and a ReSampler, Figure 11.88, which performs a similar function but in real-time. The Waves plug-ins use a proprietary dither system called IDR (Increased Digital Resolution). The recording is converted to 24-bit, processed, and then converted back to 16-bit. The optimum results are

Figure 11.83 Logic Audio's simple sample rate converter

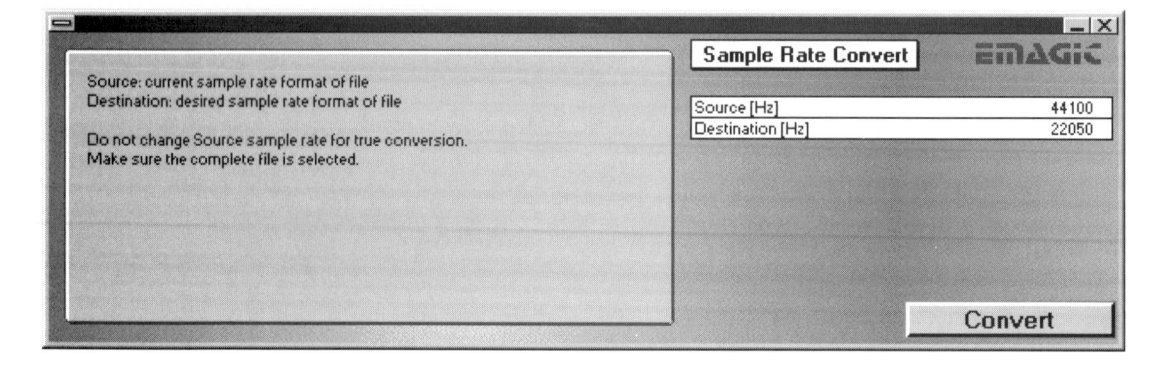

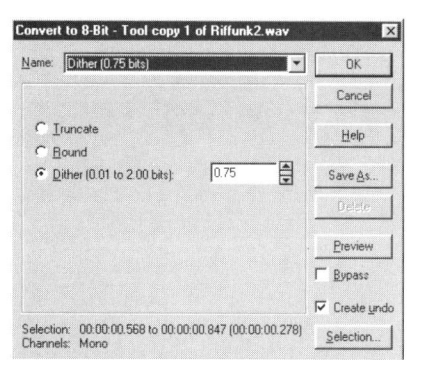

Figure 11.84 Sound Forge's 8-bit converter

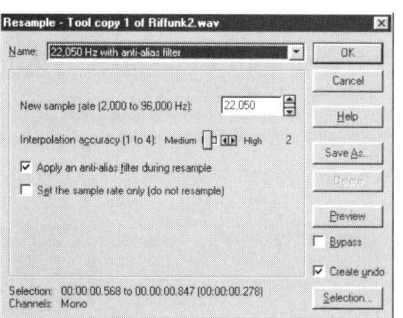

Figure 11.85 Sound Forge's resample function

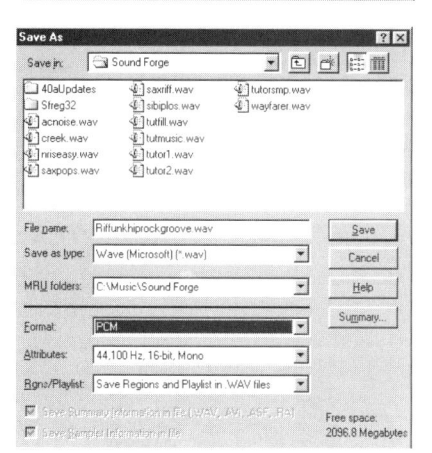

Figure 11.86 Several conversion options are available in Sound Forge's Save As ... dialog

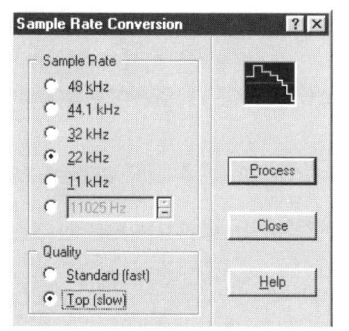

Figure 11.87 The sample rate conversion function in WaveLab

Figure 11.88 The Resampler in WaveLab

achieved with Waves' L1 Ultramaximiser, which we've already mentioned in this chapter and in Chapter 8. It offers two types of dither and four noise shaping options and produces excellent results.

## Samplers and foreign file formats

Most PC digital audio software uses the Wave format which has a .WAV extension. In fact, it is so universal among digital audio software that most musicians will rarely need to use any other format. However, if you are collaborating with other musicians, particularly those using a different computer, you may need to use files in other formats.

Many programs support a few alternative file formats but if you need to read a lot of different formats it's worth considering a dedicated program such as KCCM's ReSample Professional, which was mentioned in Chapter 8.

Sound Forge's Sampler Tool, Figure 11.89, supports both the MIDI Sample Dump Standard and the SCSI MIDI Device Interface. With a few clicks you can configure it to support a range of samplers and it has several options for fine tuning various parameters.

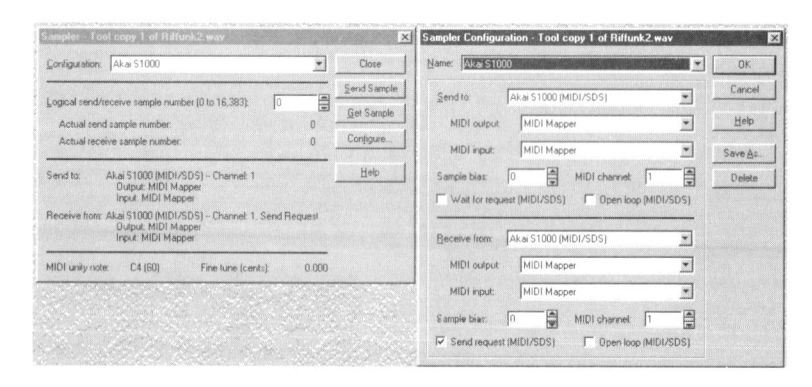

Figure 11.89 Sound Forge's Sampler Tool

## Audio and MIDI cross-fertilisation

Some software, particularly sequencers which also support digital audio, include routines which cross over the MIDI/digital audio divide.

Logic Audio has three audio-to-MIDI functions, Figure 11.90. It can convert audio data to notation. This sounds rather clever but before you start thinking you can play Beethoven's 6th in one end and get a score out the other, it really needs a clean monophonic signal. If it's not clean or it's

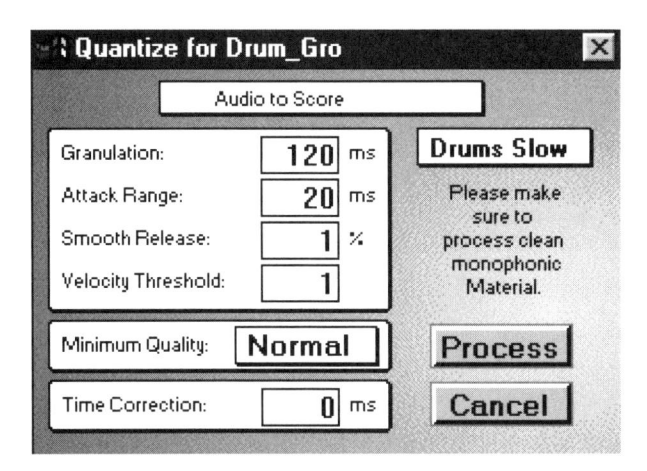

Figure 11.90 Logic Audio's Audio to score function converts a monophonic audio line into notation

not monophonic the interpretation will suffer accordingly. However, if you're more a flautist or guitarist than a keyboard player, you could use this function to record MIDI lines in real time.

## Summing up

This is one of the longest chapters in the book yet there are still effects and processes we haven't included and we haven't gone into enormous depth about any of the functions. To do so would take another book.

What haven't we included? What about Sound Forge's Grapper/Snipper which cuts chunks from the sample or inserts silence at regular intervals? Or the program's Synthesiser which can produce a simple waveform of a given shape, pitch and length and generate FM sounds. It even has a function for generating the dial tones used by telephones.

Then there's Samplitude's Convolution effect which applies certain aspects of one sample to that of another. Common overtones may be amplified while different ones may be removed. It can create reverb, delay, filter and morph effects between two samples.

MIDI opened the door to the sophisticated editing and processing of music data. Having audio in an accessible digital format means that it can be processed in a whole manner of ways. We already have software to perform all the major stock effects – and a few more besides. As developers get into gear we will start to see even more amazing digital audio processing functions appear.

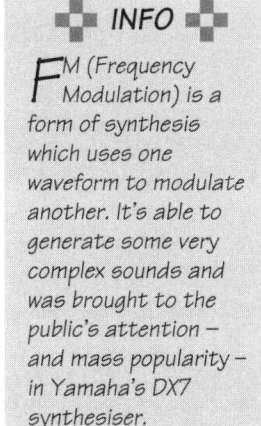

### INFO

FM (Frequency Modulation) is a form of synthesis which uses one waveform to modulate another. It's able to generate some very complex sounds and was brought to the public's attention – and mass popularity – in Yamaha's DX7 synthesiser.

# 12

## CD ROMs

> **INFO**
>
> A CD can typically store about 650Mb of data or 74 minutes of audio. Certain formats can increase the data storage capacity to over 700Mb but these are usually done with commercial systems. When writing your own CDs you shouldn't try to fit more than about 630Mb onto a disk.

For musicians and computer users, CDs are one of the best things ever invented. They are far cheaper to produce than cassettes, yet record companies charge twice as much for them. Lucky old record companies, eh?

They can store wads of audio data at 'CD quality', which makes them ideal for distributing sound samples. They can also store wads of computer data which makes them ideal for distributing music software and Wave data.

But as well as a medium for large companies to distribute their software, CDs now allow individuals to distribute their music thanks to affordable CD-R – Recordable CD. And if you have a CD-R drive you can also backup your audio files and computer data onto CD – it's the cheapest backup medium developed so far.

### Anatomy of a CD drive

You don't really need to know exactly how a CD ROM drive works in order to use it but, as ever, a little background knowledge about the gear you're using won't go amiss. We'll skip through this bit as quickly as possible but keep your eyes open for a few techy bits which may come in handy later on.

Basically, audio CD and CD ROM drives work in the same way. They use a low-power laser to read pits written into the CD which can be either audio or computer data. The CD itself consists of a reflective layer above which is the recording layer. The laser shines onto the disk and measures the reflected light. Pits reflect less light than non-pit areas and this is how the data is interpreted.

### CD ROM drive speeds

> **INFO**
>
> A CD-R disk is currently about ten times as expensive as a commercial CD.

Typically, a modern CD ROM drive will be a 12-speed, 16-speed or 24-speed drive. However, don't be mislead by the hype because there's more to fast data transfer than spin speed. The cache or buffer in a drive has an impact on performance although its usefulness depends on what sort of data the drive is reading.

The speed factor in a drive's description describes how fast it spins in relation to a, er, single-speed drive which transfers data at around

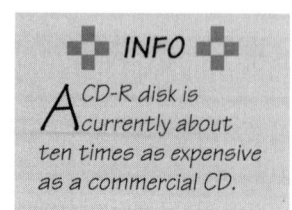

150Kb/sec. Compare this with the DTR of a modern hard disk which is measured in Mb/sec and you'll see how slow CD ROM drives are!

However single-speed drives are virtually obsolete now, along with double-speed drives. The slowest CD ROM drives commonly available commercially are probably 8-speed. The price difference between drives is getting smaller and even new 24-speed drives were launched at a little over £100.

You may think it's hardly worthwhile trying to save a few bob by going for a slower drive. It's always nice to have the latest, fastest gear but if you do want to save money, you don't need the latest, fastest drive to install software or play multimedia files.

To take an example, Teac's 24-speed CD-524E, while spinning at 24 times the speed of a single-speed drive, only claims a data transfer rate of 19.3 times – around 2.9Mb/sec. Only! That's pretty good going for a CD! But you can see that the spin speed does not automatically give you that-many times the DTR.

At this point it's worth re-affirming why we use CDs. It's nice to have a zippy drive with a fast data transfer rate, but CDs are not used in the same way as a hard disk. CDs are used for storage, for backing up computer data and, of course, you can play audio CDs. It's unlikely that you'd be using a CD for constant data access like a hard disk, so a moderately fast drive will do the job just fine.

## CLV and CAV

Drives operate in one of two modes. CLV (constant linear velocity) is the most common mode. It simply means that the motor spinning the CD varies the speed of rotation so the data passes under the read head at a constant speed so the data is transferred at a constant rate. The disk has to spin more quickly, therefore, when the head is reading the inner tracks.

The other mode is CAV (constant angular velocity) which spins the disk at a constant speed which improves the data transfer speed on disks which have been formatted with CAV in mind. These include LaserDiscs. Most CDs, however, use the CLV method so the benefits of CAV are not commonly available. Some CD ROM drives use a mixed CLV/CAV mode which uses CAV for the first section of the disk and then switches to CLV when it would benefit from a speed increase. However, the performance gains are not enormous.

Because CAV mode runs at a constant speed, it uses a little less power than CLV modes but not enough to lose sleep over. It could be useful if you have a portable PC, though. ATAPI drives, however, do use considerably more computing power than SCSI drives, and that's worth bearing in mind. At the moment, however, if you want to copy digital audio directly from an audio CD and put it on your hard disk, or if you want to write your own CDs, you probably need a SCSI drive.

## CD-R

> **INFO**
>
> If you see a gold CD it has probably been created with a CD-R. Silver CDs are commercially duplicated. The colour difference is due to the reflective surface. CD-R disks use gold while commercial disks use aluminium.

A CD-R drive has the same reading capabilities as a standard CD ROM drive but it also has a more powerful laser which burns pits into the CD so you can write or burn your own. This laser is heavier than the read laser which means that the head cannot whiz about as quickly, so CD-R drives tend to be slower than read-only drives.

Currently, CD-R drives are specified with two speeds – the read speed and the write speed. You may see 2x/2x, 2x/4x, 4x/4x or 4x/6x. Whichever is the slowest, that'll be the speed at which it writes. CD-R is still a relatively young technology – at least it was really only in the last half of 1996 that CD-R drives became affordable – so we should see some performance improvements here.

## CD formats

> **INFO**
>
> The Red Book standard was developed by Philips and Sony in 1980 and published in a red binder – hence the name.

As the CD developed as a medium, so various formats were created to allow the CD to store different types of data. This has grown into a tangle of standards commonly known by Colour Book labels, developed mainly by Philips and Sony. The most well-known is the Red Book which defines standard audio CDs. Er, and audio CDs which can store graphics...

We do our best to summarise the standards here – and bear in mind that this is a précis'd and concise rendition. Don't worry if some of the cross-overs appear confusing – most of the industry gets confused about them, too!

### CD standards

| Book | Format | Description |
| --- | --- | --- |
| Red | CD-DA | CD Digital Audio. Sound is recorded at 44.1kHz and 16-bit resolution. It can contain up to 99 tracks. It also supports the CD+G format which has the ability to store graphics. |
| Yellow | CD ROM | Yellow Book Mode 1 is a general standard for storing computer data on CDs. Mode 2 has added features for using multimedia on CD ROM. It has less error correction and can store more data. It has never been used in its standard form but in extended forms such as CD ROM XA. |
| Yellow | CD ROM XA | Stands for eXtended Architecture, an extension of the Yellow Book standard designed to add better audio and video capabilities (taken from the CD-I standard). It is also the physical format of Photo CD. |
| Blue | CD Extra | Formerly known as CD Plus or Enhanced CD, this combines CD-DA data and CD ROM data. The CD-DA is in the first section of the disk followed by the computer data which conforms to the Orange Book standard. |
| Green | CD-I | CD Interactive, a derivative of Yellow Book Mode 2 designed to allow interactive multimedia applications. |
| Orange | CD-R | The standard for CD-MO (Magneto Optical) and CD-WO (Write Once) systems – essentially the format for Recordable CDs. Includes multisession disks such as Photo CD. |

*CD standards (cont)*

| Book | Format | Description |
|---|---|---|
| White | CD-I Bridge (Video and Photo CD) | A way of recording CD-I information on a CD ROM XA disk. Photo CD is a hybrid specification based on CD ROM XA and the Orange Book. Video CD is designed to support full motion video compressed using the MPEG 1 standard. |
| | Mixed Mode | A mixture of data types on one CD, now usually CD-DA and CD ROM XA. |

The main formats of interest to musicians and computer users are Red Book, Orange Book and mixed mode CDs. The good news is, most CD-R software has options which tell you exactly what you'll be recording so you should not have to worry too much about Books and obscure CD formats.

There are, however, a few more bits of information we need to digest before we start...

## Multisession

One of the heavily promoted advantages of the new CD technology was Photo CDs – the ability to take your photos along to a Photo CD dealer who would put them on a CD which you could look at on your computer. One of the facets of Photo CD is the ability to take the one CD along to the dealer several times and get several sets of photos put on it. In other words, the data could be written to the CD in several sessions. Although storing your snaps on CD hasn't become the boom industry it was predicted it would be, it is popular in commercial areas.

Multisession capability is obviously very useful and it's a feature which must be built into a CD ROM drive if it is to be able to read disks which were written in several sessions. Non-multisession drives will only be able to read the first set of data. Fortunately, most modern CD drives are multisession compatible – but do check, just in case.

## ISO 9660

In order to put data onto a CD, the system needs a filing structure of some sort. This is ISO 9660. It's different from the file system used by other operating systems such as Windows, DOS or the Apple Macintosh, and in order for these systems to read a CD ROM they need an extra file, driver or extension which lets them understand the format. PCs use a file called MSCDEX.EXE and if you have a CD ROM drive, you'll find this somewhere on your hard disk.

A useful consequence of this is that an ISO 9660 CD ROM can be read by any computer which supports the format.

You may also hear the format referred to as High Sierra. ISO 9660 was developed from the High Sierra standard and to all intents and purposes, when someone refers to High Sierra they usually mean ISO 9660. High Sierra is virtually obsolete as a separate standard.

**TECHY BIT**

*Writing a multisession disk has an overhead as the system has to save certain information on the disk so the drive can recognise the sessions and read the data from it. The first session uses an additional 22Mb for this, subsequent sessions use about 13Mb. So, multisession is fine if you're only going to write a few sessions but you'll lose a lot of space if you intend to write lots of sessions.*

> **INFO**
>
> A group of manufacturers met at High Sierra to discuss a format for CD ROM and the format was named after the meeting place – a tough job but someone had to do it.

The Macintosh uses a filing system called HFS (Hierarchical File System) and this can also be used for CD ROMs. Some developers put both HFS and ISO 9660 partitions on the same disk so they can easily be read by both Macs and PCs.

## CD audio-to-disk transfer

If you use sample CDs, one of the nice things you can do with a CD ROM drive is transfer audio data directly from the CD to your hard disk. You can do this in several ways and we'll look at the traditional method first.

This simply involves playing the audio through the CD ROM drive's audio Out, plugging it into the sound card's In and recording it. Before digital recording became popular, samples on CD were recorded by connecting the amplifier to the sampler, so recording in this way is not as 'low level' as it may at first appear.

If the CD ROM drive has a digital output and the card has a digital input, you can bypass a stage in the digital-to-analogue-to-digital conversion process.

However, a more attractive and appealing method involves lifting the audio from the CD and depositing it directly on your hard disk without

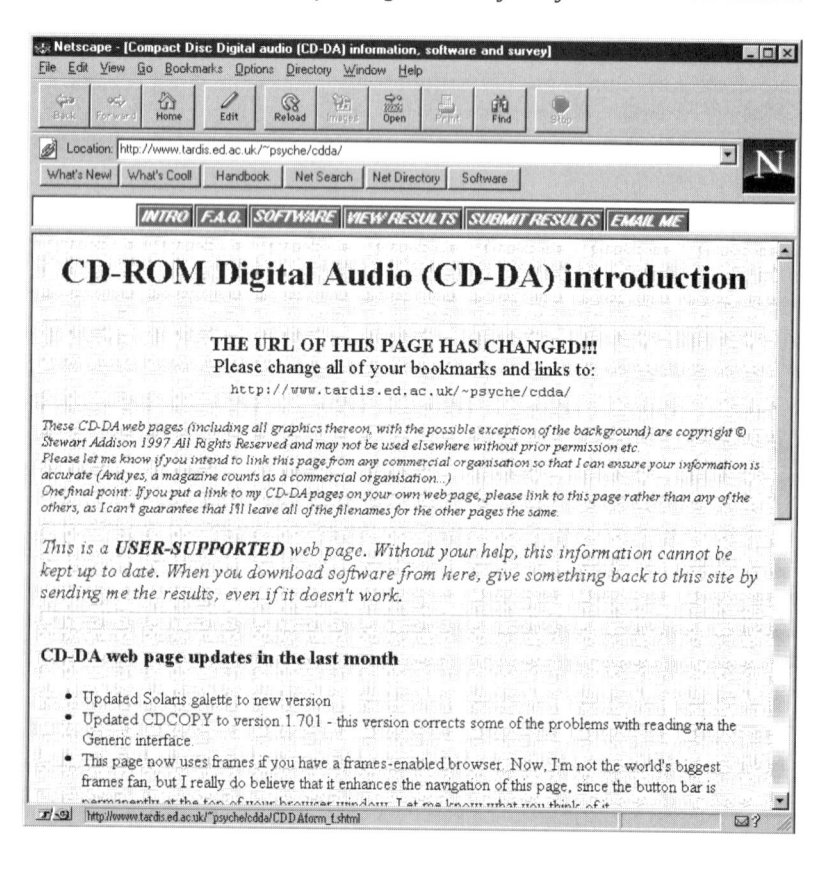

Figure 12.1 The CDDA Web site

running it through any external routes. And you can do this with a CD ROM drive. At least with some CD ROM drives and with a certain degree of success...

This area is as much a black art as a science. First of all, not all CD ROM drives have the ability to transfer audio in this way. Most SCSI drives do while many ATAPI drives do not. How can you tell?

Well, some drives actually come with an audio transfer utility. Plextor, in fact, make an issue of it and the 8Plex and 12Plex include a program called Plextor Manager which can extract digital audio data at 8-speed (the 12-speed drive doesn't extract any faster).

Unless you know for sure that a drive has the ability, you have little option but to try it and see if it works. An invaluable source of information is the CDDA Web site, Figure 12.1, which is listed in the Internet section of the Appendix. It contains listings of dozens of CD ROM drives and their capabilities vis a vis digital audio. The information was gathered by a program called ATAINF, available from the site and probably from all good PD libraries. It interrogates ATA, ATAPI and SCSI drives and produces reams of statistics which tell you everything that the spec sheets don't. It will, for example, tell you the speed of the drive so you can check if it's as fast as it's supposed to be. Figure 12.2 shows part of a dump produced by ATAINF's reading of the Cyberdrive in the Net Works computer.

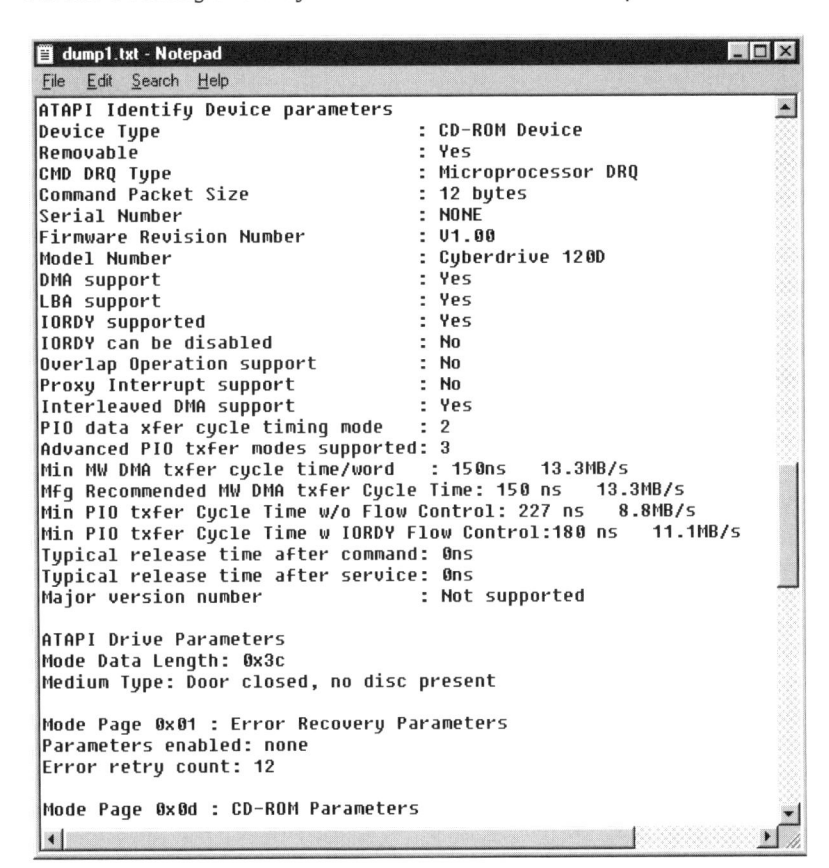

```
dump1.txt - Notepad
File  Edit  Search  Help
ATAPI Identify Device parameters
Device Type                          : CD-ROM Device
Removable                            : Yes
CMD DRQ Type                         : Microprocessor DRQ
Command Packet Size                  : 12 bytes
Serial Number                        : NONE
Firmware Revision Number             : V1.00
Model Number                         : Cyberdrive 120D
DMA support                          : Yes
LBA support                          : Yes
IORDY supported                      : Yes
IORDY can be disabled                : No
Overlap Operation support            : No
Proxy Interrupt support              : No
Interleaved DMA support              : Yes
PIO data xfer cycle timing mode      : 2
Advanced PIO txfer modes supported:  3
Min MW DMA txfer cycle time/word     : 150ns     13.3MB/s
Mfg Recommended MW DMA txfer Cycle Time: 150 ns   13.3MB/s
Min PIO txfer Cycle Time w/o Flow Control: 227 ns   8.8MB/s
Min PIO txfer Cycle Time w IORDY Flow Control:180 ns   11.1MB/s
Typical release time after command: 0ns
Typical release time after service: 0ns
Major version number                 : Not supported

ATAPI Drive Parameters
Mode Data Length: 0x3c
Medium Type: Door closed, no disc present

Mode Page 0x01 : Error Recovery Parameters
Parameters enabled: none
Error retry count: 12

Mode Page 0x0d : CD-ROM Parameters
```

Figure 12.2 Part of a dump produced by ATAINF's reading of the Cyberdrive in the Net Works computer

## Getting rid of the jitters

Sometimes audio data which has been transferred to a hard disk may have 'jitter'. This is evident by pops or breaks in the sound and it is caused by inaccuracies in positioning the read head on an audio CD in a CD ROM drive.

The Red Book says that a drive should be able to position a head with an accuracy of 1/75th of a second. Once a drive has located to a certain position, it can read the audio data sequentially without any bother, which is how a CD ROM drive plays an audio CD.

However, in the DA transfer process, the drive has to read some data, write it to the hard drive, go back to read the next piece of data and so on. The constant repositioning can lead to problems as the head could miss or duplicate 1/75th second's worth of data on each read.

One solution is for the DA transfer software to ask for overlapping sections of audio from CD ROM drive. It can then match the end of the previous section with the start of the current one, discard duplicate data and all's well with the world.

Some CD ROM drives are more prone to jitter than others and the firmware in some, particularly the Plextor drives, appears to correct jitter automatically.

Note that drives or software which use jitter correction will probably transfer the data slower than you may expect, because a proportion of the data has to be read more than once. Still, this is infinitely preferable to a poor transfer.

## Digital audio transfer software

Some digital audio software has built-in support for DA transfer. WaveLab, Figure 12.3, supports most SCSI drives and CD-R drives. You can select the transfer speed or let the program do it automatically. The program lists the tracks on the CD, you can select as many as you wish and then it will copy them as Wave files to a hard disk.

If you don't have a program which has built-in DA facilities, there are several PD and shareware programs you can try. Again, most are available from the CDDA site. In order to transfer digital audio from CD to your hard disk, the CD ROM drive must support DA transfer, the drivers have to support it and the software has to work in the operating system you are using. There can be a difference between DOS drivers and Windows 95 drivers, for example, and some programs won't work in a DOS window under 95.

Programs to look out for include:

*CDWORX*
There are versions of CD Worx, Figure 12.4, for both Windows 95 and Windows NT. It transfers digital audio from a CD to your hard disk as a Wave file with jitter correction. You can adjust and preview the selection

before you save it with 1/75th second accuracy. It can use any CD Track Lists you may have made with the Windows CD Player and it can save the data to the clipboard so you can paste it directly into an audio editor.

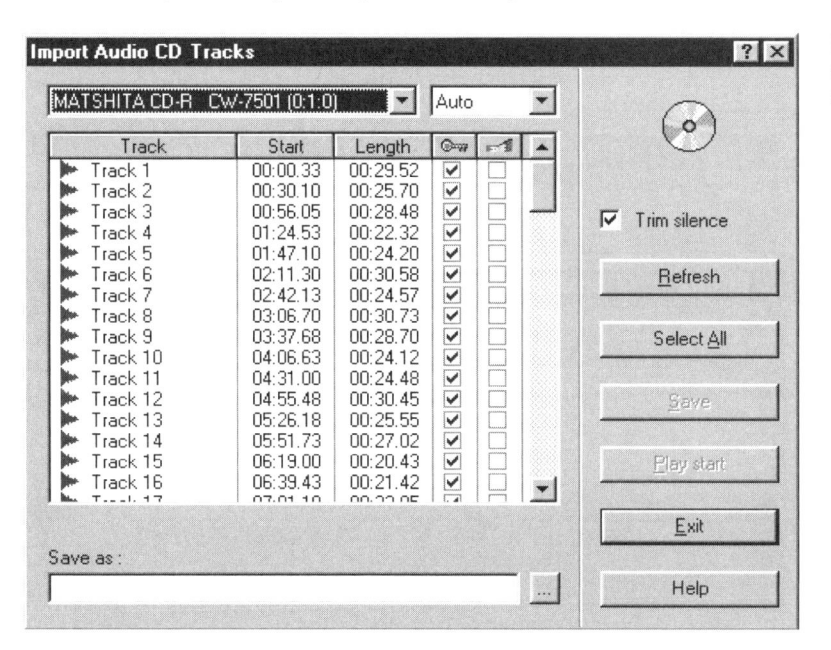

Figure 12.3 WaveLab supports most SCSI drives and CD-R drives

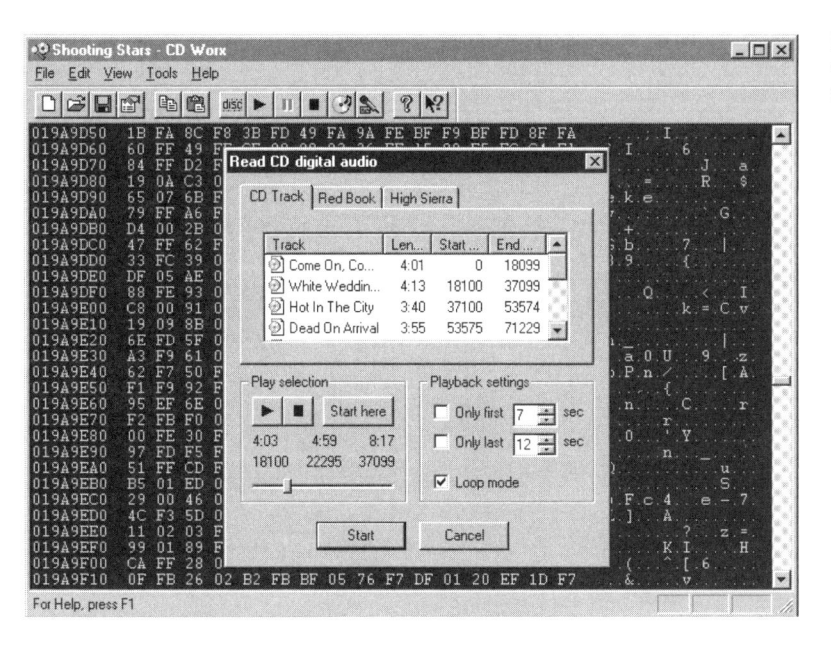

Figure 12.4 CD Worx can transfer audio data from a CD to a hard disk

### WinDAC32

Digital Audio Copy, Figure 12.5, runs under Windows 95 and NT 4.0 and above. It requires a SCSI CD ROM drive and it shows the tracks on the CDs it finds in your system. There is also a copy of DAC for DOS, Figure 12.6, which supports SCSI drives and IDE drives (strictly, ATAPI devices – see Chapter 5 for more details) via MSCDEX.

Figure 12.5 Digital Audio Copy (DAC)

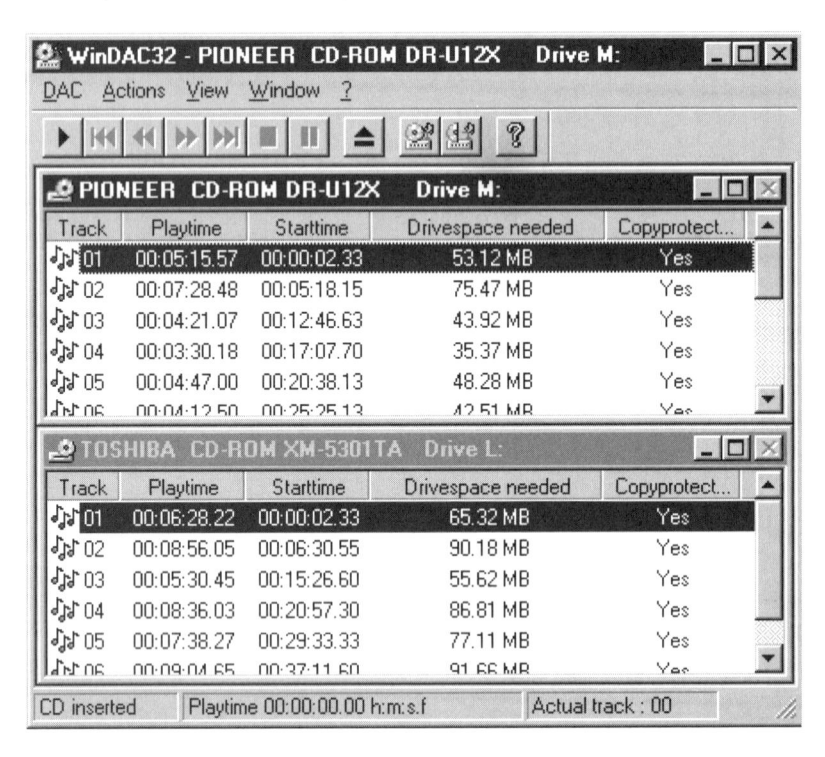

Figure 12.6 DAC for DOS

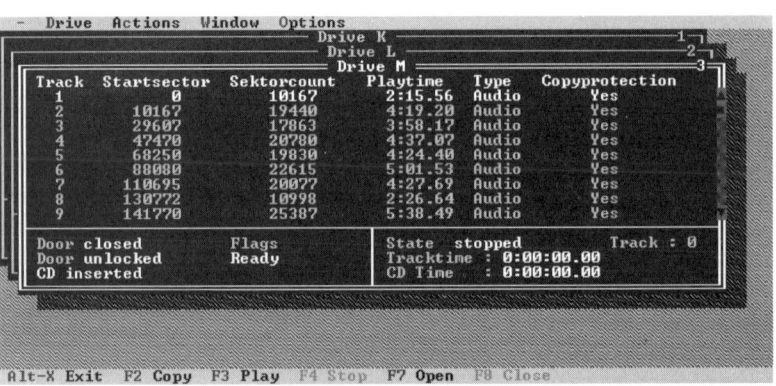

*DIDO*

Digital In Digital Out, Figure 12.7, has a rather basic interface but it's quite effective. It shows the CD's track list, you select a track and a window pops up allowing you to select the start and end times and the data format – mono, stereo, sample rate, and resolution.

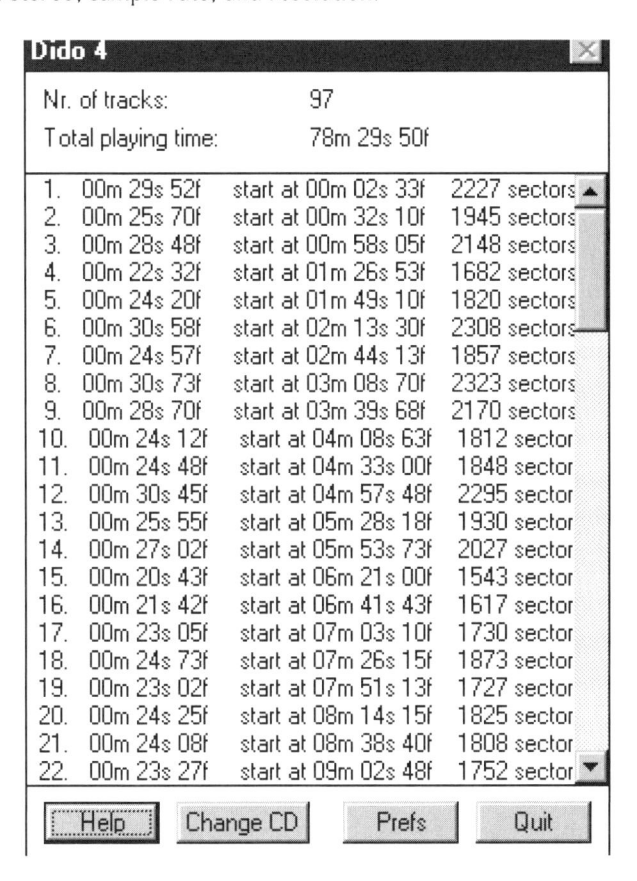

Figure 12.7 Digital In Digital Out

## Wave file CDs

Although the majority of sample CDs are in audio format, several companies are releasing CDs containing data in Wave format. These, obviously, are primarily for use with PCs and it means you don't have to faff about with DA transfer routines.

Audio CDs sell mainly to musicians with samplers while Wave CDs are aimed at multimedia users. The Wave CDs are seen in some quarters as not being quite as 'pro' as audio CDs but don't let that put you off. Most are much cheaper than audio CDs and many users will find them easier to access and use. Check out Time+Space which is one of the largest sample CD distributors in the UK. The company's catalogue is filled with sounds to suit every type of music and recording.

## Recordable CDs

CD-R technology is advancing at an incredible rate and CD-R drives are falling in price proportionally. It's now an affordable option for the musician who wants to create his or her own demo CDs. It's also an ideal medium for backing up your software and digital audio files.

CD-R stands for CD Recordable. Recordable CDs are a WORM (Write Once Read Many times) media which work just like ordinary CDs. Unlike other forms of optical media, you can read the CDs in an ordinary CD ROM drive.

You can create CDs of both audio and computer data and as both are relevant to readers of this book, we'll look at both systems. Both processes are relatively easy as long as you follow a few simple rules. In fact, with the right software, all the hard work is done for you.

There are a growing number of CD-R drives on the market, and CD mastering software, too, but for the sake of example we'll use the Plasmon CDR4240 CD-R drive and Adaptec's Easy-CD Pro for Windows 95 which comes bundled with it.

Plasmon's CDR4240 can read at 4x speed and write at 1x and 2x speed. It supports CD ROM, CD ROM XA, CD-I, CD-DA and Multisession formats. It has a SCSI 2 interface to maximise data transfer speeds and a 1Mb buffer. The pack includes an Adaptec AHA-1535A Plug and play SCSI card which uses DMA bus mastering transfer rather than PIO-mode, so data transfers are faster and it hogs less of the CPU. Beware of PIO-mode cards if you want to optimise your system.

But before we start burning there are, of course, a few other technical bits and pieces we need to become acquainted with...

> **THERE'S MORE**
>
> See Chapter 5 for more about PIO and DMA

## Preparing your system

First of all, it's important to realise that writing a CD is a real-time operation. The laser burns pits into the CD at a steady rate which cannot be interrupted. If it is, the write will fail and you'll have a beer mat instead of a CD!

To write a CD at single-speed, your system must be able to produce a sustained DTR of 150Kb/sec. Writing at 2-speed, a sustained DTR of 300Kb/sec is required and at 4-speed, 600Kb/sec. If you are writing a CD ROM XA format or an audio CD then the sustained DTR is even higher — 172Kb/sec for single-speed, 344Kb/sec for 2-speed and so on.

In order to minimise — and, hopefully, remove — any possible interruption to the writing process, disable all TSR software such as screen savers and system monitors, and disable network file sharing.

The hard disk must have a sufficiently high data transfer rate, nominally 19ms or less, to keep the buffer in the CD-R filled. This should not be a problem with a system being used for direct-to-disk recording. However, you do need some spare disk capacity which we'll get to in a moment.

Data does not go straight from the hard disk to the laser — that would almost certainly be doomed to failure — but to a buffer in the CD-R. The bigger the buffer the more scope there is for delays in the transfer of the data. The Plasmon has a very handsome 1Mb buffer.

Again, to ensure that the hard disk has the minimum amount of work to do, it should be defragmented. If the speed of the disk is hovering on the borderline of acceptability, if it performs a recalibration, it could just be disqualified. AV drives, therefore, are preferred. However, you may get by with a non-AV drive well enough although a little trial and error may be in order.

There are several ways you can transfer the data. The best is to create an image file on your hard disk of what the CD will contain and write it to the CD in one stream. The hard disk has not got to skip about looking for data and should be able to provide the CD-R with a constant and steady stream of data.

You can, however, write from a file list or a virtual image but then the software has to find the files on the hard disk, decide where they are to go on the CD and continue sending the data, uninterrupted, to the CD drive. Altogether a more dicey business, particularly if you are transmitting lots of small files, if the disk is fragmented or if the system's speed is borderline.

If you experience problems, solutions include recording at a lower speed, making an image or, if possible, increasing the CD-R's buffer.

### INFO

*The writing speed has nothing to do with the reading speed of the drive – it's simply a measure of how quickly the recorder does the job. As writing is a real-time process, writing a 74-minute CD on a single-speed CD-R would take 74 minutes, generally a little longer.*

## Track-at-Once, Disc-at-Once

These are methods of recording the data onto the CD. The Track-at-Once method records one track at a time. When it finishes recording a track, two run-out blocks are written. When it starts recording another track, one link block and four run-in blocks are written. These blocks are simply 'housekeeping' data written to the CD and they contain digital 'rubbish'.

This is not a problem for CD ROM drives as they don't read between the tracks, but most audio CD players read and play between the tracks and the blocks will probably create a click. If you want to use your CD as a master for professional duplication, many duplicators will either not master a Track-at-Once disk or re-master it.

In Disc-at-Once recording, as you have probably gathered, all the tracks are recorded in one go without stopping the laser, so avoiding the link blocks. Using this method you ought to be able to control the gap between the tracks but not all software can do this. Furthermore, not all CD-R machines support Disc-at-Once, so check before you buy.

## Gaps

If you're creating audio CDs, Disc-at-Once would seem to be essential but check that you can create inter-track gaps. This varies with the CD-R, but with most systems Track-at-Once recordings insert gaps of 2-3 seconds whether you're writing CD ROM or audio CDs. In Disc-at-Once recordings there are gaps of 2-3 seconds between all CD ROM tracks, but audio tracks have no gap between them at all.

> **INFO**
>
> A session is defined in the Orange Book as a segment of CD containing one or more tracks which can be computer or audio data.

Some recorders allow Session-at-Once recording which gives Disc-at-Once control over the gap between tracks.

Some digital audio programs, however, support the direct creation of audio CDs and include lots of the niceties you'd expect to find in an audio CD writer, such as the ability to add silence before and after a track. Again, check your requirements before buying.

### Creating a CD ROM

Let's run through the steps involved in creating a CD ROM with Easy-CD Pro. The program can create a CD ROM, an audio CD and copy an existing CD. It can create a mixed mode CD and create a CD from an image stored on the hard disk in CD ROM, XA or CD-I format.

The first step is to open a new CD project and select CD ROM from the options, Figure 12.8. Next, you enter the writing parameters such as the

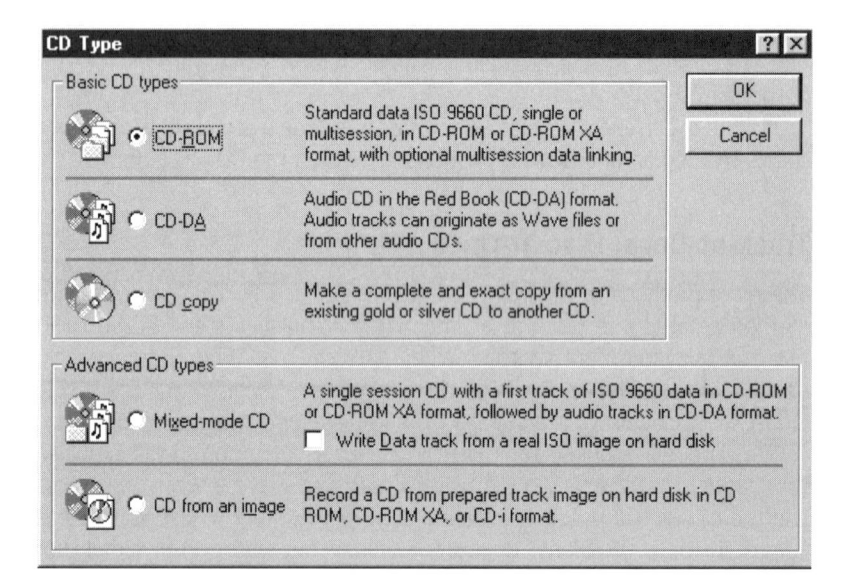

Figure 12.8 In Easy-CD Pro, select the type of CD you want to create

temporary storage area, whether you're creating the CD from an image, the write speed and so on, Figure 12.9. You also set the CD format which in this case would be either CD ROM or CD ROM XA. You can also elect to close the disk or write using the Disc-at-Once command.

The close disk command ensures that no further data can be written to the disk. It is not necessary, however, to close the disk in order for it to be read in a standard CD ROM drive.

Select a filename option, Figure 12.10, allows the use of Windows 95 long filenames if required.

There are several items of information you can enter in the Volume Info section, Figure 12.11. This includes a volume name of up to 32 characters, a system name (the operating system under which the application will run), the volume set name if you are creating one of a set of disks, a copyright name, an abstract file name which records the name of the file

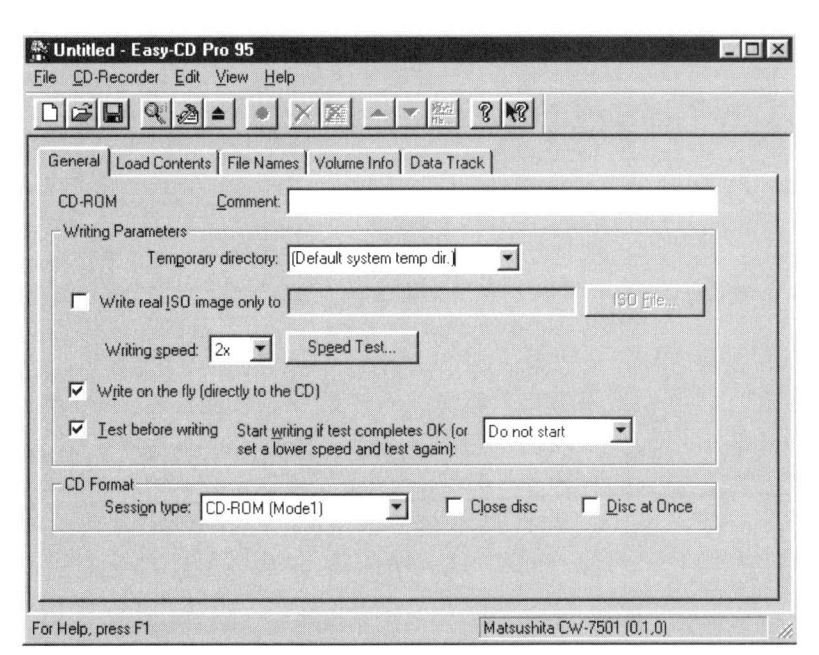

Figure 12.9 Enter the writing parameters

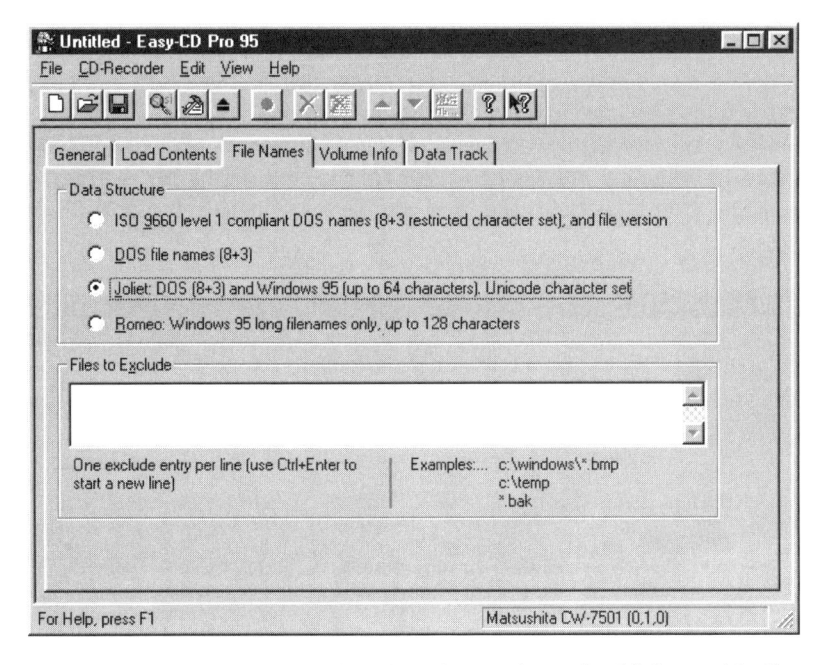

Figure 12.10 The File Names tab in Easy-CD Pro

in the root directory which describes the work, and a bibliographic filename which refers to a file containing bibliographic information such as an ISBN number.

There are copyright identifiers such as the publisher's name, the data preparer's name and the application name. There's no room for the tea lady or the dog so they'll have to share an unidentified readme file somewhere on the disk. Finally, there are lots of dates you can enter if you like to keep the records neat.

Figure 12.11 The Volume Info section of Easy-CD Pro

Then you select the Data Track tab and drag and drop files and folders into the window, Figure 12.12. You can move the files to rearrange their order using up/down buttons and exclude files or file types if they're inside folders containing other files you want to use.

Then you save the project which is simply a list of the settings you have made and the files you want to copy. Finally, click on the big red button and the writing begins. Make sure you have a suitable recordable CD in the drive, first!

Figure 12.12 Select the Data Track tab and drag and drop files and folders into the window

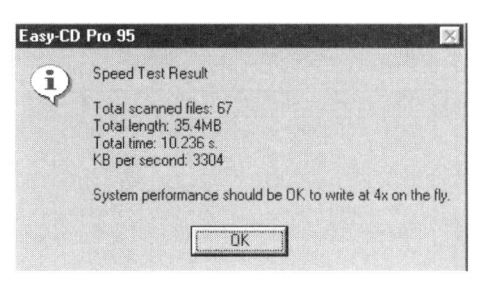

Figure 12.13 Testing the speed of your system

If you're of a cautious nature – and in any event, while preparing the first few burns – you can test the speed of your system from the General tab. The test on a number of small files, Figure 12.13, shows that the Net Works PC is well able to handle transfers at 4-speed on the fly.

That's basically the method you use to create other types of CD, too. You can create a multisession disk simply by creating another set of data and writing it to the same CD. However, it's best to decide whether a CD will be multisession or not beforehand so you can record the first session in CD ROM or CD ROM XA format.

If you want to create an audio CD, there's an Audio Tracks tab into which you drag and drop Wave files. However, for serious digital audio recording, you really need a more specialised piece of software which can handle sub codes, indexes and so on.

## Writing an audio CD with WaveLab

WaveLab includes a routine to write audio CDs. It opens a window and you add the files you want to put on your CD as in Figure 12.14. A new menu called CD Wizard appears in the menu bar and this controls the pro-

Figure 12.14 Adding the files you want to put on your CD in WaveLab

Figure 12.15 Setting the markers from the Markers window in WaveLab

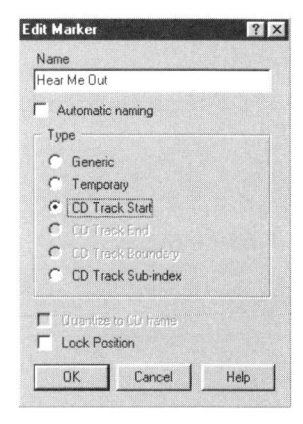

cess. The window simply stores a list of the files plus some parameters and if you change any of the files the changes will be used when you write the CD. You can add complete files or, if a file is open, select a section of it and drag it to the CD window.

If a file contains CD start and sub-index markers, these are used to define the track in the list. The markers can be set from the Markers window, Figure 12.15. If the file doesn't contain any markers, the program asks if you want to use the start and end of the file as markers. Positions can be changed so it's not a crucial decision at this point. You can change the order of the tracks by dragging and dropping, and remove tracks from the list.

Figure 12.16 Clicking on the + makes other items of information appear

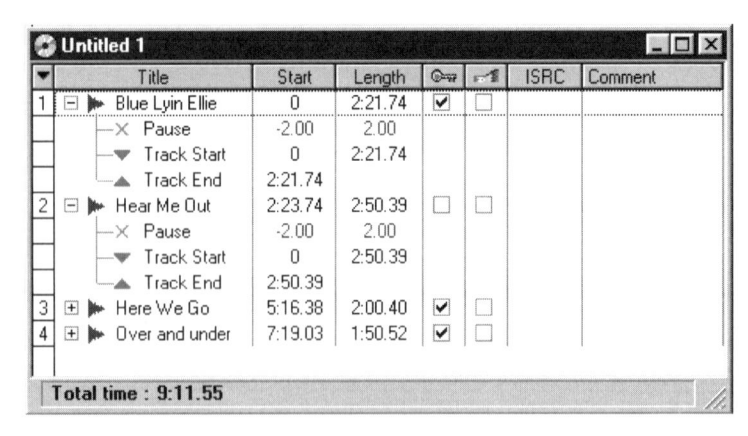

| | | Title | Start | Length | 🔑 | 🌈 | ISRC | Comment |
|---|---|---|---|---|---|---|---|---|
| 1 | ⊟ ▶ | Blue Lyin Ellie | 0 | 2:21.74 | ✔ | ☐ | | |
| | ✕ | Pause | -2.00 | 2.00 | | | | |
| | ▼ | Track Start | 0 | 2:21.74 | | | | |
| | ▲ | Track End | 2:21.74 | | | | | |
| 2 | ⊟ ▶ | Hear Me Out | 2:23.74 | 2:50.39 | ☐ | ☐ | | |
| | ✕ | Pause | -2.00 | 2.00 | | | | |
| | ▼ | Track Start | 0 | 2:50.39 | | | | |
| | ▲ | Track End | 2:50.39 | | | | | |
| 3 | ⊞ ▶ | Here We Go | 5:16.38 | 2:00.40 | ✔ | ☐ | | |
| 4 | ⊞ ▶ | Over and under | 7:19.03 | 1:50.52 | ✔ | ☐ | | |

Total time : 9:11.55

If you click on the + to the left of the track name, other items of information appear, Figure 12.16. The Track Start is how far in on the CD the tracks start in minutes:seconds:frames. Track End is where it ends and the Length is calculated from these values. Pause is the pause which will precede the track. The Start column shows negative values because the Pause starts before the track. If there are any sub-index markers these will appear here, too.

✚ **TECHY BIT** ✚

*Sub-index markers. On some CD players a track can be divided into sub-indexes (sometimes simply called indexes) which are used to mark certain positions in a track. There can be up to 98 sub-indexes in each track but as it. can be take time to search for them many CD players simply ignore them.*

## ISRC and UPC codes

ISRC is the International Standard Recording Code which is really only used on CDs intended for commercial distribution. It records the country of origin, year of issue and serial number. Many CDs don't use this at all but if you have the information you can enter it here – or you could enter some other 12-digit comment – and the program will burn it into the CD providing the CD-R supports it, which not all do.

UPC is the Universal Product Code, sometimes referred to as EAN, which you'll need if your CD is intended for mass distribution. Some CD-R drives allow you to specify this. In WaveLab it's entered in the Advanced Settings window, Figure 12.17.

## Locks and emphasis

The column headed by the key icon determines whether a track is copy-protected or not. This is the equivalent to the SCMS (Serial Copy Management System) used on consumer DATs. It will allow a user to make one digital copy of the track but that copy cannot be copied again. This is rarely used on CDs and not all CD-Rs support it, so unless you have a good reason to use, it's probably best left unchecked.

The rainbow icon to the right sets Emphasis on or off. Emphasis is a form of frequency boosting used on older DAT machines. It was applied to the recording and had to be removed on playback. Again, not something to use unless you have a good reason.

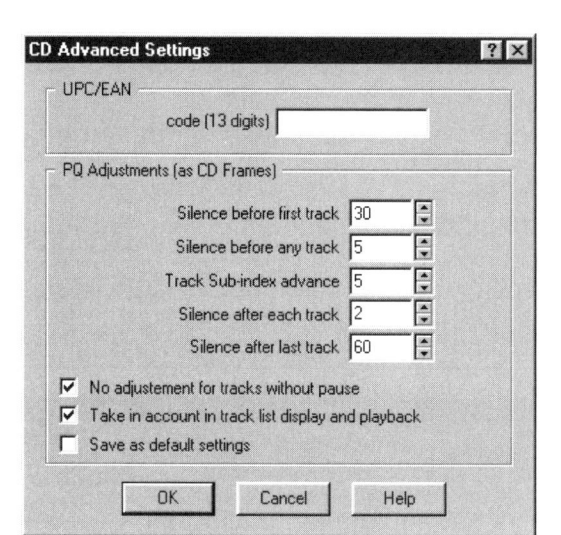

Figure 12.17 In WaveLab's Advanced Settings window

## Ps & Qs and subcodes

If you frequent the bars which are frequented by CD burners, you'll probably hear about PQs and subcodes. There are eight subcode channels labelled P to W. Most of them should not concern us, but the ones which do are the P and Q subcodes which are used to store information such as the Track Start and sub-index information described earlier.

There are a number of rules about setting PQ codes – there should be silent frames before each track, sub-indexes should be slightly early and so on – but thankfully, WaveLab handles this for you automatically from the Advanced Settings box, Figure 12.17. However, the options to change the settings are there if you require them.

Before going for the burn, you can test whether the write will work, Figure 12.18. This goes through the motions without actually writing the disc. If it passes you can be almost sure that the real write will work.

WaveLab's CD program writes on-the-fly but you can create a disk image, too. If the system is struggling to write, this is certainly an option to try.

The Select CD Recorder menu produces a brief list of the CD-R drive's properties. Figure 12.19 shows the results for the Plasmon drive which can do everything except write the copy-protection status and the ISRC code, but that probably won't worry most people.

The CDR 4240 is not Plasmon's latest drive but it is a goody and it works extremely well, having gained awards from various PC magazines.

## Buffer underruns

This is the infamous error message which turns a CD into a frisbee. As CD writing is a real-time process, the CD-R's buffer must always contain data to feed the laser. If, for whatever reason, the system slows and the buffer becomes empty the CD will be spoiled. That's one reason why a large buffer in the CD-R is useful.

> **TECHY BIT**
>
> Techy frame info. Data on an audio CD is divided into frames which contain 588 stereo samples. 75 frames equal one second of audio. Do some sums – 75 x 588 – and you'll get 44100 which is 'CD quality' sample rate. A drive cannot access an item of data smaller than a frame so if you want data in the middle of a frame it must read the whole frame. However, each frame is divided into 98 'small frames' which can each store six stereo samples. This leaves unused space which can be used for storing other information, such as encoding, laser synchronisation and subcodes.

Figure 12.18 Testing whether the write will work

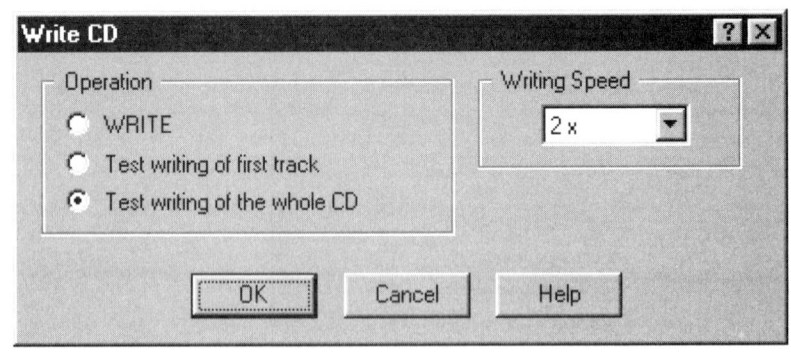

Figure 12.19 A list of the CD-R drive's properties

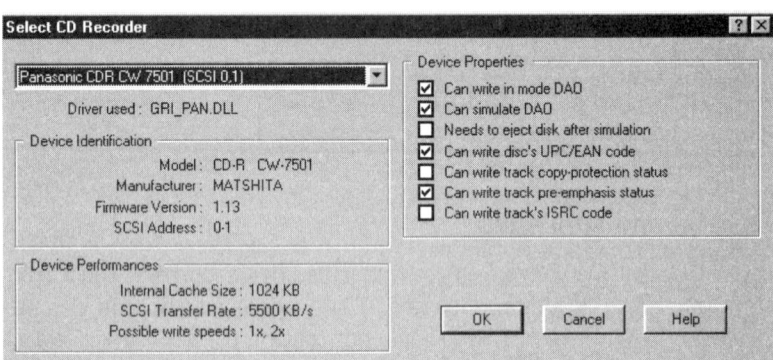

Buffer underruns can be caused by several factors including a slow computer. Here are a few typical reasons why underruns occur:

- Hard disk internal recalibration
- Fragmented hard drive
- Temporary directory has run out of space
- TSR programs kicking in and slowing down transfer
- Network access (turn it off)

And if they do, here are some solutions to try:

- Record at a slower speed
- Create an ISO image first
- Try a different brand of recordable CDs
- Turn off the Auto Insert Notification (not necessary with Easy-CD Pro v2 or later)
- Don't use 16-bit drivers with Windows 95 or NT

Auto Insert Notification lets Windows 95 know that you've inserted a CD in the CD ROM drive. To switch it off, right-click on My Computer, select Properties, select Device Manager from the System Properties box, click on the + by the CD ROM icon, select the CD drive, click on Properties, click on Settings, un-click the Auto insert notification box, breath in.

## Going for the burn

Although there may seem to be lots of things to think about when writing a CD, good software will lead you through the process relatively painlessly. The main points to be aware of are to make sure the CD-R you buy can perform the functions you require of it and write the data and codes you want to write.

You must also make sure that your computer system is up to speed – literally – as this is a potential source of CD writing failure.

Many CD-R systems are optimised for writing to a particular type or brand of blank CD. If the CD-R system recommends a brand which isn't outlandishly expensive, then do try it. This can be rather more critical than simply using brand XYZ DAT tape because the DAT manufacturer, which just happens to be XYZ, recommends it. Do try other media but be aware that it may not perform so well.

You might think that digital audio data is better written in real-time at single-speed, just as cassette duplication produces (slightly) better results if tapes are copied in real-time. Some sources say it is. Others say transfer at 2-speed produces fewer errors... It could be that the results depend on the CD-R and the media. A little experimentation may be in order.

## CD-RW

A recent development is CD-RW (CD Rewritable), also called CD-E (CD Erasable). Instead of burning pits into the CD like CD-R, CD-RW changes the state of the material in the CD from crystalline to amorphous. The disks can't be written by current CD-R drives and it's unlikely that standard CD players will be able to read CD-RW disks as the reflectivity of CD-RW is less than that of standard CDs. There are drives which can read both however, and they will probably appear with a Multi Read label.

## DVD – the future of CD?

The DVD specification has been floating around since 1995. It stands for Digital Versatile Disk and it could well be the next standard in CD technology. It essentially comes in two formats, one for use with your TV set like the LaserDisc, and the other for use in a CD ROM drive. It has a storage capacity of 4.7Mb and a double-sided version is on the cards with a capacity of 8.3Mb. Essentially, it has increased storage capacity because the data is stored in layers, one below the other.

One of its prime uses is for movies, and DVD uses MPEG-2 for high quality reproduction. DVD CD ROM drives are backwards compatible and can read standard CDs, although there is currently a question mark over compatibility with CD-R disks.

There are several steps already plotted on the evolutionary ladder of the humble CD. One possibility is the further development of DVD to a 17Mb storage capacity along with a rewritable version. Some developers are looking at multi-layer disks which can store 20 or 30 times the current DVD capacity and we could see a multi-gigabyte storage CD in a few years.

### INFO

*CD-RW disks use a different filing system to CDs called UDF which means they won't be able to be read by some operating systems. There is a limit to the number of times a CD-RW disk can be rewritten and this is likely to be between 1,000 and 100,000 times. Like most new technology, the first CD-RW devices to appear had a price premium but they are becoming as popular – and affordable – as CD-R is now. Unless something new comes along...*

### INFO

*MPEG-2 is a specification for encoding video and audio for high quality playback. It compresses the data so it can be stored on the likes of a CD but it maximises sound and video quality.*

# 13

## Digital audio for multimedia

The last 10 to 15 years have seen a remarkable increase in the number of 'alternative' music markets, especially for the computer musician. For example, in the 1980s, who would have thought that you could make a living writing music for computer games, creating sound effects, recording and designing sounds for sample CDs, creating MIDI files, scoring QuickTime movies or writing music for company presentations? Even selling music software is big business, and if you can talk as well as play – and heck, you don't even need to be able to play very well! – there are jobs in sales and as demonstrators.

Computer-based music systems have brought high quality music making to everyone. But as well as 'traditional' functions such as writing songs and music, computers have brought us music for another purpose – multimedia.

### What is multimedia?

Multimedia became a buzz word in the early 90s. It was uttered with careless abandon and few of the so-called experts who used it then knew what it meant! But now we do.

Multimedia is simply a combination of different types of media – sound, graphics, text, video, animation and so on – wrapped up in one big homogenous package. There is usually some sort of interaction within the program allowing the user to click on items on-screen to see new information, watch movies and hear sounds. In fact, the term multimedia could now be applied to a wide range of software from games to encyclopedias.

### Multimedia audio

One thing most multimedia packages have in common is poor quality audio. Not necessarily poor quality music, but audio which is the lo side of hi fi. This has been true since the early days of multimedia. At that time, most people were running a 386 – a 486 if they were rich – and compromises had to be made in order to play the videos, do the animation and play some audio all at the same time.

Video was compressed and played back at less than the ideal frame rate. Early audio was often 8-bit with a sample rate of 11.025kHz – or

22.05kHz if you were lucky. Many of these habits have stayed with the multimedia business, partly to allow older machines to play multimedia software. However, many developers are now upping the quality and, of course, the minimum PC spec required to play the titles.

One odd aspect of multimedia, however, is the relative importance placed on video and audio. If someone asked you whether you would rather watch a video with poor picture quality and excellent sound or one with excellent picture quality and poor sound, what would you say?

Without trying it, it's probably a difficult question to answer but research has shown beyond any doubt that we can put up with very poor quality video as long as we can hear what's going on. Audio has a far greater influence on our perception of an audio/visual presentation than does the video – and the multimedia developers have ignored this for years.

## Getting the right balance

If you are producing a lot of files for a project, it's important that all their volume levels have the same perceived volume. It's amazing how many projects have had files which played at different volumes levels. This doesn't happen much now with commercial titles.

Normalising is a good place to start but it doesn't automatically do the job. If a file has a strong peak but a low average volume, normalising may not make much difference to the general level as you can see from Figure 13.1. Normalising this file will barely have any effect.

Dynamics processing such as compression and loudness maximisation can be used to good effect, however, but don't overdo it – you may need to use it again if you have to convert the sample rate.

It's important to realise the difference between the actual level of a file and the perceived volume. As we know from Chapter 2, bass frequencies,

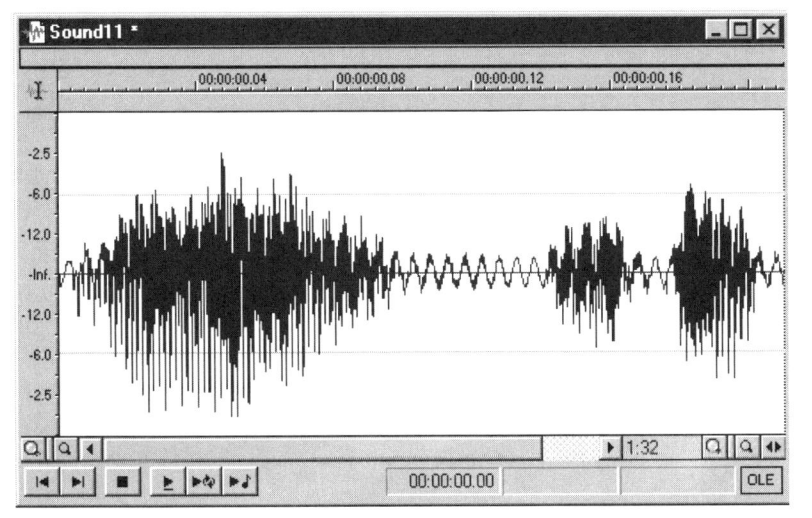

> **INFO**
>
> Many titles now have CD quality audio although the user does, of course, need a PC system capable of playing it, and that includes good speakers. The politics of the situation will doubtless be discussed until we all have a Pentium 500, but as music developers it's our job to do the best we can within the limitations of the situation, and that means producing the highest quality audio whether its 24-bit, 16-bit or 8-bit.

Figure 13.1 Normalising may not make much difference to the overall level of this file

for example, can have very high levels but we may not perceive them as being very loud. The perceived volume is something you need to check with your ears.

If some files have to be louder than others, see if the program itself can control the playback volume. If you reduce the gain of a file, the noise will increase, too.

Use a logarithmic fade rather than a linear fade to reduce noise. If a piece fades slowly, a linear fade, Figure 13.2, will give the audio lots of time to get lost in the noise towards the end of the fade. A logarithmic fade, Figure 13.3, fades more slowly at the start and more quickly towards the end giving less time for noise to become evident.

Figure 13.2 A linear fade

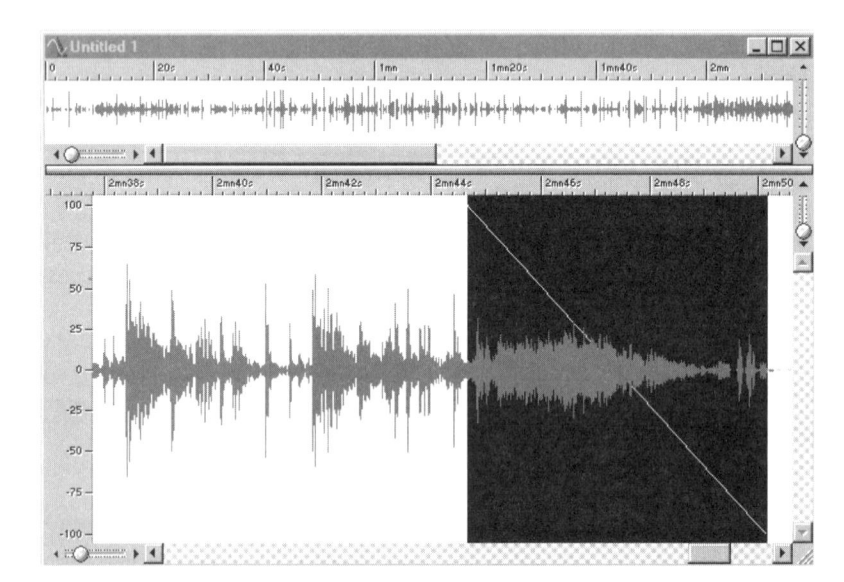

Figure 13.3 A logarithmic fade

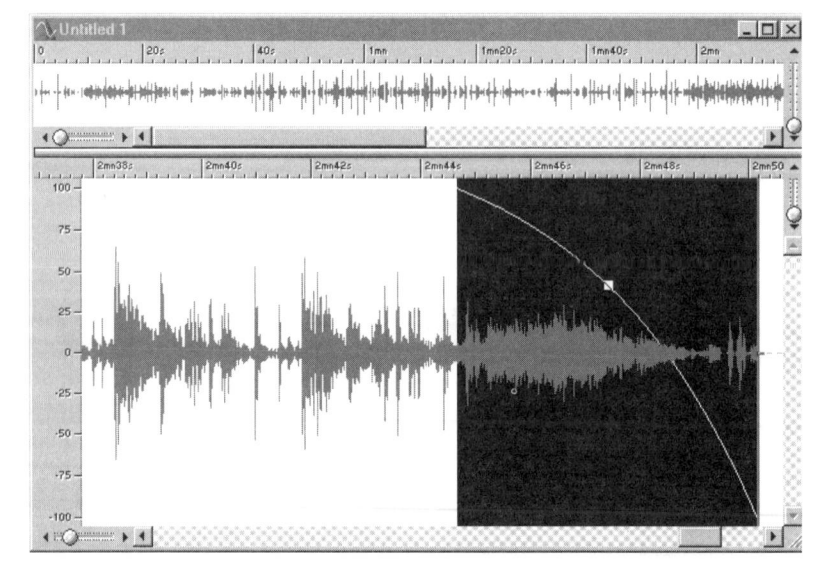

## Space savers

If you're creating music for multimedia, the first thing to do is to persuade the producer that high quality audio is important. Perhaps they will agree but the systems intended for playback won't allow it. Not much you can do there. However, if they aren't convinced of the importance of good audio, create a little presentation yourself using various combinations of good and bad video and audio and see what the reaction is.

But if, for one reason or another, you need to reduce the file size or quality of the audio, there are two options you can look at either singly or together – audio compression and file conversion.

Sometimes the choice will be determined by the systems the project is expected to play on. For example, the systems may not support 16-bit audio, they may have a mono speaker or they may not be powerful enough to deliver high quality audio along with other demands such as the video. Or it could be that the media the project will be distributed on doesn't have enough space for 16-bit 44.1kHz files, in which case you ought to look at compression.

## Stereo vs. mono

If it's a question of space, stereo files takes twice the space of mono files so it may be worth considering sacrificing stereo for smaller mono files.

But you can do so much with a stereo recording. The careful placement of sounds can heighten the overall impact of the music, and effects such as the S1 StereoImager can enhance a normal stereo image considerably. Active panning can add to the excitement of a piece, too.

The decision obviously depends on the content of the audio files, but if you want to stick with stereo there are other options to look at.

## Sample rate and resolution conversion

Most of the issues regarding the downsampling of files have already been covered but here's a summary. If a file has to be reduced to a lower sample rate and/or resolution, the usual method is to proceed as follows:

- Get the level right as described on page 132.
- Convert the sample rate, say from 44.1kHz to 22.05kHz or, if you must, to 11.025kHz. Referring to the Nyquist limit (Chapter 3), you'll notice a drop in the high frequencies.
- You may like to run the signal through a compressor or loudness maximiser at this point. And apply a touch of EQ to make up for those frequencies which were lost, but don't overdo it – you are working with more sonically-limited material.
- Convert the sample resolution, if required, to 8-bit. Using a processor such as the L1 Ultramaximiser will maximise the volume level and make the most of the downsampling with its dither facilities.

> **INFO**
>
> Archivers are widely used on the Net. They make it easy to group lots of files together for distribution and compress them en masse. The compressed archive doesn't take as long to download as the individual uncompressed files would, and grouped files help ensure that odd essential files don't go astray.

## Audio compression

Another option to consider is compressing the audio. There are two approaches to this – compress the audio data files on the distribution medium for the user to decompress on installation, or use a system which compresses the audio data itself and decompresses it during playback in real-time. There are several systems of compression in both camps.

If you want to keep your audio as high quality a possible, you'll want a loss-less compression system, which means that the data can be compressed and then decompressed back to its original form without losing any information at all. However, most systems which offer this don't compress the data by much or else cannot be used in real-time. There's usually a trade-off somewhere.

## WinZip

You can compress audio files off-line using an archiver compression utility such as WinZip, Figure 13.4. This can be used to compress any computer data including programs and it's a loss-less system. WinZip is actually a shell which makes it easy for Windows users to access a range of compression systems which include ZIP, ARJ, LZH, ARC and TAR. ZIP is far and away the most common compression system.

WinZip is useful if you need to pack a lot of data into as small a space as possible for inclusion on a distribution disk or over the Web, for example. The installation routine, which the programmer would write to install the multimedia application onto the user's hard disk, would decompress the files.

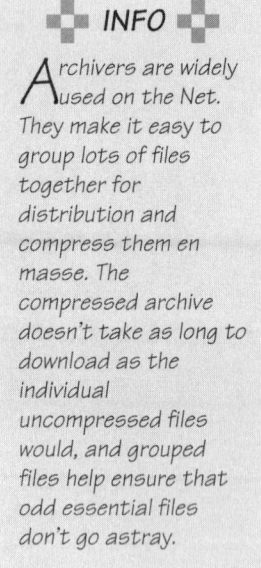

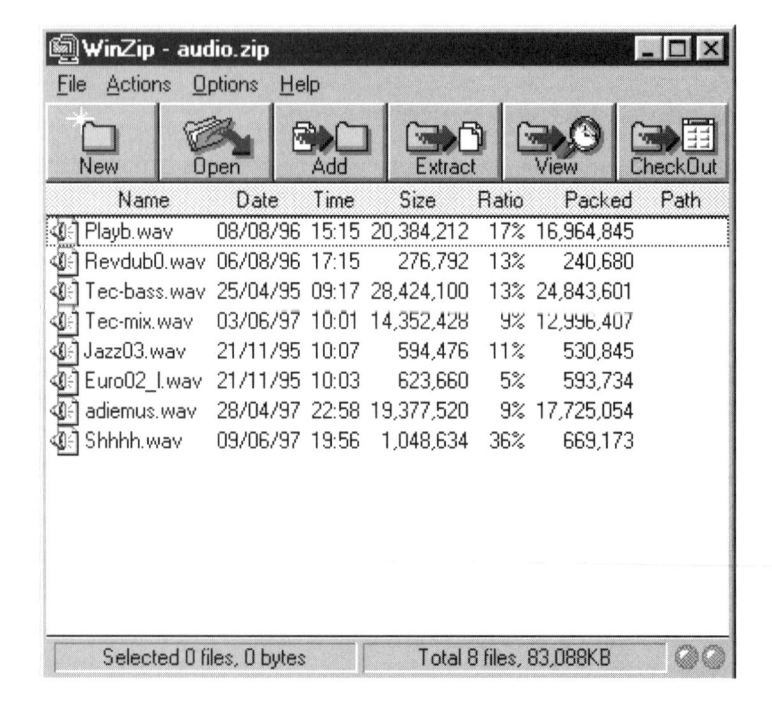

Figure 13.4 The WinZip compression utility can be used to compress any computer data including programs and Wave files

However, as you can see from Figure 13.4, this form of compression does not save a lot of space, maybe about 11-12 percent. The savings depend on the content of the file. If there is a lot of silence in it, the file will compress very well. The last file in the illustration, Shhhh, is mainly silence and it has compressed far more efficiently than the other files which contain music and vocals.

The other disadvantage of this form of compression is that the files cannot be compressed or decompressed on the fly so as a real-time playback system, it's no good at all.

## Codecs

The other option is to use real-time compression and decompression – a codec. And there's no reason why you couldn't use a codec and also wrap the whole thing up in a ZIP archive, too.

The nice thing about codecs is that the major ones come with Windows 95. Open the Multimedia Control Panel, select the Advanced tab and click on the + in front of the Audio Compression Codecs entry. You should see a list similar to that in Figure 13.5. If yours is different, it just means you have a different set of codecs to the ones installed on my machine.

If there are no codecs in your system, open the Add/Remove Programs Control panel, select the Windows Setup tab, highlight the Multimedia

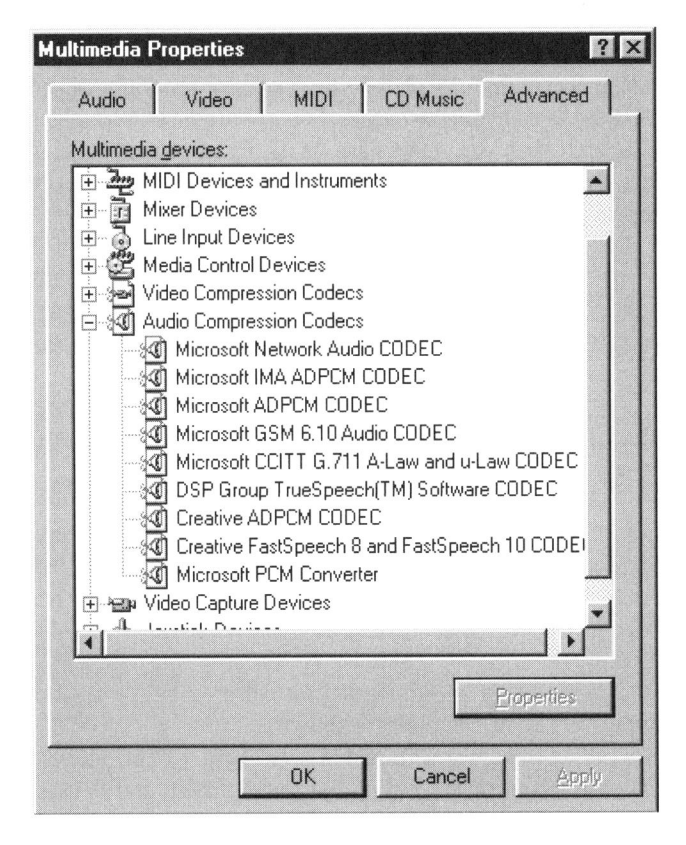

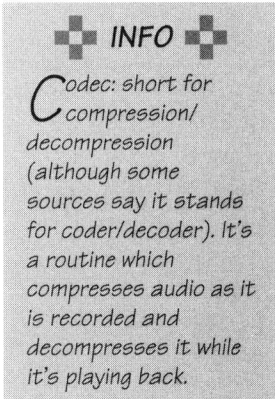

> **INFO**
>
> *Codec: short for compression/decompression (although some sources say it stands for coder/decoder). It's a routine which compresses audio as it is recorded and decompresses it while it's playing back.*

Figure 13.5 Typical list of codecs

Figure 13.6 Adding codecs to your system

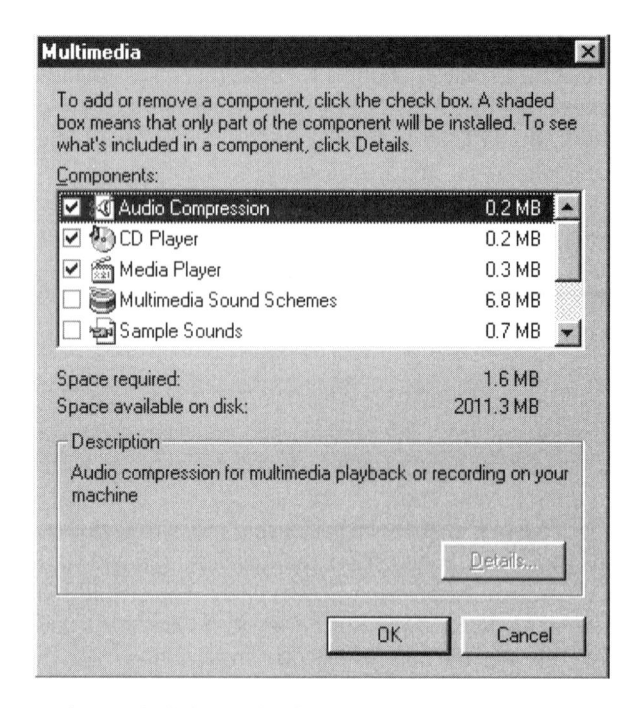

option and click on the Details button. You'll see an Audio Compression entry there, Figure 13.6. Click on the box, click on OK and follow the prompts which ask for the Windows 95 CD or disks.

Codecs are handled by the ACM (Audio Compression Manger) which is similar in concept to plug-ins in that any program which supports the ACM can use any of the codecs. Sound Forge, for example, hooks into the ACM and when you select Save As, you'll be offered a list of compression formats, Figure 13.7. If you add more codecs to your system, they'll appear here, too.

Codecs can compress and decompress data on the fly. However, Sound Forge does this off-line when loading and saving files. You probably won't notice any time difference but, as there is no hurry to compress a file, the program can perform the optimum compression which ought to ensure the best quality file possible.

Compression usually takes longer than decompression so while you may need a nippy PC to compress on the fly, decompressing can usually be done in real-time on most systems.

There are video codecs, too, which you'll also see in the Advanced section of the Multimedia Properties page. When video started to become popular as one of the ingredients of multimedia, it was necessary to compress the files because they were so large, especially when users didn't have such powerful computers as we have today.

Different codecs are suitable for different purposes. PCM (Pulse Code Modulation) is an uncompressed format used by many synthesisers which use wavetable or sample-base sounds.

ADPCM (Adaptive Differential – or Delta – PCM) stores the difference between samples rather than the sample itself, and it uses mathematical

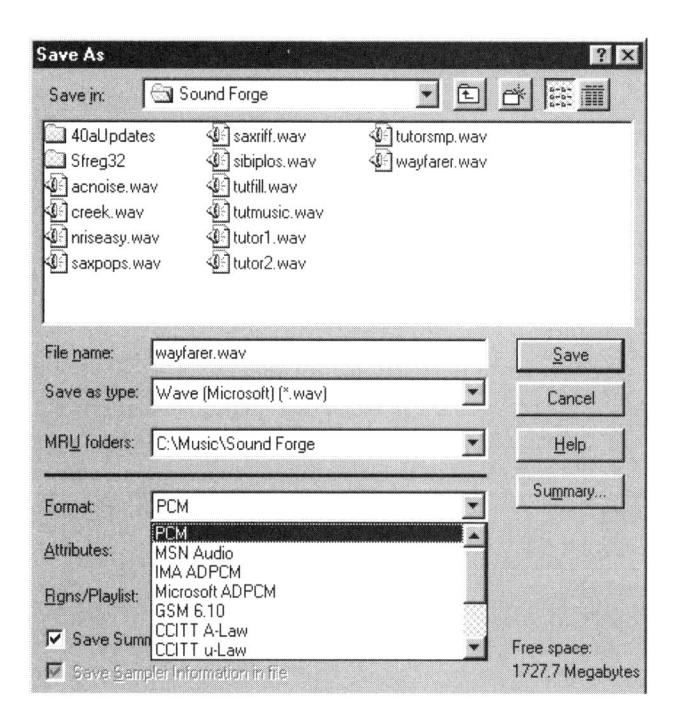

Figure 13.7 Sound Forge's Save As ... dialog offers a range of compression formats

algorithms to reduce the number of bits required to store the data. The result doesn't sound as if it had been recorded on a 4-bit system!

There is more than one method of ADPCM and they aren't always compatible. Two of the most common are Microsoft's ADPCM and IMA's (International Multimedia Association) ADPCM.

The CCITT (Consultative Committee for International Telephony and Telegraph), based in Genva, has given its name to several standards including one for audio compression which reduces the files to 8-bit.

The GSM (Groupe Spécial Mobile) standard was initially for mobile phones and in 1989 responsibility was transferred to the ETSI (European Telecommunications Standards Institute).

Here's a brief summary of some common codecs:

### Some common codecs

| Codec | Format | Comments | Size of file required to play for 1 sec |
|---|---|---|---|
| PCM | 44.1kHz, 16-bit, stereo | Loss-less, standard 'CD quality' | 172K |
| ADPCM | 44.1kHz, 4-bit, stereo | Popular codec suitable for many general uses | 43Kb |
| CCITT | 44.1kHz, 8-bit, stereo | Good quality, suitable for many files including music | 86Kb |
| GSM | 44.1kHz, mono | Not ideal for high quality music | 8Kb |
| TrueSpeech | 11.025kHz, 1-bit, mono | Very low quality, really only suitable for speech | 2Kb |

So there is a wide range of codecs suitable for a variety of purposes. But there are trade-offs:

- Most codecs are lossy types, as opposed to the loss-less compression of WinZip. That means the quality will not be as good as the original.
- Although codecs can work on-the-fly, they do take time so you may have to allow more time for them being opened and played. The exact time depends on the codec algorithm and the system it is running on.
- The system the file is to play back on must have the codec, too, which means this must be ascertained before distribution or the codec must be distributed with the software which could prove difficult if the codecs are copyrighted. Even though a codec is freely available from a Web site, it doesn't necessarily mean anyone can distribute it. And not all audio software can use compressed files. Sound Forge, for example, supports all ACM-compatible systems but other software may not.

## Using codecs

To use a codec, highlight it in the Multimedia Properties list, Figure 13.5, and click on the Properties button. This will open a box similar to that in Figure 13.8 which lets you decide whether or not it can be used. It also has a priority number which you can change. If two or more codecs could be used in a particular situation, then Windows uses them in order according to their priority number.

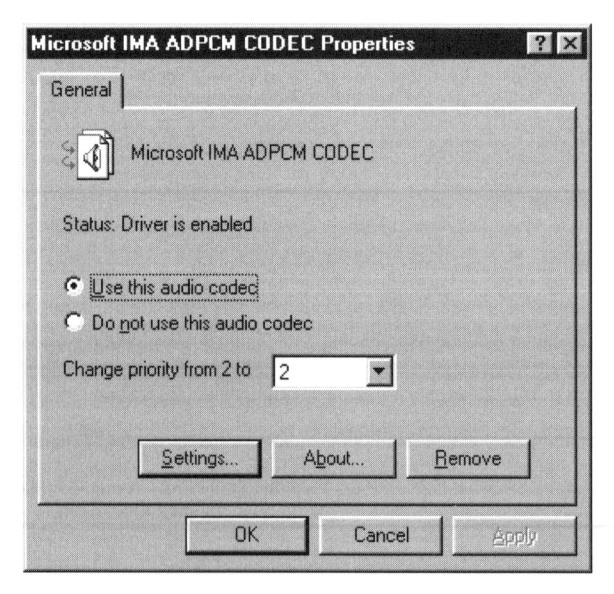

Figure 13.8 Selecting a codec for use in Windows 95

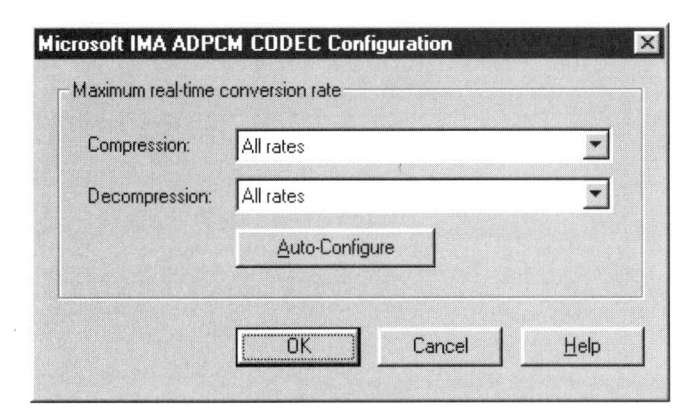

Figure 13.9 Configuring codecs in Windows 95

Click on the Settings button and you'll see a window similar to that in Figure 13.9. In the Compression and Decompression boxes, select sample rates from the drop-down menus.

If a file has a sample rate lower than that in the Compression box, then the codec will compress the data in real-time. However, be aware that higher sampling rates require more processing power and if your computer can't handle the compression there may be breaks in the sound.

On playback, any file which has a sampling rate lower than the entry in the Decompression box will be decompressed in real-time. Again, if your computer can't handle it, the playback may suffer. The Auto-Configure button sets the two boxes to values which are best suited to your computer.

## Audio files for the Internet

The Web is making increasing use of music and is alive with graphics, animations, video and audio content. All these types of data are large and require time to download by the user. Most people aren't prepared to sit and wait while a file downloads so companies have developed compression technologies for streaming this type of data over the Web. The most well-known are Progressive Network's RealAudio, Microsoft's NetShow and Macromedia's ShockWave.

They work in similar ways. The audio is saved in a special format which is transmitted over the Net when the user logs on and accesses the Web page. You need a special player or plug-in for your Web browser to play it. The essential part of the process is that the player plays the audio as it is arriving – the user doesn't have to wait until the complete file has been sent.

The RealAudio system, for example, uses an encoder, available from the RealAudio Web site (see Appendix for details), to convert Wave files into RealAudio format. The RealAudio Player, Figure 13.10, plays the file using familiar record and play controls.

NetShow, Figure 13.11, supports Microsoft's ActiveX technology and plays .ASF (ActiveX Streaming Format) files and live ASF streams. The files can be played locally or from a NetShow or HTTP server.

ShockWave can stream graphics as well as audio data and can be used

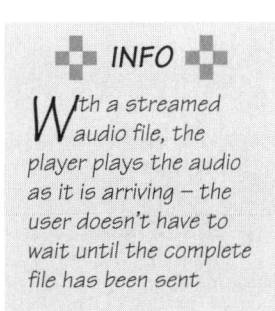

### INFO

*With a streamed audio file, the player plays the audio as it is arriving – the user doesn't have to wait until the complete file has been sent*

Figure 13.10 The RealAudio Player

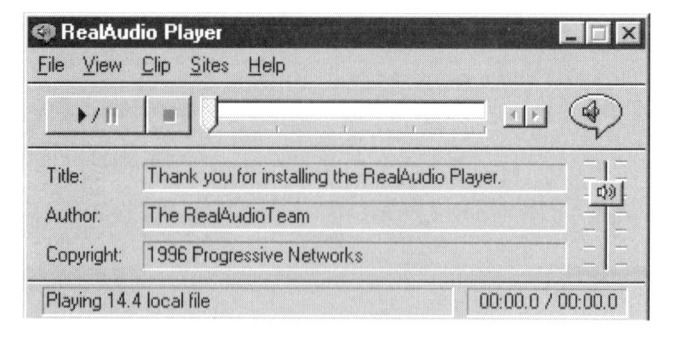

Figure 13.11 NetShow supports Microsoft's ActiveX technology

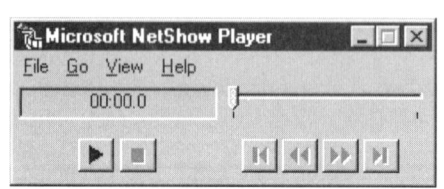

for animated interfaces, interactive demos and games as well as for speech and music. Again, the ShockWave player is free from the Macromedia Web site

As the Web develops, this type of streaming technology will become more common. However, you still need a fast and uninterrupted connection to get the most from these systems.

## Summing up

> Many of the problems surrounding the creation of music for multimedia are to do with the 'low level' system it is assumed the final users will have. We can do almost anything if the PC is powerful enough but we must bear in mind that everyone does not have the latest technology and we should create compatible audio with that in mind.
> 
> This is also a major area of concern with audio for the Web. Most Web designers and the companies which create streaming software have direct Net connections and seem to forget that the average user is linked via a BT line via a 28.8 modem or possibly a slower one.
> 
> So, when you are considering the final file format for your audio, consider what sort of system your target audience is likely to have and cater for the lowest common denominator. If there is room on the distribution media or system, include two sets of data – one for the LCD and one for a more high-end system. That way, those who have the power will be able to more fully appreciate your work.

# 14

# Audio and MIDI

Once upon a time in the early 1980s and before, all music was recorded live, as audio, onto tape. Even electronic instruments such as synthesisers were recorded onto tape a track at a time, even if many were plugged directly into a line input.

And then MIDI came along and with it the MIDI sequencer, which enabled musicians to arrange entire pieces containing 8, 12, 16, 24 and more tracks with ease. And the output was all first-generation, direct from the instrument so there were no problems with quality loss due to track bouncing, and MIDI editing was more powerful than musicians had ever seen before. Great!

But although MIDI has grown to become the major music arranging system in use today, it can't replace audio recording in many areas. These include vocals, of course, but it's also difficult to accurately synthesise many solo instruments for playback via MIDI, and there's an ambience and a quality about a live recording which MIDI can't quite capture.

Sample CDs also have a lot to offer, and the samples can often be handled easier and with more versatility in a digital audio program than by loading them into a sampler and playing them back via MIDI. The exception here, of course, is when the samples are designed to be transposed and played back over several pitches like an instrument. This is primarily what samplers were designed for. This sort of thing is not direct-to-disk's forte but d-t-d is more adept at handling most other types of audio recording including loops.

Consequently, many musicians are discovering that they need both MIDI and audio recording. Fortunately, it's usually easy to integrate the two. In this chapter we'll look at three scenarios:

- Integrated MIDI and audio software
- Synchronising music software to an external system
- Internal synchronising of separate MIDI and audio software on the same PC

## Integrated audio and MIDI software

For many users, this is the ultimate all-in-one music studio – a combination of MIDI and audio recording giving the user the best of all worlds. It is exemplified in programs such as Logic Audio, Cubase Audio (in all its various versions) and Cakewalk Pro Audio, as well as programs aimed at a more general user such as Evolution's Sound Studio Gold, Figure 14.1.

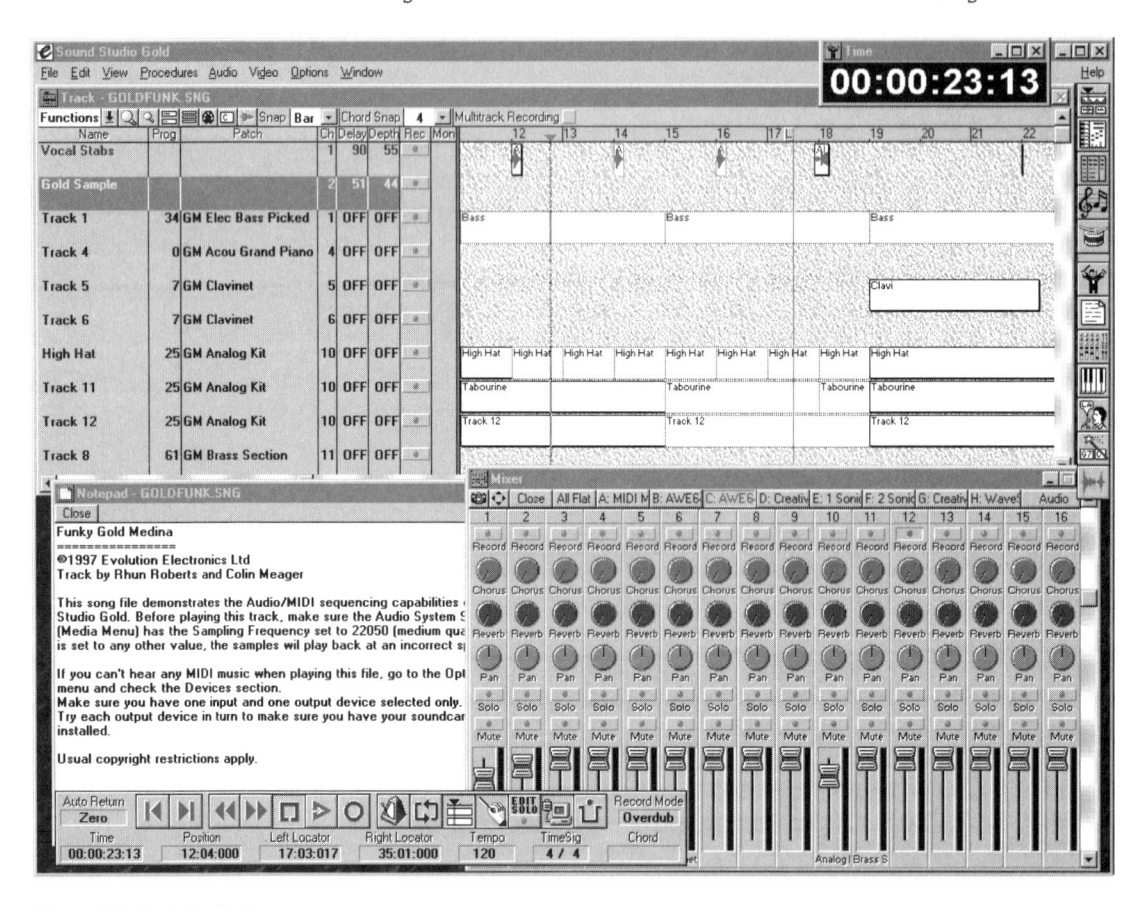

Figure 14.1 Evolution's Sound Studio Gold

The beauty of these systems is that the audio tracks and MIDI tracks sit beside each other in the same arrange page, and audio and MIDI patterns can be edited together, often in very similar ways. The tracks can usually be mixed together on playback, too, allowing you to perform a total mix of a complete song from within one program. Once that's done all you need do is press a couple of buttons and record the finished master to DAT.

This is obviously the ideal system for someone who creates pieces containing MIDI and audio in fairly equal amounts. It's also ideal for musicians who use MIDI primarily but who also need to add audio tracks occasionally. The audio facilities don't get in the way and you can use these programs simply as a MIDI sequencer when required.

The integration may seem less attractive if you don't use MIDI very often – or, indeed, if you don't use MIDI at all! The programs tend to be MIDI sequencers first and although the audio facilities, in all cases, are extremely well integrated, the programs do reveal their MIDI ancestry. But there's no reason why they can't be used purely as audio sequencers – and many people do, indeed, use them as such. However, decisions about the most suitable program for a project can be very subjective.

If you're an audiophile first rather than a MIDI-o-phile, you may prefer a dedicated d-t-d program, and it is worth bearing in mind that dedicated programs such as tripleDAT, Soundscape and wave editors like Sound Forge and WaveLab often have more to offer the audio user than combined MIDI and digital audio systems, particularly in the editing and processing department.

> **TECHY BIT**
>
> FSK records two tones, a high one and a low one, onto tape to represent the 0s and 1s of the digital signal. Don't listen to it – it sounds terrible!

## Synchronising to an external device

If you're coming to digital audio from a tape background and have some tape tracks which you'd like to combine with a MIDI sequence or digital audio material, you'll be pleased to know that you can synchronise a MIDI sequencer or a digital audio system with a tape deck. Although it may be stretching our digital audio brief a little, some of the principles discussed here are used to synchronise two software programs running on the same computer so the information will be useful.

The most basic way to keep a sequencer and tape machine together is to use a MIDI sync box. This sits between the computer and the tape machine and converts MIDI clock messages transmitted by the sequencer into a code called FSK (Frequency Shift Keying) which is recorded onto the tape. When you play the tape, the box converts them back into MIDI clock messages which the sequencer synchronises to.

Before you begin you need to stripe the tape by recording the FSK code on one of its tracks. The usual method is to record the MIDI parts first, setting the length of the song and any tempo changes required and then record the FSK signal onto the tape. The signals on the tape then control MIDI playback and you can't easily change the MIDI sequence without throwing the two out of sync.

The system works fine, most of the time, but FSK tones don't carry any positional information. If you start the tape halfway through the song, for example, the sequencer will still start playing from the beginning. If there's a dropout on the tape, it will likely throw the sequencer out of step.

One way around this is a system known as Smart FSK which records song position pointer information onto the tape so you can start playback in the middle of a song and the sequencer will know where it is. If you're considering an FSK system and are thinking of cutting costs and getting a standard FSK device, remember that you'll have to play pieces from the beginning every time you play back!

> **TIP**
>
> When recording any time code information to tape, use an outside track to minimise crosstalk. Ideally, you should leave the track next to it empty so the code is not disturbed by data on an adjacent track, but if that's not possible use it for sounds without fast transients (such as drum tracks) which could interfere with the timing information. You may also want to use sounds which will not be prominent in the mix to minimise the chances of the timecode appearing in it, too!

## SMPTE and MTC

There is an alternative. It's to use SMPTE (pronounced 'simpty'). This is a professional time code standard devised by the Society of Motion Picture and Television Engineers which divides the timeline into hours:minutes:second:frames. SMPTE data carries with it exact timing information so you can start playback at any position and the receiving unit will know exactly where it is.

Because SMPTE was originally devised to provide synchronisation with video and television, there are different frame rates to provide compatibility with the different standards throughout the world. These are:

*Frame rates*

| Frame rate | Usage |
| --- | --- |
| 24 fps | The standard for film in the UK and European film industry |
| 25 fps | Used by UK and European video and TV (PAL) |
| 30 fps non drop | Used by American black and white TV and video |
| 30 fps drop | US colour TV and video. An odd-ball but common rate. It's actually 29.97 fps but instead of trying to do the fractions it drops a frame every so-often so it all comes right in the end |

Unless you're thinking of getting involved with video, the rate you use doesn't matter much, although if you're in Europe, you may want to set your equipment to 25 fps and forget about it.

SMPTE synchronisation requires a SMPTE box, a device which is capable of generating SMPTE code. Like the FSK box, this sits between your PC and the tape deck. The PC software generates MTC (MIDI time code) which the SMPTE box interprets and uses to generate SMPTE timing information which it stripes the tape with.

The important difference between SMPTE and FSK is that FSK follows the original timing of the MIDI sequencer while SMPTE is an absolute timing reference. If the tape should speed up or slow down, the sequencer will stay with it. SMPTE timing is more solid and generally more reliable, but it's still a good idea to do the MIDI tracks first and add the tape tracks later.

Most sequencers and digital audio programs have synchronisation options which let you set the in and out ports, the frame rates and so on. Figure 14.2 shows the options available in Cubase

## MIDI machine control

Having mentioned FSK and SMPTE, it's only fair that we also mention MMC. This is an extension to the MIDI spec designed to allow MIDI sequencers to control tape and video machines, although to do so the machines must be MMC-compatible. In operation, when you click on the

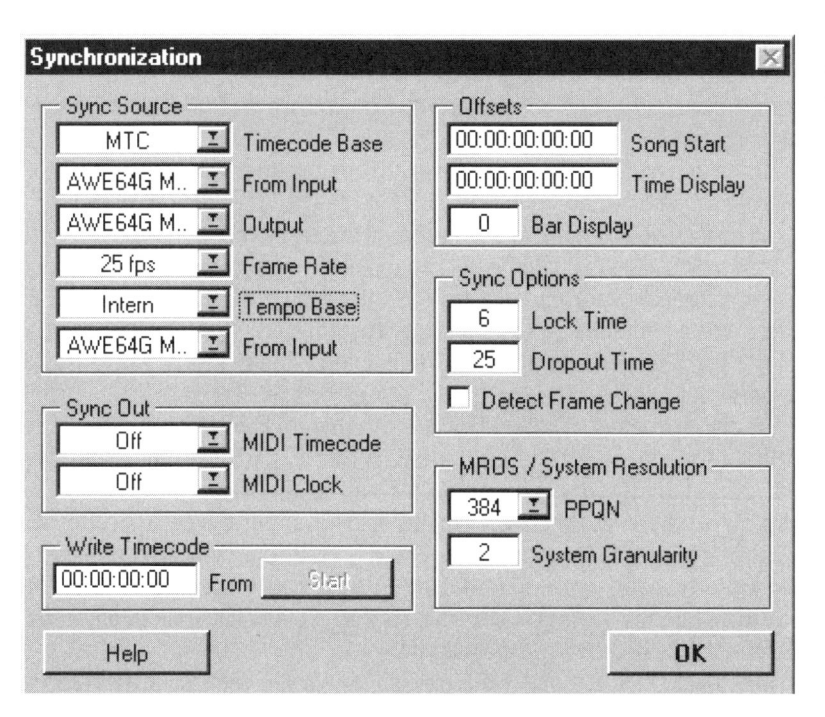

Figure 14.2 The sychronisation options in Cubase

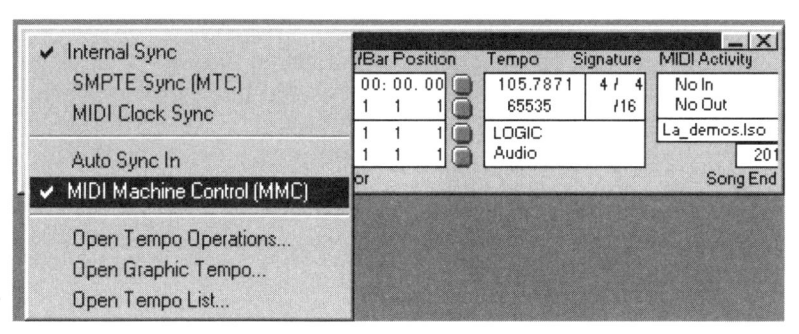

Figure 14.3 Activating MMC in Emagic Logic

play or fast forward button on your MIDI sequencer, the tape recorder follows suit.

It's a convenient way of operating the two devices from one set of controls although it does require two-way communication. The tape machine provides SMPTE code to control the sequencer. It can usually be activated very easily in software which supports it such as Logic, Figure 14.3.

## Converting tape tracks to digital tracks

If you have been using a tape recorder, you may have tracks you'd like to transfer to a digital audio system. There are a couple of approaches you can take, depending on the number of tracks on your tape machine and the capabilities of your digital audio system.

Most digital recorders can record only one track at a time which could be mono or stereo. Some systems allow two or four track recording –

tripleDAT, for example – but generally, if you have an eight-track tape recording you want to transfer to a d-t-d system, you'll be struggling to do it in one take. But no matter. You can record any number of tracks one at a time.

Ah, but what about synchronisation? Unless the tracks are synchronised during recording, won't they be out of sync in the digital recorder?

Probably, yes! But – and this is one of the really cool things about digital recording – you should be able to manually synchronise them by picking a reference point on each track and making sure they all line up. If there are no reference points such as rhythm parts, you could record a short, percussive sound at the start or end of the tracks simultaneously and use that.

There is a potential danger here. If you have a long piece and the tape drifts a little, and you line up the tracks at the start, say, they could be out of sync by the time you get to the end. If the tracks are continuous, you may need to apply a little time-stretching to put things right. Not an ideal course of action but unless the tape is really out of whack, any drifting should be very small indeed. Having said that, if drifting did occur it could well be the same for all tracks so they would all line up in any case. But a possible problem to be aware of.

Another option is to split the tracks into smaller sections after recording them and line them up individually. It's unlikely that every track will contain a recording lasting the entire length of the piece.

Perhaps the best option is to record a stereo mix which all digital recorders will be able to handle. This assumes that the recordings are in a finished state, of course.

If you have a spare track on your tape system, yet another option is to stripe it with sync code, and sync it to the PC while recording each track.

### Internal synchronisation

Returning to our main topic, digital audio, some musicians may need to produce pieces using both MIDI and audio tracks but they may not want to use an integrated system for one of the reasons mentioned earlier. If you work primarily with audio but need to add some MIDI tracks, how do you do it?

Most direct-to-disk recorders should be able to synchronise with an internal MIDI sequencer but the process is, unfortunately, not guaranteed to work with all systems. The theory is simple enough – one piece of software directs timing code to an internal MIDI driver and the other piece of software receives it via the same driver. The data is transferred internally so there should be no need to mess about with external connections. In theory.

In practice, however, there are many problems with drivers and software. Most MIDI drivers are not designed to transfer data to two devices simultaneously, so you may be able to sync two pieces of software but lose the MIDI playback facility! Not a lot of good.

When setting up the sync parameters, watch out for error messages. If

> **TIP**
>
> One thing to be aware of is the possibility of a conflict with the audio driver if you try to sync a piece of d-t-d software with a MIDI sequencer which also has digital audio capabilities. The two pieces of software may vie for the audio driver. See if you can disable this in the sequencer. Otherwise load the digital audio software first and give it a chance to 'grab' the driver. The sequencer may refuse to play because it can't find an audio driver, but it should play MIDI parts. Alternatively, it may put an error message on screen telling you it can't use the audio driver and then play the MIDI parts or, with a little luck, it will play its MIDI parts without further complaint.

you try to assign a driver to a program while the driver is already in use by another program, most software is at least friendly enough to tell you that you can't do it. But what it does next can vary. It may issue a warning then simply close the sync parameter window so you don't know what the setting is. After the warning, it may leave the setting so you could be lured into a false sense of security thinking the driver has been assigned when, if fact, it hasn't. Preferably, however, it will not allow you to make an incorrect assignment.

## Master and slave

When setting up the drivers and synchronisation parameters, there's one concept it's vital to understand and that's masters and slaves. In any synchronisation setup, there can be only one controlling application and that's the master. The application being controlled is the slave. The master generates the timing information, the slave reads it and follows the master.

It is essential that you decide which application is going to be which and set them up accordingly, otherwise the setup won't work.

## MIDI drivers

The number of MIDI drivers in your system will depend on what is installed in your PC. Some software may not recognise all the drivers or may simply use the driver assigned to the MIDI Mapper. This can be set from the MIDI tab of the Multimedia Control Panel, Figure 14.4.

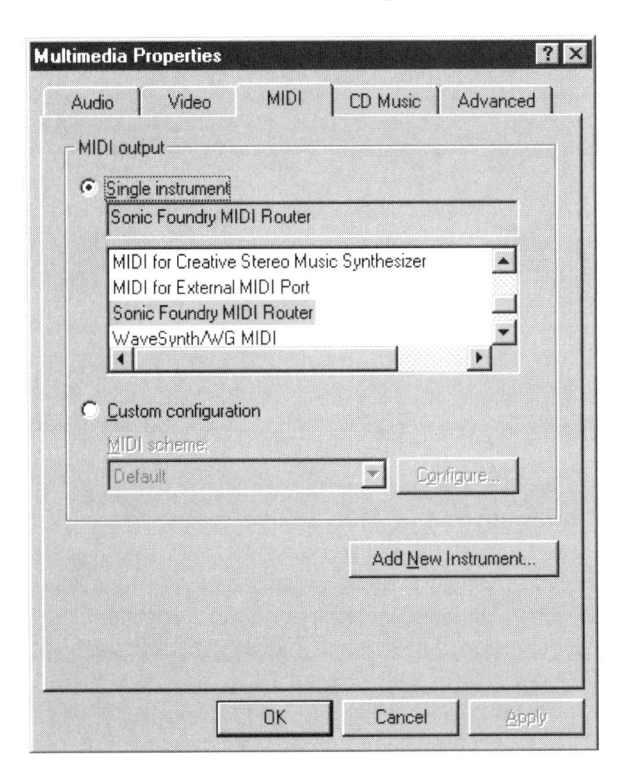

> **TIP**
>
> *It's common to use the MIDI sequencer as the master but there's no reason why you shouldn't use the audio software as the master instead, providing it can generate timing information. If you're having trouble syncing one to the other, try it the other way around.*

Figure 14.4 The MIDI tab of the Multimedia Control Panel

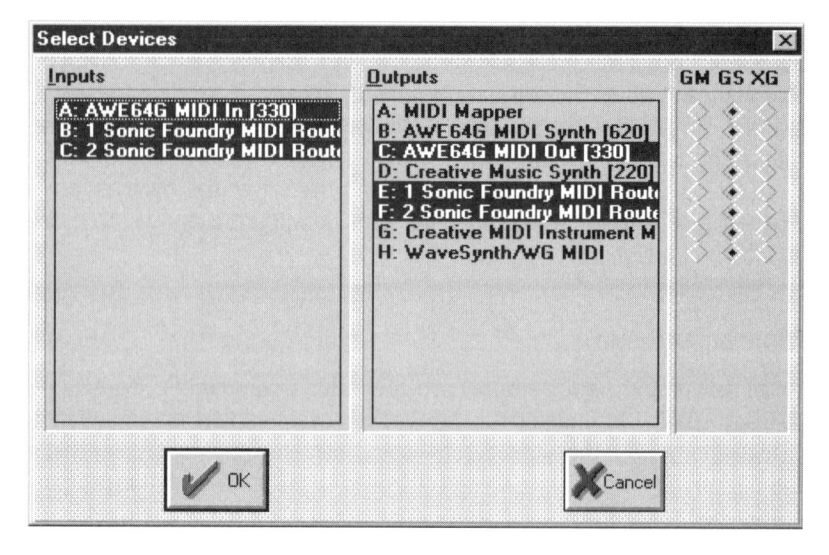

Figure 14.5 The Evolution sequencers show all the MIDI drivers in your system and you can select the ones you want to use

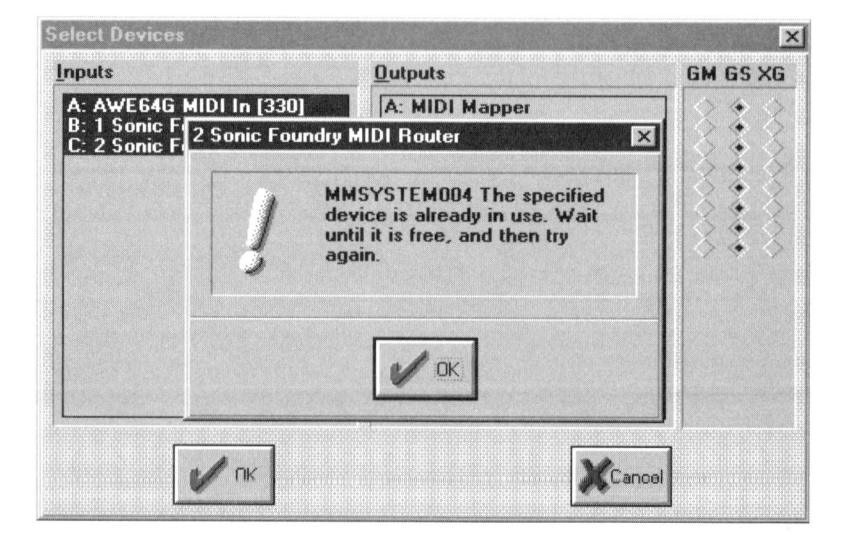

Figure 14.6 If you try to select a driver which is already in use the program will warn you

The Evolution sequencers show all the drivers in your system and let you select the inputs and outputs you want to use, Figure 14.5. If you try to select a driver which is already in use the program will warn you, Figure 14.6, although it then closes the selection window so you may not be sure what drivers are selected.

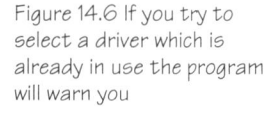

Sound Forge has a virtual MIDI router, Figure 14.7, which is specially designed to transfer MIDI data internally between programs. It can handle up to four devices and you can select how many 'routers' you want to use. They are named and numbered 1 to 4 so if one application sends data to '3 Sonic Foundry MIDI Router', for example, then another application could receive data from it by setting its input MIDI driver to '3 Sonic Foundry MIDI Router', Figure 14.8.

A routing system like this has more chance of working than using standard drivers designed to drive specific pieces of hardware and software.

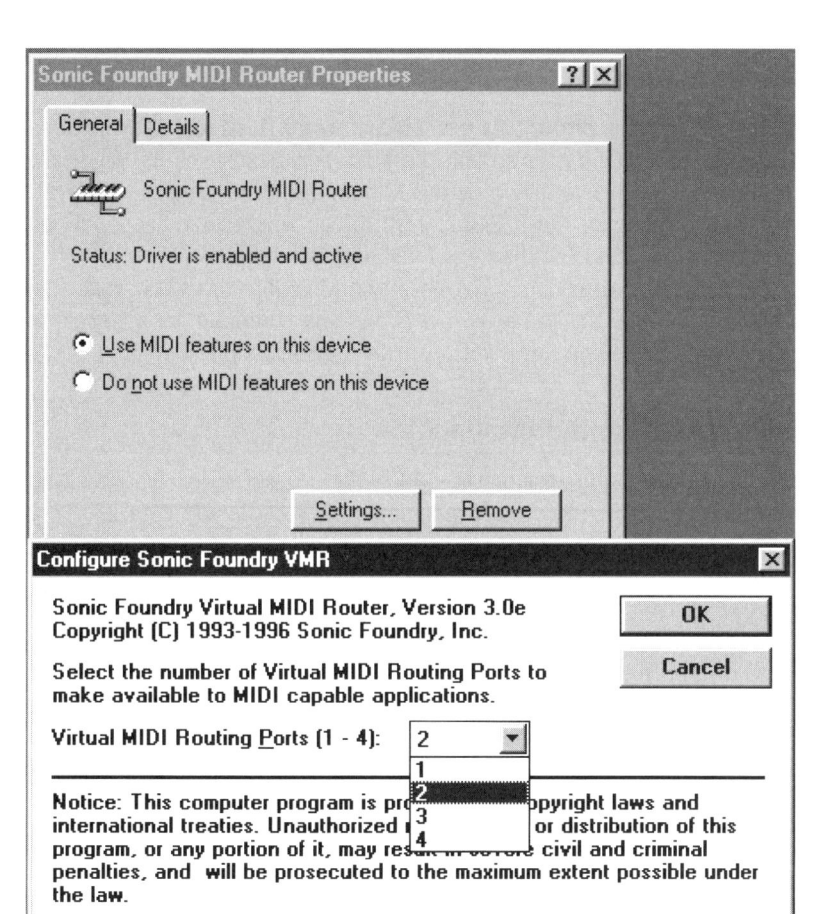

Figure 14.7 Sound Forge's virtual MIDI router

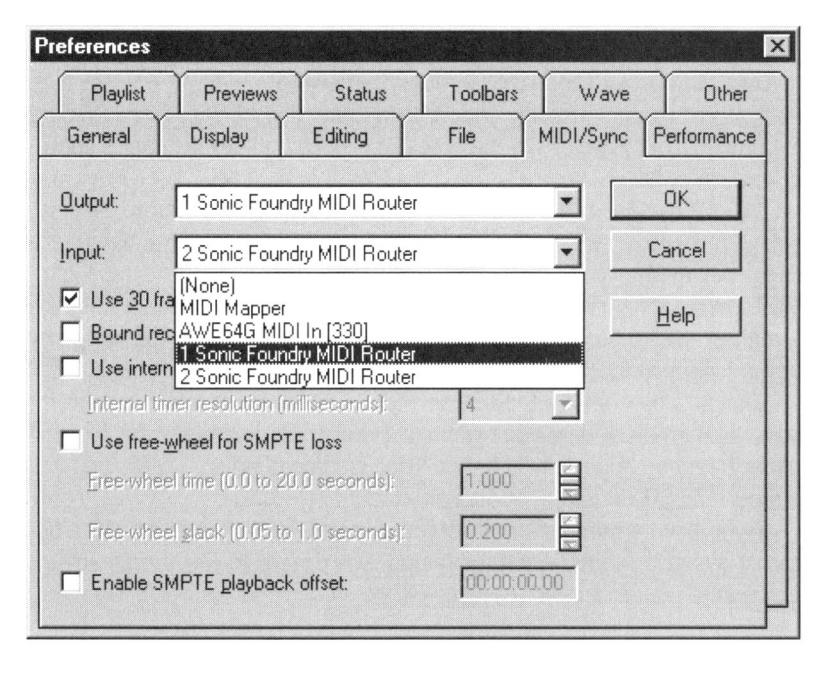

Figure 14.8 Setting the input MIDI driver to '3 Sonic Foundry MIDI Router'

### The missing link

If you're finding it difficult to get internal synchronisation to work, one option worth looking at is to link the MIDI ports externally by physically connecting a MIDI lead between the MIDI out and in sockets. However, you need to take care not to set up a MIDI loop which could happen if you connect the out and in of the same MIDI interface together.

But this is worth trying if you have two MIDI interfaces. In effect, the process would be the same as connecting the computer to an external device – only the computer is the 'external' device, too!

### Mixing MIDI and digital audio

Whether you're using an integrated MIDI/d-t-d program or synchronising separate programs, the ability to combine MIDI and audio data is a very powerful one. With most systems you will be able to record and add MIDI or audio data as you wish. However, there are a few potential problems to be aware of.

Most are concerned with tempo changes. You can easily change the speed of a MIDI recording by a factor of two or more with no side effects at all. However, as you will be aware, you cannot change the tempo of an audio recording without changing its pitch – you can, of course, using a time stretch function but you can't change it by much before the sound loses its character. This is particularly true of vocals.

So, if you're working with both MIDI and audio, the general rule of thumb is to record the MIDI parts first then fit the audio to the MIDI. You don't have to record all the MIDI parts, but you certainly ought to try to plan the general structure of the piece and include any tempo changes.

### Using sample loops

In Logic Audio you can insert an audio pattern into a track and set it to loop. It will continue to play until it encounters another pattern. In Figure 14.9, the Groove pattern in the first track loops until it encounters another pattern at bar 4.

Logic Audio also has a function to match the tempo to a loop. Let's say you've recorded a two-bar drum loop and want to use it as the basis for a song, but in the Arrange page it's a little longer than two bars, Figure 14.10. You could change the tempo manually, slowing it down until the sample seems to fit. Or you could use the function to adjust the tempo by object length and locators.

Sounds a bit complicated but all you do is set the locators to encompass the number of bars you want the drums to fill and select the function from the menu, Figure 14.11. You'll see it's ended up as a really odd-ball tempo – 73.5909 bpm! – but it's an exact fit.

If you have a number of loops you want to use in the same piece but each plays at a slightly different tempo, you'd have to use a time stretch function to make them all the same tempo.

> **TIP**
>
> *E*ven if your software doesn't have an audio loop function, you can still easily play loops by copying a pattern to the end of itself. Audio patterns aren't 'real' data like MIDI patterns, but simply pointers to the audio data on disk, so this doesn't use any additional memory or disk space.

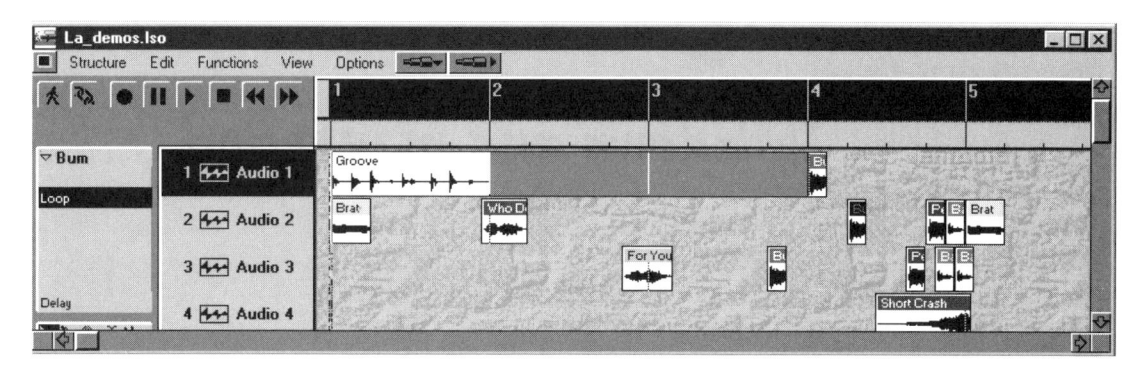

Figure 14.9 The Groove pattern in the first track loops until it encounters another pattern at bar 4

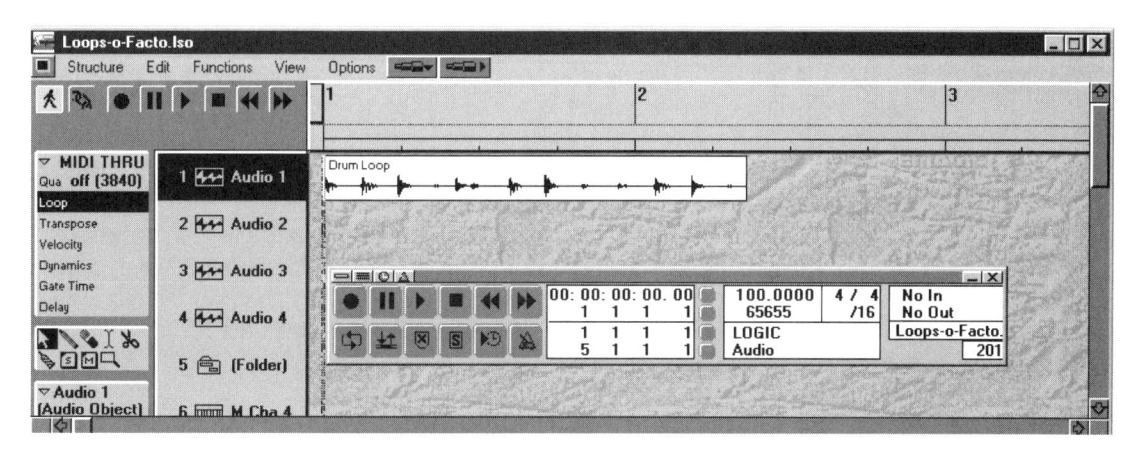

Figure 14.10 The two-bar drum loop is longer than two bars

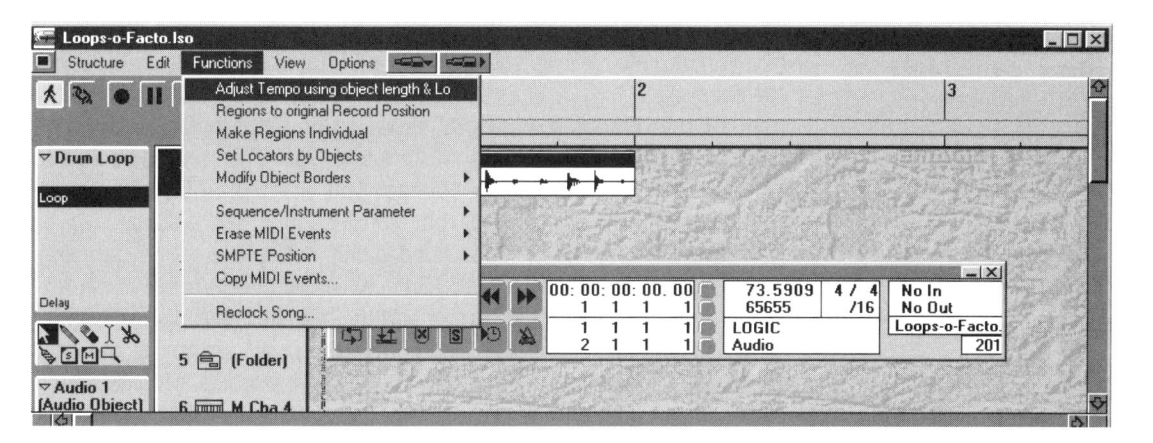

Figure 14.11 Set the locators to encompass the number of bars you want the drums to fill and select the function from the menu

# 15

# Mixdown and mastering

> **INFO**
>
> Technically, the term 'master' should only be applied to the glass master produced at the pressing plant from which the mass production CDs are made. The DAT or CD you take along to be copied is more correctly called the PreMaster. However, 'master' is in such common widespread use (except, perhaps by the people in mastering houses and pressing plants) that we won't try to rewrite the audio dictionary here.

Whatever project you're working on and whatever media and format it will eventually end up on, there comes a time when you have to acknowledge that it's finished – or there's no time left to do any more work with it. All the tracks need to be combined and mixed down into a final format – in the case of music this will usually be 16-bit 44.1kHz stereo.

This mixdown is usually called mastering – creating a finished 'master' recording from which copies will be made. It must be the very best version of the recording possible.

Having spent six days, weeks, months or years on your project, you may think that the hard work is over and that mastering is simply a matter of dotting a few Is, crossing a few Ts and laying down the mix. There is actually much more to the mastering process than that.

## In praise of mastering houses

If you have created music for mass distribution on CD or cassette, the best advice – and take it if you dare – is to leave the mastering up to a professional mastering house. There are many reasons for this, some of which will become clear as we explore the DIY approach – which is yet not to be dismissed.

One of the reasons for using a mastering house is that they will have had more experience at creating masters than you. They should be able to spot problems in the recording. Perhaps you boosted an EQ band which sounds great on your speakers but terrible on other systems. Maybe you've overdone the compression and didn't notice the subtle pumping. Perhaps you mixed one track at 10am when your ears were fresh and another at 10pm when they weren't and the balance is wrong.

A mastering house will also check that the levels are right, the gaps between the songs are correct and the fades are good and consistent. Which brings us to another reason for using a mastering house – their equipment will be better than yours, and any changes they make should retain the audio quality. This is particularly important if your system is a little less 'pro' than you'd like.

Let's take fade outs, for example. You know that as you reduce the volume of a recording, the noise increases (see Chapter 10). A good mastering house ought to be using 20-bit or 24-bit equipment which will maintain the audio quality far better than a 16-bit system.

## Creating your own master

If the final mix isn't for mass production or if you want to run off your own copies onto cassette, CD or MiniDisc, then you may prefer to create the master yourself.

This book has covered the various processes which can be used in the creation of a master – mixing, compression, EQ, fades and sample rate conversion. However, having normalised, equalised, maximised and compressed sections of your music on the path to the perfect recording, beware of repeating these processes on the final mix, or at least overdoing them.

If you are assembling a collection of recordings such as songs, the primary concern is the overall sound and comparative levels of the individual pieces. When you listen to them one after the others do they 'fit' well together?

Compression is the great leveller and can be used to 'even out' differences in levels across tracks. However, a recording can be over-compressed and once you start messing around with volume levels you're in danger of losing the sonic quality of the material.

Likewise with EQ. Tweak a little here and there if you must but don't overdo it. You won't brighten a dull recording by whacking up the EQ, you'll only tire your listeners' ears.

But as ever, it's your ears which make the final decision. However, if you're working alone, this is an ideal time to enlist the comments and opinions of a fellow musician who has not lived with the project as you have and who is not so close to the work that he can't make objective comments about it.

> **TIP**
>
> *If you can bear to wait, put your recording away for a couple of weeks and then come back to mix it with fresh ears. It's amazing what a little distance can reveal. If you can't wait, ask the opinion of a trusted musician – an honest soul who knows music and recording and who will be truthful – not a close friend or relative. And play the mix on as many different hi fi and music systems as you can – you'll be amazed how much different systems colour the sound.*

## Mixing a combined MIDI and digital audio recording

If you have a recording which uses both MIDI and digital audio data, you can do a mixdown in one of two ways. The easiest is simply to set everything to playback, do the mix and record the result to DAT. This is probably the most common method.

An alternative method is to record the MIDI mix into the digital audio software alongside the audio material. Benefits include the ability to apply digital processing to the MIDI tracks and control the entire mixdown process from within the computer.

It's not always easy to recreate the MIDI setup used on a project after the sounds and settings have been changed, perhaps for another project. If you have MIDI equipment on loan or hire, when it goes back you may lose access to the sounds altogether. Recording the parts into the audio program captures them and saves them from loss although it also makes it impossible to perform any MIDI tricks on the parts or substitute alternative MIDI sounds.

Similar considerations apply when recording MIDI tracks as those described in the section on converting tape tracks to digital audio tracks in Chapter 14. If you're happy to do a stereo mix, you can probably record

> **TIP**
>
> *Compression warning. If you have applied compression to several tracks and then mixed them together, the resulting output level could cause clipping due to the combination of several highly compressed sounds. Keep your eye on the meters and an ear open for possible distortion.*

the MIDI section in one go directly alongside the existing digital audio parts. Otherwise you may have to record the tracks one or two at a time and adjust their positions manually within the program.

## What speakers?

If you're producing music for mass distribution, it needs to be mixed so it sounds good on the listener's system. But what will your listeners be using? It could be anything from a set of headphones, a £10 pair of computer speakers, or a ghetto blaster to a £5,000 hi fi system. And your recording will sound different on each of these.

Most studios have two sets of speakers – a large pair, very hi fi, and a smaller pair of monitor speakers, sometimes called near-field monitors. These were originally used by recording engineers to give them a feel for how the music would sound on a cheap radio or hi fi system.

The main problem in getting a good balance on different systems is the size of the speakers. Small speakers simply cannot reproduce bass frequencies as well as large speakers. It's basically because bass frequencies need a large speaker cone in order to vibrate to their full extent, and although there is a range of modern technologies to compensate for this including the infamous bass boost button, the difference between small speakers and large speakers is still usually quite apparent.

So, if you listen to a recording through small speakers, the bass will be less prominent so there's the temptation to boost it to compensate. Play the result on a good hi fi system, however, and the resulting bass levels could be overwhelming.

Ideally, you ought to listen to your recording through a pair of hi fi speakers and monitors. If that's not possible, then play the mix on a few different systems to make sure there are no glaring problems.

## Last orders

If you are compiling an album you may prefer to wait until the pieces have been mixed down before deciding on the final song order. So mix them individually, concentrating on the sound, the balance and the level rather than any fancy processing effects. Then you can load them *en bloc* into an audio program and play around with the order.

This gives you added flexibility. You may decide it would be better if two pieces were segued or one faded out as the other faded in. Or perhaps you want to adjust the length of a fade. All these things are far easier to do – while retaining quality – if you still have the full, original material. Add a touch of EQ or compression if really necessary.

## The final master

The final stage is to create a master. If you are going to burn CDs you may prefer to create a single image on disk from the assembled pieces in the digital audio program. If you are copying the master to cassette or

MiniDisc you may prefer to master the recording to DAT and make the copies from that. In any event, you ought to back up the recording to DAT anyway. Make a couple of backups and store them in a safe place. DAT tape and CDs are cheap.

Having taken so much care over the creation of your project, you do not want to lose any of the quality you strived so hard to maintain by letting your recording escape into the analogue domain until it has to. The recording is on your hard disk in digital format and it should stay in digital format until the listener puts it in his or her hi fi system and presses play. This means that all editing, processing and mixing done during the mastering process should take place on the hard disk or be transferred to another system digitally.

> **THERE'S MORE**
>
> *See Chapter 12 for more on burning your own CDs*

## DAT

The industry hoped that DAT would replace the humble cassette but it never happened. Record companies were fainting at the thought of a system which could make perfect digital copies of CDs. But when they were launched, DAT machines were too expensive for the consumer, there were no pre-recorded DAT tapes to buy and the average user simply wasn't interested in a super hi fi quality medium – if they wanted hi fi they could buy CDs and it all sounds like junk through a pair of walkman phones anyway! So DAT sort of fizzled out as a consumer item.

But the recording industry loved it. Cheaper than quality analogue tape, easier to use, and the results are good enough to master from directly. Certainly for the next few years, DAT will be the mastering medium of choice, although CD-R is growing in popularity, too.

A couple of things to beware of with DATs. There are professional models, consumer models and models which fall in between. The professional models are recognisable by their price tag. They are designed to work day in, day out, every day and have all the bells and whistles you'd expect in a piece of pro gear.

Consumer models have fewer features, aren't as robust and they may only record at 48kHz. Apart from the desirability to record at 44.1kHz (which may not be so important to you, depending on what your final purpose is), many models are fine for home and semi-pro use, but bear in mind that you usually get what you pay for, and the A/D and D/A converters in cheaper models will not be as good as those in more expensive machines.

And consumer models invariably have a system known as SCMS (pronounced 'scums'). It stands for Serial Copyright Management System and was instigated by paranoid record companies who expected all and sundry to copy their CDs and give perfect copies to their mates.

SCMS allows a digital copy of the tape to be made but that copy can't be copied digitally. You can, of course, copy the tape as many times as you like using the DAT's analogue sockets and this is almost as good. And SCMS can easily be defeated. It works by inserting a 'copy inhibit' message onto the tape and more than one company is selling SCMS boxes which remove the message while letting the data through untouched. Functionally, SCMS is a complete waste of time and does nothing more than annoy the user.

The mid-range models should be able to handle 44.1kHz, have better A/D and D/A converters and a more robust transport mechanism although they may still have SCMS.

DATs can be used for creating your own masters and for assembling pieces to take to a mastering house. If you are using a mastering house, ask if they have any special requirements. They may like a test tone on the tape so they can check various aspects of your system. Don't start recording until after 2 minutes into the tape. Also, it's not necessary to put the songs in the finished album order or to get the correct gaps between the songs or even to do fade outs. You don't even need to put all the songs on one tape.

You will need to explain exactly what you want to the mastering house but they will assemble a master quicker than you and with better quality than a 16-bit system.

If you're producing your own DAT master then you will have to do this yourself. If you can prepare the finished product on your hard disk and record it to DAT in one take, that's ideal. If you can't then make sure not to get any clicks on the tape while starting and stopping it. You must also make sure that the gaps between the pieces are silent and uniform.

Later on, if you decide you'd like to re-order some of the pieces, you can transfer the DAT back to your PC, perform the edits and then record the album again.

> **TIP**
>
> Needless to say, if your sound card has a digital output, you should use it.

## CD-R

Recording to a recordable CD has been covered in Chapter 12 but it's mentioned again here to remind you that, along with DAT, it produces a true 16-bit copy of your original material.

If you want to burn CDs for mass distribution, be aware that it's a (very) slow process and if you want to produce a lot it's worth considering getting them duplicated professionally. Most mastering houses will accept CD-R format although the majority still prefer DAT.

## DCC and MiniDisc

The digital alternatives to DAT and CD-R are Philips' DCC (Digital Compact Cassette) and Sony's MiniDisc. They both use similar technology, they're both 18-bit systems and they both use lossy compression.

They use a system called psycho acoustic masking, which analyses the frequencies in the recording and removes ones which are quieter and overshadowed by louder frequencies. If you've heard one of these systems you'll know that they sound very good. In fact, many people find it difficult to distinguish between them and DAT.

However, the fact remains that they do remove parts of the original and while a listener may not be aware that anything's missing, you may.

So they give you 18-bit quality on the one hand (hooray!) but take away the advantage on the other by using lossy compression (boo!).

As the object of the exercise is to retain the full content of the recording all the way through to the final product, do you really want to throw bits of it away when creating the master? But if you have one of these systems and are happy with it, fine.

Whether or not either of these formats will catch on and replace the ageing cassette – or the pro-oriented DAT – remains to be seen. The jury's still out but there's a lot of activity in the MiniDisc market...

> **INFO**
>
> *Many mastering houses can't or won't accept DCC or MiniDisc formats for mastering.*

## MiniDisc 2

Several manufacturers such as Yamaha, Sony and Tascam have backed the format and have released MiniDisc four-track recorders. Whatever you think of the quality, they are streets ahead of cassette multi-trackers and they could well herald the death knell of cassette based systems, particularly in the mid-to-upper range of the market But they're still nowhere near as flexible as a computer-based d-t-d system.

The latest generation of MiniDisc machines has improved on the quality of the original MiniDisc recorders so if you really don't want to use DAT or CD-R you may like to run your ears over the latest models. But check the price of the writable MiniDiscs. They're currently several times more expensive than CD-R media, although the price is likely to come down if enough people start using them...

## Cassette

It's probably fair to say that you should not master onto cassette unless you really have to. Quite simply, it's not up to the job. You may think the quality is okay but in comparison with digital systems it's not. Such is the price of progress. Anyone using a gramophone to play vinyl records, particularly 78s, would have been stunned by the quality of a modern cassette but now that we've tasted digital, it's no longer considered up to scratch.

But if you do want to use cassette and you're looking for a cassette deck, you may be tempted to go for one with dual decks. This does make cassette copying easier (while adding to the inherent noise) but you'll get a better quality deck if you opt for a single deck costing the same amount. However, if you're looking for a professional cassette deck, you can probably get a low-end DAT machine for the same price...

It's probably best not to use noise reduction. If you must use it, use Dolby S although not all cassette decks have this. Using noise reduction may sound fine on your deck but you don't know what sort of decks the finished product will be played on, and head misalignment between machines can produce different frequency responses on playback. Leave it off and record at the highest level you can without distortion. Make sure to mark the tape 'noise reduction off'.

Do use a good quality tape and don't be tempted by special offers of

> **TECHY BIT**
>
> *The MiniDisc system works very much like a CD although as the discs are smaller, they cannot hold as much data as a CD so it needs to be compressed. It's possible that developments in CD-R may filter through to the MiniDisc and we may see a non-lossy system. But that's just idle speculation.*

'cheapies' in the high street stores. Use chrome tape and if your cassette deck doesn't support chrome get another deck!

Keep the tape heads clean – use a cotton bud and special cleaning fluid or a bottle of isopropyl alcohol (sold at all good chemists). Be very, very wary about using a cleaner cassette. It can sweep the grunge into the machine or possibly even scratch the heads. And remember to demagnetise the heads regularly.

Many mastering houses will accept cassettes but they don't like doing it.

### Packaging, artwork and promotion

Just a few words about the final stages of production. If you are creating music for distribution, it needs to look the part. You may think that as you put so much time, effort – and money – into the music that the packaging is not important. But it is! Your product has to compete with all the others out there so it has to have something special going for it. The outside needs to attract customers otherwise they'll never get to hear the inside!

It need not cost an arm and a leg to get quality CD or cassette inserts printed. Colour is more expensive than black and white but many striking designs have been produced using just black and white. You have a computer and there are many good drawing, painting and design packages available for it.

If that's not your forte, many printing companies, especially those who print music inserts, offer a design service. Alternatively, contact a local design college or put the word out on the Web. There are many budding designers who would be happy to design a cover for the credit or a small fee.

And just because you've produced the best album in the entire history of the known Universe, the world, alas, will not beat a path to your door unless you tell everyone about it. If you gig, promote the recording on the posters.

Send press releases to the newspapers. Send review copies to every music magazine and reviewer you can think of. Send copies to DJs in clubs and on radio. Don't forget local radio stations. Some are happy to give new artists an airing, especially local ones, and they may even do a short interview with you discussing your music, how you put the project together and so on.

Again, use your computer to produce professional-looking letters. Check and double check the spelling and grammar, and if English is not your strongest subject ask someone to check it for you. Nothing shouts 'amateur' louder than a badly-written or grammatically incorrect letter.

Music may be what you're about but promotion is even more important. Sad but true. The music business is littered with bands who were manufactured, with artists short on musical ability but high on style and with songs which have nothing going for them but hype.

No, it's not intended to sound depressing, but to illustrate the power of promotion. It often is more important than the music. And if you really do happen to have the best album in the known Universe, it certainly won't do your chances of success any harm at all...

# 16

# Troubleshooting

## System problems

### It doesn't work!!!
- The most common cause of all problems involving music and audio is poor connections. Check the cabling. Check the plugs. Check that the mic is in the audio In socket and not the audio Out socket (yes, we've all done it!). If the connections look okay but it's still not working, change the cable for one you know works.
- Cut out the middle men. As your system becomes more complex, more things can go wrong (what a reassuring thought!). If you have leads from the audio card to a line mixer to a patch bay to a mixing console, check each link in the chain. Start by plugging the card's output directly into the amp or a set of headphones and then check each stage of the audio route.

### The system won't record and playback at the same time
- This is a function of the soundcard. In order to record and playback at the same time it needs to be full duplex. Most moderns cards, certainly those with half an eye on the music market, are full duplex. If you have an older card, check the specs and check with the manufacturer.
- If a card is full duplex but still won't record and playback at the same time, make sure you have the latest drivers. Some full duplex cards were released with half-duplex drivers, which means they can only record or playback but not do both at the same time.

### The program says the computer or hard disk is too slow
These messages are given by several programs if they are asked to perform a function and the system hasn't got enough power to do it. The problem is most often caused by trying to play too many tracks or using too many processing functions in real-time. You may think you need a faster system and this is the obvious solution. However, there are several things you can do to ease the load.
- First of all, check that the turbo switch on your PC is activated. They are often next to the reset switch and are easily pressed by mistake.
- Virtual memory allows the computer to use the hard disk as temporary

storage space if it runs out of RAM. This can make a crucial difference to the performance of your system so check the software documentation to see what it says about the VM setting, Figure 16.1. WaveLab, for example, tells you to set the virtual memory to a fixed amount. Try setting it to 2-3 times the amount of RAM in your PC or at least to 20Mb. See if this improves performance. Make the minimum and maximum values the same.

Figure 16.1 Check the virtual memory setting

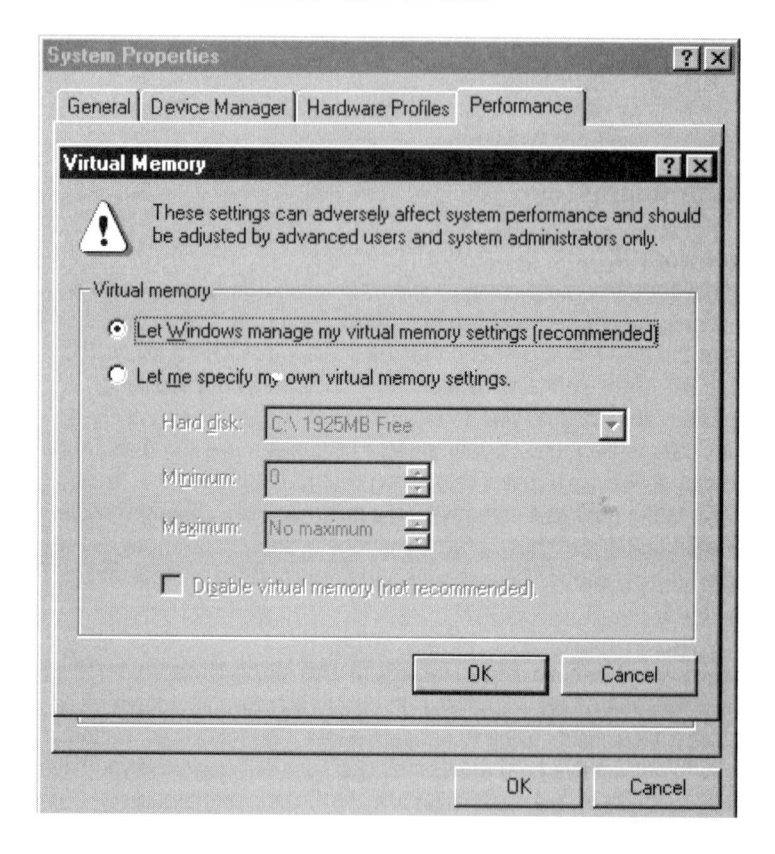

- If you have a drive dedicated to audio data, assign virtual memory to another drive.
- In Control Panel/System/Performance/File System set the 'Typical role of this machine' to network server, Figure 16.2, as this setting has a better performance configuration than the 'Desktop' setting.
- Some sources also say you should set the 'Read-ahead optimisation' setting to 'none'. See what your software's documentation says about it (probably nothing), see what the software's tech support team says about it (should be interesting) and try it both set to 'none' and 'full' and compare performances yourself.
- If you get continual errors which suggest that lack of memory is a problem, it's probably time to add more RAM.
- If you are using real-time processing functions, apply them to the file off-line so you can disengage the effect during playback.
- Check that the software is optimally set up for your system. Many

# Troubleshooting

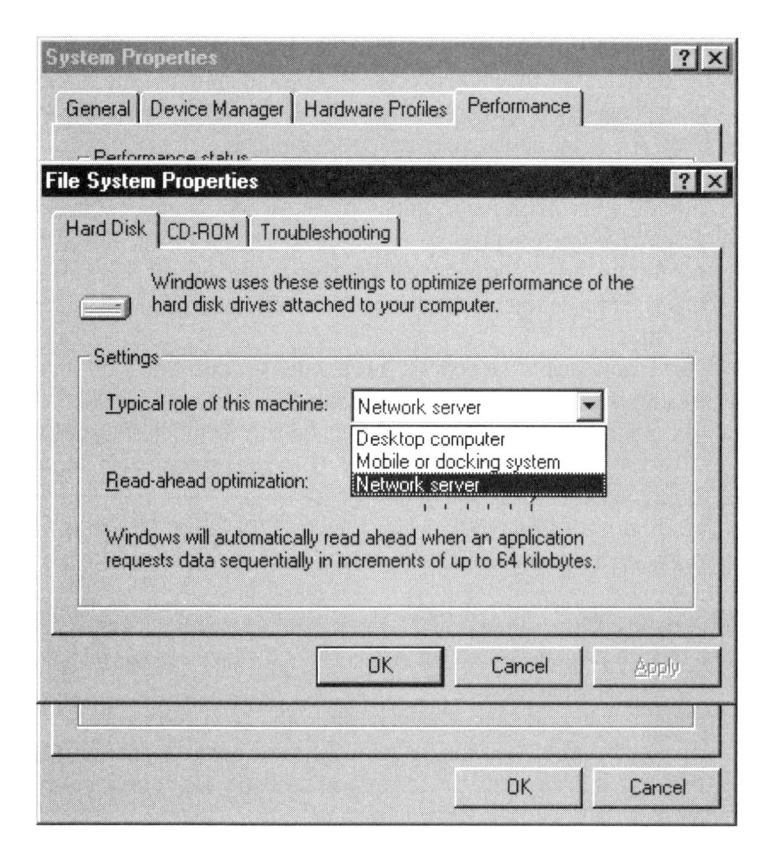

231

Figure 16.2 Set the optimum role of your PC to 'Network server'

programs use buffers to improve data throughput and these need to be configured to your system. Read the software documentation.
- Reduce the number of real-time updates. Many programs have performance-related options in a preferences window. Reduce the demands on the system by removing some of these. They typically include real-time screen updates, waveform displays in the tracks, and you may be able to set the system performance of the PC as in Cubase, Figure 16.3.

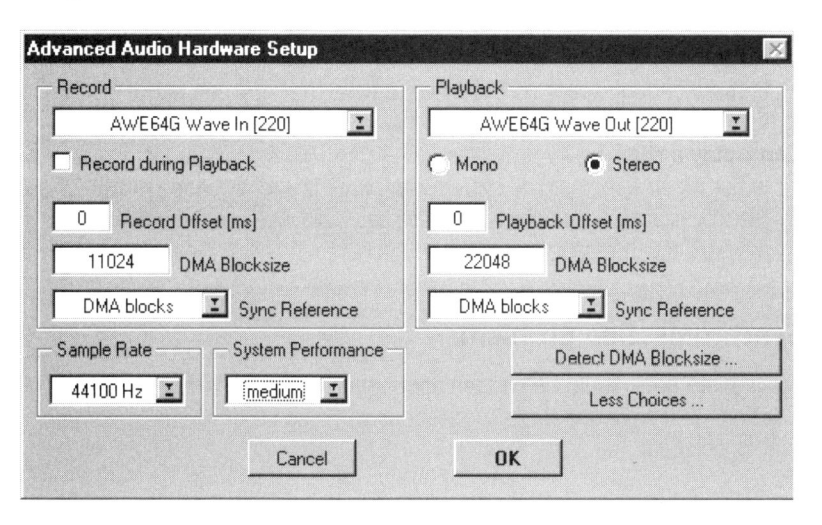

Figure 16.3 Setting the system performance in Cubase

- Remove all TSR programs such as screen savers. They sit in the background but they hog processor time and interrupt the system to see if their 'event' has occurred.
- Close any other applications which are running.
- Reduce the number of tracks by bouncing two or more tracks together.
- Check the hard disk for fragmentation and defragment it. Check the cluster size (see Chapter 5).
- In a multi-track recording, split the tracks over two or more disks. This will reduce the work each of the drives has to do in order to read the data.
- If you can specify a temporary storage folder, put it on a different drive to the one used for the main data.
- Add or increase the second level cache in your computer. Contact the software manufacturers to see how much they recommend and the performance increase you might expect.
- A SCSI drive is likely to be faster than an EIDE drive. Use an AV drive to maintain a sustained data transfer rate.

**Can't save a file**
- Is there enough space on the hard drive? It's very easy to fill a drive with digital audio files.
- If you're using removable media, is it in the drive and on-line?
- Are you trying to save the file with the same name as another file? If the original file is write-protected you probably won't be allowed to do this so save it with a different filename.

**Can't record**
- Check that you have the latest drivers for your soundcard.
- Do the software and soundcard support the sample rate and resolution you are trying to record at? Some systems won't record at less than 44.1kHz, for example, and some soundcards can't record at 48kHz.
- Check that the correct recording input is selected. Most systems let you select mic, line or CD input.
- Check that the soundcard is installed correctly and working by playing a Wave file using the Media Player and recording a file using the Sound Recorder.
- Is there enough space on the drive to save the recorded file to?

**Can't play a file**
- Is the file in a format the system can play? If you've loaded a 48kHz file, for example, and the soundcard can't playback at that speed you may get this message.

# Synchronisation problems

A complete book could be written about synchronisation, its problems and solutions, but here are some suggestions to fix some of the most common sync problems:

- When syncing to tape make sure the timecode is well recorded, at a sufficiently high level and with no dropouts.
- Don't use EQ if you're running the code through a mixer. In fact, don't run timecode through a patch bay, use a direct cable to the recorder.
- Check if the tape deck has a special track for timecode. If it has it will probably have a Noise Reduction Off switch for it. Put the timecode on an outside track.
- Make sure both devices are set to the same SMPTE frame rate (make sure one's not set to 30 drop and the other to 30 non-drop, for example).
- Make sure one device is clearly the master and the other clearly the slave.
- Many systems can use SMPTE or MTC. Make sure the slave is expecting what the master is transmitting.
- If the system is working flat out, you may get drop outs and lose sync. Many systems have a freewheel mode which lets the program carry on playing even if it loses sync for a short while. Increasing this may help keep the two systems together although when you increase the freewheel setting you decrease the tightness between the two systems.

## Audio problems

### The recording crackles and pops during playback
- Check for spikes in the audio data. If you can't manually cut out the spike (you may be able to do this if it's in a 'silent' section at the start or end of a file) use a noise reduction or spike reduction processor.
- Make sure edits are at zero crossing points (see Chapter 10).
- Check the levels of each of the tracks. An overdose of EQ can cause a track to clip.
- Several heavily compressed tracks played at the same time can cause clipping. In fact, the meters may suggest that all the tracks are playing at low levels but in combination the output could be distorting.
- If the file has no spikes or glitches, the problem could lie with the soundcard's drivers. Some cards produce a click when starting or finishing playback of a file. Check that you have the latest drivers.
- Make sure that the card has no IRQ or DMA conflicts. Open Control Panel/System/Device Manager/Computer Properties and check the IRQ and DMA settings, Figure 16.4.
- Do not used a disk compression utility such as DriveSpace which compresses data as it is being saved to disk. This takes processing power away from the program. Also, if something should go wrong with the system, it reduces the chance of recovering any data. If you need more disk space, buy another disk - they're cheap.
- If you are playing a file from a CD ROM, the CD ROM drive must be fast enough to transfer sufficient data in real-time.

### The recordings are noisy
- Make sure you are recording with a good level. See Chapter 9.
- Check that playback is set to 16-bit. Some systems can playback at 8-

Figure 16.4 Check for IRQ conflicts

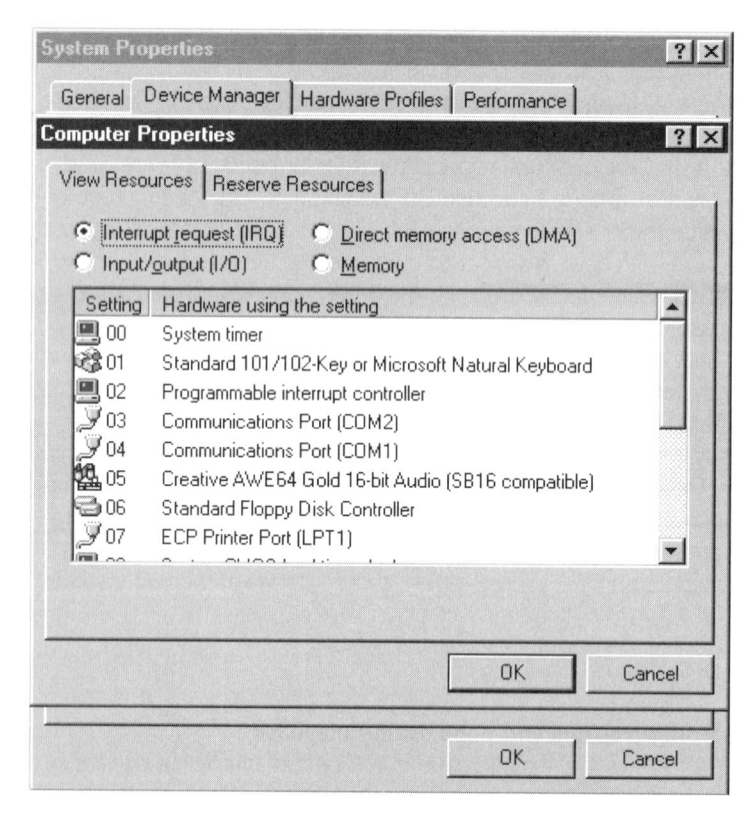

bit and do the conversion on the fly which will result in lower quality.
- Use a good microphone. The ones supplied with soundcards are not high quality.
- Check that you're using the correct input - connect the mic to the mic input and a line signal to the line input. See Chapter 9.

### There's no audio output
- Check the cables and connections first.
- Make sure the mixer in the program and any mixer used by the soundcard have their levels turned up sufficiently.
- Make sure the software itself and then the audio parts and tracks are assigned to an audio output.

### The mix sounds muddy
- Muddiness is often caused when several tracks or sounds are in the same frequency band. There are several solutions. If the parts contain MIDI sounds or a solo instrument, change the sound to one which contrasts with the other parts.
- If that's not possible, see if you can remove any of the parts. Sometimes arrangers get carried away and add more and more parts and often it's a case of less is better.
- If that's not possible you'll have to dust off the EQ control and EQ the tracks so they are prominent in different frequency bands. Use cut

more than boost. Remember the first rule of creative EQing – it's better to take than to receive.

### The bass guitar sounds terrible
- The straightforward way to record a bass guitar is to run it through a DI box and into the recorder. It often helps to add a bit compression at this stage although not all digital audio programs let you process incoming data. If you can, fine, if not, you may have to ride the levels and compress the track after recording.
- Don't EQ the bass in isolation. Wait until the rest of the recording has been done and EQ it - and the mix - in relation to each other.

### The guitar parts are noisy and the level are out of whack
- Use a DI box to reduce hum.
- Use a noise gate (in the software during recording if possible, or an external FX unit if not) to reduce background noise.
- Use a compressor to even out the level, again in software if possible.
- Don't be afraid to use EQ to get the tone you want. For solos try boosting between 1-4kHz.

### The vocals are flat, noisy, uneven and poppy
- The same principles for recording instruments apply to recording vocals, too.
- Use a good studio mic. You won't get a good recording with bad gear and the mics supplied with soundcards are not up to the job.
- Use a pop shield to avoid popping on Ps and Bs and/or sing these potentially dangerous sounds across the mic rather than into it.
- Most vocals need compression (on the way in is best) and a touch of EQ.
- Good microphone technique is essential to keep the volume even and minimise the breathing noises.
- Break the song down into sections. Record and perfect them one at a time. It's easier and less soul-destroying on the vocalist than asking them to sing the complete song several dozen times.

## Calling for help
- If all else fails, it's probably time to call in technical support. Read the documentation which came with the software or hardware and see what information you need. You may have to supply a registration number and almost certainly a description of your system. If telephoning, it will help if you are sitting in front of the system when you call. As most problems are caused by a combination of software and hardware, who do you call first? Software developers are more likely to have experience of a wide range of audio cards, often through feedback from their users, than the other way around.
- Check the Web for user groups. The chances are someone in the group has had a problem similar to yours and these groups are full of hints, tips and information.

# 17

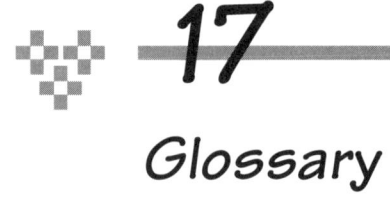

## Glossary

**ACM** Audio Compression Manager. Windows software which handles audio compression and signal processing which can be 'tapped into' by audio programs.

**ADC** Analogue-to-digital converter. A hardware device which converts analogue sound from a microphone or a line input, for example, into digital data. Often abbreviated to A/D or A-to-D.

**ADPCM** Adaptive Delta (or Differential) Pulse Code Modulation. A method of compressing audio data by storing the differences between samples rather than the values of the samples themselves. There are different types of ADPCM (Microsoft and IMA, for example) which are not necessarily compatible.

**AES/EBU** Audio Engineering Society/European Broadcast Union, societies which gave their name to a professional digital audio connection standard which uses XLR connectors.

**AIFF** Audio Interchange File Format. A file format designed for transferring files between computers. It's the most popular audio file format on the Apple Macintosh but many PC digital audio programs can read it, too.

**Aliasing** A distortion commonly caused by sampling frequencies at a low sample rate. If you sample a sound at less than half its highest frequency (the Nyquist frequency) the higher frequencies can be misinterpreted causing frequencies to appear in the sample which were not present in the original.

**Anti-aliasing filter** A filter commonly use by ADCs to remove high frequencies which could cause aliasing.

**Balanced line** A cable with three connectors used to transfer audio signals which reduces noise and interference that a two-connector cable may pick up. Usually uses XLR connectors.

**Bit** Short for **B**inary Dig**IT**, a single digit in a binary number which will be either 0 or 1.

**Byte** A collection of bits, usually accepted as being eight bits. The maximum value of an 8-bit byte (11111111 in binary) is 256.

**Clipping** Distortion caused by recording or playing a sound at a higher level than the system allows. Values of the sample above this level are chopped off or clipped resulting in the loss of information and causing distortion.

**Codec** Short for compression/decompression (some sources say

coder/decoder), a routine which compresses audio as it is recorded and decompresses it during playback.
**Compressor** (1) A processing function which compresses or reduces a signal's dynamic range. See also Limiter. (2) Data compression used to reduce the storage space required by data. It includes ADPCM. The MiniDisc system uses compression.
**CPU** Central Processing Unit. The chip inside the computer which does the processing, essentially its 'brain' but also often used to mean the computer itself.
**Crossfade** Fading out one sample while fading in another.
**Cutoff frequency/point** The frequency at which a filter starts filtering. A low pass filter, for example, passes the frequencies below the cutoff point and attenuates those above it.
**D-t-d** Short for direct-to-disk, usually meaning direct-to-disk recording. The process of recording and playing audio data direct from a hard disk.
**DAC** Digital-to-analogue converter. A hardware device which converts digitised audio back into analogue sound. Often abbreviated to D/A or D-to-A.
**DAT** Digital Audio Tape, although DAT usually refers to the machine which uses it and the tape is usually referred to as DAT tape. Such is the perversity of the acronym. There are two types of DAT machine – one for recording digital audio and one used to backup computer data.
**DAW** Digital Audio Workstation. Another name for a direct-to-disk recording system which could be a self-contained hardware unit or a computer-based system.
**DC offset** This occurs when a device such as a soundcard adds a DC current to the signal. In an editor, the waveform will appear above or below the centre line. A small DC offset may go unnoticed but it could cause a glitch, especially if joined to a recording with no offset.
**Decibel** Usually abbreviated to dB, a unit of measurement used to represent a ratio between two numbers. It's a logarithmic ratio used in audio because we hear logarithmically. A 6dB increase in a level will double the volume of a signal.
**Dither** The process of adding noise to a recording in order to reduce quantisation noise. It increases the low-level noise in the signal but this is generally more acceptable than the distortion.
**Downsample** To reduce the bit rate and/or resolution of an audio file, say from 16-bit 44.1kHz to 8-bit 22.05kHz.
**DSP** Digital Signal Processing/Processor. In digital audio it's usually a software routine which alters a signal, say by creating reverb or chorus. Some systems have a built-in DSP chip designed to handle the audio processing to take the strain off the CPU.
**Dynamic range** The difference between a recording's loudest and quietest sections, expressed in decibels.
**EIDE** Enhanced IDE (see IDE), essentially a faster and more efficient version of IDE.
**EQ** Short for equalisation. The process of increasing (boosting) or cutting (reducing) certain frequencies in a recording to change their timbre or tonal characteristics.

**FSK** Frequency Shift Keying. A set of tones recorded onto a tape which are used to synchronise the tape with another device such as a sequencer.

**Hard knee** Hard knee and soft knee describe the curve produce by dynamic effects such as compression. A hard knee effect applies the compression as soon as the level reaches the specified point. A soft knee increases the compression gradually. When viewed on a graph, the dynamic curves appear angular (hard knee) or round (soft knee).

**Headroom** The gap between the volume of a signal being recorded and the maximum possible volume level.

**Hertz** Usually abbreviated to Hz, the same as cycles per second, used to measure frequency.

**IDE** Intelligent (or Integrated) Drive Electronics. A system for connecting hard drives to a computer where the controller circuitry is in the hard drive itself. The motherboard only needs simple interfacing circuitry making the system easy and cheap to use.

**ISA** Industry Standard Architecture. The connection system used by PCs which allows additional hardware in the form of plug-in cards to be connected to the motherboard. These are the so-called expansion slots in a PC. ISA was originally designed to work with 8 bits of data but was extended to handle 16 bits. Most modern PCs have 16-bit slots although some cards only need 8 bits and may be shorter than the 16-bit slot. However, they will still work perfectly well in a 16-bit slot. See also PCI.

**ISO 9660** The filing structure used by CDs.

**Limiter** A device or software routine which produces a severe form of compression. It sets a maximum threshold level or limit, and any signal louder than that is reduced to the threshold level.

**Mb** Short for megabyte. In computing terms, mega is a prefix which normally denotes $2^{20} = 1048567$. A megabyte, therefore, ought to be 1048567 bytes. However, it is sometimes simply used to denote a million. Hard disk manufacturers commonly use it to describe the capacity of their disk drives.

**MIDI** Musical Instrument Digital Interface. A standard for communicating messages carrying music information such as note on and note off events, pitch bend, program change messages and so on.

**MTC** MIDI Time Code. Essentially a MIDI representation of SMPTE code which can be used to synchronise two MIDI devices. A MTC/SMPTE converter can be used to synchronise a MIDI device with SMPTE code recorded on tape.

**Noise shaping** A process for minimising quantisation noise by moving it to a less audible frequency band.

**Non-destructive editing** A system of editing which uses pointers to reference the audio data on the hard disk. Editing functions such as cut and paste do not actually cut or move the audio data. Instead they tell the software what section to skip and where to start playing by adjusting the pointers.

**Normalise** A process which raises the level of a recording to the maximum possible.

**Nyquist frequency/rate** Half the sample rate. It represents the highest frequency which can be recorded at a given sample rate without aliasing. Although it's commonly taken to be half the sample rate, it's actually a little less.

**PCI** Peripheral Component Interconnect. A type of expansion slot on the motherboard of modern PCs which allows other devices (including graphics cards, soundcards, a SCSI card, an internal modem, network cards and so on) to be plugged in. It's a more recent standard than ISA and provides faster access to the CPU for demanding peripherals such as graphics and soundcards. Most PCI devices are Plug and Play compatible which makes them easier to install.

**Quantisation noise** The noise produced as a result of converting analogue signals into a discrete series of numbers. The lower the sample resolution, the more noticeable quantisation noise will be as fewer values are available for storing the information and the more the analogue values will have to be rounded off.

**RAM** Random Access Memory. Not a very memorable name; it simply means data can be written to and retrieved from any part of the memory.

**RPM** Revolutions Per Minute, in the case of a hard disk, the number of times the disk completes a revolution or a spin in one minute.

**S/PDIF** Sony/Philips Digital Interface. A consumer or semi-pro standard based on the AES/EBU standard for transferring digital audio signals. It uses phono (also called RCA) connectors.

**Sample rate/frequency** How often a sound is measured or 'sampled'. A sample rate of 44.1kHz, for example, samples the sound 44,100 times every second.

**Sample resolution** The number of bits used to store sample data. On most digital audio systems the sample resolution is 16-bit which enables the data to take one of 65,536 values. 8-bit systems offer 256 values. Some pro audio systems have a resolution of 20-bit (1,048,576 values) or 24-bit (16,777,216 values). As a rule of thumb, each additional bit gives another 6dB of dynamic range.

**SCSI** Small Computer Systems Interface. A standard communications protocol for connecting devices to a computer including hard drives, CD ROM drives, samplers, scanners and so on. The standard spec allows up to seven devices to be connected to one SCSI bus, but additions to the spec such as Wide SCSI support up to 15 devices.

**Soft knee** See hard knee.

**Signal-to-noise ratio** The difference between the highest level of a recorded signal and the noise inherent in the signal, measured in decibels. Some manufacturers quote 'signal-to-noise' (without the 'ratio') which is how much lower the noise is compared to the signal. In this instance the figures have a '-' in front of them. A signal-to-noise ratio of 86dB (or a signal-to-noise spec of -86dB), for example, means that the signal is 86dB higher than the noise. Essentially, it's a measurement of how quiet a system is.

**SMPTE** Society of Motion Picture and Television Engineers. A timecode standard developed by the society for synchronisation, particularly between film and video devices. It takes the format hours:minutes:seconds:frames where frames are fractions of a second based on frame rates. These vary from continent to continent and include 24, 25, 29.97 and 30.

**Take** A colloquial term for a performance which is recorded in the studio. It's usually, but not always, a short section of music rather than the complete piece. If the performer or recording engineer want to do it again they'll say 'Let's do another take'.

**Wave** Microsoft's audio file format for Windows. Wave files have a .WAV extension. It is the *de facto* standard for audio files on the PC and can be read by all digital audio software, including many programs on other computer platforms such as the Apple Macintosh.

**XLR** A three-pin connector, often called a Cannon, usually used for carrying balanced audio signals or AES/EBU digital audio signals.

**Zero crossing** The point at which an audio file crosses the horizontal, zero amplitude axis. Making edits to a file at this point helps ensure a glitch-free edit, although you should also ensure that the slopes leading to and from this point are compatible, too.

# Appendix 1

## Copyrights and wrongs

The ins and outs of copyright and copyright law could fill several books – and if you have a few months with nothing to do you could pop down to a library specialising in the law and read them! However, the general principles can be described fairly concisely. While a lot of the following applies to most copyrightable material, it is slanted towards recorded audio material.

### What's copyright?

Copyright is, as its name suggests, the right to copy. It applies to all forms of artistic endeavour. As soon as you commit a work to paper, tape, disk or perform it in public, you have staked your claim to the copyright. Unlike some countries, you do not need to specifically register copyright in the UK. The essential part, however, is being able to prove that you did, indeed, write the material, and this is usually done by being able to prove that you were in possession of the material before anyone else.

There are several ways to do this. A common method is to send the material to yourself by registered mail. It can then be opened in a court of law to prove that you were in possession of the material at a specific date. Some banks will hold material for you, as will solicitors, and if you have a record deal your record company will be one step ahead of you on copyright material anyway.

### What's a breach of copyright?

Copyright has been broken when copyrighted material is used – copied – by someone who has not been granted permission to use it. At which point solicitor's letters usually start flying around.

### Who owns the copyright?

To make the situation more complex, there is often more than one copyright owner. In fact in the case of recorded music there are usually three – the record company, the music publisher and the owner of the moral rights.

The first two, being part of the music industry, can generally be bought and will usually give their permission to use a sample in exchange for a suitable amount of dosh or a percentage of the royalties from the sale of a record on which the sample appears. You can usually come to some agreement although it may take a little time.

> **INFO**
> Please note that what follows does not constitute legal advice and neither the author nor the publisher can be held responsible for any issues arising from the information contained herein.

> **INFO**
> You cannot copyright a title or an idea.

> **INFO**
>
> If you want to use a sample, you need permission from all copyright holders.

The owner of the moral rights is more problematical. This will usually be the composer who has the right to refuse permission to copy their work by invoking the Integrity clause. This basically means they can refuse permission to copy if they don't like your face or the football team you support, but it's usually dressed up in more technical terms, something to the effect that it brings their material into disrepute. Many artists use this as a way of refusing any of their material to be sampled, full stop. So okay, it's theirs they can do what they like with it, after all.

### Copyright and audio material

Copyright exists in all recorded material, so if you're thinking of lifting a section from an album and using it in your own song you need permission from the copyright holders. The exception to this is the samples on sample CDs. Technically, you don't 'buy' the samples at all but pay a license fee which gives you permission to use them on a commercial recording. This is why sample CDs tend to be so expensive compared to the cost of music CDs. However, you need to read the small print very carefully because there are some sample CDs out there which demand a further payment if the material is used for commercial purposes.

### How long does a sample have to be before clearance is required?

Technically, any sample, no matter how short, must be cleared.

### How do I get clearance?

You must contact the copyright holders and get permission in writing. The MCPS (Mechanical Copyright Protection Society) has a special department – known, usefully, as the Sample Clearance Department – which will help. Tell them what recording you want to sample from and they'll tell you who owns the copyright and probably give you a phone number and contact name. They won't arrange clearance for you but they'll give you a few hints and a hand up the ladder.

### How much will it cost?

Ah, the big question. It depends on the sample, who owns it, how important they think it is, how big a part it plays in your recording, how famous the copyright holder is, how famous you are, how much money the copyright holders think it will make, how much money you have, how much money they think they can squeeze out of you ...

In other words, it varies. The MCPS Sample Clearance Department may be able to give you an indication of the sort of fees being paid for the type of sample you want to clear.

> **TIP**
>
> If you think a recording may get an airing, better arrange a percentage deal than risk losing the lot, eh? **You have been warned**

### Keep it legal

There is always the temptation, of course, not to get clearance for a sample. But if the recording is released or made public and you're found out you could be in deep doo doo. As well as demanding a large share of any income you may have already received from the recording, the copyright holders could claim massive damages, have existing stocks of the material confiscated and generally be a bigger pain that you ever imagined possible.

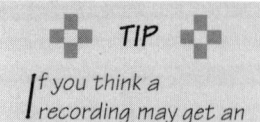

# Appendix 2

## Using the Net

The Net is an excellent place for the musician. One you start using it you'll wonder how you ever managed without it. It has several uses including:

- Email. Electronic mail, the communication medium of the 90s! Some people hate it. Most people love it. You can send messages immediately to anyone anywhere in the world for the cost of a local phone call. You can read your email at a time convenient to you, not the sender - unlike a telephone call - and reply at your leisure.
- Software. The Net is crawling with free software covering every imaginable computer application - including music and digital audio, of course. There are also demo versions of software products so you can try before you buy. And you can get them now, without waiting a week for someone to send you the disk.
- Software updates. Many software companies have a Web site where they post updates to their software, often free of charge - especially if they fix bugs! And these, too, are available instantly.
- Technical support. Many companies now offer technical support via email. It's not as immediate as a telephone call but you won't be hanging on the end of a phone for an hour listening to musak.
- News. Many manufactures post information about new and upcoming products on the Web. And you can get the information as soon as it's been posted - you don't have to wait four or six weeks to read about it in a magazine.
- Information. There are lots of user groups on the Net devoted to music, recording, MIDI and specific products. Users exchange ideas, offer hints and tips and help each other with problems.

## What's the Web?

The Web, WWW or the World Wide Web is actually only one aspect of the Internet but it's what helped make the Net so popular and people tend to use the terms Web and Internet as if they were the same thing.

The Web is a system which lets you jump - or surf! - from one Internet site to another by clicking on hyperlinks which appear in Web pages. They are usually underlined text but they can also be buttons or graphic images. The links can take you to another page on the same site or to another computer on the other side of the world.

## Getting on the Net

To get 'wired' you need an account with an ISP (Internet Service Provider), a modem and some software. You use the modem to dial a number given to you by the ISP which plugs your computer into the Net. The ISP usually provides all the software you need. That's it! Make sure that the ISP has a dial-in number local to you so you only pay for a local call.

There are hundreds of books and over half a dozen magazines about the Net and how to use it. Pick up one or two at your local newsagent. They periodically run features on how to get started and include information about ISPs. Details can change rapidly!

### Web sites

You can surf the Web by clicking on hyperlinks to go from site to site but if you know exactly where a site is you can go straight to it by typing its address into your Web browser. Every site has a unique address, technically known as the URL - Uniform Resource Locator (don't ask!). They may look strange at first but you'll soon become familiar with them. Most begin:

http://www.

Which is followed by the unique details of the site. The address for most sites can be entered in upper or lower case but it's common practice to use lower case so stick to that. Some sites have an address which is case sensitive so watch out for that, too.

Because sites can, literally, be set up and put on the Web and removed again within minutes (although that's not a common occurrence!), site addresses are prone to change. Established companies are most unlikely to change their address but sites run as a hobby and for fun may change or cease to exist altogether.

> **TIP**
>
> *The sites mentioned here were up and running at the time this book was written but don't be surprised if a few have moved or ceased to exist when you try them.*

### Some useful Web addresses

| | |
|---|---|
| Akai | http://www.akai.com |
| Arboretum Systems. Developer of digital audio software and Plug-ins | http://www.arboretum.com |
| Cakewalk. Developer of Cakewalk Pro Audio and other music software | http://www.cakewalk.com |
| CD Information Center. US site full of essential information about CDs | http://www.cd-info.com |
| CDDA  CD ROM info and transferring CD audio to hard disk | http://www.tardis.ed.ac.uk/~psyche/cdda/ |
| Creamware. Developer of the tripleDAT digital audio system | http://www.creamware.com |
| Creative Labs. Manufacturers of Sound Blaster sound cards | http://www.creaf.com |
| Cubase for Windows Users Site. Independent site with lots of goodies | http://www.instanet.com/~thedusk |

## Some useful Web addresses (cont)

| Description | URL |
|---|---|
| Digidesign. Developer of the Audiomedia III digital audio card | http://www.digidesign.com |
| Digital Audio Labs. Manufacture the range of CardD digital audio cards | http://www.digitalaudio.com |
| Digital Domain. Lots of info about digital audio and CD mastering | http://www.digido.com |
| Disc Makers. Wealth of information about CD-R and duplication | http://www2.discmakers.com |
| Electronic Music Foundation. For electronic and avant garde music | http://www.emr.org |
| Emagic. Developer of MIDI and audio software and hardware | http://www.emagic.de |
| Emagic Users Page. Unofficial site for Emagic products | http://www.mcc.ac.uk/~emagic |
| Et Cetera. A wholesale PC music software company | http://www.etcetera.co.uk |
| Evolution. Distributor of Evolution MIDI and audio software | http://www.evolution-uk.com |
| FutureNet. Future Publishing's site includes mags and Musicians Net | http://www.futurenet.com |
| Hyperreal. Home to alternative culture, music and expression | http://www.hyperreal.com |
| IQS. Developer of SAW digital multi-track software | http://www.iqsoft.com |
| IRCAM. Information about alternative and avant garde music research | http://www.ircam.fr |
| Macromedia. The multimedia specialist, developer of Shockwave | http://www.macromedia.com |
| MCPS. Information on copyright issues | http://www.mcps.co.uk |
| Microsoft | http://www.microsoft.com |
| MIDI Farm. A vast collection of MIDI, music and audio links | http://www.midifarm.com |
| Musicians Net Links. Links to music instrument and software companies | http://www.musicians-net.co.uk/MIDI.html |
| MMA. MIDI Manufacturers Association | http://www2.midi.org |
| Music Search. References and links to sites on all aspects of music | http://www.musicsearch.com |
| Musician's Union. Info on contracts, royalties, gigging and copyright | http://www.musiciansunion.org.uk |
| Opcode. MIDI and digital audio software and hardware | http://www.opcode.com |
| Passport Designs. Developer of Mastertracks and other music software | http://www.passportdesigns.com |
| PC Publishing. Publishers of this and other books on music technology | http://www.pc-pubs.demon.co.uk |
| Pro Audio Net. Pro audio, product news, info and marketplace for gear | http://www.soundwave.com |
| Progressive Networks. Developer of the RealAudio streaming system | http://www.realaudio.com |
| Prosoniq. Developer of digital audio software and Plug-Ins | http://www.prosoniq.com |
| QSound. Developer of 3D sound processing digital audio software | http://www.qsound.ca |
| Roland UK | http://www.roland.co.uk |
| Roland US | http://www.rolandus.com |
| SEK'D. Developer of Samplitude and CD recording software | http://www.sekd.com |
| Sonic Foundry. Developer of Sound Forge and digital audio Plug-ins | http://www.sfoundry.com |
| Sonic Solutions. Developer of the professional Sonic Solutions DAW | http://www.sonic.com |
| Sonicstate. Classifieds, news, information about software and hardware | http://www.sonicstate.com |
| Sound machine. A collection of sources and addresses of music sites | http://alpha.science.unitn.it/~oss/sourcese.html |
| Sound Solutions. Mail order PC music specialist with on-line catalogue | http://www.soundsol.com |
| Sound Technology. Distributor of Emagic, Alesis and other products | http://www.soundtech.co.uk |
| Soundscape Digital. Developer of the Soundscape DAW | http://www.soundscape-digital.com |
| Steinberg. Developer of Cubase and other music software | http://www.steinberg.de/english |
| Stirling Audio. Hi tech retailer, on-line catalogue and second-hand gear | http://www.stirlingaudio.com |
| Studiobase. A collection of info for the UK pro recording industry | http://www.demon.co.uk/studiobase |
| Synth Zone. A collection of resources for synthesisers | http://www.synthzone.com |
| Time & Space. Distributor of vast range of sample CDs | http://www.timespace.com |
| Turnkey. Retailer of a wide range of musical hardware and software | http://www.turnkey.uk.com |
| Turtle Beach. Developer of a range of sound cards and music software | http://www.tbeach.com |
| Waves. A range of digital audio Plug-Ins for the Mac and PC | http://www.waves.com |
| Yamaha UK. Currently mainly devoted to XG software and products | http://www.yamaha.co.uk |
| Yamaha USA | http://www.yamaha.com |
| Yamaha. Japan | http://www.yamaha.co.jp/english |
| ZDNET. Source of up-to-the minute stuff on the computer business | http://www3.zdnet.com |

## Useful contacts

Adaptec UK
4 Archipelago, Lyon Way, Camberley
Surrey GU16 5ER
Tel: 01276 854500
Fax: 01276 854505

Akai
Haslemere Heathrow Estate
Silver Jubilee Way, Parkway
Hounslow, Middlesex TW4 6NQ
Tel: 0181 897 6388
Fax: 0181 759 8268

AL Digital Ltd
Voysey House, Barley Mow Passage
London W4 4GB
Tel: 0181 7420755
Fax: 0181 7425995

Arbiter Pro MIDI
Wilberforce Road
London NW9 6AX
Tel: 0181 202 7076
Fax: 0181 202 7076

Audiovirtual
72 New Bond Street
London W1Y 9DD
Tel: 01256 701889
Fax: 01256 701580

CreamWare UK
24 Chalcroft Gardens, Liphook
Hampshire GU30 7PW
Tel: 01428 724594
Fax: 01428 722177

Creative Labs
Unit 2, The Pavilion, Ruscombe Bus. Park
Ruscombe
Berks G10 9NN
Tel: 01245 265265

Digidesign UK
Westside Complex, Pinewood Studios
Iver Heath, Pinewood
Bucks SL0 0NH
Tel: 01753 653322
Fax: 01753 654999

Et Cetera
Valley House, 2 Bradwood Court
St. Crispin Way, Haslingden
Lancashire BB4 4PW
Tel: 01706 228039
Fax: 01706 222989

Evolution Electronics
8 Church Square, Leighton Buzzard
Beds LU7 7AE
Tel: 01525 372621
Fax: 01525 383228

Harman Audio
Unit 2, Borehamwood Industrial Park
Rowley Lane, Borehamwood
Hertfordshire WD6 5PZ
Tel: 0181 2075050
Fax: 0181 2074572

HHB Communications Ltd
73-75 Scrubs Lane
London NW10 6QU
Tel: 0181 962 5000
Fax: 0181 962 5050

M. Hohner
Bedwas House Industrial Estate
Bedwas, Newport
Gwent NP1 8XQ
Tel: 01222 887333
Fax: 01222 851056

Karnataka Group
Blackfriars Foundry, 156 Blackfriars Road
London SE1 8EN
Tel: 0171 721 7021

Korg UK Ltd
8 Newmarket Court
Kingston, Milton Keynes MK10 0AU
Tel: 01908 857100
Fax: 01908 857199

MCMXCIX
9 Hatton Street
London NW8 8PR
Tel: 0171 723 7221
Fax: 0171 262 8215

MCPS
Sample Clearance Department, Elgar House
41 Streatham High Road
London SW16 1ER
Tel: 0181 769 7702
Fax: 0181 664 4698

Midiman UK
Hubberts Bridge House, Hubberts Bridge
Boston, Lincolnshire PE20 3QU
Tel: 01205 290680
Fax: 01205 290671

Natural Audio Ltd
Suite 6 Kinetic Centre, Theobald Street
Boreham Wood
Herts WD6 4SE
Tel: 0181 2071717
Fax: 0181 2072727

Net Works (GB) Ltd
103 Cozens Road, Ware
Hertfordshire SG12 7HP
Tel: 01920 425388
Fax: 01920 425389

Plasmon Data Ltd
Whiting Way, Melbourn
Hertfordshire SG8 6EN
Tel: 01763 262963
Fax: 01763 264444

Roland (UK) Ltd
Atlantic Close, Swansea Enterprise Park
Swansea
West Glamorgan SA7 9FJ
Tel: 01792 702701
Fax: 01792 700130

Sound Technology plc
15 Letchworth Point
Letchworth
Herts SG6 1ND
Tel: 01462 480000
Fax: 01462 480800

Soundscape Digital
Crichton House
Mount Stuart Square, Cardiff Bay
Cardiff CF1 6DR
Tel: 01222 450120
Fax: 01222 450130

SSEYO
Weir Bank, Monkey Island Lane
Bray
Berks SL6 2ED
Tel: 01628 29828
Fax: 01628 29829

Stirling Audio
Kimberley Road
London NW6 7SF
Tel: 0171 624 6000
Fax: 0171 372 6370

Symantec (UK) Ltd
Sygnus Court, Market Street
Maidenhead
Berkshire SL6 8AD
Tel: 01628 592222
Fax: 01628 592384

Time + Space
PO Box 306, Berkhampstead
Herts HP4 3EP
Tel: 01442 870681
Fax: 01442 877266

Unity Audio
Upper Wheeler House, Colliers End
Nr Ware
Herts SG11 1ET
Tel: 01920 822890
Fax: 01920 822892

WOW Sounds
2 King Edwards Road
Bath BA2 3RD
Tel: 01225 313219

Xyratex
PO Box 6
Havant
Hampshire PO9 1SA
Tel: 01705 498851
Fax: 01705 498853

Yamaha-Kemble
Sherbourne Drive, Tilbrook
Milton Keynes MK7 8BL
Tel: 01908 366700
Fax: 01908 308872

# Index

A weighted, 70
access time, 38, 45
ACM, 206
active filters, 134
ActiveMovie, 91
ActiveX streaming format, 209
ActiveX, 91
actuator arm, 45
Adaptec Easy-CD Pro, 190
Adaptec, 42, 48, 50, 52, 66
adaptive differential – or delta – PCM, 206
ADCs, 30, 70, 114
additive synthesis, 18
ADPCM, 206
AES/EBU, 72, 73
AIFF, 30
aliasing, 23, 111, 115, 155
AMD, 35
amplitude, 9, 11, 19
analogue recording, 2
analogue-to-digital converter, 30
anchors, 123
anti-alias filter, 154, 155
archiver, 204
artefacts, 167
ASF, 91, 209
AT Attachment, 47
ATA, 36, 47
ATAPI, 47, 181
attack time, 141
attenuation, 132
Audio Architect, 106
audio CDs, 40
audio channels, 84
audio compression, 204
Audio Compression Manger, 206
Audiomedia card, 76, 95
Audiomedia III, 95
Audiowerk8, 77
Auto Insert Notification, 198
AV drives, 52, 191, 232
average access time, 45
AWE32, 73
AWE64, 73
AWE64 Gold, 74

balanced connections, 110
band pass, 138
band reject, 138
bandwidth, 133
bell, 138
bi-directional, 64
BIOS, 35, 46
bits, 24, 112

Blue Book, 182
Boot Manager, 58
bounce, 3
breathing, 141
buffer underruns, 197
burst rate transfer, 45
bus, 35
bytes, 24

cache, 34 – 36
Cakewalk Pro Audio, 95
Cannons, 111
CardD, 95
CardDplus, 75
cardioid, 111
cassette, 227
CAV, 181
CBX-D5, 78
CCITT, 207
CD audio transfer, 87
CD formats, 182
CD quality, 71
CD ROM drive, 40
CD start marker, 195
CD-E, 66, 199
CD-R, 41, 42, 65, 182, 190, 226
CD-RW, 199
cents, 153
change gain, 147
chipset, 35
chorus, 163
click removal, 170
clip, 233
clip indicator, 113
clipped, 111, 170
clipping, 28, 112, 139, 223
clock speeds, 35
close disk, 192,
clusters, 55, 56, 232
CLV, 181
CMOS, 46
codecs, 205
compression, 139
compression ratio, 140
concurrent PCI, 35
constant angular velocity, 181
constant linear velocity, 181
Consultative Committee for International Telephony and Telegraph, 207
copyright, 241
Corel CD Creator, 66
CPS (cycles per second), 15
CPU, 34, 35
CrashGuard, 62

Creamware, 76
Creative Labs, 73
cross-linked files, 61
crossfade, 83, 127, 128
Cubase, 93
Cubase VST, 94
cut or boost, 18
cutoff frequency/point, 132
Cyrix, 35

DACs, 30, 70
damping/frequency attenuation, 157
DAT, 67, 114, 225
DAT machines, 68
data transfer rate, 38, 40, 65, 190
daughterboard, 71
DC offset, 151
DCC, 226
de-esser, 145, 146
decibel, 12
declicker, 99, 169
defragment, 60, 62
defragmented, 191
delay time, 160
delay, 160
DeNoiser, 98, 169
density/width, 157
DI box, 111, 235
diffusion, 157
Digidesign, 76
Digital Audio Lab, 75
Digital Compact Cassette, 226
digital enhancing, 29
digital input, 114
Digital Only CardD, 75
digital output, 116
Direct Memory Access, 46
DirectX, 91, 96, 149
Disc-at-Once, 191
distortion, 69, 166
dither, 116
dithering, 29, 175
DMA, 46
DMA 3, 50
DMA conflicts, 233
Dolby S, 227
DOS, 57
DOS FAT, 56
downsampling, 24, 203
DPMA, 35
DRAM, 38
DSP (digital signal processing), 75, 77
DTR, 181
dump, 105

*247*

duplex, 70, 229
DVD, 199
dynamic range, 5, 14, 27, 29, 69
dynamics processing, 139

early reflections, 157
Easy CD Pro, 66
ECC, 35
echo, 160
EDO, 35, 38
EIDE, 36, 47, 52
EIDE, Mode 4, 50
Emagic, 77
email, 243
emphasis, 133, 196
enhancers, 150
enharmonics, 18
EQ, 20, 131, 234
equalisation, 20, 131
ETSI, 207
European Telecommunications Standards Institute, 207
Evolution Sound Studio Gold, 84
expander, 145
expansion, 139
exponential, 127

fade curves, 127
fades, 127
Fast ATA, 47
Fast Fourier Transform, 173
Fast SCSI, 49
FAT32, 56, 57, 62
FATs, 55
FDISK, 57
feedback, 160
FFT, 19, 173
fibre channel, 52
file allocation table, 55
filepool, 82, 119
FireWalkers, 90, 102
FireWire, 51
flanging, 164
flat frequency response, 17, 69, 70, 117
flip, 152
FM (frequency modulation) synthesis, 72, 92, 179
formants, 155
Fourier transform, 19
fragmentation, 232
fragmented, 59
freewheel, 233
frequency analysis, 19
frequency decay, 157
frequency response, 69
frequency shift keying, 213
frequency, 9, 15
FSK, 213
fundamental, 18, 138

gain, 134
gain control, 142
gaps, 191
gate, 100
General MIDI, 7
graphic EQ, 134
Green Book, 182
GSM (Groupe Special Mobile), 207
handles, 122
hard disk, 38, 44
hard knees, 143
harmonic correction, 155

harmonic distortion, 69
harmonics, 16, 17
harmoniser, 156
headroom, 29
hertz, 15
HFS (Hierarchical File System), 184
high pass, 138
high shelf, 138
High Sierra, 183
hits, 123
host adapter, 48
hot plugging, 50
HTML, 102
Hurricane architecture, 75
Hz, 15

I/O, 36
IDE, 36, 46, 47
IDR (Increased Digital Resolution), 76, 99
IEEE-1394, 51
impedance, 111
input/output, 36
Intel, 34
inter-track gaps, 191
intermodulation distortion, 69
internal synchronisation, 216
International Standard Recording Code, 196
Internet Service Provider, 244
invert phase, 152
Iomega, 65
IRQ, 233
ISA, 35, 37
ISO 9660, 183
ISP, 244
ISRC, 196

Jazz, 65
jitter, 186

L1 Ultramaximiser, 100
Level 1 cache, 36, 134
Level 2 cache, 36
limiting, 143
line out, 116
linear fade, 127, 202
logarithmic fade, 202
logarithmic, 127
Logic Audio, 77, 94
Logic sequencer, 77
loops, 126, 128
loss-less compression, 204
lossy compression, 226
loudness' maximisation, 148
loudness, 11, 13
low pass, 138

magneto optical drives, 65
markers, 122
master and slave, 217
master, 233
mastering, 90, 222
MasterPort, 76, 89, 102
Maui, 74
MaxIT, 65
MCPS, 242
Mechanical Copyright Protection Society, 242
megabyte, 54
memory, 37
MFT, 57
mic inputs, 110
mic line level, 110
mid-side recording, 172

MIDI, 6, 178, 192
MIDI clock, 213
MIDI drivers, 217
MIDI Machine Control, 214
MIDI router, 218
MIDI sample, 105
MIDI sample dump, 87
MIDI sync box, 213,
MiniDisc, 226
mixdown, 90, 125
mixer, 114
mixing, 125
MMC, 214
MMX, 34
MO, 65
monitor speakers, 117, 224
motherboard, 35
MPEG-2, 199
MS recording, 172
MTC, 214
multi-band dynamics, 145
multi-tap, 102, 160, 162
multi-tasking, 35, 42, 47
multi-track recording, 1
multi-track recording software, 86
multimedia, 200
multisession, 183

net, 243
NetShow On-Demand, 91
NetShow, 209
noise, 28, 71, 111
noise gate, 144, 235
noise print, 97, 167
noise reduction, 167, 227, 233,
noise shaping, 70, 149
non-destructive editing, 81, 118
normalise, 142, 148
normalising, 201
Norton Utilities, 57, 62
notch, 138
NTFS, 57
Nyquist, 22
Nyquist Limit, 24

on-site warranty, 42
optimisation, 59
optimise, 60, 62
Orange Book, 182
OSR2, 42, 56, 63
over driving, 5
oversampling, 24, 70
overtones, 16, 17

pan envelopes, 120
paragraphic EQ, 136
parallel bus, 49
parametric EQ, 135
partials, 18, 155
Partition Magic, 58
partitioning, 55
partitions, 42
parts, 119
passive filter, 134
PCI, 35, 37
PCM, 206
peak, 113, 133, 138
Pentium, 34
Pentium Pro, 34
phase cancellation, 153
phasing, 164
phono, 110

Photo CD, 182
Pinnacle, 75
PIO, 46
pipeline burst, 36
pitch shifting, 153
pitch, 15
Plasmon, 42, 190
platters, 44
playlist, 82
plosives, 140
plosives, 145
Plug and Play, PnP, 37
plug-ins, 96
poles, 132
polyphony, 73
PQs, 197
pre-delay, 157
Pro Tools, 76
PSU, 41
psycho acoustic masking, 226
pulse code modulation, 206
pumping, 141
punch in and out, 3

Q points, 123
Q, 133, 135
Q10 paragraphic EQ, 100
quantisation errors, 176
quantisation noise, 28

RAID arrrays, 51
RAM, 6, 37, 46
RCA phono, 72
RealAudio 3.0, 91, 209
ReBirth RB-338, 107
recording level, 112, 113
Recycle, 104
Red Book, 91, 182
regions, 119
registry, 62, 63
release time, 141
removable disks, 65
requantiser, 149
ReSample Pro, 105
resampling, 155, 176
resolution, 26, 115
resolution conversion, 203
resonance, 133
reverb, 157
reverb/decay time, 157
reverberation, 157
reverse, 153
roll-off, 132
room simulators, 158
rounding, 175
RTB (return to base), 42
S/PDIF, 72, 75
S1 Stereo Imager, 100
sample CDs, 40
sample conversion, 175
sample dump standard, 92, 178
sample loops, 220
sample rate, 21, 68, 115, 203
sample resolution, 24, 29
SampleCell, 105
samplers, 5, 178
Samplitude, 86
SCAM, 50
ScanDisk, 61

SCMS, 196, 225
SCSI, 35, 48, 181
SCSI 2, 49
SCSI 3, 49
SCSI ID number, 48
SCSI MIDI Device Interface, 92,178
SDRAM, 35, 38
second level cache, 232
sections, 119
seek time, 45
SEK'D, 86
Serial Copy Mangement System, 196, 225
Serial Storage Architecture, 50
session, 87, 192
Session Software, 77
Session-at-Once, 192
ShockWave, 209
sibilants, 145, 146
sigma-delta conversion, 70
signal-to-noise, 69
signal-to-noise ratio, 14
silence, 129
slave, 233
slope, 132
Smart FSK, 213
SMART, 47
SMPTE, 214, 233
snap to, 122
soft knee, 100, 143, 144
Sound Forge, 91, 97
sound pressure level (SPL), 11
Sound Tools, 76
sound vibrations, 10
sound, 9
Soundscape, 78, 95
Soundscape Digital, 52
Soundscape SSHDR1, 88
Soundscape SSHDRT1, 84
speakers, 117, 224
spectrum analyser, 98
spectrum analysis, 173
SpeedRate, 57
SPL (sound pressure level), 13
SSA, 50
stereo expansion, 171
streaming, 209
sub-index markers, 195, 196
subcodes, 197
sustained DTR (Data Transfer Rate), 45, 52, 55, 57
SVGA, 38, 39
synchronisation, 232
synchronising, 213
SyQuest, 65

Tahiti, 74
tap, 102
tape hiss, 17
tape recorder, 4
tape streamer, 64
termination, 48
THD, 69
threshold, 140
timbre, 9, 18
time code, 213, 233
time stretching, 153
tone, 9, 18
total, 69
Track-at-Once, 191

tremolo, 165
tripleDAT, 73, 76, 89, 102
Tropez, 74
TrueVerb, 100
truncation, 175
Turtle Beach, 74

UDF, 199
Ultra 2 SCSI, 49
Ultra ATA, 47
Ultra SCSI, 49
Ultra Wide SCSI, 42
Ultramaximiser, 100
unbalanced connections, 110
uni-directional microphone, 111
Uniform Resource Locator, 244
Universal Product Code, 196
UPC, 196
URL, 244
USB, 35

varispeed, 68, 89, 115, 154
VGA, 38, 39
vibrato, 164
video graphics card, 38
video, 124
vinyl restoration, 170
virtual memory, 229
virtual tracks, 3, 84
volume, 120
VST, 96

wah, 164
warranty, 42
Wave, 30
wavetable synthesis, 72
WaveConvert, 102
WaveCraft, 105
waveform formats, 30
WaveLab, 90, 98
WaveLab Lite, 93
Waves Native Power Pack, 99
web, 243
White Book, 183
Wide SCSI, 49
Windows 95, 34, 37, 41, 56
Windows 3.1, 41, 57
Windows NT, 35, 42, 50, 57
WinZip, 204
words, 26
World Wide Web, 243
WORM, 190
Write Once Read Many, 190
write-back, 36
write-through, 36
WWW, 243

XG, 7
XLR, 73, 110
Yamaha, 78
Yellow Book, 182

zero crossing, 125
zero crossing points, 233
Zip, 65

16 bits, 5
20, 24 bits, 5

# newtronic

## creative tools for music programmers

Music production has undergone great change in the last few years. Music computing has opened the door to production for many aspiring musicians. Professionals have had the opportunity to rethink their production techniques resulting in the creation of many new musical genres such as the Dance explosion breaking both conventional ideas and borders. Newtronic is proud to be part of that global culture.

We have created a range of new products that aid the production process of music including up-to-date Dance styles such as Drum'n'Bass, House, Techno, Trance, Trip Hop, Rave and Dreamhouse. Our midifile loop & tool disks, sampling collections, midi software & midi books are the essence of a 7 year long successful track record in supplying tools for music programmers. Whether you are a professional or a hobbyist, using our products results in a new experience of **creative control & inspiration**.

When you make music, you want it to come out the way you hear it in your head. With the pro studio loops series we introduced a range of midifile disks which give you the freedom to choose, use or abuse the various grooves it contains. Make fresher, more creative, original, professional tracks. You can analyse the complex dance grooves of the Newtronic loop & tool disks and you have all the space you need to make them part of your sound. Each disk is style specific - you get what you ask for. If you are into dance music you can't afford not to talk to us.

**newtronic ltd.**
62B Manor Avenue
London SE4 1TE

Tel. +44 (0)181 691 1087
Fax +44 (0)181 691 2284

email sales@newtronic.com
online shop

**www.newtronic.com**

### pro studio loops
house garage
breakbeat house
original jungle
intelligent drum'n'bass
funky classics
swingbeat breakbeat
dance percussion

### pro studio tools
arpeggio kit
midi gates
filter kit
xg/gs wizard

### construction kits
techno & dance kit
trip hop kit
trance kit
funk factory kit
dreamhouse kit
electronica & big beat kit

### creative groove tools
dance, deep house + new movements
post-jungle & beyond

### production libraries
club nation
hip hop nation
jungle nation
rave nation

### pro studio elements
club bass
rave bass

### midi busker disks
acoustic guitar vol.1
acoustic guitar vol.2
electric guitar
latin guitar
beat busker